THE RANSOM

"I have found a ransom."
—Elihu

The Cross and the Tomahawk

The Rain From God
The Ransom

The RANSOM

Historical Fiction by
MARK AMMERMAN

CPL

HORIZON BOOKs
CAMP HILL, PENNSYLVANIA

Horizon Books
3825 Hartzdale Drive
Camp Hill, PA 17011

ISBN: 0-88965-135-3

97 98 99 00 01   5 4 3 2 1

Cover art by Ed French

Interior illustrations:
Pencil artwork by Kit Wray
from layouts by Mark Ammerman;
Map by Mark Ammerman

This book is dedicated,
with gratitude and joy,
to my brother and friend,
the Reverend Roland Mars,
and to his wife Starr and their youngest daughter Silvermoon.

Just as John Eliot was New England's "Apostle to the Indians,"
leaving the warmth and comfort of his Roxbury home to tread the
dark paths to the towns and tents of the soul-needy Native American,
Roland Mars—an apostle in his own right—climbs into his car many
times weekly to travel the black pavement from his home in the
Narragansett Indian reservation in Charlestown, Rhode Island, to his
inner-city pastorate in Roxbury, Massachusetts. In God's Kingdom,
the good that goes around comes around.

Keep the love rollin', Rolly!
"I'm your brother."

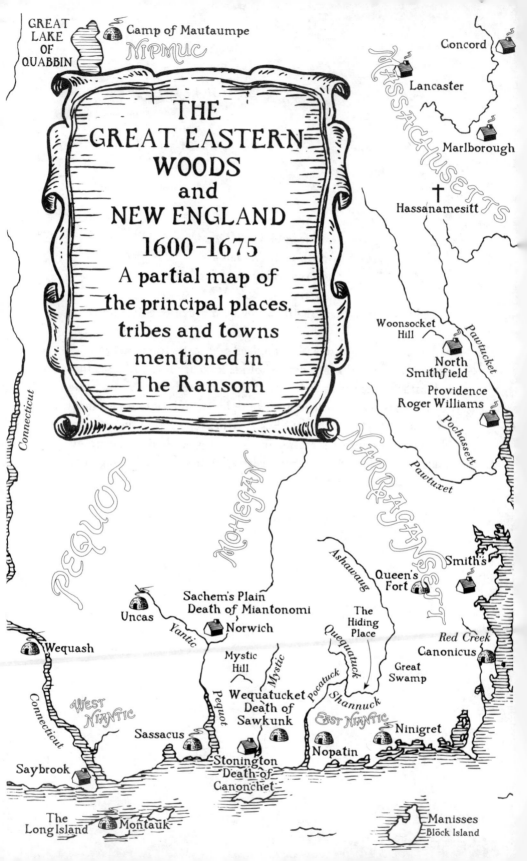

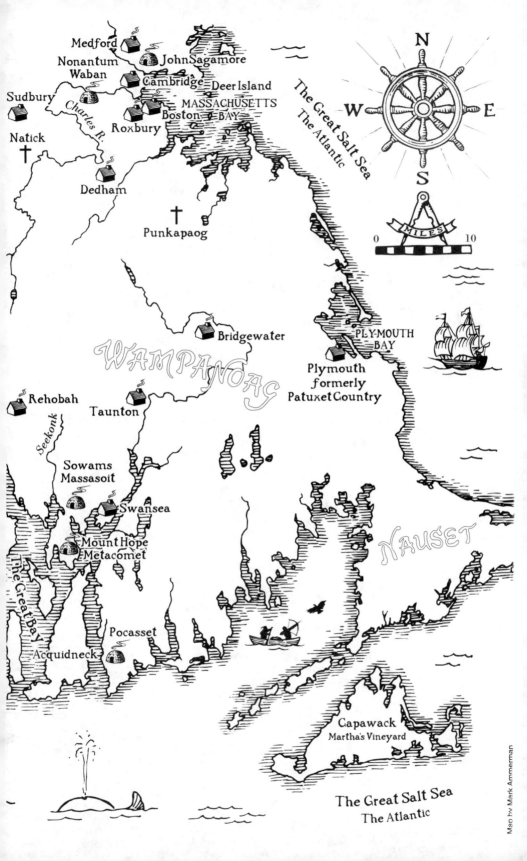

Medford
Nonantum
Waban
John Sagamore
Cambridge
Deer Island
Sudbury
MASSACHUSETTS
BAY
Boston
Roxbury
Natick †
Charles R.

Dedham

† Punkapaog

The Great Salt Sea
The Atlantic

N
W   E
S

MILES
0   10

PLY-MOUTH
BAY

Bridgewater

WAMPANOAG

Plymouth
formerly
Patuxet Country

Rehobah
Taunton

Seekonk

Sowams
Massasoit

Swansea

NAUSET

Mount Hope
Metacomet

The Great Bay

Pocasset

Acquidneck

Capawack
Martha's Vineyard

The Great Salt Sea
The Atlantic

Map by Mark Ammerman

Table of Contents

Part Three   The Blood

No Comic Book

A merican Spies—*Real Life Stories of Undercover Agents in Our History*: ten short, pulse-pounding, true adventures that any boy would want to read over and over. But it was Jo's book, and it was on her bookshelf. I never opened its pages.

Ten years ago—and twenty years after I first saw it in my sister's room—I pulled *American Spies* off my own shelves while looking for an easy read before bed. Many books that belonged to my three sisters have found their way mysteriously to my own shelves over the years. Most of them have been returned. But not this one.

The first story in the simple collection was about a Praying Indian (a term I had never heard) named Job Kattenanit, who spied for the English colonists in a late seventeenth-century New England conflict called "King Philip's War" (a bitter bit of history of which I was totally ignorant). It was a fascinating story, and I pored over it several times, thinking to myself, "This would make a great comic book!"—(which is the first thing I always think when I read a tale I like). I told my wife about it, saying, "I'd like to find out more about the Praying Indians someday."

From time to time as the years passed since that first happy discovery, my eye would catch an article here or a quote there concerning the Praying Indians of colonial New England, and I'd jot down the reference or photocopy the article and stick it in one of my many "comic book wannabe" file folders in my big, old, tank-green, metal file cabinet.

Then, in 1994, while working on a first chapter for a hopeful book on comics and the gospel message (I draw pictures for a living, my soul breathes life from the gospel of the Lord Jesus Christ, and I dig comics!), the doors opened for me to write, instead, a small children's book about the unsinkable Puritan divine and founder of Rhode Island, Roger Williams (who is also my great-great-great-great-great-great grandfather on my mother's side). In researching the life and times of my compassionately bull-headed grandpa, I discovered a treasure chest of information on the Praying Indians. "This stuff would make great comics!" I declared. But God decided that it would make great (well, *you* be the judge on how great it is) paperback fiction first.

The book you are now holding—and *The Cross and the Tomahawk* series of which it is the second volume—is the latest fruit of those adventurous images that played in my mind as I lay awake in my bed after my initial perusal of *American Spies* by Richard Deming. That fascinating tale of Job Kattenanit, America's "first spy," is the story around which this whole novel is wrapped. Kattenanit, the narrator and leading character of *The Ransom*, was a real man, a real Indian, a real Christian—as can be discovered in historical sources centuries older than Mr. Deming's delightful book. Job's larger story, and the story of the preaching and the progress of the gospel among his fellow Native Americans in the middle of the seventeenth century, is a fascinating and essential piece of our national heritage. In telling anew the story of the Praying Indians of New England, I wandered down paths first walked by compassionate and courageous colonists such as Edward Winslow of Plymouth, Reverend John Eliot of Roxbury (the Apostle to the Indians), Major-General Daniel Gookin of Cambridge (Superintendent of the Praying Indian Towns of Massachusetts), Governor Thomas Mayhew of Martha's Vineyard and his son the Reverend Thomas Mayhew Junior, and Roger Williams of Providence Plantations and Rhode Island. Shortly after King Philip's War, Daniel Gookin wrote a history he entitled "An Historical Account of the Doings and Sufferings of the Christian Indians in New England." Though my work is a computer-keyed armchair fiction, it owes its essence—in large part—to Gookin's hard-won, footsore, firsthand history. And though folks may think it unlikely that a man with cable television who lives in a city of 55,000 in a house heated room-to-room by electricity can relate to a man who lived in a town of 500 at the edge of a vast and unknown wilderness in a house heated with firewood from trees that he cut down with his own hands, the following words—first penned by Gookin with goose-quill and ink three hundred twenty years ago—speak for my own heart as well: *Forasmuch as sundry persons have taken pains to write and publish historical narratives of . . . the English and the Indians of New England, but very little hath been hitherto declared (that I have seen) concerning the Christian Indians . . . I thought it might have a tendency to God's glory . . . to give . . . right information how these Christian natives have demeaned themselves in this hour of tribulation. And therefore (through divine assistance) I shall endeavor to give a particular and real account of this affair.*

Mark Ammerman
March 1997

For a further discussion of research and terminology, be sure to see the historical notes at the end of the book. You may find the glossary of terms and the bibliography, also at the end, helpful as well.

Acknowledgments

Giving Thanks

My deepest appreciation is due to my wife Terri Lynn for cheerfully, prayerfully, and faithfully holding down the fort so well and so long. And to Jandy, Bethany, Jonathan, Keysha, Margaret, and Sherry for picking up the slack and for patiently awaiting for Daddy (Dad, Mr. Mark, Mark) to finish the last chapter so that they can actually see if he looks like the same man who entered his study two years past.

My thanks are also sincerely declared to the following:

• My father, Clifford S. Ammerman, for lovingly and patiently cooking all those meals that I only sat at for a few brief minutes before disappearing again into his guest room to bang away at my Macintosh keyboard (and all this on my vacation!).

This book is finally done, Dad, and now I can actually come to *visit!*

• David Fessenden, Dr. K. Neill Foster and his wife Marilynne, Janet Hixon, George McPeek, and the rest of the gang at Horizon Books for their commitment to ministry first, and the machinery of book publishing second.

Thank you so much for your willingness to stretch our deadline on behalf of the needs of my family and our church.

• William Scranton Simmons for giving himself to the task of professionally chronicling the cultural, spiritual, and social evolution of the New England Indian.

Again, Bill, without your excellent books, I'd be lost in the woods.

- Lancaster County Public Library for their commitment to continually shelve books that reflect our true national heritage and for walking the winding paths of interlibrary loan in search of the obscure titles that supplied me with so much of my primary resource material.

- All who prayed for me while my nose was stuck between the brittle pages of old historical records and my eyes were glued to the back-lit grey of the computer screen, and all who helped us fix up one house to sell, moved us, and helped us fix up another house to live in: David and Mary Kulina, Sherry Hill, Chris and Jen Ruch, Tom and Loretta and the Willow Street Home Group, David and Steve and Carol Erk, M.C. and Keith and Bruce and Tom and Vernon and Reggie and Gayle and Kathy and Kathleen and Glenn and Andy and . . . so many more, God's people all!

- Chris and Jen Ruch for letting me hang out late at night to deplete their ice cream supply ("I can always eat.") and use their printer and crack silly jokes and insult their favorite musical groups.

- Roger Williams, John Eliot, and Daniel Gookin for a lifetime of commitment to the temporal and eternal well-being of the New England Indian.
  I pray that this novel will be a small tribute to the great sacrifices you made on behalf of the "least of these" of Adam's children in old America.

- Job Kattenanit and all my Praying Indian brothers and sisters for their incredible, uncompromising, and selfless service to God and to the English—even in the unjust fires of prejudice and war. Great is their reward in Heaven!
  My dear brethren, you are among my first American heroes! You ran the Straight Path to the end, and now the prize is yours. I look to the day when we sit and sing together by the River Of Life.

- Jesus Christ for everything.
  Without You, I can do nothing.

THE RANSOM

Part One

THE NAME

" The Name of the Lord
is a strong tower."

—Solomon

Some Many-Colored Leaves

In the bright autumn that follows each full summer, the world is filled with the scattered, fallen leaves of the tall trees of the deep forest. Where once each leaf had clung to its own bough, proudly hailing itself an Oak or a Maple or a Birch, now it gathers in the Great Council Of Many Colors, mixing with the Poplar and the Willow and the Ironwood as together they tumble before the east wind across the forest floor.

My life is like the autumn leaves—a carpet of many colors that shifts restlessly beneath the dark trunks of the forest in the fall. There is beauty upon its face as the sun bathes it in warm light. There are secrets beneath its skin where the snake and the salamander slither under its damp, darkened cover.

If I squat upon the many-colored carpet and lift each leaf before my eyes, I no longer see the whole but the pieces of the whole. And the pieces call to my remembrance the voice of the wind as it walked through the trees when still the leaves were green.

I am Job Kattenanit, son of Jacob Katanaquat who was The Rain From God. In a past season I told you the story of Katanaquat my father. Now I would tell you my own.

But the whole of my trail is long, and to shorten the path for you, I would hold at first before your eyes some many-colored leaves.

"Your bloody deeds will come upon your own heads," cried the strange and pale man, spitting forth his curse like broken teeth, with accents that betrayed the words as only lately learned. "For God is sorely angered with you," the little man croaked, "and in His hot displeasure He will smite you!"

The tall sagamore and his scant band of warriors laughed with wide mouths, scorning the small man's words as foolishness, and pushed the poor fellow forward through the woods. He stumbled over roots and rocks, his arms laden with wooden fuel for the evening fire. His cruel companions picked up timber as they walked and added it to his load.

"If you wish to practice with our words," said the smirking sagamore, "choose those that bless! Or we may take your tongue and make ourselves a tasty soup!"

The warriors laughed again, and slapped the bared and burdened arms of the unhappy doomsayer.

The pale man was a French, a black-bearded creature from across the Great Sea, the last of five survivors of a battle with the men of the Massachusetts. Warclubs and arrows and fire had won against the thundersticks of the French traders. Even the great French canoe, its white wings wrapped in crimson flames, had sung its own dirge and sunk smoking beneath the dark waters of the salt sea. A mighty victory for the warriors of the Massachusetts!

The five French prisoners were distributed as slaves among the tribes of the Massachusetts and the Wampanoag and labored among them for several summers until only one was left alive.

My father Katanaquat, The Rain From God of the Narragansett, had traveled the path to Sowams—the chief city of the Wampanoag—as a boy. And there he saw the French slave.

"He worked as the squaw* works," said my father, "hoeing

---

*   *Squaw*, a very "popular" Indian term in use across our nation, is in reality and origin a preseventeenth-century Narragansett word. First heard by the European from the lips of the Indian of New England—and thus made part of the initial English-Indian vocabulary—*squaw* has worked its way west (all the way to Hollywood!) through the centuries. Though some present-day Native Americans consider the word offensive and an English invention, it is in fact an Indian term. In *The Ransom, squaw* takes its place in our narrative in a way that is linguistically, culturally, and historically accurate.

and planting and hauling wood and water. He was hardly a man."

But this hardly-a-man cursed the Massachusetts like the strong powwow* does. And though the warriors mocked him, his curse came home at last, like the barking dog after it has cornered the skunk. For when the poor slave was finally redeemed from the Massachusetts by an English boat captain named Dermer, the Great God of the French unleashed his wrath.

First this Great God made a second moon—a comet, as now I understand—rise in the night sky beside our old moon Nanepaushat. This brought much fear and wonder to all who saw it. Yet Askug our powwow said that it was good, for it came at a time when our people were celebrating the rising of a new ruling prince in our midst—Miantonomi, son of Mascus of the mighty Narragansett. And both the rising of the new sachem and the rising of the new moon were indeed good for the Narragansett.

But the second moon was not a good omen for the tribes of the Massachusetts or the Wampanoag or the Patuxet or the Pennacook—for to them came the Dying, and the woods to the east of the Great Bay of the Narragansett were filled with weeping and mourning. And the smell of rotted flesh. And the bones of great men and small men, women and children,

---

* *Powwow* is a word which originated with the pre-European Indians of America's Northeast (the Narragansett in particular) and has since spread in use across all of North America. Yet time and travels have nearly erased its first meaning. The current and most common use of the word denotes a large tribal or intertribal gathering. More colloquially, the word is used as slang for "gettin' together to talk things over." But in the historical context of *The Ransom, powwow* means "medicine man" or "shaman." In short, the powwow was the tribal healer, prophet, magician, and priest of the New England Indian. Interestingly, among the Amish of Lancaster County, Pennsylvania, "powwowing" (also called "conjuring" or "charming") has sustained its original Indian "witch doctor" connotation. To the Amish, powwowing is folk-rooted faith healing, and some Amish condemn the practice.

whose stinking, yellowed bodies were devoured at last by the birds and the beasts.

After this, most men did not mock the French God or fall so quickly in violence upon the god-men—either the French or the Dutch or the English—who came more and more from over the Great Sea.

Yet the Narragansett escaped the plague, and so we declared our medicine to be strong. And we gave thanks to our great god Cautantowwit and to dark Chepi and the spirits of the winds and the waves and the beasts and the trees. And this was five summers before I was born.

"Askug our powwow is close with the spirits," said Katanaquat my father as we lay one night together upon our bed. "They hear him even when he snores."

"Do they hear him only?" I asked, for I was very young and had many questions about such things.

"No," said my father, "but they hear him best."

"How is it that they hear him best?" I asked, for I wished them to hear me, too. The powwow was my great-grandfather, and should I not also be a great powwow one day?

"When you lie quietly upon the bed in the shadow of the moonlight, do you hear the beating of your heart?" questioned Katanaquat my father.

"Yes," I replied, "and it sounds in my ears like the chant of the bullfrog in the marsh."

Silvermoon my mother laughed quietly.

"So, too, do the spirits hear Askug," said my father with a wide and sighing yawn. "For they long ago swallowed him, and now he beats like the heart within their unseen breast."

Swallowed by the gods! How could this be? I did not ask, for my heart was chanting like the bullfrog—and my father was snoring.

When my summers numbered six, I went to Plymouth of the English with my father and his great friend, our prince Mian-tonomi. As we arrived, the English were sending away—against his will—a wicked man called Morton. They put him upon one of their great-boats, and they sailed him out to sea.

Many more went with him—to cross the sea for trade and travel—but he alone was sent from them for his wickedness. He shouted many things that I could not understand, but I knew that he mocked the English for the way his face was twisted and the way his words were tossed.

"What has he done to be thrust from his people thus?" I asked Katanaquat my father.

"He is the weed that is torn from among the corn," replied my father. "For he sells guns to the tribes of the Massachussetts, and strong water to the children of their sachems."

"Why is this wicked?" I asked. "Are not guns good in the hunt, and better than our bows? For Canonchet says it is so."

My father looked about him at the soldiers of Captain Standish as they stood staring out upon the rolling, blue-black waters of Plymouth Bay and the fluttering, wide white wings of the English great-boat. "Young Canonchet is not yet as wise as Miantonomi his father," said Katanaquat. "For the little brave heeds the bark of the dog quicker than he hears the song of his elders. Though guns are good in the hunt, they are not better than our bows." At this my father's hand moved toward his shoulder, but his bow was not there, for the English required that our weapons be laid outside their towns when we came to traffic and to trade. His long fingers twitched anxiously, seeking the comfort of their friend, the strong bent oak.

"Our bows are like the wind while the English guns are like the thunder," explained Katanaquat my father. "The beasts do not flee from the whisper of the wind as they bolt from the bellow of the thunder. And so the bow is better in the hunt.

"But the powder and the shot are better on the warpath than the bow and the arrow," he continued, "for they spit death faster and farther." And he looked again upon the English soldiers and their muskets. "I would have a gun myself," he whispered to his own heart and my ears alone.

"But now you may not have one from Morton!" I cried. "For he is sent away upon the salt sea and you cannot walk the path to meet him in the trade."

"No. For I am not the giant Weetucks that I can step into the waters and wade out to the islands!" laughed Katanaquat my father, and he lifted me up so that I could see the great-boat as it turned upon the wind and moved slowly out to sea.

"And strong water?" I asked, as I watched the gulls glide war-ily above the whitewashed spray, crying like charging warriors as they dove toward a leaping band of silverbacked fish.

My father sighed—that brow-bent, tight-lipped sigh that meant his thoughts were brewing like the soup within the kettle of Silvermoon my mother. Then he turned his hard, dark eyes upon mine. "Kattenanit my son," he said. "Strong water is filled with the spirits. I know, for I have seen them swimming there."

And I looked anew upon the leaping fish. And I thought of the great porpoise and the giant whale beneath the dark salt sea. And I pictured their silent, black shadows moving through the green waters like the blacksnake slides through the grasses of the marsh. And I shuddered for the moment.

"Those who drink strong water swallow the spirits in great number," said my father. "And the more they drink, the more they are filled with the gods of the drink. And the gods do play with the mind of the man like the cat plays with the ball."

Father set me upon the pebbled shore and took my hand. I kicked a small stone and watched it spin and stumble toward the feet of an English soldier. It leapt over a large clamshell and smacked the shin of one of his great, black boots. He glanced for a moment at his foot, then at my wide-eyed stare. Seeing me pull myself back behind my father, he smiled a broad-faced, knowing smile, his teeth flashing white behind his brown beard—*like the tail of Noonatch the deer*, I thought, *as it turns in the dark thicket to flee from the falling foot of man.*

"The ball is muddied and dizzied and beaten by the cat," I heard my father say, as the English soldier turned his hairy face once more toward the sea, "and it no longer knows whether the sky is blue or the earth is black. Those who are drunken with strong water do many bad things, for their hearts open up like caves out of which the beasts of the night do rage and roar."

And I knew then that it was good that Morton be sent from the English, for how could the children of the sachems of the Massachusetts be safe upon their paths if their hearts did rage and roar like Pussough the wildcat?

"Then it is better to be swallowed by the spirits than to swallow them," I declared.

"It is all the same!" said my father, lifting me again in his arms and pushing us forward through the crowd to the edge of the shore. The waves slipped quickly in and slid quickly out again, back and forth, in and out—*like our great friend Assoko the Fool*, I thought, *as he rocks to and fro while sitting upon the floor of my father's wigwam.*

"It is all the same," repeated Katanaquat my father. "For whether the man swallows the Great Salt Sea or the Great Salt Sea swallows the man, the end is the same: the man drowns, for the sea has slain him."

"But Askug lives!" I cried.

"As the great whale lives," answered my father, "too often in the cold, dark deep, and too little with its head above the waters toward the sun."

"I would not wish to live as the whale," I said, "for I love Keesuckquand the sun too well. He chases the shadows from me and warms me when I'm chilled."

Thus I understood that the spirits were such that a man must be wary of them. And I ceased in my wishes to be swallowed as Askug our powwow had been swallowed. For I did not wish to drown, or to live beneath the sea.

In the eighth summer of my life, the English came upon the shores of the Massachusetts as the numbers of the shells that are spit from the sea. Their great-boats rose out of the waters in the east like Keesuckquand in his dawning. Their flat-walled houses rose out of the ground like the woodchuck from its lair. Their children rose from their beds to run and play like the children of all men in all places. And I longed to join them, for their games were new and full of great wonder to me. But we did not go often among them, for our powwows and our sachems were darkened in their hearts toward them.

This darkness was none of the doing of the English, for they looked well to our good, and never came against us in their strength except that the threat or the taunt came from us first. And then they desired only peace after the wrong was righted, for they said that their gods were princes of peace and desired all men to live in peace. This was good, and we said so.

But the Wampanoag their neighbors—Massasoit their sachem and his people our subjects—when they saw that the English were a strong arm to hold to, separated themselves from the cloak of the Narragansett and held to the coat of the English. For the English traded many good things with them, and asked no tribute besides. Thus the English were foes though they meant not to be.

"Each new dawning finds us more like the weak, old sachem whose people will not bow," said Katanaquat my father. "And our subjects hide our tribute in their own baskets, for they no longer fear us with the English by their side."

"And how many more of our tributaries will run like hungry dogs to the bones that are cast from the doors of the English?" cried Askug our powwow. "We must beat the dogs sorely and bind them once again beside our wigwams!"

"The dog that is sore beaten loves its master less," warned Miantonomi our prince. "And we are too few to surround the dogs of Massasoit, for they need only bark and their English protector comes running."

"Let him come!" said my father. "And we will nip at his heels ourselves."

"No!" declared wise Canonicus. "We have nipped at his heels too often already, only to have him turn and kick. Do not our teeth hurt still?"

"Miantonomi is right," said an old warrior who was sitting at the council. "We are not a large enough pack of ourselves. But if we join with the Massachusetts, who love neither the English nor Massasoit, then we may bring the stray dogs home, and chase their new master besides."

And so Canonicus our great king and Miantonomi our prince and many of the smaller sachems and sagamores of our tribes, with my father and his father Nopatin and many warriors, went to the Massachusetts to speak of dogs and war. Among the Massachusetts were many chiefs and lesser men who had bowed to us after the Dying, for they no longer had enough warriors to stand against us in the battle.

"The English—though their weapons are terrible—are not so many yet that we may not together cause them to flee from their houses and return to their cities across the sea," said Canonicus our grand sachem as he sat at the council fire of Cutshamakin of the Massachusetts. "Many birds, though they are small, can chase the great hawk from the skies."

"And then the birds are free to fly as they will?" asked Cutshamakin our vassal, for he wished his leash were longer or his wings once more his own.

"More so than this present day," nodded Canonicus with a strong smile. "Yet not without limit," he added. And the Massachusetts sachem seemed pleased with as much.

Then the mighty Narragansett and the ancient Massachusetts embraced shoulders against the English to push them back into the sea. But John Sagamore, an undersachem of the Massachusetts and one who always loved the English, took our plot to the pale princes of Salem and made it known. Thus when our warriors were at last man-behind-man upon the warpath, the great cannon of Salem of the English began to roar and echo in the trees so that the ground shook and men's hearts failed them for fear. Thus we found the English knew our coming. And thus they warned us of their might.

The Massachusetts ran to their wigwams as rabbits to their holes, and the Narragansett returned across the Great Bay to their old men and their children and their squaws.

And I knew then that the gods of the English were very strong, for they only had to shout in the forest and my people ran.

But in our pride we thought ourselves to be men who stand at the top of the mountain. For we were the Narragansett. We were the people of the inlets and the bays. We were the children of the great god Cautantowwit, who looked afar upon us from his gardens and his courts in great Sowanniu to the southwest. Like Cautantowwit, we faced east. We saw the great spirit Keesuckquand rise red each morn out of the dark bay. We stood where we stood. And thus my father taught me.

But my heart, like my eyes, faced east as well.

East, beyond the land of the Narragansett.

East, to the English with their strong medicine and their marvelous machines, their mighty weapons, and their clever tools.

East, where men in warm clothing and black shoes rode high and fast upon great moose with no antlers—called horses. Where children in long trousers drank sweet milk from great horned beasts—called cows. Where the tribes of the English rested one day out of seven to gather in song and prayer to their gods—to their One God, they said.

And my tongue longed for the sweetness of that milk, my soul for the medicine, my heart for the song.

"As the sun that breaks through the grey clouds of winter, so did the Song On The Wind pierce my heart," said my father. "It sang without words of a dream beyond waking, a land of no ending, a joy beyond telling. And it called to the heart as the father calls the son to the harvest feast and to the games."

My father stared up into the star-splashed sky as he spoke.

"Yet I knew not how to follow," he said to the stars and to the night and to my heart that was wondering.

Many other braves from many tribes throughout the hills and valleys also heard this Song On The Wind. It sang one summer night to the whole country round, said Father, and many were called beyond the moonlight toward the morning dew. But some who heard it were ill affected, and thought it a curse and an omen of evil.

"It was all one song," said my father, "but every tongue tastes the berry for itself. And some tongues find things sour that other tongues find sweet."

And this Song was one summer before the Great Dying, four summers before the English of Plymouth had come to us over the sea. Yet after they came, my father heard the Song once more.

"At Plymouth, in their Sabbath-house, there I heard the melody anew. The same Song—I am sure!—but with words of the English," he told me. "Nopatin your grandfather, and Assoko our Fool heard it too."

When the words were made known to him in the Narragansett tongue, my father understood the Song to be a chant of praise to the great gods of the English.

"To the father and to the son and to the holy ghost," Katan-
quat my father told me. "And the son is a god who walks as a
man. And all three gods are yet one!" he said. "Though I know
not how such things can be . . .

". . . and indeed I doubt that they are!" continued my father.
"For how can three be one? And how can a man be a god? And
why would a god wish to walk as a man?

"Does Keesuckquand leave his bright path in the sky to
stumble as a man among the mosquitoes and the serpents
within the cold swamp of Chepi?

"Does Nanepaushat bid the cool stars farewell to sweat as a
man in the autumn wigwam, picking fleas and cracking them
between his teeth?"

But I marveled that a god might walk as a man. And I
thought that it could be so. For did not the giant Weetucks
walk once among us, doing us great good? And so could not
another by a new Name do as much? Or more?

The Name of this son was Jesus, said Miantonomi our
prince, who wondered much about this god and asked of him
whenever he had the ear of the English.

And the Name called me often, like the Song had called my
father. And It woke me sometimes from my dreams.

"Do not turn too quickly toward your dreams," warned
Katanaquat my father. "Nor come very near them without the
long axe in your hand. For often they are snares and deceits of
the spirits. Build your wall against the gods, my son, wisely and
quietly. Thank them for their favors, but open your eyes wide
about you. Keep your arms held out before you in the night.
Stand where you stand."

I stood. And I lifted stones with which to build my wall. But
I stopped to listen always when I chanced to hear the Name.

Canonchet was my friend, the son of our prince Miantonomi. His summers were as many as mine, and we grew to
manhood each tied to the belt of the other. All that young
braves do we did together. We breathed the air as brothers.

And though my father cared not to speak much of the
Name, while Canonchet's father longed to hear of it, yet
Canonchet himself scorned the news of any gods but the gods

of the Narragansett. And this was the only stone in our moccasins as we walked the paths of the seasons together. But it was
not a stone that caused us to stumble, for we knew that each
man must speak his own heart—for how else will he know his
own name? And how can one man know another to call him
Friend, if each does not declare what lies within his soul?

At times the stone would lodge beneath the heel, and we
would sit beside the path and pull it from our shoes to look
upon it more intently. Then it held us both—but it never held
Canonchet long, for he would soon and often say to me, "One
day I will be sachem like my father and his father and his father yet before him. And I will look upon many new things to
judge them. Until then I must cling to the old ways—the ways
of the Narragansett—for those ways are sure, like the earth
and the sky."

Our enemies. They were many and all around us. The Wampanoag to our east across the Great Bay. The Mohawk—
dreaded man-eaters whom all tribes feared—to our northwest
above the Nipmuc, the Pocumtuc, and the Mohican. The spirits themselves were counted, by my father, in the number of
our foes—yet this war was his own, and none outside our wigwam yet knew it. But Askug our powwow hated most of all the
wicked Pequot whose lands were on our west across the cool
waters of the rolling Pocatuck.

The Pequot sachem—Sassacus—was powwow as well as
prince, a great warrior, and a strong ruler. Many thought him a
god and that he could not die. Under his hand were also the
western Niantic and some men of the lesser of the River Tribes
along the Long River of the Connecticut.

Among the Pequot was one named Uncas—of whom I am
sure you have heard, for great infamy often lives longer than
righteousness in the memory of men. He was a cousin to
Miantonomi, and when he was a boy he would come to play
with our prince and with my father and our Fool. But none
could love him, for his heart was rotten and his soul was sour.
In later seasons he brought much deep and dark and grievous
sorrow to many. Askug despised him, even when the summers

of Uncas were few, more for his Pequot blood than his blackened heart.

Askug hated next the God of the English—and especially the
Name.

"My spirits warn me often against these English gods!" he argued one evening in the wigwam of Miantonomi, as Canonchet and I sat eating grapes and chipping arrowheads. "When
they wake me with their warnings, they raise such a rattle that
my head aches for days."

I wondered that his head did not ache always for his own rattling and dancing and whirling and shrieking. But how else
could we know the favor of the gods? How else could we be
cured of our illnesses? How else could we know the outcome
of our hunts and of our warrings if our powwow did not rattle
and wail? So when Askug called the chant, we joined him in it.
When Askug started the dance, we set our feet behind his.
Sometimes all our heads ached. But we knew when the spirits
had heard us. For they would tell us in our dreams, and Askug
would tell us in our waking. He was their heartbeat. He was
their voice.

"Why should the spirits fear the English gods?" asked Miantonomi. "Do not all the spirits—ours and those of the English
as well—work together to break each dawn and to set each
evening in its bed at night? Does not each spirit walk in its own
path as always it has?"

The powwow did not like the queries of our prince. He
growled and bared his broken teeth, like the hungry dog that
wishes to be left alone to chew upon its bone. "Even the souls
of the fathers of our fathers cry out against us," argued Askug.
" 'Why do you forsake the gods of your fathers?' they moan.
And my head and my heart ache the more!"

"We do not forsake the gods of our fathers!" declared our
prince. "To learn of new gods is not to cast off the old. When a
new papoose comes into the wigwam of the Narragansett,
does not the whole tribe rejoice? Yet we love still the children
who run at our feet as always!"

Miantonomi cast a small stick into the fire in the center of
his house. It sat for a moment upon the blaze, rose up sud-

denly in a burst of yellow smoke, and settled down at last beside its brothers in the crackling chant.

"I do not understand this fear of new gods," said our prince. "But I will call a feast day for the city," he declared. "We will give thanks to the spirits for their many gifts and their much-watching-over our people."

Askug looked pleased. "I will fast while the people feast," said the powwow.

"As will I—and Canonicus our king," replied Miantonomi as he looked intently upon the crooked smile of the powwow. "Yet will you not also give thanks to the English one-god for the strength of his axes and his hoes, his knives and his tomahawks?" asked our prince. "All these things—and many more—he has given to the English. And have they not then traded them to us to our great good and to the increase of our crops and all that we put our hands to?"

"Let the English thank their gods!" spoke Askug coldly. "We have thanked the English and paid them in full with skins and wampum. That is enough!"

While the people feasted and our sachems went without meat, Askug danced himself into a fever to the songs of our gods. He cursed our enemies the Pequot. He railed against our enemies the Wampanoag. But he did not curse the Name. For he was afraid to, I was told. For though all the sorcery of all the powwows of our enemies the Wampanoag had once been tried against the English, it had not so much as caused the English to stub their toes upon their doorsteps! And was this not the protection of their great gods and of the Name? asked many.

Thus Askug did not curse the Name, but neither did he give it any thanks. And this, I thought, was foolish—for was it not a strong Name? And does not every strong warrior receive the honor he is due when he comes home from the battle with his arms rolled in blood and the scalps of his foes upon his belt? Who would dare to look the other way and say, "Let another man praise him for his victories, but not my lips!"? None would dare! For this would be a great injustice, and the offended warrior would lie upon his bed in shame, his heart plotting mischief against the rude offender. *Why call such blood upon our own heads?* I thought.

But Askug was the heart of the spirits, and the spirits themselves had counseled him thus.

"Let the gods fight it out among themselves!" said Katanaquat my father when I spoke to him about it. "And we shall praise the victor when the fight is over."

"Can we not know what they please?" I asked.

"Sometimes," said my father, "when they wish to tell us. Yet even then a man must try their words, for who can know when they speak the truth?"

"I wish I could search their hearts, as Mother does mine when she wonders at my thoughts," I said.

"The gods have no hearts!" declared my father. "And searching for their purposes is like looking for the drop of rain that has fallen into the sea.

"Build your wall, Kattenanit. Keep your eyes open. Stand where you stand. Be the man when your day comes.

"The spirits will do as they please."

In the summer that followed, the spirits did as they pleased. Seven hundred of the Narragansett fell by a silent dying in the midst of the fever and the small red pox.

Askug and Canonicus blamed the English and their gods for sending the plague, yet it was the English who then came among us in our suffering and did us much good. They fed us and clothed us and helped with our harvest. They tended our sick and buried our dead. They sat with us in our sorrow, and welcomed our orphaned at their own tables. I heard the Name upon their lips, and I called it once myself. Though many of my friends were laid beneath the mourning earth, the dying neither touched me nor my house. Neither did it touch but two houses of all the English, though the plague slew many thousands of Indians from the southern shores of the Pequot to the Piscataqua River of the Pennacooks.

In this once more I saw the strength of the God of the English. And afterward I often spoke the Name in my heart. Also I saw the courage and compassion of those who called upon the

Name, and this was more than I was used to finding among my own.

These were hard things to see, for I was a Narragansett. And I knew, too, that my own heart was harder than the hearts of the English in their doing good. This was a burden on my soul, and I did not want to own it even to myself. But I opened the matter to my mother, for I knew that she loved me. And cannot a young boy lay these things before the one who bore him?

"The heart is a difficult thing to know," said Silvermoon my mother, as she added green wood to the fire which warmed our wigwam in the Moon Of The Melting. The stubborn fuel hissed and stiffened in the flames, crying tears of protest as its sap boiled out like the blood of the meat upon the spit. "It is hard to look into the heart of another, even when it has beaten at your side for many long summers."

"Is my heart like the heart of my father?" I asked.

"Let it not be so," she said quietly, her lips drawn thin and her brow wrinkled sadly. "The heart of your father is a hedge and a wall, and it grows stronger and taller and thicker every season. I fear that it will close him all about until none can find him."

"Is he changed by the seasons?" I asked, for my father was my father, a warrior, and a great brave. I knew him in no other way.

"He is changed," said my mother, and I thought she brushed back tears as she pulled her long hair from her face to fasten it behind her with a piece of leather that it might not feed the fire.

"And my own heart?" I asked.

"Your heart is made of bits of stick and rock and fern and flower and sunshine and song from beside every path you have walked, Kattenanit my son," smiled Silvermoon my mother, as the wrinkles gathered around her eyes. She suddenly seemed an older squaw. But then—with a laugh—the well within her soul bubbled up like the fresh waters of the springs at Matantuck. It lent beauty to her clean, dark eyes. Those eyes were everything to me.

"But what of my wall?" I asked.

"Your wall is your own," said my mother, "made of those same sticks and rocks and ferns. But be careful how you raise it." She took an English iron pot down from a great hanging hook, brushed it clean with a small strawed broom, and set it on the floor. "Make your wall strong to protect those who are weak, but do not lay the brambles at the door where the friend would come to sit and laugh and talk."

She sighed. "And do not make it so high that the old man—or the old woman—cannot climb it to share with you the wisdom of the years."

She straightened her bent back for a moment and seemed much taller than herself. For an instant I felt like a very small child again, looking up at the baskets on our wigwam wall, out of reach and filled with curious pebbles and stones, feathers and bones, shells and clubs, knives and hatchets, needles and nuts, arrowheads and thin straight shafts of elm and ash.

Much is still too high for me, I thought, *and far beyond my reach*.

"And the gods?" I heard myself ask, as the eyes of my heart squinted at baskets that hung upon the sky above the sun.

"Honor them all and always," said my mother from a world far away.

Father came back after fighting the Pequot along the Pocatuck. He hung his bloody trophies upon a high pole. I was proud. "He will soon have more scalps than your father our prince," I boasted to Canonchet.

Nopatin my grandfather was a hero in the conflict, as was Assoko our Fool. None fought like our Fool!

Our warriors had pushed the Pequot back across the Pocatuck with much slaughter. Eighteen heads of the men of Sassacus now swallowed flies upon the palisade of Canonicus. I hungered for the stories of the battle, and I shouted in exultation at every turn of every tale of blood and victory. Yet my hands did not itch for the war itself—and this was something that Katanaquat my father could not understand.

"Do you not wish to run with me upon the warpath?" he asked.

"I do, and I will, when I am of the age," I said.

"Your heart must beat to the pulse of the spilled blood of our foes," he warned, "for no other heart will give you strength when you face the warclub of the enemy!"

"I am not afraid of the foe," I said to my father. And I set my eyes upon his. "You know that I am not afraid of the foe."

He knew this to be so, for it was only nine days past that I stood with him against Uncas when the crooked once-Pequot—now sachem of the Mohegan—challenged him beneath the pines. My bow was readied then, and its shaft had found its target though I had not aimed at flesh. I pinned the mad dog to a tree by his loin clothes! I drew no blood, but I had stood my ground. I was not afraid of the foe.

"Your heart is not as my heart," sighed Katanaquat.

"Yet my heart is for your heart, my father," I replied. "And when my days are come, I will run with you upon the warpath."

We embraced.

And this was in the Moon Of Midsummer of my thirteenth year.

The Rain From God built a new and larger wigwam and took another wife, for Silvermoon had borne him only one child in all their summers together. And I began to see the changes of which my mother had hinted. But what can the small stream do to alter the course of the great river?

And though my father continued to take me into the woods to put strength into my heart against the spirits—to walk the hunt with me, to draw the bow, to swing the tomahawk, and to stalk the shadows of Pussough—still I dreamed of something beyond the rivers of the Narragansett and the blue-black waters of the Great Bay. Something above the tall pines and the strong oaks of the familiar hills of our ancient lands.

Was there not a new world to be known among the English? Were there not many lands across the Great Salt Sea? Were there not greater gods than our own? Was there not One Great God? The God who walked as a man? The Name?

Come unto me, cried the Name. And it was the strong voice of Wisdom. But no matter which way I turned, I could not see the path.

Chapter One

White As Snow

He must have ridden upon the blasting, bitter breath of Nanúmmatin the North Wind. For how else could he have crossed the miles in the midst of the pelting sleet and the blinding snows?

He must have walked like the spirit walks, untouched by the cruel elements that fly upon winter wings to assail the senses and oppose the staunchest flesh of the strongest warrior. For how else could he have survived his trek through the raging wild white of the hardest winter that my tribe had ever known?

And we were amazed when he stumbled into our city in the cold, grey twilight. And we thought him a madman or a dead man or a god. But when at last he sat enwrapped in warm blankets by the bright fire of Canonicus, sipping soup from a carved wooden bowl, he looked like any other man.

Roger Williams was born across the Great Salt Sea—Miantonomi told me—in that great city which the English call London. He grew to be a man there. And because there were few trees left beneath which a man may walk and hunt and raise his wigwam, he longed for a country where the wood was tall and the forest deep. Thus he crossed the dark, salt waters in a great sailing boat and came to our shores to live among his own at Boston and at Plymouth and at Salem. He knew to come here because of the Name. For the Name had crossed over ahead of him, calling to him from afar.

19

After his crossing, Williams walked the paths to the Narragansett to trade pots and pans and knives and hoes and hatchets for beaver skins and wampum. He loved us much, he said, and desired to know our tongue that he might better learn our ways. Very quickly he began to use our words, though very simply at the start, like the young child when he first begins to speak. Canonchet and I laughed to hear his tongue stumble. But we were delighted and amazed to hear our own words falling from the lips of an English, for it seemed somehow as if we had taught one of our dogs to speak!

But we did not think of Williams as a dog—or any other beast—but as a very other kind of man. Yet he was not a very other kind of man, except that his heart beat to the quiet rhythm of some strong and unknown chant beyond the treetops.

"I wish to speak as the English speak," I told him one day when he was trading words with Miantonomi our prince. Many in the wigwam grunted their assent to my desire. Thus, while Williams practiced our tongue, he also instructed us in his own. And as he told us tales of gold-gilded carriages and great stone castles and scarlet-robed kings, he spoke, too, of the Name.

The Name was the chant that beat with his heart. I could hear it even when his lips were silent. But they were seldom silent. We called him "the God-preacher," for he boasted of his God as often as the warrior exults in the scalps he has taken or the battles he has won.

And now the preacher was among us to stay—and not to return to his own, he said. He would send for his wife and his children after the final Moon Of The Melting, when the Moon Of The New Green rose to signal the coming of the spring.

Yet how could this be that an English should cleave to the cloaks of the Narragansett?

What strong song had called the God-preacher from beside his laughing fire within his thick, wooded walls at Salem?

What deep dream beckoned him out into the wicked, drifted white of winter to follow the shrieking gale to the half-buried tents of the shivering Narragansett?

"Love is the song," he said, "sung by the Father through the Son.

"Your souls are the dream," he said, "trapped in darkness and awaiting the light of God."

Love! "Do the gods ever sing of love?" scoffed Katanaquat my father. "Never!"

Our souls! "Is the Name greater than Keesuckquand that he can shine light even upon the soul of a man?" cried Askug our powwow.

"The Narragansett have one Fool already!" laughed the warriors of Canonicus and Miantonomi. "Must we lodge a mad English among us as well?"

Assoko the Fool was the friend of my father. Born one day apart, of mothers who were sisters, Assoko and Katanaquat grew as brothers.

The Fool was my friend, too. I loved him for as long as I could remember. For his heart was clean, his eyes were warm, and his tongue was kind.

I did not complain when his strong arms embraced me too tightly or his small hands got tangled in my hair as he absently fingered my locks while he rocked. For I knew that he loved me. As if I were his own son, he loved me. Even when children were born to him at last—of a squaw given to him for his great fighting at Nopatin's victory along the Pocatuck—still he loved me.

And I did not think it strange that he seemed sometimes the child himself. That he did not think so quickly or speak so well as other men. That he cried—like the papoose—when none should cry. That he laughed—like the fool—when none should laugh.

Though many thought him a shell full of spirits, my father taught me well that Assoko was his own man—a man whose soul was strong of itself, for it had to work much harder than the souls of other men. When Assoko was young, he could not even walk as other children walked. Nothing came easy for the Fool. Yet he learned all things at last, and in the learning he won great patience.

While other men stood at the fire, spitting out words in haughty praise of their own thoughts and deeds, Assoko sat humming, smiling out of one side of his face and frowning with the other, privately fishing the deep waters of his own soul, waiting quietly for the tug at the line, rested and ready for the wrestling match when at last the eel takes the bait. "This one swam fast," Assoko liked to say while licking the bones of some great fish he had caught. Then he would grin. Even as the swiftest fish will hang at last upon the hook of the hunter who waits, so do the wisest words rise at last from the lips of the long-silent listener.

"Too many words," he once mumbled during an especially long and hot and smoky council in the wigwam of Miantonomi our prince.

"Too many words, Assoko?" asked our prince, whose ear was always open to the heart of his friend the Fool.

"Too many arrows on one bow!" Assoko exclaimed. "None hit the target!"

None danced like our powwow. For none were so full of the winds that they could whirl above the earth like so many dry leaves in the tempests of autumn.

Canonchet and I sat in the shadowed corner of the wigwam of Miantonomi his father. Like the house of Canonicus our grand sachem, the tent of Miantonomi was long and held three great fires. Many squaws lived with our prince, and many children—young and old—slept the cold nights upon the low, blanketed beds. Tonight, the wives and children of Miantonomi were scattered in small bands against the matted walls, while old men, wise men, great men, and warriors filled the center of the tent.

Around the central fire—which burned highest and hottest on this midwinter's eve—danced our powwow.

Askug was an old warrior. An old hunter. An old sorcerer. And yet he seemed no older each year than the last, and no more so than when I first saw his dark face above my bed as I lay in my mother's arms. I did not know if ever he was young. For can the spirits be born? And can they be young? And do they grow old? And had they not swallowed my grandfather? And did he not beat as their heart?

Yet old warriors do not dance! They sit and watch with sad eyes while the young men leap and turn. And they do not shriek like the wildcat at midnight or howl like the lone wolf upon the hillside. They groan like the ancient willow when the strong wind blows upon its back. They growl like the aged dog who hears the foe at the door of his dreams.

But our powwow danced. He shrieked. He howled. And should he not? And must he not? For how else could the spirits be honored? How else could they be called to our side? How else could they hear and heed and grant us their favor, if our powwow did not dance?

This night he danced for the snows to recede, for the winter was hard, long, and heavy, and the Narragansett lay cold and hungry beneath it. I was sure that either the winter must melt or the powwow must melt, for nothing apart from the vast, crackling blaze burned hotter than Askug of the Narragansett.

His eyes glowed with the lusty thirst of the heart that is kindled for the battle. His face and arms glistened with a flowing sweat that ran blood-red in the light of the roaring flames. His mouth coughed up smoke from the hot, ashen depths of his burning soul. He wailed with the dark and grizzled cry of the warrior who is about to gorge himself upon the charred and smoldering flesh of some great foe who has died valiantly upon the fiery stake of torture.

And he danced.

Twisting his painted body like the dog that chases its tail. Coiling his limbs about him like the serpent that is ready to spring. Leaping into the smoky air like the wildcat that bounds into the tall sycamore. Waving his arms like the willow in the hurricane. Prancing and leaping like Noonatch when he smells the doe in heat.

He danced. And many were the men who joined him in the dance.

"Great Cautantowwit!" cried the powwow.

"Hear us as we cry!" chanted the warriors of the dance.

"Great Cautantowwit!" cried the powwow.

"See us as we dance!" echoed the warriors.

"Great Cautantowwit," prayed the powwow, "stand upon

your great mountain in the warm Southwest and look to the
east! Call the gods around you and tell them of our plight! We
are made to run the long gauntlet of Nanúmmatin the North
Wind. Our feet are frozen and our legs are wearied. Nanúmmatin blows upon our heads, and our eyes close fast in the
sleep of death. Clap your hands, great Cautantowwit, and
wake Sowwanishen the Southwest Wind. Wake Sowwanishen
and point him to our doors."

"Come, Sowwanishen, and chase the North Wind home to
his bed!" pled the warriors.

"And will you not rest for a time, Nanúmmatin? For a season?" continued the powwow, as he beat his arms about him
like the wings of the frighted partridge, chasing the shadows,
dispelling the smoke. "Take your rest, great Nanúmmatin! For
every warrior must close his eyes in sleep, that he might rise up
renewed to fight again. Sleep! Sleep! And when you have slept
long—when the moon has rolled over the mountains many
times—awake at last to blow again!"

Late into the night the powwow my great grandfather
danced. Until his sweat was gathered in such fullness that it
might have quenched the fire had it fallen upon it. Until his
long hair had tied itself in more knots than I was used to seeing upon the fishing nets of Katanaquat my father. Until he
swooned as one wounded on the field of battle. Until every
warrior who had joined him lay wasted on the floor or had
stumbled home to fall upon his mats to dream of sunshine and
pear blossoms. Until none were left in the tent of Miantonomi
but the household of Miantonomi. And Katanaquat my father.
And the croaking, reeling medicine man of the mighty Narragansett. And me.

And still the hard winds blew.

"The spirits harshly yank his leash this night," sighed my father quietly, "while they sing their own cold song in the barren
treetops." I heard the cruel, unceasing howling outside our
smoky shelter, and I shuddered.

"Williams!" coughed Askug, tottering over to where my father
and our prince were seated. "The god-preacher!" he gasped.

I looked to the wind-rattled mats that clung tightly to our

door, thinking to see the good English man pass through them. But he did not.

Miantonomi looked upon the sweat-soaked powwow, but our prince did not speak.

"Williams has cursed us!" hissed Askug. "And so the gods do not hear us."

The tired fire yawned brightly for a moment, throwing the long shadow of the powwow over the troubled faces of Miantonomi and my father, then it lay itself down upon its amber, ashen bed and closed its eyes. The room fell into a violet darkness, and I shivered. A papoose cried on the other side of the wigwam, and someone shuffled through the shadowed dimness to feed another log to the slumbering fire. It opened its warm eyes again and waved its weary arms once more above its bowed head.

Sleep! the wavering flame whistled.

Did it counsel us? Or did it beg on its own behalf? I turned to Canonchet and saw that he had made up his own mind in the matter. But I was not tired. Not tired enough. Not yet.

I was cold though. Leaning tight against the snoring Canonchet, I pulled his mat upon myself as well.

Our prince pursed his lips and sighed through flared nostrils. "Williams does not curse us," I heard him say.

"The winds yet howl as they have all day!" argued Askug. "And my spirits cry the name of Williams! If he does not curse us, then why do the gods shake their warclubs at him?"

"The gods shake their warclubs at any man who does not fear them," said Katanaquat my father.

"You are worse than the Fool!" scoffed Askug his grandfather. "For you shake your own warclub at the gods!"

"I stand where I stand," said Katanaquat. "And must not the warrior look about him for the foe? Must not the hunter watch each thicket for the beast of the hunt?"

"The spirits are not beasts that we hunt them! They . . ."

"They are the hunters?" offered Katanaquat.

"They are the gods!" declared the powwow, his bloodshot eyes opened wide in desperate anger. "Do you not fear them?"

"I fear them," admitted my father.

"And who does not fear them?" asked Miantonomi to the shadows and to the powwow and to my father and to the gods who lurked listening.

"Williams," answered my father.

And I wondered in amazement that a man did not fear the gods. And I pulled the mat over my face for the fire had fallen low again. And the frost of my own breath fell upon me like a cold mist.

At length I slept.

"The wind blows where it will," said Roger Williams, "and no man can hold it in his hands!" And the wind blew where it willed as the snow piled high against the tents of the Narragansett.

"I do not say that any man can hold the wind," declared Miantonomi to the preacher. "Only that a man might hold the ear of the wind. That the wind might heed the man and either blow or cease to blow on his behalf."

Williams sat beside the hot, sputtering fire of our prince and pulled his round-brimmed, black hat down about his ears and eyes, causing his long, wavy hair to stick out at the sides like two rivers of falling, brown water. Though the low blaze was strong before him, the storm was stronger still behind his back. Though the walls of Miantonomi were thick with the bark of the birch and the skins of the bear and the beaver and the moose, the sharp arrows of Nanúmmatin found each weak spot, each crack and crevice, and forced their way inside. Though the flesh upon our faces threatened to blister as we leaned into the flames, the clothes upon our backs might well have been ice for the bitter breath of the merciless north wind.

The smoke of the fire rose resolutely toward the ceiling, but it could not exit, for the wind beat it back upon us until it hung like a black cloud about our heads. We could see little— at times—of the dark familiar forms that sat next to us in the red glow of the fiery fog.

"You speak of the wind as though it were a god," said Williams. And the wind spoke for itself, with an unceasing moaning, outside the wigwams of the Narragansett.

"And so it is!" declared Miantonomi.

"Nay!" argued the preacher. "For the winds are but a part of the great creation of the One Great God."

"Friend, not so!" countered our prince. "For how can the wind, if it blows where it will, not be a god? It rises from the sea on its own wings. It sings in the trees and howls in the valleys. It has great power to do both good and evil. It can lift the waves of the Great Bay out of their bounds and fling them into the forest. It can rage and roar and topple the wigwams of men. It can push the clouds of the heavens from one side of the black sky to the other. How can it not be a god? And what is it otherwise?"

"It is the wind, and nothing more," declared the preacher, "for God has made it so." And he rose to his feet, stood over the fire, and hid his hands in the black billows that climbed stubbornly above the low flames.

"I am not the wind," said Williams, "but I can make some!" And he swung his arms vigorously across the path of the rising smoke. The grey vapors leapt back from the preacher's whirling arms, separating into small, bewildered clouds that fled in all directions. As the air cleared for a few heartbeats, I looked upon the men who sat about the fire. At Katanaquat my father. At Assoko our Fool. At Miantonomi our prince and Canonchet his son, my friend and my companion.

My father grunted, a grim smile upon his lips. "A man can do much that the gods can do," he said, "but the gods can do much that a man cannot do. The man may make a little wind with his hands or with his lips, yet it is but a shadow of the real thing. It is but a faint echo of the gods themselves."

The Fool belched, and grinned a hissing grin which quickly faded to a silent frown. He rocked slowly next to the fire, his eyes ensnared by the slow-dancing flames. As the smoke settled once again about our eyes, he seemed to be lost in a world of his own. Yet I knew that he listened to every whisper, every word.

"There is truth in your mouth, my friend," said the preacher to Katanaquat my father. "For men were created to be echoes of God. Yet I say that only One God made all things—even those things that seem to be gods. And he made even the mighty winds that blow where they will. It is not their power that makes them gods; it is God that makes them powerful."

"You speak often of this one god," said our prince. "And you say that he is god alone. Yet you worship three gods: the father and the son and the holy spirit."

"The three are one . . ." began Williams, but our prince raised his hand to call the preacher to silence.

"I have thought on this much, Roger Williams," said Miantonomi. "I will tell you my mind on the matter."

The tall sachem stood in the midst of the hovering, brown clouds, wrapping his strong arms around themselves. The smoke moved away from him for a brief moment, and he set his clean eyes upon the warm face of the preacher. Stooping beside the fire, Miantonomi picked up a small stick that had escaped the flames. He broke a piece from it and laid it at the feet of Williams. "You say that the son is a man. And yet you say he is god! So, I count one god," he said, pointing to the piece of stick upon the floor.

"But you also say that the father is god," declared our prince, and he snapped the remainder of the bough in half and laid a second piece upon the ground.

"And then there is the holy spirit!" he declared, laying the last bit of stick on the mat before the preacher. "Three gods cannot be one god. One god cannot be three. These things are out of the path! They wander! I cannot know them. If there is only one god, then which of the three is the one true god?" He threw his hands in the air, tossing the question to the bewildered smoke and the snickering spirits who mocked this mad talk of one god only.

"Is the father god only?" continued Miantonomi. "And is the son just a child and not truly a man that he cannot yet be a god? And is the spirit not a god at all, but a ghost or a phantom, like the wandering soul of one who has died and cannot find entry through the gates of Sowanniu into the gardens of Cautantowwit?"

Miantonomi poured his heart out before the god-preacher. His questions flowed as waters from the clear spring. And I longed to follow those waters to the Great Sea where surely the answers swam at last beneath the rolling deep. For there a man might set his hook into the mouth of the Great Truth and pull it from the black depths!

But might it not pull the man instead beneath the dark waters where no eye can see the heavens? echoed my heart with the warnings of Katanaquat my father. *And might it not, like any spirit that is given the chance, swallow the man into its own dark belly where no cry can reach the land of the living?*

"Look upon my hand," said Williams, pulling back the sleeve of his grey shirt. He stretched a bared arm out toward the fire. It glowed red in the captured light of the smoke-shrouded blaze. "What do you see?"

A hand, of course, spoke our stinging eyes in unison. *But something more is in your heart, no doubt. Speak on.*

"It is one hand only," said the preacher, and he folded it into a solid fist. "Yet it has more than one member." He unfolded his fingers and slowly flexed them before our gaze. "But no . . ." he said, faltering, and pulled his arm back into the shelter of his clothing. He shook his head. "For though God is one and yet three, His unity and His trinity are a mystery. The mind cannot know it, nor can the tongue tell it— the heart alone can hold it! It is like the wind itself," mumbled Williams. "A mystery."

"If your god is like the wind," declared our prince triumphantly, "then surely our winds may be gods. For though your one god has made the winds that blow through your lands across the Great Salt Sea, yet our gods have made us and the heavens and the earth that we see here. And thus Nanúmmatin sings as he wills and blows as he wills. And if he would but cease his howling long enough to hear our pleas, perhaps . . ."

But I did not hear the rest of the words of my prince, for the Mystery was howling like a storm within my soul, its wide, warm winds advancing like armed warriors against the wary clouds of winter. My heart beat hard for the battle, and it pounded in my ears like summer thunder. A Fist was raised high within me, higher than the clouds of the heavens, and it flexed its strong fingers in the face of the cold and gleaming midnight stars.

I am! it cried.

When the Name walked as a man, said Roger Williams on one cold morning of the day that the English called the Sabbath, He often crossed a wide sea called Galilee in a large canoe. During one such crossing, He fell asleep upon a mat in the back of the boat while his friends paddled.

While the Name slept, said Williams, great winds came sweeping across the waters, exciting the waves and disturbing the sea. The waters rolled high and the canoe was in danger of going under. Everyone might have died.

But the friends of the Name woke Him with frightened cries and called on Him to save them. Yet He wondered at their fear, and rose to face the blowing blast.

"Be still!" He commanded the winds. And they stopped their blowing and bowed their heads before the voice of the Name.

"Be still!" He commanded the waves. And they stopped their rolling and lay quietly at the feet of the Name.

And the friends of the Name were filled with more fear now than when the sea had beaten upon their faces, and they said to one another, "What kind of Man is this? For even the winds and the sea obey Him!"

White as snow.

What could be whiter than snow?

Even the paling power of the bright eye of Keesuckquand is not white like the snow. Yet when the sun in its glory spills its vast, uncovered light upon the shoreline spread with the whiteness of winter, there is nothing under the heavens that equals the brilliance and the purity of its clean, hard gaze. Then only are the snows made whiter than snow.

"I am the cannon!" shouted Canonchet, and with a loud, bellowed "Paughm!" he flung a great, hard ball of snow high into the branches of the white-covered pines.

"Pahgh!" he cried as his cannonball collided with the boughs above us, bringing an avalanche of heavy wet coldness down around our ears.

"We are caught in the fire of the cannon bomb!" cried Sawkunk the son of Weetakitch, as he clawed the fallen snow from his shoulders and his arms. "We will roast alive! Aieegh!" And he rolled in the wet drifts in an effort to extinguish the deadly blaze.

"Baugoom!" shouted Canonchet, as he tossed another ball into the overhanging trees.

Several other boys began to roll their own cannonballs in the wet, fallen snow, and I was doing the same when I had a sudden thought. Slipping from the clearing into the shadowed woods, I plodded through the deep white to the hidden base of the massive pine that stood tallest and fullest above the playfully warring band of young braves.

The lowest branches were normally beyond my reach, for the tribe cut them clear to allow full sight of enemies and game. But the winds of winter had piled the snow to within a few feet of the bottom boughs. I decided to mount the white drifts and pull myself into the pine.

The lean-to of snow was higher than my head, and climbing it was like scrambling up a slide of loose mud. But I managed, with some pushing and packing of the wet stuff, to make my way high enough that I could grasp the sticky, rough bark of the pine giant's lowest outstretched arm.

Taking hold with both hands, I walked the trunk as I pulled myself up, and soon I was seated in the boughs. From there, my climb—though slippery—was like mounting the ladders of the English. Soon I was as high as a young man might throw a stone, and I began to edge my way out upon a thick branch that hung low with a great load of the last night's snow. The bough pointed its wearied fingers out above the clearing where my friends were bombarding their imaginary foes with terrible death and great shrieking joy.

I will position myself above the pack of them, I laughed within my heart, *and shake down such a fall of snow that it buries them all at once! I will shriek like the Mohawk, and they will flee like rabbits! Then I will tell of my victory around the fire tonight, and Katanaquat my father will lift his eyes and smile long for his clever son Kattenanit the almost-warrior!*

No sooner had I found the perfect perch than the winds began to rise and the boughs began to sway. Below me, as the slow-bobbing branches began to shake loose their heavy, wet burdens, my friends danced and howled with increased delight.

"The sky is falling upon us!" cried Sawkunk, and I saw him sweep a small boy off his feet and hold him up as a shield before his own face.

Sawkunk is a coward! I thought. I would cover him first with my hail! But the winds were already at work to that end.

"Put me down," screamed the squirming little shield, as a great load of snow careened down upon him and his bearer.

Snow was falling on me, too, wet and heavy, from the many boughs about me and above me. I found it harder each moment to hold to my sloughing, swinging branch. Suddenly a great weight pressed coldly and heavily upon my back and legs, and my bough bent low beneath it. Lower. Lower. Lower it bowed.

No longer was I lying flat upon my perch, but hanging head-down in the midst of a scraping, sopping barrage of snow and falling pine.

The force of the wind grew stronger, as the dull sounds of cracking and complaining branches were mixed with the cold whisper of hundreds of heavy white blankets slipping from their beds to tumble below upon the wet carpet of the white earth.

My own bough moaned pitifully—once—and let go its hold on the trunk that had mothered it so long.

Down we went, and I let go my own hold to wrap my arms about my head. The tumble through the pine was over in a pained and frightful instant as the soft hill of slush at the foot of the trunk took the brunt of my fall. But I could not get up! For my descent had sent me to the very earth itself, and the wet drifts closed around my bent form like the sucking, suffocating muds of the swamp of Chepi. More snow fell upon me from above, with a great shower of splintered boughs and severed branches.

My hands clawed at the tight and tangled web of wood about my head. My lips spat cold slush from the door of my mouth. My eyes stung with the blows of the white and pressing foe—I could not keep them open. Wet snow slid against my face and entered my nostrils as I breathed. My legs were pinned to my side and I could no more kick them than if Weetucks had held them in the grip of his great hand. I screamed the Name once in terrored desperation. A blackness filled my soul as frigid death poured into my open mouth.

Jesus! I cried once more within my bursting heart. *The spirits swallow me! And the storm takes me now beneath the cold, eternal waves! Save me!*

I gasped. I wretched in cold agony. I forced my trapped hands from the top of my head to the front of my face and spread my raw fingers across my nose and eyes, pushing my palms a thumb away from my sputtering mouth. I opened my eyes. And I saw, just beyond the palisade of my shaking hands, a solid and surrounding wall of shaded, shifting blue.

Helplessly I lay encased within a tomb of unbearable coldness. But the shower of pine and snow had ceased. The wind, too—unless I could hear nothing within my white grave. But, ho! for the muffled sounds of my shouting friends came to my straining ears.

So, then, I was neither dead nor dying! Yet my snare was such that I dared not make a single wrong move.

To the right of my face—though I did not turn my head or move my hands for fear of a shift in the snows—lay a shadowed tunnel, large enough only for the chipmunk or the field mouse. Through it flowed a precious stream of cold air which kissed my cheek and slipped into my anxious lungs.

"Kattenanit! Kattenanit!" came the cries from the outside world. Closer at times. Further at others. Always muffled by the white walls that pinned me to the earth. Could they not follow my tracks? Had the loosed and fallen snow covered all signs of my trek to the pine?

"Here!" bellowed Canonchet, and his cry was once more near. I felt, rather than heard, the searching feet of my friends upon the snow about the pine. I determined I would risk a shout myself. But my cry rose the same moment as a united call rang out from my companions.

"Kattenanit!" their voices thundered, and my own shout was drowned beneath theirs. In mocking answer to my lost appeal,

the soaking mound shifted slightly near my right ear, pressing
its frozen mass against my cheek.

One more sound out of you, it whispered threateningly, *and I
will lay my full mantle upon you. I will darken the windows that let
light into your soul. I will close the door that lets breath into your
body. I will silence your heart forever. The wolf will find you first in
the Moon Of The Melting. The rains will wash your bones. And
your mother will wail unceasing.*

Who is this that pours ice upon my soul? my heart cried. And a
chill not born of winter rose within me like the copper-headed
serpent that rises out of the spring grasses to peer into the eyes
of the crawling papoose. Terror followed like a flood, until I
nearly choked to death within myself.

Katanaquat my father! my heart pled. *The spirits climb over my
wall! And I cannot repel them!*

"Kattenanit!" cried Canonchet again. And if I were
crouched within the summer brush beneath the tree instead
of tied to the earth by winter's cruel, uncaring load, I could
have reached out and tugged the loin clothes of my dear
friend.

"He is not within the wood!" Sawkunk declared.

I am here! shrieked my darkened, desperate heart.

"Perhaps he is gone home," said another.

"No!" I heard Canonchet say, from a distance. "He is here."

Save me! my soul cried to the Name and to Canonchet and
to the searchers in the snow.

"Save me!" my lips echoed, and a sudden, last, and desperate
strength surged through my frozen limbs. My legs wailed with
the cry of battle and strained with futility to lift my trunk toward the dying dream of light and life.

You dare! hissed the Terror which shadowed my tomb, and it
tumbled my small tunnel down around my face. My own stale
wind—my only air!—rose and fell within me, pacing to and fro
from stiffened lips to frozen palms that stood before my
pained and unbelieving eyes.

"I dare!" I cried aloud, leaning with all my waning strength
toward the heavens that my heart declared were watching.

And the Terror laughed as it stepped once more upon my tomb, forcing the snows of the slippery mound between my fingers and my face. I closed my mouth to the drowning, cold tide.

Holding my breath as my head pounded horribly, I opened my eyes one last time to the world as I knew it. The white wall that pressed against me was as black as night.

So darkness shall win at the last! I declared. And I stood tall within myself to await the loss of all things.

Here! came the cry. And I knew it must be Death.

Where else? I replied. *For I have ever been here. I stand where I stand.*

And the sky opened up to receive my soul. And a hand reached forth to pull me into another world.

And my eyes fell shut for the brilliance of the day. And my lungs caved in for the force of the winds.

And my ears shouted loudly, *This is not as you dreamed!*

And my heart cried with joy, though my thoughts reeled like madmen.

And my flesh was warmed by many coats and the touch of many hands.

And my tears fell like rain as my head throbbed in agony.

And my friends carried me through the white, brilliant forest to the warm impossible of the wigwam of Katanaquat my father.

And I cried with my mother.

And I laughed with the Fool.

And I slept long and soundly.

"The sun fell upon your mound as my eyes swept the trees," said Canonchet as we sat sipping soup upon my father's bed. "I saw a small patch of snow sink within the hill. I heard a cry within my heart. And I knew that you were there beneath the drift."

"The spirits betrayed themselves!" I declared. "For it was their death stomp that you saw."

"I do not understand them," said Canonchet with fear in his strong eyes.

"The Name," I whispered to his softened heart. "I believe it saved me."

"The Name? Why should it care for you?" said the son of my prince. "No! Bright Keesuckquand chased the shadows! His eye saw what mine could not, and thus he led me to you."

When the Name walked as a man, said Roger Williams one cold morning of the English Sabbath, He once trod like Weetucks upon the very waves of the sea.

He walked the waters as surely as the hunter walks the wooded path, and came near to His friends who were striving against the winds in their great canoe. He would have passed them by to the other side, but they saw Him upon the waters.

"It is a ghost!" they cried out, for they did not know it was the Name, and their hearts failed them for fear.

"Do not fear!" replied the Name. "It is I!"

There was one within the boat named Peter, said Williams, who loved the Name. "If it is You, Master," declared Peter, "then call me out upon the water!"

"Come," said the Name.

And Peter stepped out upon the waves.

He walked—he truly walked!—upon the sea.

But his eyes cried out to him in fear, *The flesh of a man cannot stand upon the waters of the sea!*

And the winds cried out to him in mockery, *Fool! Fool!*

And as surely as the rock sinks in the waters of the Pocatuck, Peter went down beneath the tides.

"Save me!" he cried, before the sea had fully claimed him.

And the hand of the Name reached out and pulled him from the deadly depths, set him in the boat, and carried him to the safety of the solid shore and the sure warmth of the fires of his people.

"To everything there is a season and a time to every purpose under heaven," said Williams to Katanaquat my father. "This you know, my Rain From God. The snows will end. The spring will come."

"And when the Melting comes," suggested Askug our pow-wow as he stood staring out from the wigwam, "you will be leaving us?"

"He will not be far from our fires," said Canonicus our grand

and aged sachem, rising to his feet to join the men who conversed at the door.

He laid his firm and gnarled hand upon the wide shoulder of the god-preacher. Turning toward the sachem, Williams smiled. And the sun broke forth in my heart.

What was in the man that made me love him so? That caused the hearts of our sachems to cling to him in love and friendship? That held Miantonomi at his side through endless discussions that filled the long, cold nights? That captured heart and soul of Assoko the Fool, so that his eyes rolled up toward the heavens in questioning wonder? That caused the eyes of my father to drop from their own proud heights to gaze in warmth upon the pale, strong visage of the English man? That brought young children to his lap? That caused our maidens to smile and blush when he looked upon them with the care of a father? That made even the shadows fall from the form of Askug our powwow, so that the old serpent appeared straightened like a man?

"My heart is for you all," declared the preacher. "And I am grateful to God that He has opened your own hearts toward me as if I were your own."

"You are as my son!" declared Canonicus. The old sachem held Williams more tightly, and turned the preacher's strong form to face us all.

"I have given Roger Williams a piece of my woods to the north of the Seekonk," announced Canonicus. "There he will raise his house. There he will set his corn. There he will gather his squaw and his children. There he will make his home upon the lands of the Narragansett."

Grunts and hums of warm approval rose from all who were assembled in the great wigwam of our grand sachem—all but Askug, who groaned as one who takes a hard blow to the belly. And the shadows returned to surround him.

"There he will truck with us in English goods," continued Canonicus, "for there we will travel to trade our skins and our corn and our venison." The old chief halted for a breath and looked to Williams. "You will have sugar in your stores?" he asked, and his eyes were as those of the child that begs his mother for the honeybiscuit.

"Always—for you, my wise and sour-faced friend!" laughed the preacher. And we bent our heads to chortle and to share in the jest.

"Long winters and many summers make a man wise and sober," spoke our prince Miantonomi, "but never sour so long as he walks his paths in honor and in peace with all his strong friends!

"I pledge you my heart," said our prince to the preacher. "And I ask for no sugar," he added, as he embraced his English friend. More laughter rolled through the great tent.

"It is my tongue that asks for the sugar," Canonicus quickly explained, "not my heart! And should not the tongue of a grand king taste some sweetness near the end of its troubled days?" He looked about the great room, and all heads bobbed in amused assent to these rightful and kingly desires. "Yet my heart is yours as the heart of Miantonomi my nephew!" he declared to Williams, stepping back to raise a chant.

"Welcome always, friend, to the fires of the Narragansett!" he sang.

"Welcome, friend!" declared the joyous wigwam.

"Welcome always, friend, to the table of Canonicus!" cried our king.

"Welcome, friend!" chanted the household of the great chief.

"Welcome always, friend, to the hearts of the First People Of The Forest And The Bays!" sang Canonicus. And he set his face soberly, bowed his silver-braided head, and held his wide palms out to the English preacher.

Williams could find no words, and I knew that his heart was weak for the true love that came upon it from our people. Is it not a strange thing that strong words of love make the heart faint? Yet afterward, the soul stands taller than before.

He opened his mouth at last to speak, and his tongue, though it stumbled, did not fail him.

"Grace, mercy, and peace be unto you all in the name of the Lord Jesus Christ," he said quietly. And a great shout arose as more logs were fed to the fire.

Men slapped one another upon their arms, women warbled

like birds, and Canonicus led Williams to the central fire where they sat in tight quarters with many glad warriors, and ate.

"What is Grace?" I asked of Canonchet my friend the son of our sachem the prince. And he did not know. For he was not yet a sachem, he said, that he might know such things.

"And why must a man wait to know of Grace? Of Mercy? Or of Peace?" I asked him. And he said that Mercy could be known by all. And Peace. But of Grace—his father did not even know.

"Then the knowing comes not to the man or the sachem merely by years or by honor!" I declared.

"Perhaps the spirits grant the knowledge," said Canonchet my friend. "Perhaps the powwow may tell us."

But the powwow did not know, and declared Grace a curse if it came from the Name. And I scoffed at the powwow and went with my friend to my father, for he was the wisest in things yet unseen—though his was the counsel I hoped to avoid.

"Grace?" he said. "It is not for men who breathe. For there is no such thing in the land of the living! The Grace of Williams is a shadow and a dream. Can any man touch it?"

"But the gods! Cannot they give what no man can give?" I asked. "And have you not declared it so in all the fourteen summers of my life?"

"The gods give as they see fit to give!" declared Katanaquat my father. "You can build your wall, my son, and hide from their hand behind it, but you cannot force their hand in the field."

"You have seen them, Father!" I argued. "When your eyes held theirs, was there no plea within your heart?"

"None!" declared my father. "For the warrior does not plea with the foe who holds the knife to his neck."

"Is there none among them that cares for us truly?" I cried.

"None!" answered The Rain From God.

"Not even great Cautantowwit?" I begged. "Not even the Name?"

"I do not know the Name!" he cried angrily. "And why should you wish to lay your head before the axe of any god? Have I not warned you? Do you not see? Must you be laid beneath the snows again to feel their icy claws and hear their threats of death? Are you not my son? The first son of my loins and the mirror of my years?"

"I am your son," I proudly declared.

"Then hold back your hand from treating with the gods!" he commanded. "Stand where you stand!"

"Your father thinks that treating with the gods is like striking hands with lightning," said Canonchet as we walked thoughtfully together in the Moon Of Late Winter.

Chapter Two

Providence

The sound of English axes mixed with the twittering of the busy birds and the intermittent hammering of the hungry, hunting woodpecker. The fragrances of early summer rose from the reawakened earth to ride upon the soft breeze in the company of the wafting odor of the punkwood fire. A small, pale-faced man with curled red hair and a bristling brown beard whistled a melody that he had carried with him from across the Great Salt Sea. A large, black-bearded fellow hummed in unison, and swung his axe in rhythm with the sorrowful tune.

The great oak fell. And the hard maple beside it. The cherry, too. And the ash. With terrible crashes they shook the forest, then shed their limbs before the sharp command of English iron.

I watched the men work, and I thought it wonderful.

The trunks of the giant oaks became thick, squared beams which were laid in piles to one side of the sunsplashed clearing. The great legs of the maples were likewise transformed. The limbs of each felled tree were chopped into lengths twice that of a man's arm and piled beside the great beams. The red-haired English called us to inspect the ash, that we might take some of it for our bows and our arrows. Some of the maple was split into firewood and stacked beneath an ancient spruce that pointed its proud head toward the drifted grey clouds of the heavens. The many chips were gathered and added to our fire.

Then the men began to dig, and it seemed so like fun that
Miantonomi got up from his tobacco and his pipe and joined
them. Could we sit and watch as our prince shoveled dirt beside the English? Canonchet and I, with my father and our
Fool, set aside our smoke to lay stiff hoes and iron shovels to
the soft earth.

"Is this not the woman's work?" asked Canonchet as the
sweat of his labor dampened his long black hair. Assoko
looked suddenly surprised, for yes! it was the work of the
squaw to turn the soil—yet now the Fool was turning the soil
himself! Was he as a woman? He sat down in the deepening
hole and frowned.

"Nay!" declared Roger Williams, who had barely rested since
the hard day had dawned. "This is not work for women!"

"Truly does the preacher speak!" laughed our prince, as his
shovel spat a mouthful of dark earth upon the lap of the troubled Fool. "For when has the squaw of the Narragansett ever
raised a house of the English? Up! Up, Assoko, and subdue
the earth!"

The Fool stumbled to his feet and wiped the dirt from him.
"Woman's work!" he mumbled, climbing from the pit. He
walked to the fire and sat down with his head between his
knees. *He must think his slow thoughts,* I said to myself, *and come
to a decision in the matter.*

When the hole was all dug, it was the height of a man, wide
and long and squared like the houses of the English, and this
too was wonderful. But the day was spent, and thus we retired
to a bark-roofed dugout that lay against the hillside just beyond the clearing. There, packed tight like many clams in one
shell, we feasted on venison, corn soup, and bread.

"Though I thought to live in these woods with my family
alone," said Roger Williams to Miantonomi our prince, "men
came to me from Salem pleading to raise their houses beside
mine in peace. I could not turn away them who came to me as
beggars asking only to share the land and live in freedom as
brothers."

Williams spread his hands out toward his English friends.
The red-haired man, named Wicks, grinned with his mouth full

of meat. Beside him sat Thomas Angell, a young man of my own years, looking very tired after the long hot day of unending labor. On a bench behind Wicks and Angell were the humming, black-bearded John Smith and a sweaty, weak-looking, light-haired fellow called Harris.

"It is good that you will not be alone," said Miantonomi. "For it takes many braves to make a tribe. And it takes many arrows to bring down the herds of Noonatch. You will be glad to have brothers by your side."

"Tomorrow we will line our cellar with stone, and will build a stone chimney for our fire," said Williams. "The next day, the Lord willing, we will lay our floor and raise our walls. Then we shall split timber for clapboard and shingles, and finish our windows and our doors. Within a week, a good English house will stand where yesterday the black bear scratched his back against the oak. Will you stay to watch and help?"

"I will stay," said our prince, for he liked much the company—and the ample supper table—of the preacher.

"I wish, one day, to build an English house of my own, for my squaw and our children," I said to Canonchet, as we lay upon our coats beneath the cool and wide-eyed gaze of Nanepaushat. The stars blinked at us from above the great spruce and winked at us through the gently waving arms of the wooded sentinels that surrounded the clearing of Williams. The soft music of the low-singing waters of the Seekonk rose from over the next hill and walked the woods to whisper in our ears. An owl hooted somewhere beyond the river.

"The wigwams of our people will keep my children warm," said Canonchet sleepily. "But first—no matter what our walls are built of—we must get us some squaws!"

"And before that," I said to the distant stars and the tireless moon, "we must take our first scalps."

"I have been dreaming of the warpath," said Canonchet.

"I have been dreaming of Aquinne," I heard myself say.

"Of peace?" asked Canonchet, and he rolled to face me.

"Of the maiden whose name means 'peace,'" I answered. "Aquinne, the daughter of Wussuckhoso."

"Ah!" replied Canonchet, and he turned upon his back again to stare into the star-sprinkled heavens. "The one of whom all the boys dream!"

"Yes," I said.

"And will you go to war soon that you may win Peace?" he chuckled.

"As soon as you," I sighed. And I stretched out my arms toward the dark woods and yawned.

"Love can only be bought by blood," mumbled Canonchet. "And we are not yet warriors that we may barter blood for love."

The owl hooted once more, and Nanepaushat stared down upon the sleeping Narragansett.

After the house of Williams was raised, more trees were felled. More homes were built. Walls of stone and fences of timber sprang up about each house and lined the widening clearing. Much corn was planted along the river and in a meadow that stretched upon the ridge that overlooked the village. Cows and pigs were sent over from Plymouth. They grazed in the tall grasses or rooted among the brush beside the English houses. Mary the wife of Williams came from Salem, with their young daughter Mary. Another girl-child came forth to them from the womb. They called her Freeborn.

And the village grew suddenly, like the fir tree which is one day but a seed within the ground and the next day a sapling that is already stretching its long fingers toward the clouds.

Providence. Williams called his village Providence. For it meant that his God had watched over him well and surprised him with good.

"Hearken to me," cried Williams, above the rattling chatter of the hunters of the Narragansett. The seated braves jostled their shoulders against one another, shifted their forms upon the matted, wooden floor, and lifted their curious eyes to behold the preacher. It was the Sabbath, and that meant god-talk. Meat and drink would have to wait for the preacher to expound his gods.

"Hearken to me as I tell you of the One God and His Heaven," said Williams. "Of the One God and His Hell."

I had heard from Williams of this Heaven and this Hell. And my heart longed for Heaven, while my soul feared for Hell. But so had it always been within me, for my father had taught me the ways of our people: that when a man dies his soul flies to Sowanniu in the Southwest—to the gardens of Cautantow-wit. There, a great fierce dog guards the gates of Summer. If a man is worthy, the dog will let him pass into the courts of Cautantowwit. Within those courts lie pleasures and peace for days without end. Yet if a man is wicked, the dog will chase him from the doors. And the soul of that man must wander without hope and without love, eternally.

"All men must die," declared Williams, and our heads nodded sadly in dark and troubled consent. "Englishmen die. Dutchmen die. Indians die. And when they die," said the preacher, "their souls go not to the Southwest."

"You lie!" cried many. But my own lips were still.

"Though the English may go elsewhere," fired a bent, old hunter from the back of the warm room, "yet our souls sprout wings for Sowanniu!"

Grunts of hard assent rose from the small congregation, and faces were lifted arrogantly toward the beamed ceiling. *If this be the talk of the English, let us eat his meat and be gone!* was the silent cry of many who sat in the house of Williams.

The preacher ran his coarse fingers through his wavy, dark hair. His clean, brown eyes walked the room to look upon each face. As he caught my gaze, he nodded, and my heart reached out to him. I could not grunt against him, for I knew that his tongue was straight. And I knew that he had books and writings—and one Book that God Himself made—concerning men's souls. Because of the God-book—Miantonomi our prince had once said—Roger Williams might well know more than we who must trust upon the dim-echoed word of our forefathers.

Williams began again, for he knew that we would listen. Each man must hear the heart of the other, whether he walked the same path or not. This was right. This was our way.

"All that know the One God," said Williams, "all that love and fear Him, go up to Heaven. There they live ever in joy in God's own house."

"Does the One God live in an English house or in a wigwam?" asked Canonchet my friend.

"And how can any man love the gods?" coughed Katanaquat my father.

"And who can know this god as though he were a man of flesh?" challenged a young brave who sat upon the table of Williams.

"This god is no god!" spat a tall warrior—a Mohegan of Uncas—who stood at the door. "This god walks as a man! He lets himself be taken in the battle and hung by his arms upon a tree. He is tortured. He dies. He is no god! He is a flea!"

"You will not speak thus in my house, Wequash," said Williams firmly but quietly. "Have I or my God done you any ill that you kick at us so?"

"I do not kick at you, Roger Williams," said Wequash stubbornly, with his face to the floor, "but at this god who dies. For the gods do not die."

"The gods do not die!" echoed the hunters of the Narragansett.

The preacher stood up taller for a moment, and sighed. He raised his arms out above his head to call us to silence.

"When a great and hated warrior is taken in battle, do not his enemies rejoice in the catch?" Williams asked.

"Yes!" we all shouted. And I saw that Wequash had slipped out of the house and closed the door behind him.

Miantonomi stood suddenly and faced the preacher.

"Miantonomi, beloved prince of the Narragansett," said Williams. "Will you speak?"

"My friend," said our prince to the preacher, "I wish to hear more of the god who walks as a man, but I must speak with Wequash before he fades into the forest. I beg your pardon and your leave."

"You will return?" asked Williams earnestly.

"I will return," said our sachem. And several hunters began to rise to follow our prince. "I would go alone," said Miantonomi to the restless braves. "And if you wish to eat the soup of Mary Williams, I think you must listen to the words of her husband." With a wry smile, he strode through his men, opened the door, and disappeared into the daylight.

"Tell us of this great and hated warrior who is taken in battle," shouted the young brave who sat upon the table of Williams.

"His name is Jesus," said the preacher. And I felt of a sudden that the Name was among us.

Katanaquat my father shifted uneasily and looked from window to window of the small house. Did he see Wequash and our prince outside? Or did the spirits peer in upon us?

"Jesus is like the great warrior taken in battle by his foes, who dies courageously and in great honor upon the poles of torture," said Williams. And we knew that no man who dies thus is a flea. But neither is he a god.

"Yet Jesus dies not for His own honor," continued the preacher, his warm eyes filled with strength and strange medicine. "Nor does He die because His foes are stronger or swifter and have thus caught Him at war."

In the corner of the room, beside the chair of Mary Williams, little Mary and tiny Freeborn played with small blocks of wood and giggled quietly.

"He dies because He willingly gives Himself up to the foe!" said Williams, his eyes walking from one visage to another of those who sat listening. And we wondered at the warrior who surrenders to the foe.

"He gives Himself as a ransom for His tribe," explained the god-preacher. "His people—every man, every woman, every child—have been captured by the enemy. Not one of them roams the forest free. All are in bonds within the tents of their foes."

"What will become of them?" we asked aloud. But we knew what would become of them. Some braves would be tortured and die. Some would be made to be servants and slaves. Some children would be adopted into the enemy tribe. Some squaws would be taken as wives. And some—the old men, with some women and their children—would be allowed to return to their village as vassals and tributaries of the victorious foe.

"They will all go free," replied Williams. And we scoffed. We laughed. And we wondered more greatly at this strange tale.

"They will all go free," repeated Williams, "for their great sachem, Jesus, gives Himself up to die in their place—a ransom for them all."

"What tribe would set so many free for the blood of one man?" we asked, unbelieving.

"No tribe upon earth," answered the preacher.

"You mock us!" shouted the old hunter from the back of the room.

"Nay!" cried the preacher, raising his arms again. "I do not mock you. It is your gods who mock you!"

"Our gods!" we cried aloud. And Katanaquat my father smiled a knowing smile, and looked upon me with a grim eye.

"Your gods mock you," said Williams. "For they hold you captive within their tents. They keep you from the One God who alone can save you. They keep you from Jesus who has given Himself to ransom you from Hell. And though no foe of flesh would set you free, yet the One God has accepted the ransom of Jesus, and His anger will no longer fall on those who love the Son.

"But the thief, the liar, the idle man, and the murderer," continued the god-preacher, "the unclean person, the adulterer, the oppressor, the violent man, the worshiper of many gods who are no gods: these will go to the Hell where they shall ever lament!"

"Who told you so?" coughed many coarse tongues.

"God's Book tells me so," said Williams, holding up a great and heavy book for all to see. And we were silent.

"Friends," appealed the preacher, leaning toward us with his heart in his hand, "when you die without Jesus, you are everlastingly undone."

"The ransom," I heard myself say, and all eyes turned upon me. "Is this what buys us the love of God?"

"God loves you now, Kattenanit," said Williams. "But you cannot know His love, for your sins are a wall against that love." My father turned to stare at me full. *Be wary*, his heart spoke.

"The ransom," I heard myself say once more, and my father sighed through flared nostrils. "Does it buy me safety outside my wall?"

"It tears down the wall," said Williams. And Katanaquat my father rose to face the preacher.

"The Rain From God of the Narragansett," bowed the preacher respectfully.

"A man builds a wall to keep out his foes," said my father. "And he is a fool who lets another tear it down." And he sat back down beside me, crossing his arms against the counsel of the god-preacher.

Make your wall strong to protect those who are weak, but do not lay the brambles at the door where the friend would come to sit and laugh and talk, spoke the words of Silvermoon my mother in my heart.

Can this One God be the friend of a man? I said within myself. And I heard a shadowed chorus chanting, *No!*

And I heard the heart of my father crying, *Take up your war-club and stand where you stand!*

And I heard the voice of Askug my great-grandfather saying, *Cursed be the Name!*

And above it all—with a clean voice that cut through the babble like a sharpened tomahawk through a yearling birch—I heard the Name say, *Come.*

And I feared for myself.

"I am no longer a Mohegan," said Wequash as he stood with Miantonomi in the tent of Katanaquat my father. "Your prince has won me and made me to see that Uncas is a dog and not a man that I can follow him."

"Could you not tell a dog from a man before now?" scorned my father. "For one walks on four legs and barks at his master's door, while the other walks on two legs and holds out his hands in peace to his neighbor. And dogs run in packs! How do we know you do not still bark like your sachem?"

"Uncas is no longer my sachem," declared Wequash. "I have shaken his dirt from my moccasins."

"As you shook off the dirt of Sassacus your sachem before him!" fired Katanaquat.

"I was born under hard Sassacus," said Wequash, "and with Uncas I fled him as Noonatch runs with his brothers before the hunter. Sassacus is a cruel man of claws and blood, but Uncas . . . !"

". . . is a stinking snake and a mad dog!" exclaimed my father. "Has he bitten you? Or do you tire of scratching because of his fleas?"

"I have not come to your tent to be insulted!" said Wequash.

"You are among friends," said Miantonomi our prince. "Though some of them may growl a bit at first." And he looked with hard eyes upon my father.

"I growl because Uncas is a skunk whose scent clings to all who crawl the woods with him!" argued Katanaquat.

"I have washed my clothes clean of the skunk!" spoke Wequash firmly. "And I would smell his hide nevermore unless it meant my knife could cut off his tail!"

"Ha!" cried my father, convinced of a sudden. And his eyes softened.

"You are welcome here among us," said our prince, embracing the shoulders of the once-Mohegan. "And for a house, you may share my own."

"I am your servant," spoke Wequash quietly.

"One wife? Why?" asked Katanaquat my father as he counted furs and wampum at the table of Roger Williams.

"Your men have only one wife, for the most part," said Williams, as he set the pelts to one side.

"But there are those of honor and achievement among us who have taken several squaws," answered Katanaquat.

"And you are one of those great men, my friend," said Williams.

"I am," said my father.

"But many squaws is not the way of God," said the preacher, leaning back upon his stool. I watched the eyes of both my father and the English man. Both are men indeed, I said within myself.

"It is the way of the Narragansett," answered my father. "And if it were not, how could a great man be known above his brothers?"

"By his heart," said Williams.

"My cold heart can never warm me in the Moons Of The Snow as my squaws can!" bellowed The Rain From God.

"Do you not want me?" she asked.

The dusk was balmy with the soft mid-summer wind, as the first stars of evening opened their blinking eyes in the blackening heavens. The gulls cried their lonely cries, and the song of the sea rose strong with the salt-scented spray that misted our forms as we sat upon the warm rocks of the shores of the Great Bay.

Aquinne was a dark and beautiful dream—unwaking and untouchable—beside me. I feared that my eyes might fully open and that she would be gone.

"More than anything," I whispered to the sea breezes and the phantom of my heart's desire.

"We are alone," she said, staring out upon the dark and gently rocking waters.

I could not speak, for to speak would be to wake. Yet to sit in silence was to sit in hiding with bow pulled tight, watching as the doe walks the open glade and passes once more into the cover of the thicket. I must loose the arrow—somehow—and risk the waking! For how else might I know if my aim were true?

"I . . . I have no blood on my hands from the scalp of any foe . . ." I mumbled.

My dream laughed quietly. The dawn had not broken. Blood could wait. For love was stronger than blood.

My face flushed cold. My hands shook. And I thought that I must have eaten bad meat, for my stomach turned like the bay beneath a storm.

"More than anything," I whispered again. But my fear betrayed my tongue, and I slid nervously from the rock to pace before the quiet, darkness of my waiting dream.

She is marvelous! my heart cried. *And none of the stars of the heavens is the equal of her deep, sparkling eyes! She is more desirous than the ripest berry or the sweetest drink! Her heart calls me like the song of spring and the sunshine of the morning!*

*And there she sits!—a warm and welcoming fire upon the rock—
and waits my words.*

"We are alone," whispered Aquinne. And the night winds
drew my heart.

*But I am a wallowing fish in a mud pool! A strange pup who runs
from the hand that would feed it! A blind man! A deaf man! A
bleeding, dying fool! I cannot find my tongue to attach it to my
heart! And if I do—surely it will spill out sounds that mock the
night and shame the moment!*

"I cannot have you, dearest Aquinne!" my tortured tongue at
last confessed. "For the Great God commands that we wait for
the day of our pledge. Then . . . then I may lie with you and
quench my thirst upon your ever-singing sweetness." My voice
trailed off like the wind into the forest behind us. "Only then."

My dream grew darker, her image shadowed in the muddled
thoughts of waking. But she did not rise and fade like the mist
of the morning. Instead she laughed again, quietly, nervously.

"Others have had me," she said with no shame. "And I am
not yet pledged to any."

Others! Who am I among so many others?

*And what—indeed—does it matter to the Great God that I hold
myself to the fast while others feast? Am I not a man that I may take
and eat to the satisfaction of my soul?*

*And have I not tasted of lesser fruits? So why should the best fruit
be spoiled while I wait?*

*And why do I now feel the leash of the Word where once I was free?
I will cut this leash!*

I stood up behind my wall within myself. And I lifted my axe
to sever the troubling strands that chained my heart to the
Unsingable Song that rang above the stars beyond the midnight sky. And I swung my axe against the ropes.

But a Hand held the ropes, and my axe struck the Hand so
that a wound opened wide in the palm of the Hand. And I fell
back in fear as the Hand took my hard-beating heart in its hot,
crimson fingers.

I was held—undeniably held—to the bonds of a conscience,
a strong, watching conscience, that would no longer let me
roam. The leash could not be broken.

"I . . . I know that I love you, Aquinne," I said at last. And the truth put strength in my heart. "Yet there is One whom I wish to love more."

"Oh!" whispered my dream, and the light went out of her eyes.

"Not another like you!" I pleaded, leaping once more upon the rock and taking her hands in mine. "No other maiden!" I whispered. She pulled herself from me.

"I speak of the Great God!" I spat. "But I am no doubt a fool! For who can love a god? And who but a fool can believe that a god could love a man? And how could one such as you love a fool such as I! I love you, Aquinne!"

"You are mad," she said, her face filled with troubled lines that I had never seen before.

"I love you, Aquinne," I spoke more softly, taking her hands again. And she gripped them weakly, shaking.

"Who is this great god that he asks you to wait for the day of our pledge?" pled the maiden bitterly to the cold stars and to the drifting gulls and to my trembling, tripping heart.

"I don't know," I said.

Thou shalt not kill.
What could this mean?
A man must kill to live.
He must slay the beasts for the meat of his household, or his household will starve.
He must kill his enemies in the battle or his enemies will kill him.
He must take vengeance when vengeance calls, or the souls of his own departed will know no rest.
He must even—at times—lay the knife and the fire to the captives of war, or the spirits will doubt that he honors them. And in their anger they will bring calamity and sickness and death upon him.
What could this mean, *Thou shalt not kill?*

"Murder and justice for murder are one thing," said Williams as we sat about his table in the Moon Of Late Summer in my fourteenth year. "But war is quite another."

"Blood is blood," said Katanaquat my father.

"Blood is blood," echoed Assoko, rocking so close to the table that I thought he must hit his head upon its wooded edge at any moment.

"But now the Pequot spill the blood of both the Narragansett and the English," said Miantonomi our prince. "They fall upon the scattered houses of the English along the Connecticut. They crawl across the Pocatuck to tomahawk my people in their beds. Canonicus and I have pledged to stand with the English as one against this enemy."

"Yet many among you fear the Pequot sachem Sassacus, do they not?" queried Williams.

"They do!" answered my father. "For they think him a god, and that he cannot die."

"He is no god," said Wequash. "I know this, for I was raised in his shadow. My own Pequot blood cries against him that he is both man—and murderer. I did not join Uncas against him for the love of Uncas!"

"Sassacus is wise," said Miantonomi. "And he is a great warrior. But I do not fear to face him."

"Nor do I," said Wequash the once-Pequot, once-Mohegan. "Though the medicine of Sassacus is strong, he is no god. I have seen him bleed. I would like to see him die."

"Blood is blood," said Katanaquat my father.

"Blood is blood," echoed Assoko our Fool.

"An eye for an eye and a tooth for a tooth," muttered Williams. "Soon we shall all be blind and unable to chew our supper!"

He rose to pace the timbered floor of his house. Back and forth before the fire he walked, like the wolf in its cage when it is caught and penned.

"We must counsel the English," said Williams at length to the golden flames that clawed their way up his stone chimney, "for they do not know how to fight as the Indians fight. They do not know how to find the fox in its lair."

"I will show them how to fight!" declared my father, "for they are weak women but for their great weapons!"

"They are not weak women," said Williams, holding my father with his strong eyes. "And they fight quite well, as you shall see! I simply meant that they do not fight as the Indians fight."

"I will show them how Indians fight!" declared my father anew.

"And I will lead them to the fox!" pledged Wequash. "For his lair was once my home."

"Very well," said Williams, seating himself once more. "Let us talk about how one might catch the fox and his brood sleeping. When our counsel seems good to us, I will write it down. I will send it to Boston for the eyes of my friend Winthrop. He is the under-governor and can bring our words to the ears of the governor."

"Will the governor listen to the counsel of Williams?" asked our prince.

"I will pray that he will," said the preacher grimly. "For otherwise the fox may run wild with fire on its tail. And then might we all burn!"

Chapter Three

The Fire Of God

"She is a precious little bundle," whispered Silvermoon my mother, holding the newborn child of Ohowauke and Katanaquat in her arms. Tears mixed of pain and joy trickled down her cheeks and fell like raindrops from the end of her handsome nose. Ohowauke sat, exhausted, upon the bed. Her lips moved in a quiet chant of gratitude to the spirits.

The tiny papoose stared, silent and unblinking, at the smoky ceiling of our wigwam. Her mother named her Quanatik, which means Little Fish. "For the sea is filled with little fish like this one," said Ohowauke weakly. But Silvermoon my mother bit her lip, for her own sea was empty. Her own womb was closed. And the children of the new wives of Katanaquat would fill her wigwam instead.

Katanaquat my father was not there, for the war with the Pequot was begun.

Jûhetteke! Jûhetteke! we cried. *Fight! Fight!*
And we loosed our shafts into the air upon the foe.
Nissníssoke! Nissníssoke! we shrieked. *Kill! Kill!*
And we fell upon each other with the blood lust in our hearts and the scornful cry of battle on our lips.

Yet we were neighbors. Brothers. Friends. Cousins.

For this was our way. The way of the young almost-warrior of the Narragansett. This was the path to the battles of manhood. The trail to the scalps of our foes.

Canonchet and I, with Sawkunk, Kuttowonk, and the four sons of Eatawus, fought for our honor and the eye of the maidens against a dozen other young men of our tribe.

Our cries were like those of our fathers. Our blows were like that of our fathers. Yet we did not fight to kill. Our arrows were blunt that they might not pierce. Our warclubs were rounded wood that they might not bite.

And we pit flesh against flesh.

Lips were split and bloodied. Eyes were blackened. Limbs were bruised. And a cracked skull was a trophy of honor to both the one who cracked it and the one whose skull was cracked.

"Let me go!" cried Sawkunk, as two boys sat upon him, pummeling his arms and legs with the flat of their fists. "I am killed!"

"We have not killed you yet," complained Tawhitch, one of the assailants, as he continued to pound upon the legs of Sawkunk.

"We have only begun to wound you," explained Waumausu, the second of the attackers.

"I will slay two!" I cried, kicking sod into the air, warning Sawkunk's foes that I had come to the rescue of my friend.

Tawhitch rose to meet me, a vengeful grin upon his face. A dark gap in his smile announced the outcome of a fight he and I had joined in the summer past. Three teeth less for Tawhitch. A bloody nose and headache for Kattenanit.

"I would not smile if I were you!" I goaded. "For the once-smitten target invites another blow!"

"I show you my wounds that you might anticipate your own!" cried my lively opponent. And we swung our clubs in unison.

The cudgels met with a force that stung my hands to numbness, but I held on in pained silence. No sooner had our wood kissed than Tawhitch spun round and swung his leg violently against the back of my knees. For a breath I tottered, and that was all the weakness that my foe required. Another kick to my lower legs brought me to the dust, and Tawhitch was upon me.

He had thrown aside his club to lay both hands on mine. His knee punched my stomach and stole my wind. His forehead smacked my temple and stole my reason. But I held to my weapon like the roots of the sycamore hold to the depths of the earth. And I rolled.

It was a weak maneuver, and all that my spinning senses could conceive, but it won me a brief moment, for Tawhitch rolled with me. We fell into the thicket of the blackberry, and though I barely felt the sharp claws of the grasping vines, Tawhitch yelped suddenly in pain—and let me go.

"Bees!" he cried, as an angry, winged band of black and yellow warriors rose with a hair-raising whine from their lair beneath the earth. My eyes grew wide as I watched the daggered demons gather above us like a circling whirlwind.

"Run!" I bawled, scrambling madly to my feet. But Tawhitch needed no such exhortation. The thicket tore at us as we stumbled out into the field of our former battle.

Pursue them! sang the wicked whirlwind, and it swooped after us like the osprey that falls upon the field mouse.

"Bees!" shouted Tawhitch anew, as we bolted past wrestling boys and giggling maidens.

I heard the whirling, buzzing storm behind me, the alarmed and fearful cries of the many maidens and the almost-warriors.

I saw the safe waters of Red Creek just beyond Old Willow, and my heart cried *Strength!* to my feet as my strides widened.

With one final, thoughtless leap, I crashed into the rippling coolness of Red Creek, striking at once for the deeps. Tawhitch flayed the river beside me. With the waters up to our necks, we stood with arms flying, filling the air around us with a shield of cold and constant spray.

Soon—very soon—howling young men and shrieking young women of the Narragansett crowded with us into our strong fortress, and two score of hands was added to our tireless, desperate drenching cannonade.

At length, with no strength left to heave Red Creek into the air, we sank to eye level, like so many turtles in a marsh, and glanced warily about us at the blue sky and the waving green locks of Old Willow. The whirlwind had passed, and the stream was now quiet but for the sleepy gurgle of water over rocks and the breathless gasps of the victorious defenders.

We fought while we might win. We fled when we might lose. We fought again united against a foe that would annihilate us all. This was the way of the warrior of the Narragansett.

"I would run against the Pequot like the head of the wolf pack runs after the deer!" declared Sawkunk, as we sat beside our cookfire with our catch above the flames.

"Then why do you always bay at the back of the pack in our games?" asked Tawhitch, turning his fish over the licking blaze.

"I wish to see how it is that others fight," said Sawkunk, pulling the meat of the trout from the bones. "For Pussough the wildcat watches his prey before he leaps."

"Yes," said Tawhitch, "but he does not let others leap first, for what will he say to his mate and his cubs when he returns to his lair without supper?"

"Oh, he will say, 'I leapt so magnificently today, my darling, my dear!' " laughed Canonchet in jest.

"And his mate will then say, 'But you leapt last again, did you not?' " I added. "And then she will have to go out hunting for herself!"

"You will see!" barked Sawkunk. "When our summers are full and we run on the warpath at last, I will run fastest and first."

"And we shall sit back like women and watch how you fight!" declared Tawhitch.

"You will see," mumbled Sawkunk, his mouth filled with trout.

The air was cool and the northwest wind bent the birch on a clear morning in the Moon Of The New Green. The sails of the English held the breeze as it pushed their great-boat into the Great Bay of the Narragansett. But the wind howled so that the English dared not set their canoes in the churning waters to make for the shore. Not until the sun sought its bed on the third night did the sea sit still. Then the ship spat out its cargo, and the soldiers of Mason and Underhill, with the warriors of Uncas the Mohegan, marched from the stony beach to the city of Canonicus and Miantonomi.

"I hate the sight of Uncas," said Katanaquat my father as we stood with our warriors and our grand sachem to receive the men of Mason. The arrogant sachem of the Mohegan stood painted and armed for war, his eyes lifted high and his feet planted firmly upon the soil from which my father had chased him only one summer past. With him were sixty armed braves.

"Yet he is here with our friends the English and stands against Sassacus our enemy," I replied.

"I would rather strike hands with a water moccasin," said my father, "than walk the warpath with Uncas!"

I turned my gaze from the Mohegan to the soldiers of Mason. They were men of many statures, who stood like the trees of autumn, some with heads of gold, some with heads of brown, a few with heads of red, and some with heads of grey and silver like the underleaf of the rippling maple. Some were bearded like Winthrop. Some had scraped their faces clean like Williams. Some wore hats with wide brims and high roofs. Some wore coats of bright steel, which flashed red in the setting sun. All were clothed with long pants that were tucked into great boots. All carried muskets. All had sheathed knives of many lengths. Some had guns that could be held in one hand, which were strapped at belts around their waists or over their shoulders like the Indian carries the bow.

There were ninety English warriors in all. They did not look like weak women. But even Williams said that they did not fight as the Narragansett fight. Did not the Narragansett fight bravest and best of all?

"We have come to you with much love," said Captain Mason to Canonicus our king. "And we beg the right to walk your lands to the country of our common enemy, the Pequot. There, with God's help, we will fall upon the foe to revenge the wrongs that he has done to our people and to yours."

"How can so few go against so many?" asked Canonicus our great sachem. "For the men of Sassacus are as the trees of the wood!"

"Walk the warpath with us," encouraged Mason, "and we will be an army indeed! But whether you follow or no, we shall go forth. And by the hand of God, we shall prevail."

"You will need the hands of many gods!" declared our king. "For Sassacus is a great captain among many great captains, and he will not run like the rabbit to his hole!"

Canonicus held us back from the march, for Miantonomi and many of our warriors were upon the warpath elsewhere, fighting with Wequash and the English Captain Patrick against some Pequot on Block Island. Yet Katanaquat my father was like a mad dog upon a leash as he waited for the return of our prince. For though he loathed to set his moccasins in the same path as Uncas, still his tomahawk thirsted for the blood of the Pequot.

When Miantonomi returned with tales of great victory and slaughter, he learned that Mason had departed only that morning for the country of Sassacus.

"It is as we counseled in the house of Williams," said our prince, "but the English have gone on without us!"

"We shall follow them!" said Katanaquat my father, throwing off the leash. "For though they have the once-Pequot noses of the hunters of Uncas, still they will need the hands, hearts, clubs, and medicine of the Narragansett!"

Miantonomi hesitated, for he did not wish to walk beside Uncas any more than did my father. And though he now knew that the English could fight, he knew not Mason.

"I would rather walk the path with Patrick," said our prince, "for I know his heart and I trust his men. But when we parted at Block Island, he sailed for Providence. Williams will send him to us, no doubt, but . . . "

"Wait for him here," counseled Wequash our friend. "For he will be glad to have you with him on the path. And I will run ahead of you to Mason. For I know the trails of the Pequot, and I can lead many warriors through the forest to their doors. Without us, the English will fall as the great flocks of the pigeon before the shafts of many hunters. For they are weak and must cover their weak hearts with shirts of steel! Their god is a flea and can do no more than cause the Pequot to scratch at their ankles!"

"Go then," said our prince. "And take as many as will follow you."

But none would run without the blessing of our powwow. For who could enter the swamp if he knows not the way out? And who could show the way but Askug and the spirits?

Askug danced, the spirits spoke, and the powwow declared that a victory would be ours. At his bidding, nearly two hundred of the fighting men of the Narragansett took to the warpath in the heavy tracks of Mason.

"When our summer comes at last, I will run first and fastest," declared Sawkunk as we watched Wequash and Assoko and my father disappear into the dark green at the head of the long, silent line. "You will see."

It was not many days when the humbled warriors of the Narragansett began to wander back into our city from their western trek. They had seen no warfare. They had taken no scalps. They had captured no foe.

They had met with Nopatin my grandfather in his lands among the Niantic just east of the Pocatuck. Nopatin and many warriors joined them in their march.

But some then saw visions in the night. And strange birds in the forest. And a dwarf with a serpent's tongue. Some dreamed dreams that warned them not to cross the Pocatuck. Some remembered the wounds of wars past. Some saw Chepi frowning in the dark clouds of midnight. And the strong words of Askug failed them.

Who would step into the snare if he saw it before his feet? Should any man close his eyes and bare his breast before the foe? And if Sassacus was a god indeed, who could stand before him? Thus many decided to turn back and not to stand. This was no shame, said the wanderers-home, this was no stain upon the honor of the warrior who wished to live to fight another day. Yet Askug called them cowards all.

But neither The Rain From God nor the Fool of the Narragansett fled like the dog which tucks its tail between its legs. Nor did Wequash come limping back to the wigwam of Miantonomi. They crossed the Pocatuck, for my father had sworn that if Uncas crossed, he would cross. And thus his feet were wet with the waters that stand at the door of the Pequot our foe.

"Could Sassacus be a god?" I asked of Canonchet as we sat beside the fire and listened to the chanting of the women for their braves.

"If the gods can walk as men," he replied, "then it might be so."

"The Pequot are burned in the fire of the One Great God!" groaned Wequash, his own face black with the ashes of the death pyre of the warriors of Sassacus. "He is no flea—but a ravening wolf! A mad and charging moose! A storm of lightning and hail . . . and fire!

"And I am a dead man walking," he cried, "for I spat in His face and cannot now find Him to bow at His dreadful feet and beg His mercy." Wequash moaned like the autumn wind as it passes through the harvest corn.

"They fight like demons," said Katanaquat of the English. "Like phantoms without fear."

And he told me of the great fort of the foe, sitting high among the trees upon the hill of Mystic. Filled one night with the mocking laughter of the braves of Sassacus. Filled the next morning with the charred bodies and the spilled blood of seven hundred souls of the proud Pequot.

He told me of the guns of Mason. Of the fire of Mason and the breath of God upon it. Of the tears and prayers of Mason as he knelt at last upon the mountain of the slaughter.

And of that one eternal moment when the mountain was swallowed in flame as men became torches, and women melted like wax, and the souls of children rose shrieking upon the smoke of the fire of God.

Yet Sassacus lived, for he was not upon the hill when the fire of God came upon it.

And I wondered at the power and the terror of the Name. For Williams had told me that the Name held great and awful fire in His hand, and that one day His fire would swallow the forests and lick up the waters of the Great Salt Sea. I trembled with fear, and I watched as Wequash paced the village a ruined man.

Chapter Four

Ten Words

War with the Pequot continued for a season, until the angry sparks of the Fire Of God had spread from one village to the next of the scorched and scattered people of the once-god Sassacus.

The great sachem himself, having fled far from his own, fell at last beneath the hungry tomahawk of the monstrous Mohawk. His scalp and the scalps of many of his chief men were brought from the north to the English at Hartford. There his ragged flesh was nailed to the side of the Meetinghouse. Long after his name had died upon the lips of those who knew him, young children of pale skin stared vacantly at his tufted memory and played in the dirt beneath his shriveled, leathered pate.

Wequash looked me in the eyes. His own sorrowed gaze was clouded with a fearsome mist that rose from his tortured soul. Never had I seen a man so full of the terror of the gods—of the One God—nor so desperate to cast his fear from him into the heat of the Dreadful Fire.

"I must . . ." he stammered. "I must find the path that leads to the Name! Or else I must throw my flesh into the bog of Chepi so that my soul may flee to Sowanniu for refuge! Yet even there, if the world should burn, how could I hide from the Fire That Eats Mountains?"

"Is it the Name that you fear?" I asked, for I wondered that the Name could be our ransom and our terror all at once. How could the vengeance and the slaughter of the Fire Of God be at one with the surrender and the torture of the Son Of God?

"Or is it the great dying of the Pequot that causes your heart to sink?" I wondered aloud.

"The Name!" cried Wequash. "For who are the Pequot but ashes upon the wind? It is the Name I fear! The Fire! The Anger! The Power." And he dug the palms of his hands into his red and maddened eyes. "I am a toad beneath His heel! I am a dead man!" cried Wequash. And he wept bitterly.

"It is a terrible thing to fall into the hands of the living God," said Williams gently, as Wequash and my father and I sat at the table with him at the trading house of Smith at Cocomscussuc.

The English house of Smith stood closer to the city of Canonicus than even the houses of Providence. It sat upon ground that Canonicus traded to Smith for much sugar and many pipes, for blankets and wampum and a little toy cart with wheels. I thought it a strange and wonderful thing to emerge from under the dark limbs of the elm and the oak and see this English fortress standing strong and tall within the bright and conquered glade. The smoke of its warm fire tumbled from the peak of the great stone chimney. Its small, papered windows looked out like many eyes upon the surrounding forest. Its great, planked door opened in glad welcome, day and night, to any friend or stranger who happened to knock upon it. Its large rooms—for it had several, unlike many of the houses of the English which were all of one room like the tents of my people—were filled with the wonders of the English. Most amazing of all to me was the music that was made by the young son of Smith as he pulled a small thin bow across the strings of a strange, wooded object called the violin.

"Manitoo!" I declared when first I heard it. For surely the violin was a god with the voice of a beautiful woman! In sorrowful tones it sang to us as it was stroked by the bow of the son of Smith. And I wept in joy and wonder as the music filled the room.

"Is this the Song On The Wind?" I cried to Katanaquat my father when first I heard it.

"No," replied The Rain From God, "for the Song On The Wind was a song on the wind, and came not from the hands of any man."

"But this song cannot be of the hands of man!" I exclaimed as the full, strong strains of the violin sank deeply into my hungering heart.

"It is as the wind which came from the hands of Williams over the fire of Canonicus," said my father.

"It cannot be!" I countered.

"Do you not pull music from your own bow when you loose the arrow into the forest?" asked Katanaquat my father. And I said that I did. But I marveled at this magic of the English, and I fell with gladness beneath the spell of its clear, sad melody.

"It is a terrible thing to fall into the hands of the living God," repeated Williams. "But His wrath is laid aside from all who kiss the Son."

"Show me His face that I might kiss it!" cried Wequash. "Show me His paths that I might walk them!"

"Come and lodge with me at Providence awhile," said Williams to the once-Mohegan. "And there we will speak of the face and the paths of God."

Wequash walked to the house of Williams. For four days and four nights he stayed with the God-preacher, pouring his anguish into the cup of the English man, drinking the words of the prince of Providence, weeping for his sins, crying out to the One Great God. When he came home to the Narragansett, he was a man with two hearts. One for our people, the other for the Name.

"You have swallowed the Name?" I cried.

"I have swallowed the Name," said Wequash, "and now He dwells within me by His Spirit. He brushes the tears from my eyes. He holds me to Himself."

"I see no shadow!" said Katanaquat my father.

"He is all light," said Wequash, "and has chased the shadows from my soul."

"Even the bright day of Keesuckquand cannot touch the black depths of the soul," declared my father. "And how can any spirit warm the heart of a man?"

"My own heart is a black thicket and a crooked path," said Wequash, "but the Name is a torch to show the way for my faltering feet. I cannot see His face in the forest, but I hear His song in my heart. I have drunk from His pipe. He is the smoke of peace to my soul. My terror is gone."

"The war with the Pequot has been good for everyone!" said Katanaquat my father as I reclined with him beneath Old Willow upon the leafy banks of Red Creek. "Nopatin and I have many more scalps. The Fool has a quiver full of Pequot arrows. Wequash has the large coat that he was given by Winthrop for his services in battle. Miantonomi has his fine suit of English clothes. And Uncas . . ." Father spat into the murmuring stream, ". . . Uncas has two new Pequot wives that he lured from the house of the Boston governor!"

"And more than two new warriors within his tents," I added.

A great, black and shining dragonfly rose from the reeds to my right and hung motionless for a breath in the hot evening air. Then, like a drunken arrow, it ran a swift and crooked path up Red Creek toward the crimson, setting sun.

"Many more than two!" growled my father. "Ten handfuls of runaway servants and weakhearted warriors of the Pequot! All hiding beneath the skirts of the squaws of the Mohegan!" He threw a small, flat stone upon the face of the creek. It skipped over the walking waters, racing upstream after the reeling dragonfly.

"Roger Williams declares that he will go with our prince to the city of Uncas to retrieve the servants of Winthrop," I said, watching the great winged needle as it stopped upon its path and suddenly leapt like lightning back in our direction. *It moves like Askug the powwow when he dances for war*, I thought.

"Williams would do well to beg a Pequot servant or two for himself and let it rest at that," said The Rain From God. He sat up in our grassy bed, squatted with his toes in the dark blue waters of the creek, cupped his hands, and scooped himself a drink.

"But Uncas accuses us to the English," I complained. "And tells the lie that we are harboring the Pequot within our own wigwams. Our prince was called to Boston to answer the lies of the Mohegan!"

"He walked to Boston like a king. He spoke the truth," said my father. "And he declared anew his love and faithfulness to the English."

"But still Uncas lies!" I cried.

"Lying is as breathing to the mad dog," snorted my father.

"Our prince must go to Uncas as Williams has declared," I said, "to see with his own eyes the Pequot paint upon the faces of the new guests of his Mohegan cousin. And to make a count of the many murderers of the English who sit smoking tobacco beside the waters of the Long River. I will go with him! I will carry the count to Boston myself! Then the English will believe!"

Father wiped his wet lips with the thick locks of his long hair.

"Uncas will slide away like the snake before Miantonomi even gets near him," said Katanaquat. "And the Pequot hares will hop around behind the Mohegan so that Williams will get dizzy looking for them."

"Why do the English believe Uncas rather than us?" I asked, turning to look into the eyes of my father. "Why do they not believe Williams when his tongue speaks on our behalf?"

Father raised his head toward the darkening dusk and sighed. "It is because the Narragansett are many and mighty. It is because we walk strong beneath the tall pine and the ancient oak, like the great herds of Moosoog that wander the endless hills to the north. It is because our feet must walk many mornings before they find the paths that run down into the towns of the English," he said. "We are like the wolf to the English, the wild beast that howls in the deep wood and causes the little papoose to cry upon its bed.

"But Uncas sleeps at their door, the dog! He wags his tail when they open their windows to throw him a bone. He barks at their foes for them. And he comes when they call."

"Do they not know he is a murderer, a liar, and a thief?" I asked.

"He barks at their foes and bites them as well," said my father.

"And did not the Narragansett bite the foe of the English in the war against the Pequot? And have we not declared our love?" I argued.

"We are the wild wolf," said my father. "Uncas is the wigwam dog."

"Can none chase the dog without angering the master?" I asked.

"Sometimes the dog runs alone in the woods," said Katanaquat. "And there the wolf may find him."

Uncas continued to accuse us before the English of harboring Pequots, of plotting war against the English, and of killing English horses and cattle. And we, to silence the lies and to uphold our honor, threatened to send arrows and death into the city of the Mohegan sachem.

Governor Haynes of Connecticut desired that Uncas and Miantonomi come to meet with him, for he wished that a peace should be made between the Mohegan and the Narragansett.

"Let us go up to Hartford at last," said our prince, "and throw the lie back into the lap of Uncas. Then the English will see that it sits upon him as his own!"

We set out from Narragansett in the Moon Of The Fall, one hundred fifty Narragansett warriors and sagamores, with Miantonomi and his wives and children. Our prince was painted as the king he was, with his hair in one long, many-feathered braid. He wore his suit of English clothes, with a Narragansett robe about his shoulders and his best bow slung over his left arm.

My father—though he did not dance for the battle—had painted himself for war, and his quiver was full of arrows fashioned by my own hand. "Though your heart sings of peace," he said to me, "your hands work the straightest shafts and fit them with the finest feathers that a warrior could ever wish for."

Roger Williams, with two other men of Providence, walked at our head as our tongue to the English.

For three days we trod the paths. For three nights we slept beneath the tall trees. And always we came upon Narragansett who were hunting or trapping or wandering the woods. Their words were full of complaint against the Mohegan and the Pequot.

"I was robbed and beaten upon this very path," said one old

sagamore.

"Our squaws were threatened and their clams taken as they came home from the bay," said some of the men of the village of Ashawaug.

"Six hundred fifty Pequots and Mohegans robbed us and spoiled twenty-three fields of our corn," cried a group of angry Wunnashowt. "Where is the strong shield of Canonicus over us?" they moaned.

"The men of Uncas lie in wait to stop Miantonomi's passage to the Connecticut," said some.

"They say they will boil our prince in a kettle!" said others.

Williams desired that we turn back, for we could travel more safely by ship, he said, and then no blood should be shed.

But Miantonomi and his council resolved—being nearly half the way upon our journey—that not a man should turn aside, but rather that we all resolve to die. "Should the oak tree bow before the birch? Should the warrior flee for the barking of the dog?" he said.

We went on, keeping a strict watch by night. By day, our sachem and his family kept to the path, while fifty men spread out into the woods on the left and on the right. In the front marched Williams and his company, with Wequash and Assoko and Katanaquat my father at their side. Canonchet and I often joined them at the head.

On the Sabbath of Williams, we did not move from camp, for our prince wished to honor the heart of the preacher his friend.

"It is God whom we honor by our resting on this day," said Williams as we sat by our fire in the new morning. The many-colored leaves of autumn skipped and tumbled with the chill breeze that rolled through the rustling forest. The yawning fire waved its crimson arms in the restless air.

"Tell us tales of your God," said Miantonomi, unwinding his legs from themselves and stretching them out toward the warm blaze, "and we shall rest!" He lay full-length upon the cleared ground, hands behind his head, staring up at the cold, blue face of the vast, clean dawning sky. Wawaloam his first-squaw came to his side with his tobacco and pipe, and lit it for him. His daughters brought water from the nearby Shannuck and set it to boil. Soon we would have hot nokehick for breakfast and perhaps some boiled venison left from the last night's supper.

"Ten things!" said Assoko, as he dropped a handful of dried leaves onto the fire. They hovered for a moment above the grasping flames, their brittle sails vibrating in the pulsing heat, then sank together into the consuming blaze. Their colors melted into one last brilliant flash of blinding gold as their souls followed the sparks that wandered with the dark smoke toward the bare and bending treetops. "Ten things!" the Fool repeated.

And Williams nodded, for he seemed to know what the Fool had on his mind. We waited for more words. Assoko fed more kindling to the fire.

"Ten things God wants!" Assoko said at last, a furrowed frown upon his brow, a toothy grin upon his face. And I understood. *The Ten Words,* I said within myself, *the Ten Commands.* For Wequash had told me of them once before. It was Wequash who rose now to stride about the fire.

"Tell us of these ten things," said Miantonomi to Wequash. And Williams sat back against a log to listen with the rest of us.

The two-hearted once-Mohegan held up his hands before us, spreading his fingers wide. "Ten things," he said. "Ten things God has commanded all men to obey."

Many curious warriors rose from their fires and walked to join us at ours, sitting within our circle, standing at our backs.

Katanaquat my father sat cross-legged, his arms upon his knees, his face set hard, the stones of his wall set firmly within his heart.

The Fool rocked slowly to and fro before the fire, quietly chanting, "Ten things," and I thought that the flames might lick his long locks as they swung about his cheeks like the thin boughs of Old Willow.

Canonchet looked upon the once-Mohegan, the firelight dancing in his dark and quiet gaze.

Sawkunk rubbed his eyes as the smoke of our fire fell from the heights and whirled around our crowded circle. A cold wind came behind the smoke and kicked up the ashes at my feet. Though the fire was hot before me, I pulled my cloak up over my back against the sudden, bitter breeze.

"Ten things God spoke upon the mountain to the Moses

Man who saw His face," said Wequash, his strong visage strangely lit in the glow of the crackling blaze. "And the mountain was filled with thunder and lightning.

"And God came down in smoke and dark fire. And the mountain quaked greatly! And the great tribe of the Moses Man heard it and saw it. And they stood far off, for they feared the fire of the Great God."

This mountain sounded to us like the mountain of Machemoodus that stood at the meeting of the Moodus and the Salmon rivers. The English called it Mount Tom. But the people who had always lived about it feared it much for its rumblings and its shakings. "It is the house of Chepi," many said. And none dared go up to it in the night or on the sunless day.

"And you, my brothers!" cried Wequash. "Do you not fear the fire of the Great God? Do you not remember the hill of the Pequot at Mystic? Did you not see the Great Death that fell upon our foes? Did you not run afar from the mountain in its melting?

"I saw it! I felt it! In the deepest places of my heart! Burning, burning! Choking me, blinding me, clawing at my soul! It was terrible! Terrible! Terrible! But Jesus . . ." And Wequash fell of a sudden upon his knees in the circle of the wondering Narragansett, and wept.

"Burning!" he wailed. "Burning!"

A murmur rose among us, and fear called to our hearts. Many braves shouted to the spirits for mercy. My father gripped my arm. *See to your wall!* his eyes said, but I stood upon an open field within my soul. The Fire Of God danced before me in the flames that swallowed the kindling of the Fool. The Name stood within the fire, a formless, beckoning presence.

Williams stood, his palms held forth in a gesture of peace. For many moments men wailed, but at last all tongues grew still and all eyes turned upon the English preacher.

"It was the fire of men—not the fire of God—which fell upon the Pequot," he said, placing his hands upon the shaking shoulders of Wequash. The weeping man of the two-hearts crawled slowly to the edge of our circle and seated himself, sobbing silently, beside our prince. "But it is true that the fire of God fell upon the mountain of Moses. And there it was that God himself spoke the Ten Words."

"Tell us of the Ten Words," said our prince, purposefully calling us back from our fear to the strong words of Williams.

"The first word," said Williams, "is this: *You shall have no other gods before me.*"

"But we have many gods!" we cried. "And who can say which is greatest or which should be first?"

"Cautantowwit is the greatest of gods!" declared an old warrior, and many shouted their assent.

"Chepi is a great god!" cried another old brave, and many more chanted their approval.

"But the Great God of Heaven says that your gods are no gods," declared Williams above the din, "and that He will blow on them and they will fall like the dead leaves of autumn." And we howled against this strange and awful word.

"And the second word is this," cried the God-preacher. "*You shall not carve and then bow down to any image of anything that is in heaven above or in the earth beneath or in the water under the earth. You shall not bow down yourself to them to serve them, for God is a jealous God, and will punish the children for the sins of the fathers, even to the fourth generation of them that hate Him.*"

And we shouted that this word was a good one, for we did not make images as did the tribes to our north and to our west. We were not children to bow down to the work of our own hands. It was the gods whom we feared, not some mask carved by our knives or some doll sewn by our squaws.

And that the gods were jealous—this we knew! For did we not fast and chant and dance to honor them and to humor them and to pay them our respect? And did not our powwow throw his very life at their feet?

We would never hate the gods! For what man hates the sun for shining or the wind for blowing? No, this second word was a good word, we said, and one we did keep.

"The third word," said Williams, "is this: *You shall not make the Name of the Lord your God an empty thing, for the Lord will hold him guilty who makes a small thing of His Name.*"

And we cried aloud that all the names of the gods were

great. And that none should be made small. For the gods were in all places and their ears were open to hear what men did say for or against them. But as for the god of the English, we did not mean to think small of his Name, but we knew him not and saw him not. Nor did our powwow hear his voice in any dream or see his form in any vision. Yet he must be great, for he gives great things to his people the English, and they are strong in war.

And I looked upon my father, and I wondered, concerning him, *Do the gods hold him guilty for his warfare and his wall against them? Does the Name stand against him? And can any man stand against the Name?*

"The fourth is this," said Williams. *"Remember the Sabbath day to keep it holy. Six days shall you labor and do all your work. But the seventh day is the Sabbath of the Lord your God. In it you shall do no work, nor shall your son or daughter, your squaw or servant, or any stranger that is within your tents."*

And we loved this word much, for we would gladly lie beside our fires and smoke our tobacco. We would happily rest upon our mats and tell great lies and boasts. But someone must tend the fire and prepare the stew, and this was women's work—thus the Sabbath must be for men! "Yes, we love this word. Now tell us the fifth!"

"Honor your father and your mother, that your days may be long upon the land which the Lord your God gives you."

"Another good word!" we cried. "And a true one." For the man who scorns his father soon scorns his people as well. He wanders from the lands of his fathers, and who then will be his father or his mother? But were his days shorter than the days of him who honored his father and mother? And we wondered at this.

"The sixth word," said Williams, "is, *You shall not kill.*"

And we said that this was a hard word. For though murder was a terrible thing, only blood could pay for blood. And sometimes a man must kill a man for his honor and his own soul's good. And without the scalps and the blood of the foe, how could any man know that he is a man? How could his medicine grow strong? How could he win the heart of a woman? How could he be great among his own? How could his vengeance sleep or his anger be quenched? How could justice be done? How could lands be held?

"And the seventh word," declared Williams, "is, *You shall not commit adultery.*"

And we knew this word to be a just one, though it shamed us. For the strongest among us took what our hands could hold, and the weakest wished for what only the strong dared take. Yet men killed men for the taking of their wives by another. And was adultery not stealing and worse? And did our sachems not condemn it? My heart cried out against the man who lay with the squaw of his brother. Uncas was such a man. And many of his own hated him for it.

The eighth word was a harder word still: "*You shall not steal.*" For many among us took what we could from those who did not see or could not stop us. And we stole most of all from the English, for they had much to steal.

"*You shall not bear false witness against your neighbor* is the ninth word," said Williams. And we said this was good, for our neighbors were as our brothers and sisters and our tongues must be straight with them. Yet against our enemies we would speak whatever our hearts called us to speak. We would curse our foes. And our lies—like our arrows—would be fully loosed against them. In war, any weapon is a fair one.

"There is nothing false in our hatred and our vengeance," we said.

And the last and tenth word was, "*You shall not covet your neighbor's house or his wife or his servants, or anything that is your neighbor's.*"

And we grumbled against this word, for our eyes and our hearts were like flames in the woods which never cried, *Enough!*

More medicine. More strength. More scalps. More blood. More houses. More lands. More women. More baskets and bowls and warclubs and arrows. More shoes and coats and knives and hatchets.

And should not our eyes and our hearts desire the good things of another? Should they lie down in hunger and sleep while their neighbor has meat? No! To covet is to breathe. What other call can raise a man from his warm dreams to face the cold dawn?

This was a hard word indeed—*You shall not covet!*

"Your god asks too much," we said to our good friend the preacher. And we ate our stew and lit our pipes and remembered the Sabbath as we lay in our blankets and blew our smoke to the wandering wind that carried our daydreams upward and over the tallest pine to the god of the English who sat on his mats in a wigwam of blue near a path made of gold in the far-off country of Heaven.

We arrived safely in the English town of Hartford on the Connecticut, having seen none of the warriors of Uncas in our march. There had been rumors, we were told, that great numbers of the English had walked with us from our country. And the rumor had been as a wall and a shield to us, keeping the Pequot and the Mohegan at bay.

Governor Haynes greeted us well and gave us meat and drink. But Uncas sent a message that he was lame and could not come.

"A lame excuse!" said the governor, and he sent earnestly for the sachem again. At last the Mohegan came.

"What do you answer to the testimony of so many that your armies are robbing and pillaging among the Narragansett and the river tribes?" asked Haynes of the Mohegan king.

"I have been with my men in the hunt these many moons," said Uncas plainly. "We numbered no more than one hundred braves. I did not see any violence being done, nor fields being spoiled. We roasted some corn, that is all!"

"You promised to boil our prince in a pot!" cried Katanaquat my father.

"Not so!" said Uncas coolly, "For I am not welcomed at the table of the Narragansett."

And thus began much shouting between the men of Uncas and our own. While the Narragansett and the Mohegan traded threats and taunts and tales of trespass and treachery, Haynes drew Williams aside to counsel for a time. At last, they called Miantonomi to them.

"Will you sit with Uncas to talk of a peace between your people?" asked Haynes through Williams.

"I will," said our prince, "if the Mohegan will give up the Pequot who hide in his towns."

"We will speak to him of it," said Haynes.

Miantonomi returned to the fray and ordered us to withdraw from our arguments. "For we must speak of peace now," he said. He walked then into the ranks of the Mohegan, and the men of Uncas stood aside as he passed through them. Taller by a hand than most, our prince was like the oak, hard and strong and full of the deep medicine of the ancient earth.

"Uncas," said our prince as he stood before his cousin. "I would sup with you, if you will. For my hunters have killed some venison. Call some of your chief men together and we will dine."

"I am not welcomed at the table of the Narragansett," declared the Mohegan. He stood as the maple beside the oak, more broad but not so high, his boughs stretched wide about him. Beneath his powerful limbs the dark thicket spread, and none could see within it. His heart was as the clinging vine which rests by day and rises at night to creep about the forest, encircling and entangling all that sleeps within its path.

"You are welcomed at the table of the English," said Miantonomi. "And I would sit with you as in our youth. Come and join me at our venison. There is much we must speak of."

"I will speak to the governor if he wills it," said Uncas, "but I have no hunger for your venison. I am quite filled with corn at the moment."

Williams called Miantonomi to himself again, and together the two friends went into the house of the governor. There, in company with the English magistrates, our prince gave the names of the Pequot sachems and murderers of the English whom he knew to be among the Mohegan.

Then Uncas was called in, and was asked the names of any Pequot who might be among his people. He knew not their names, he said, but was sure that there were many on the Long Island, and some among Ninigret's Niantic. And he himself had only twenty.

A principal man of the English named Stanton, who knew well the Indian tongue, accused Uncas of dealing falsely. "We know that you have many more Pequot than twenty," said Stanton, "and that only lately you have fetched thirty or forty to yourself from the Long Island."

"Yes, I have thirty," said Uncas simply, "but I do not know their names." And he would speak no more.

"We'll give you ten days to bring in the exact number and names of your Pequots and any runaway servants of the English," said Haynes. "And if you don't deliver, we will come fetch them!"

And thus a kind of peace was struck in which the Narragansett and the Mohegan agreed to sheath their knives and bury their tomahawks. And if any quarrel should arise between the two tribes, neither side would begin war without first appealing to the English, whose decision would be binding. And the tribe in whose favor the decision was made would thereafter know the support and arms of the English.

Yet Uncas continued to breathe his lies against us. And he surrendered no Pequots, for he said that they were all gone to the wigwams of Canonicus and Miantonomi. But Haynes did not go to fetch them as he had said he would, for the English were busy with many things. And the wigwam dog made sure to wag its tail whenever it happened to wander the streets of Hartford.

Chapter Five

The Shield Of God

"**P**lease, send these gifts to Governor Winthrop at Boston," said Miantonomi as he laid a basket and a bundle of wampum upon the wooden table of Williams at Providence. "Here are ten fathom of wampum from Canonicus, twenty fathom from me, and a basket as a present from Wawaloam my wife to the wife of Winthrop."

The small daughters of Williams put drink upon the table for our prince and his braves. Our men took it thankfully, speaking many kind words to the little maidens.

"The governor will be very glad for this expression of your love," said the preacher, running his fingers through the strings of white and purple beads. "And what shall I tell him besides?"

"That we desire three things of him," said our prince. "His sure and constant friendship; the free use promised us, after the war against the Pequot, of the Pequot country for our hunting; and . . ." our sachem paused and looked for a moment toward the sun that peered brightly in through the English glass windows that faced south.

"There are many Pequot sachems and captains that have survived the war," said our prince grimly. "And this you know," he said, looking once more upon Williams his friend. "Many who murdered the English, and three who have slain some of our sachems, are still free in the forest and and in the tents of other tribes.

"Mr. Haynes has done nothing to take them captive, and Uncas lays the lie at our door that we gather them all to ourselves against the English. Yet I fear that the Pequots—and there are many hundreds of them—will do more mischief to us and to the English if they are not destroyed or made to bow the knee."

"And what do you desire of Winthrop in this?" asked Williams.

"That Winthrop and Haynes might agree together to allow me to pursue those Pequot princes and captains whom I named when we traveled to Hartford to treat of peace," said Miantonomi plainly. "And we shall not harm so much as a Mohegan or a Niantic in all of our business!"

"I will send Winthrop your gifts and your words," said Williams. "Is there nothing else you desire?" he added with a smile.

"Canonicus begs of Mr. Governor a little sugar," said our prince with a wide grin.

"You are no Narragansett!" shrieked Askug the powwow at Wequash the god-preacher. "You were born a Pequot serpent and you are yet a Pequot serpent. You say that you love us, but I look in your eyes and I see the poison of your heart that rises to your fangs whenever you open your mouth to speak of your 'great god'! I see the fork in your tongue! I see the rattle at your tail! You are the serpent who lies upon the rock, waiting for the careless traveler to take his rest beside you on his way!"

"I am none of this!" stuttered Wequash, his eyes red with the fire of his proud and angered heart. "And I have done you no wrong, bitter Askug! I have walked with your sachems in peace and brotherhood. I have taken wounds at their side in the wars of your people. I have laid many a Pequot relative dead in the dust. I have left my wife and children behind me in the tents of the Mohegan. And though I am nothing in the eyes of the Great God, still He loves me!"

"He loves you because you are as he is, a serpent who hisses in the shadows and strikes at the heels of men!" fired Askug.

"My words are not whispered in the night!" cried Wequash. "I speak true and openly of the one Son of God. It is you who are the serpent, you slippery snake! You are the slave of that devil the Great Serpent himself! Your evil spirits will choke you in your sleep one day, and you will wake only to wander in the utter black places forever. In the everlasting night your tortured soul will cry out in the dark fire that can never be quenched!"

The powwow rose up before the once-Pequot preacher like the great she-bear when it is cornered with its young. His eyes rolled wide in his reddened, maddened face, and his mouth hung open in a ghastly, growling gape. "May the four winds crush you in their arms together!" he howled. "May the sea rise up and take you in its icy limbs! May the beasts of the wild descend upon you as you walk your crooked path! May the warriors of Chepi sink their blades into your flesh and cut out your heart to cast it into the Great Swamp! Die in your dreams, Pequot dung! Die in your dreams!" wailed Askug. And Wequash stepped back from him in fear and amazement.

Would the once-Pequot burst into flame beneath the fiery curses of the powwow? Would the four winds rush upon him even now and crush him like the beetle that is ground beneath the heel of man? Would his skin slide off like the snake which sheds? Would his blood pour out like the cup that is spilled? Surely he could not stand before the great and bitter sorcery of Askug! Surely we would witness a terrible retribution this dark and awful day!

But the God of Wequash was a strong shield. And the preacher stood his ground.

"The Lord is my guard," he chanted. "I shall lack nothing.

"He makes me lie down in green grasses.

"He leads me beside the cool waters.

"He restores my soul.

"He leads me in the paths that are right for the sake of his own Great Name.

"And even when I walk through the Valley Of The Shadow Of Death, I will fear no evil, for He is with me.

"His club and His spear are my comfort and protection.

"He prepares my meat in the presence of my enemies.

"He blesses me for the battle.

"He fills my cup with water until it overflows.

"Surely goodness and mercy shall follow me all the days of my life, and I will dwell in the house of the Lord forever."

A knife appeared suddenly in the upraised hand of the pow-wow, and it flashed in the light of the fire of Katanaquat my father. *It is the lightning of the gods!* cried my heart. *And it will fall upon Wequash!*

"Hold, powwow!" cried our prince, stepping between the lightning of the gods and the chanting servant of the Great Name.

"I will cut out his heart myself and eat it!" shrieked my great grandfather as Miantonomi took the bladed arm in his own strong hands.

"Hold, I say!" shouted our prince, and he bent the crooked limb of Askug backward until the knife fell from its choked and weakened fingers.

"You stand as a man who would take the charge of the bull moose!" coughed the powwow to our prince. "For the anger of the gods are against this Pequot pea!"

"My own anger would take you by the throat and rattle you hard and long, you old gourd!" cried Miantonomi as he released Askug. The powwow crumpled in a brittle heap upon my father's floor.

"Wequash may chant! He may preach!" thundered our prince, and I thought I had never seen him so angry. "He may run with my warriors on the hunt and in the battle! He may eat my soup and sleep in my bed! He is as my brother and my son! He is under my tent and my protection! Canonicus has blessed him! Our people owe him much! And you—you jealous and pitiful old bag of spells and potions—you will cease in your curses and your threats, or I will cast you from us like the carcass of the dead dog that is thrown to the buzzards and the birds!"

Askug rose from the floor like a strange fire that has somehow awakened without fuel, blazing hot and strong in his shame and in his wrath. His eyes lit up with a dark power that filled his frail form with the illusion of a great and ancient strength. A cold hiss blew from between his teeth as he gathered his robes about him. He bent to take up his knife, which seemed a long claw that fitted his hand like a sharp talon on the paw of Pussough the great cat. He shook his head, and his tangled locks swung like the branches of a towering elm in the midst of a summer storm. He stood tall for a breath, taller

than his own legs should ever raise him, and swept the door
open with one swift motion of his shadowed arm. Like the
wind when it turns in violent circles upon the sea, Askug
whirled from our midst into the darkening night.

"Lift up your heads, oh you gates," chanted Wequash.

"Lift up your heads, you everlasting doors, and the King of
Glory will come in.

"Who is the King of Glory?

"The Lord! Strong and mighty in battle!"

"Your words will lay you in your own blood one day," said
Miantonomi to Wequash, sitting down hard upon my father's
bed, wiping the sweat of his anger from his paling face. "I have
made an enemy of my own powwow this day on your behalf,
you Pequot pea! I hope you remember me to your god tonight
when you chant yourself to sleep!"

Few gave any heed to the preaching of Wequash. For though
we loved him for his heart toward us, we feared turning to his
god because of the railings of our powwow, because of the
teachings of our father's fathers, because of the terror of our
own jealous gods. And who could say which god was the greatest of all gods? Did not Cautantowwit watch over us always?
Did he not carve our first parents from the great oak that
stood upon his mountain in the Southwest? Did he not
breathe life into their forms and set them in this land? Did he
not send our first corn, beans, and squash upon the wings of
Kaukant the crow from his own great garden in Sowanniu? Did
he not build many wigwams for us in his courts? And did he
not wait for our souls to join him there when our days in this
flesh were done? Could we turn our backs to him simply to
please this strange god of the Ten Words and the Son Who
Walks And Dies As A Man?

Perhaps Wequash was mad, said some. Perhaps the fire of
the hill at Mystic had burned its way into his soul and he could
no longer think as his fathers did, as the Mohegan do, as the
Narragansett in their wisdom and their great and ancient traditions.

Perhaps the once-Pequot, once-Mohegan was now a once-

Narragansett. Perhaps he was an English and could no longer hear the voices of the spirits of his people and their neighbors.

Perhaps he would burn down at last, like the fire without wood, and be still.

Miantonomi asked fewer questions about the Name, and Canonchet would not speak of Him at all. "I will follow no god which sets the sachem against the powwow," he said. "For the sachem and the powwow must walk as one or the spirits will not bless our people. Wequash may speak his heart all that he wishes, for Canonicus and Miantonomi my father have so declared. But I will not listen, for not every song is meant for every ear. Does Katanaquat your father sing the same song to you that he whispers to Silvermoon your mother?"

And I said he did not. But then no longer did he sing us any song at all. And I wondered how the song of love could be stilled in the heart of a man. Perhaps, in the same way, the new song of Wequash might grow still one day. Yet though it sang only for a time, still it was a strong song which rang with a sure melody, like the arrow that leaves the bow to fly true to its target. My own heart hummed its harmony, and it longed for words with which to give the song wings that it might fly beyond my wall to my anxious, waiting tongue.

But I could not sing the song aloud. It was not mine to sing.

"I do not know why you have ears for the words of this new god," said Aquinne as she walked with me beside Red Creek. The cold air was full of the drifting flakes of the First Moon Of Snow. I put my hand upon the shoulder of my love, but it was as cold as the day. Her eyes were deep grey like the dark, clouded skies.

"My heart opens to the One God," I said simply. "My eyes see His shadow when I wake. It is not my doing, Aquinne. I am not running down strange paths to discover what lies there. I am walking as ever I walked, yet there He is in all places that my feet find me."

"But he asks things of you that our fathers have never asked!" she said, tossing her head to chase the settling snow. "He asks you to wait for my love! He asks you to love our enemies! He asks you to let men strike you on your face without letting you save your own honor by striking them back! He asks you to be a woman, Kattenanit, and not a warrior!"

"I will be a warrior," I said. "But a warrior does not have to chase every dog that barks at him or kick every dog that nips at him. If someone were to strike you or another whom I loved, I would surely strike them in return! But my cheek can take the blow while my heart remains my own. I can stand where I stand. I will be the man."

"But this is not being the man!" cried Aquinne. "For strong medicine comes only by blood and much favor with the gods! And our gods oppose this English god. Askug says it is so. And I believe it is so. How can a brave protect his woman and his children if the gods are against him!"

I stopped and stood for a moment in the falling snow. The tall pines on the far side of Red Creek stood like blurred giants in the midst of the gentle storm. The gathering dusk cast blue shadows across the white carpet at our feet.

"I know men who stand against the gods and are still men," I said to the cold creek and the wondering woman. And I thought of my father. And I knew that a warrior could stand where he stands, even against the gods. "And the English are warriors and men," I said. "And do they not protect their women and children? And do they not shed the blood of their enemies when they must? And so a man may love his enemies in times of peace yet lift the warclub to protect his own in times of war."

"I do not know if I can be the wife of such a man," said Aquinne quietly, and her voice shook like the boughs of Old Willow in the cold winter wind.

"But I love you!" I cried, taking her in my arms and turning her to me. "I love you and I will always love you!"

"You are not the only one to say these words to me," she said, turning her tear-streaked face from mine.

"But we have spoken our love to each other," I stammered, "and we have spoken of our love to your parents and to mine. Many among our people know that you will be mine. Though others say they love you, it is not they who will have you!

"I will be your man! I will be your warrior! I will be the father of your children and the hunter of their meat! I will build your wigwam and fill it with plenty as the gods give me favor and the Great God gives me medicine!"

"But the great god will not let you have any other gods!" cried Aquinne as she pulled her shivering form from mine. "He will chase the others from you, says Wequash! And then he will be your only god. Who would we turn to if the great god closes his eyes to us? Who would we call upon if the great god turns his back to us? How would we live if he lowered his shield when all other gods opposed us?"

"He is faithful," I said, with the hope that arose from the echo of the words of Wequash and Williams. "He is good. He will not let His own fall that they cannot rise again. He will be their shield always."

"How do you know?" fired Aquinne.

"I—I just know," I said. "That is all."

"Askug says it is not so!" cried Aquinne. "And none can ask me to sleep in the tent of the man who will not shield his squaw from the anger of the gods!"

"I will shield you!" I declared. "My bow will be ready always! My tomahawk will be sharp! My eyes and ears will be open. My heart will be yours!"

"Mine?" asked the maiden of my soul's dreams. "Mine? How can your heart be mine if you must love this great god first?"

"I will have two hearts," I declared. "As Wequash does. One for the Great God and one for you, my love! Only for you!"

"It cannot be," she said to the paled, pleading form of the almost-warrior, myself.

I could not bear the warfare in my soul. The howling of the spirits of my fathers rose above the whisper of the fast-falling snow and rushed about my head like a swarm of summer bees. The song of Wequash rose above the howl and played upon the soft wind that sent the white sky tumbling down in small, wet pieces. My wall called my name. My father stared down upon me from the high faces of the dark pine across the waters. My heart cried out the name of Aquinne. And the evening grew still.

A cold and frozen piece of dreaming was this moment.

Aquinne stood before me, beautiful and chill, dark and inviting against the white wall of winter. Our quiet, rhythmic breathing slid from within us into the chilled air and hung like clouds between us. A dog barked, once, in the distance. My heart beat loud in my ears.

"I will love you first," I heard myself say, as my words turned to frost before my face and drifted away upon the north wind.

A new Dying came upon us, but it was not as the last Dying in which so many Narragansett slept without waking. Yet it took some to the grave and left many weak and weary from the fever and the pox.

"Wequash brings this upon us!" cried Askug to Canonicus our king. "The spirits are angry because of his preaching. They came to me in a vision, a pack of black wolves, and howled against the Pequot and his English god. I saw them chase him through a dark wood until he climbed a tree to escape them. They surrounded the tree, and one by one they began to climb it after him. He coughed at them, like our sick ones cough in the Dying, and they all of them fell from the tree as though dead.

"Then one rose up among his brothers and cursed the god of the English, at which Wequash lost his hold and fell from his perch into the midst of the slumbering wolves. They awoke as one and devoured the wicked Pequot. Praise them! They devoured him bones and all!"

"Why would Wequash send the plague among us?" asked our grand sachem as his fingers drummed absently upon the wooden lid of the small sugar box given him by Winthrop. It was long empty.

"Because we do not turn to his god!" replied the powwow, turning his head from side to side as though to read the shadows that danced within the wigwam of Canonicus. I watched his own shadow, which gestured and twitched with a life of its own. Perhaps it was its own.

Canonicus rubbed his thick hands across his greased chest. The firelight pulsed in his dark, thoughtful eyes.

"Williams often wonders that we turn not to this god," said

our king. "And I tell him always that no one god will hold my allegiance alone. For the sea is made up of many drops of water, and the forest is full of many kinds of trees. There cannot be one god above all, for then there is no *all.*"

"I do not doubt the love of Williams for our king and our prince and our people," said Askug, rolling his fingers over the fire, "but he loves his god more! And would not any man punish those who spurn the one he loves? Perhaps it is Williams who brings this upon us! But no! It must be Wequash," declared the powwow, for his hatred of the Pequot led him down this path anew.

"Williams told us long ago that the Dying was in the hands of this great god," said Canonicus, "so your words may be true. This is a sour grape! For I trusted Wequash as I trusted my sons."

"Never trust a Pequot!" sneered Askug, peering around upon the men who sat at the fires of their king. We loved not the Pequot, but neither did we hate them as our powwow did. His hatred was born of deep wounds, long since scarred but never healed for the powwow scratched at them daily.

Many seasons past, when Nopatin my grandfather was but a boy—and a Pequot boy at that!—his father and a small band of Pequot warriors crept one dawn into the city of Mascus and Canonicus. They came to murder the powwow of the Narragansett, but they slew his young son instead.

In vengeance, Askug and Mascus, with many warriors of the Narragansett, fell in battle upon the Pequot village, slaying some and capturing a boy-child named Waupi. The Pequot lad was adopted into the family of Askug and became Nopatin of the Narragansett, my grandfather and the father of Katanaquat my father. Thus my own blood was traced to that of the Pequot, and thus my heart rose up against the wrath of Askug.

I stood.

"Kattenanit the Night Wind," said Askug with a clumsy bow of his dark, matted head. He sat down awkwardly beside our king.

"Could not the plague be sent by our own gods?" I asked. "And if not, are they not strong enough to chase it from our doors? And if they will not, should we not call upon the God of Wequash and Williams to aid us in our sorrow and our need?" I had risen to defend Wequash, but my words fell out on the side of the Great God instead.

"Son of your father!" barked the powwow, leaping to his feet as swiftly as the dog who is poked with the sharp head of an arrow. "Should we call the wrath of the spirits upon us in concert with the plague of the English god? No! We will curse this English god and watch as Wequash falls from his tree! When he is devoured, then will the English god flee and the Dying with him!"

The Snake began to dance and coil himself around the central blaze, twisting his limbs about him in ways that astounded us all—for even the tree must break when it bends itself against itself! But the powwow was like the sea which could lift its waves high and push them low, over and under themselves forever.

A sudden chill came over me, and I thought for a moment that Askug had conjured the gods, but then I realized that someone had entered the house at my back. Miantonomi.

"My prince!" I blurted. "The powwow dances against Wequash and the One Great God!"

Then Wequash himself stepped into the tent. And Askug froze in midleap and glared at the once-Pequot god-preacher.

"Canonicus my uncle," said Miantonomi with a grim smile and a sincere bow of his head. "Do we dance against our brothers here tonight?"

"Against the Dying," answered the grand sachem with a troubled wave of his hand.

"Against the Pequot poison in our cup!" cried Askug, swinging his painted arms through the rising smoke of the fire of Canonicus.

Wequash stood for a breath in the door of the wigwam, one foot in the warm room, the other upon the white winter floor of the cold outdoors. His clean gaze walked the tent in an instant, and then fell sadly to the mats at his feet. He came fully in, but only by a step, and looked up once more at us all.

"I am Wequash of the Narragansett," he said quietly. "And my love for you is as the love of a child for its mother. What I once was, I am no more. What I am, I will remain until the day I close my eyes to open them in Heaven."

And he bowed his head to us and backed out the door into the bitter night.

"We dance against the Dying," repeated Canonicus our king. "And not against our brother," he said, looking hard at Askug.

"I will dance as the spirits bid me dance," said the powwow, his eyes dulled in cruel resolve.

"But not against our brother," affirmed Miantonomi, standing still and tall before the jittering form of the medicine man. "Wequash is my brother," said our prince. And then he too passed out into the hard starlight.

"I am going home," said Wequash.

"Is this not home?" I asked.

"No longer," he answered. "For the spirits oppose me on every side, and no man will hear the words of God. Askug would have my scalp upon a pole, and Canonicus no longer sees the love in my heart."

"Where is home?" I asked.

"Along the Connecticut, north of the Mohegan, where I was born," he said. "I have lands there that were once under the sachemdom of my great grandfather. They are now hunting grounds, fishing holes. I will build my wigwam, send for my wife and children who are with Uncas, and raise young braves and maidens who will call on the One Great God."

"Will you be safe?" I asked.

"God is my shield," he said.

"Will you not fear?" I asked.

"When I am afraid, I will throw myself on Him," said Wequash.

Wequash left us, but Askug did not let him go within his heart. For the hatred of the powwow was a master stronger than our kings, harder than the gods.

Many moons waxed and waned, and Wequash raised his wigwam as he promised. I walked to him once, with Williams and my father and Canonchet and our prince. His gardens were full, his tobacco strong. His house was filled with children and glad sounds. The song of the Name was strong upon his lips.

But the wolves followed him into the woods at last and found him up his tree. When he breathed upon them, they fell as in the dream of Askug.

The wolves were the warriors of Uncas and the powwows of the Long River. They opposed Wequash's claim to the land of his great grandfather, but he withstood them with the help of some neighboring tribes, and the Mohegan turned back bitterly in defeat.

But then the Snake of the mighty Narragansett rose up in the wake of the conquered wolves, and inwardly muttering oaths against the One Great God as he slithered up the trunk, he shook his rattle in the tree of the once-Pequot. When Wequash turned at the sound of the rattle, Askug spat poison in his face.

"Where has the Snake gone?" I asked.

"Westward into the woods," replied my great grandmother his squaw. "To visit Nopatin your grandfather."

But when he slithered home at last, the word had flown ahead of him that Wequash our friend had been bitten by the fangs of Askug.

"The shield of God has fallen," I said to Katanaquat my father with great and bitter sorrow in my heart.

"Even the gods must blink," said The Rain From God.

"It is murder," said our prince, with darkness in his eyes. "And it must be life for life."

"The powwow is our health and our strength with the spirits," said old Canonicus. "For all my days he has danced for our people. You would be dead yourself if not for his medicine and his magic!"

"It is murder," said our prince. "And it must be life for life. The poison was mixed in the tent of the powwow and poured into the cup of Wequash my brother. As they ate together at the table of Wequash! A bitter, wicked deed! Must I cover my own cup when I sit at meat with the powwow?"

"His hatred for the Pequot is buried now with Wequash be-

side the Connecticut," said Canonicus. "Askug will not spill his
wrath upon his own."

"Wequash was his own!" declared our prince. "For we made
him our own and he pledged to be our own. Did his battle
scars mean nothing? The blows he took on our behalf against
our foes? Did his bow in the hunt mean nothing? The meat he
laid upon our tables? He was our own! It is murder! And it
must be life for life!"

Canonicus laid his head in his heavy, gnarled hands, and a
deep sigh pushed itself from his thick, wrinkled lips.

"You are the man," said the chief sachem. "Do what must be
done."

And the man followed the snake into the woods one day and
did what must be done. For murder must not go unpunished.
Life for life.

"All men die," said Katanaquat my father, "no matter which
gods they bow to."

"All men die," I echoed, and my tears fell for Wequash my
friend. For he had loved me, and I had loved him.

But my heart grieved little for the powwow, the old gourd,
my great grandfather. For he had never loved me, as I knew
most fully now that his cold shadow no longer fell upon my
face. Worse, he had slain one dear to me! And thus I now
hated the name of the powwow.

Love your enemy, whispered the Name to my torn, embittered
soul.

Impossible!

The wolves rose up again, as in the dream of the now-dead
powwow, and fell upon the house of Wequash. They plundered
his gardens and dug up his grave. They cut up his body and
scattered his bones.

But his squaw and children were safe within the tent of
Miantonomi, for our prince brought them to us to live among
us as our own.

Chapter Six

The Terror

It was a time of tragedy and sorrows upon sorrows for my people. It was a time of terror in my soul.

Williams was gone across the Great Salt Sea to England of his birth, to speak with kings and princes, to ride horses across stone bridges and climb stairs in tall houses. I thought—when the Terror came upon me—that the Name had gone with him.

Miantonomi conspires against the English, said the old lie that Uncas loosed once more in the woods. The rumor was whispered in the ears of many, and it spread like fire in the leaves of autumn.

"With or without the consent of the English, I will take to the warpath against the Mohegan," declared our prince, "before his crooked tongue calls the soldiers of Boston to our shores!"

"I would not be so swift to paint for war against the mad dog," cautioned Canonicus. "For he will surely bark at the doors of the English at Hartford. And when they open to him, he will run inside. Then you will find yourself facing muskets instead of bows."

"I would rather chase him to their doors than have him lead them to ours!" said Miantonomi. "Yet I pray rather to catch him sleeping behind his own."

"You may find him lurking instead in the shadows along your path!"

"This also would please me," said our prince. "He has hidden

too long in the shadows! The hearts of my warriors have borne
his taunts and lies for many seasons. Our quivers are filled with
angry arrows. Much blood goes unavenged."

"Let vengeance rest awhile longer," counseled Canonicus,
"for the English master may soon tire of the Mohegan dog
who begs too often for too much. Then we may chase down
the dog without fear."

But the dog ran unleashed in the woods. It stole more than it
begged—and never from the English.

In the Moon Of Late Summer in my twenty-first year, Uncas
crossed the Pocatuck and fell upon the village of Nopatin my
grandfather. He plundered the harvest and burned many wigwams. Eight of the warriors of Nopatin were killed in the first
light of dawn. Many more were wounded. The cries of their
mourning rose with the smoke of their fires and blew east
upon the wind to our tents beside the Great Bay.

"I will dance tonight around the fire of war," said Miantonomi.

"I will dance with you," said Canonicus grimly. "Though my
old legs are too weak to run straight on the warpath, I will
dance. I will chant. The dog must be whipped!"

I had shed the blood of beasts from my seventh summer on-
ward. I had beaten blood from my friends in the games, and
had licked my own blood during the same. I had seen the foe
die inch by inch upon the poles of torture, the red juice of life
a thick puddle at his feet. I knew the stain of death that clings
to the warrior who stumbles home from battles fought over the
rivers and beyond the Bay. But though my sharp arrows had
tasted the hearts of our enemies, the shafts had been sped by
the hand of my father. War had not yet called me to the field
of death myself.

But now I walked painted, burdened with vengeance, and
armed with the long-crafted work of my own strong hands.

This was the end and the purpose of youth. This was the
sure path of every young brave. This was the strength of the
gods of our fathers. This was the medicine every boy
dreamed for. This was the door into manhood and honor.

This was our hope and the day we all longed for—to walk with our fathers to war.

The day had only dawned as six hundred warriors of the Narragansett forded the Shetucket one whoop north of where it strikes hands with the Quinnibaug.

The birds and the beasts of the wood seemed to know that we hunted for something other than themselves, for they went about their chirping and their wandering and their grazing as if we were mere shadows upon the mists of morning. But the laurel on the hills sheltered watchmen of the Mohegan, and we heard them whisper, we saw them run. Uncas would soon be aware of our coming.

What would he do? Flee like the frightened hare? Take to the trees like the wary squirrel? Stand and coil like the angry rattlesnake? Strike like the hungry wolf?

And what would I do?

This was not the Great Hunt Before The Snow. This was not the Games Of Harvest. This was not the play of battle where arrows were dull and warclubs were rounded bats of white birch.

Katanaquat my father walked before me, his face painted red from the middle of his nose to his left ear, yellow from the middle of his nose to his right ear, with black circles around both eyes. Straight silver streaks fell from his chest to his loins, for this was the sign of The Rain From God. His hair was pulled back in a long braid, a single black feather of Kaukant tied at its end. Over his right shoulder hung his weapons belt, with his English knife under his left arm, his quiver and backbag behind him. His warclub hung at one side from the belt of his loin cloth. His oaken bow was armed and in his hands. Around his neck he wore a small bag of English gunpowder. He had no gun with which to use it, but "It is strong medicine against our foes," he said.

Katanaquat my father was my own strong medicine. How glad I was to set my moccasins in his step! He was the strength of my heart upon this path. Without him, I felt that I might have fled homeward at the first cough of the crow.

In front of Katanaquat and behind our prince walked Canonchet, a strong and confident reflection of his father. I wished that we were walking side by side, for that was always our way in the days before this long morning's trail to manhood.

Behind me walked the Fool, humming quietly in a constant pitch that sounded like the buzzing of a fly. *Today I will see the Fool fight!* I thought, for I had heard a thousand tales of his courage and his skill. None dared run into the enemy as our Fool—laughing, reeling, leaping, shooting, he was like a warclub with wings. His arrows always flew true. All foes feared our Fool, for they thought him a god or a man filled with ghosts. His scalp belt was the fullest of our tribe.

I will bring you the fresh scalp of a Mohegan warrior, I heard myself say to Aquinne. The memory, though new, seemed a far-distant dream as my feet fell in rhythm with twelve hundred more of the moccasined feet of the strong Narragansett. *And we shall be wed before autumn comes falling*—the thought gave me strength, cleared my eyes, stood me taller.

The Yantic was cold as we waded its waters. The hilltop above it was empty of life, but I felt that its trees were a door that, once entered, would lead to the contest at last.

As we topped the hill and walked out of its woods on the other side, a wide, level valley stretched out below us—the Great Plain of the Pequot. Here great herds of deer often grazed—but not on this morning.

Across the divide, in scattered clusters of tens and twenties, in the trees and along the treeline, stood the fighting men of the Mohegan. They were many, I could see, but we were many more. My heart beat loud enough within me that I thought it might be heard even across that great and terrible field.

All of my days had been walking toward this one. This was the high and one day of my first blood, the moment of manhood, the reason for living, the full cup of medicine—strong, red, and welcomed. My soul stretched its arms toward the heavens in anxious longing and fearful joy.

My hands moved unconsciously across my body. They found my weapons readied, my bow fitted with the straightest and best of my shafts.

My eyes moved intently from the ranks of the enemy to my

father, to Canonchet, to our prince, and back again to the grassy plain before me.

My ears keened themselves for the whisper of the sliding arrow, the thunder of the throaty warcry.

Hawks drifted, circling, high above the great divide.

A lone figure came forward from the line of the Mohegan, his palms held out in peace. A parley at the dawn of peril.

Our prince sent one of ours to meet him, and a message was relayed that Uncas would come to Miantonomi in the valley between us. The sachems would speak their hearts first. This was our way.

I watched our prince walk down the hill of my manhood. Tall and with grace in his step he moved onward. Uncas came forth from his forest of warriors and stood in the valley to treat with our prince.

You are a dog and a worm, declared my heart to Uncas, as it loudly spoke for Miantonomi my prince. *I have come to kill you. So fight as a man or run like the dog that you are. Either way, I will crush you beneath my foot as the heel crushes the worm.*

But nothing could be heard of the meeting in the field. The two men stood still as trees. Their tongues spoke to each alone. All eyes were upon them.

Suddenly Uncas threw himself upon the ground, and my heart cried, *Treachery!* In the same moment, the Terror came upon me, and I froze like the stone upon the hillside.

As in a dream, I saw the Mohegan warriors draw their readied bows as one. A blurred shower of sharp death leapt from their ranks and sped across the morning sky toward the astonished warriors of the Narragansett. I heard the great cries of my brothers as they reeled back into the trees. I heard the whistling descent of the dark storm of Mohegan shafts. They bit into the earth at my feet and rattled against the stone and wood behind my back. Still I could not move.

I saw Uncas roll forward and leap to his feet, his mouth open in an ugly gape. The sound of his cry came next upon the wind, its shrieking syllables calling for the bloody slaughter of the foe. In concert with that awful command, I saw the men of the Mohegan pour out into the field, their bows once more readied, their own mouths wide in a great, shrill cry of murder and war.

Miantonomi fled. Toward us he bounded like the deer that leaps before the racing hunter. We needed no cry to send us flying home!

Still I could not move! Though my heart shrieked to my feet to flee, they were rooted to the earth.

My prince raced past me. My father was gone. The Fool was nowhere to be seen. Not a shadow of Canonchet.

A painted, swirling flood of Mohegan demons rolled up the hill toward me. A feathered shaft passed by my face. Another glanced off the warclub that hung at my belt. A horrible roar—like the sound of the mighty sea storm when it comes ashore to shake the forest in its wrath—filled my ears and blackened my eyes. The scream of my heart burst forth from my lips as my feet tore themselves at last from the clinging soil. Before me was a charging monster of a thousand legs, a thousand eyes, five hundred gaping, howling mouths. I felt my fingers let go of my drawn bowstring. I saw my shaft sink into one eye of the thousand. I felt my form turn like the fallen leaf before the mighty storm. And I tumbled upon its awful winds into the wild wood.

The fire burned low within the wigwam of The Rain From God. I sat in numbed fear in the shadows behind our bed.

"The spirits have taken his heart," they said of me. And I did not doubt it. For my heart would not beat as it should, and my sleep was short and filled with dreams of death and terror.

"He brought home no scalp but his own," they said of me. Aquinne would not look upon me, and Silvermoon my mother could not comfort me.

The new powwow among us, Nickeétem by name, danced over me, but I would not rise from the shadows. Canonchet could not pull me up. The Terror held me there.

For where was my father? Our prince? Our Fool?

Twenty-three men were missing, besides the known dead who numbered nine. The city of Canonicus wailed with the loud mourning of two thousand angered, sorrowed souls. Ambassadors were sent from Canonicus to the country of Uncas to treat for peace, to bring home our dead, and to offer ransom for any who were captive.

While they were gone, others of our scattered warriors wandered home, mumbling tales of blood and slaughter. Miantonomi was a captive of the Mohegan, they said. We chanted and stomped for the safety of our prince.

Two men came last to the city of Canonicus, two dead men walking—the form of my father and Assoko our Fool. They too had been captive, but Uncas had finally set them free into the forest. My father, though not wounded, seemed a man without a heart. The Fool was a bloody and terrible sight to behold.

"He is gone from us!" we cried when we looked upon the Fool.

"The soul of Assoko is flown!" declared Nickeétem.

"It is gone with his scalp at the hands of Uncas," mumbled Katanaquat my father in the darkness of his own despair. For the Mohegan sachem had made the Fool race in the gauntlet. And when brave Assoko had mastered the run, Uncas met him man to man.

"The Fool fought as the wildcat fights," said my father to the shadows and the failing fire. "But Uncas slid his knife across his head. You see it for yourself! He lives—yet it is no longer him."

The great ghastly wound of the Fool stood gnarled and red upon his hairless forehead. We wept to behold it, for surely our Fool was now a man without a soul. For the soul is in the scalp! And when the soul has flown, is not the man dead?

"Not dead!" said the once-man firmly to his family and friends. But they wailed and wept and would not speak to him.

"I walk," said the once-man quietly to the children of our city as he wandered among them, his short, thick arms wagging like the wings of an English hen. But the children ran from him screaming.

"I am the Fool," he said sadly as we sat in the tent of Katanaquat my father. But I did not know how to speak to the once-man, and my father turned from us both to tend the fire. The Terror gnawed at my soul.

"Sawkunk fled first," said Kuttowonk.

"Our prince fled first!" Sawkunk declared. "And should we not follow his lead?"

"We followed your lead," said Kuttowonk. "For everyone was shouting, 'There goes Sawkunk. He knows the way home. Follow him!' "

"If Miantonomi had raised his hand against Uncas," argued Sawkunk, "I would have been first into the valley to aid him!"

"Had he raised his hand against Uncas," jabbed Waumausu, "you would have thought it first a signal to flee!"

"If our prince were here," cried Sawkunk, "he would speak for me!"

"He is not here," we said darkly, "and so none can say what he might speak."

"If Williams were here, he could plead for our prince!" I said.

"He is not here," we said sadly, "and so we must wait for word from the Mohegan."

"We have paid Uncas a great ransom!" declared Sawkunk.

"And if he will not take it?" wondered Tawhitch.

"He has taken it already!" I said. "But he makes no promises!"

"And if he harms our prince?" cried Kuttowonk.

"I will run first against the foe!" declared Sawkunk. "You will see."

"It was for his well-keeping while I had him among us," sneered Uncas concerning the ransom. "None ever spoke of release."

"He was arrogant and hard-set against us," said the Hartford English concerning our prince. "His friendship was feigned."

"He was given by the Mohegan into the hands of the English," said Katanaquat my father, "and they gave him back into the hands of Uncas. 'Kill him,' they told him. And gladly the dog took the bite for its master!"

"But our prince said he loved them!" I cried in confusion.

"They thought him a liar."

"The dog is the liar!"

"It bites when they bid him. It comes when they call."

Sachem's Plain we now call it, the place where the brother of Uncas buried his tomahawk in the head of our prince. The place where Uncas cut a piece of the dead sachem's shoulder and ate it, declaring, "It is the sweetest meat ever I tasted!"

Williams was over the Great Salt Sea when it happened. His eyes did not see. His ears did not hear. He could not run to the rescue. He could not plead for the life of his friend.

I wept upon the stones that covered the rude grave of our dead sachem. But my tears were as ashes compared to the storm that fell from the eyes of The Rain From God. My father had loved this great man from his childhood. Now he was gone. Forever and always. The forest was empty of light. My father was darkness itself.

Assoko would leave us, he said.

"Why?" I asked.

"To find a new soul," said the once-man who walked in the form of the Fool. And my father wept the more, for he knew in his heart that the once-man was still his Fool. He could not bear his leaving.

"Where will you go?" I asked the Assoko-man.

"To the English," said the once-man. "To Williams."

"But he is not home," I said. And our Fool did not know what to say or do.

"God gives a new soul!" he insisted at last, and would have walked north to search alone for the One God.

"We will go with you to Providence," said Katanaquat my father, and we walked him once more to the house of the preacher where Mary the wife of Williams took him in.

"He will be well with us until Roger's return," she said. And we left him sitting at that fine table before that fine fire with his scarred head in his hands, rocking to and fro, humming a quiet tune of his own making.

"Will the Great God give a new soul?" I asked of my father as we journeyed southward home.

"Does a man rise from the dead?" replied The Rain From God.

I woke in a cold, clammy sweat. The Terror slept. Beside me on the bed slept also Winaponk, my younger brother by Ohowauke. Shadows danced low in the warm wigwam. The midnight moon peaked in at our smoke hole. A fire burned outside. Men chanted softly. Women wept. Our prince was dead. It would be long seasons before our tears were done.

Where was the Name? Where was His shield upon the ones I loved?

Where was the Fire Of God upon our foes?

Where was the love of God in the hearts of the English?

Where was the Call that once woke me in wonder from my sleep?

Who gave the Terror such reign in my soul? And what was it? Why did it dog me? Where was my medicine against it?

Had my wall fallen? Had the spirits crept over it? Long I had left it untended, unfinished, unmanned.

Katanaquat my father moaned in his bed.

"Father?" I said. He rolled on his mat to face me.

"Hnggh . . ." he grunted.

"Are you awake?"

"I would not be but for your words!" he grumbled roughly.

"How does a man chase the spirits from him?" I asked.

"Two ways," he said absently, rubbing his fists in his eyes. "Either he dances and howls like the powwow, cutting himself with knives and throwing his best tobacco into the fire, or he hires the powwow to howl and cut himself and throw his best tobacco into the fire. Why do you wish to know?"

"My wall," I said.

The Rain From God sat up in his bed.

"Are you well?" asked Silvermoon my mother in her dreams.

"Your wall?" said Father.

"Something has crossed it," I said.

"I have seen the shadow of fear in your eyes," my father said.

"The Terror of Death," I said.

"Is it a god?" he asked.

"I do not know," I replied.

"Have you seen it?" he asked.

"No," I replied.

"Has it spoken?" he asked.

"Not with words," I said.

"Spit it out!" said the Rain From God.

"I would gladly!" I declared. "But I cannot force it."

"Blood will force it," said Father. "Blood of the Mohegan. Strong medicine will send it flying from you. The medicine of your own strong heart.

"Rise up in the battle, Kattenanit! Slay the foe! Be the man! The spirits cross your wall because you sit at it carving bowls!

"Rise up and cast this Terror from you with loud shouts of war. With the sharp edge of your knife at the scalp of the enemy. With the heartbeat of the warrior. Be the man. Show yourself my son!"

"I am a man, Father," I said in my pride. "I stood on the field of battle when all others fled! When you had fled! I loosed my bow upon the Mohegan! I am a man!"

The Terror opened its eyes within me. I felt its cold gaze upon my soul. Then I heard its voice!

You stayed in the field because I held you there! it hissed. *And you fled like the hare when I finally let you go! A man! Ha!*

"A man!" echoed Katanaquat my father mockingly. "Let me sleep," he said. And he lay down once more and pulled his mat over his head. "Our prince was a man!" I heard him whisper quietly, bitterly, and then he said no more.

It spoke! I said within myself, my heart beating wildly. But now it slept again, and all was still. I dared not close my eyes until the dawn.

Pessacus, the younger brother of our murdered prince, ruled now with ancient Canonicus, and the Narragansett plotted hard and hot against the murderous Mohegan.

"Let us call all our tributaries to us here at Narragansett," counseled Katanaquat my father in the wigwam of Canonicus. "And with our numbers as many as the trees of the wood, we will march once more into the country of Uncas as the English marched upon the Pequot. We will chase the foe onto some high hill and set fire to his bed!"

"No," said old Canonicus, shaking his wise and whitened head. "For the English would rise up against us. They will not sit still if we take to the warpath in force."

Many somber heads nodded assent to the words of our grand sachem.

Pessacus stood.

"If we cannot come against Uncas as the trees of the forest," said Pessacus our sachem, "then we shall sneak upon him as the vine that encircles the oak. We will be like the serpent that strikes him in the legs and then slides away in the grass to wait for another day to strike him anew. In this way our poison will weaken him little by little until at last he falls!"

We bit the dog's legs and it ran to its master. *A truce!* cried the master, his heel on the head of the serpent. We promised the peace for one year and no more. I was glad for the year, for the Terror did not wake within those days. *Sleep still!* I said.

The seasons walked on. I fished the Great Bay with Canonchet and Sawkunk. I tended the eel weirs on the Shewatuck and Matantuck. I hunted the forest for bird and beast. And I carved bowls and spoons for the further winning of Aquinne, for our marriage was put off by the cooling of her heart toward me. But my bowls did not impress her—she wanted warclubs instead.

"I have carved three already," I said.

"Where are your scalps?" she asked.

"Upon the heads of the Mohegan," I said, "waiting for my knife to kiss them."

"Will they wait forever?" she asked.

"They wait only for war," I replied.

"The truce is ended," she reminded me.

Though I longed for Aquinne, I had no heart for the war-path. But my father could think of nothing else. His days and nights were filled with dreams of vengeance against the Mohegan. He grew rough and rude with everyone, especially those within his own wigwam.

"Why do you not make new arrows?" he asked me one day as I sat at soup.

"I have many," I replied, "and more." Winaponk sat beside me. He was nine summers old.

"I have many arrows, too," said Winaponk, holding up the small shafts he had whittled with my English knife. Father ignored him.

"Why do you not take Aquinne as your wife?" he blurted at me, taking a bowl from Silvermoon my mother without thanks. "My tent grows crowded!" he growled.

"Would it not be still more crowded with Aquinne in my bed?" I said.

He looked at me darkly.

"You could have her love and a wigwam of your own if you'd wash your hands in Mohegan blood!"

"I saved your life from one Mohegan, Father, when I was not yet a man," I said, reminding him of his fight with Uncas those many summers past. "And I have blinded or killed another since."

"You have not the heart of the warrior!" snorted Katanaquat.

"I have not the heart of the killer!" I corrected him coldly, for my pride had risen against him.

He stood before me suddenly, his face dark with anger.

"*Thou shalt not kill!*" he scoffed. "Is that what your heart is chanting? Do you sing these empty words of the English god while you lie in the tent of your Narragansett father? Are you such a fool that you suck on the dry bones of the murderous English?

"They gave our prince over to the mad dog Mohegan!" he shouted. "They laid the highest and the best of the Narragansett beneath the butchering, black axe of Uncas!

"And you! My own son! You dare to sit in my house and carve spoons and chant *Thou shalt not kill.*"

"Father," I said quietly. "I mean no dishonor to the name of our prince! I will take up my bow against the . . ."

"You will take up your bowls!" he shouted, tossing his own bowl aside while the soup splashed into the fire.

"Katanaquat, my lord!" cried Ohowauke. "The broth is rare! We have so little." And she took the soup pot from the fire to protect it from my father's rage.

He turned on her, and in the moments that followed, his anger gave vent to violence. He cursed at us all, scattering Winaponk's arrows and bow at our feet. My brother ran to stand behind his mother.

As my father moved toward the boy, Ohowauke stood in his way. Katanaquat struck her, and the boiling pot turned full upon her. It spilled upon her limbs, splashing the form of the crouching child.

"Aieyagh!" cried Winaponk my brother as the scalding liquid painted his small face.

"No! No! No!" cried his mother, flailing her pained arms in the smoky air, wailing for help for her wounded son.

Many came running, and the tent was soon filled with the busy hands of caring neighbors. Songs for healing rose from Silvermoon my mother, Quanatik my sister, and many of the squaws of the village.

I followed my father out into the night.

"Go back and wipe up the soup!" he said.

"Go wipe it up yourself!" I cried. "A man is not a man who strikes the doe for protecting the fawn!"

He swung his fist at me, and I caught it in mine. We were both men now. I held him fast.

"I am a warrior, Father," I said to The Rain From God. "Not a daughter!" And I pushed his hand from me. "I will run the war-path! I will take my scalps! But I will not drink blood as water!"

"You drink soup instead!" he spat. "And chant *Thou shalt not kill* to my children!"

"You are wrong, Father," I said, my heart cooling slowly with the chill night breeze. His eyes flashed hot, and he raised his hand to strike at me again. I turned my back against him.

"You mock me!" he cried.

"I do not mock you," I said with a heavy sigh. And I walked away alone to sit and think beside Red Creek.

Why did the Name call me to His words?

Why did His words turn my loved ones from me?

Why did I care for Him at all who would not show His face to me—or let me take my woman—or come into my heart to chase the Terror from my soul?

Was the Name a dream?

Did His Song die upon the cold lips of Wequash?

Would the Fool ever find Him?

Would He give the Fool a soul?

And who was the fool? I was the fool! For I sat beneath Old Willow in my sorrow and my pain while I could be lying in pleasure and peace in bed beside Aquinne!

Scalps—and only one at that! In my hands, warm and dripping! That was what I needed. Not the cold and distant twinkling of some far off Star!

Chapter Seven

The Ransom

At the foot of the Shannuck, where it empties into the Pocatuck, we camped high in the rocks that hid beneath the
ever-green boughs of the mountain rose. Nine young warriors
of the Narragansett, we promised each other to never turn east
until we had strengthened our medicine on the blood of the
Mohegan. Canonchet was not with us. This was my foray.

One whoop to our south, the widening Pocatuck turned a
slow bend near a deep pocket of backwater that formed a large
pool surrounded on three sides by a tousled hedge of cattails
and a sloping bank of tall grasses. Many fish swam within that
pocket, lazily, sleeping among the river reeds that stood in the
shallows, dreaming in the deeps where the gaze of Keesuckquand was dim. The Mohegan came often to hook and to
spear them.

It was my turn at watch.

"Don't laugh so loud around the fire this time!" I scolded.
"You sounded like a pack of crows when last I went on
watch—yet not so much like crows as to fool a Mohegan warrior! Laugh into your clothes if you must, and keep the smoke
thin!" I pulled myself out of our pit and crawled through the
thicket to the watch-rock that looked south.

The day was new, and the sun had not yet climbed to where
it might look upon my hiding place, but the trees that rose
above me stretched their arms toward the sky to dip their fingers in the warm light that slowly blanketed the earth.

The woods were alive with the movement of morning in summer. Deer wandered carelessly along the Shannuck to my right, walking their path to the Mohegan fishing pool. Its waters were quiet and to their liking. A band of skinny turkeys sauntered through the brushless tract of thick pine that stood across the Shannuck to the north. They flushed out a grouse that had been resting at the edge of the pine, and it flew from its nest with a wild whirl of humming wings. A small, thin salamander climbed my rock to take watch with me, settling upon a soft mat of moss as if it were its bed.

Will they come? I wondered.

By the time bright Keesuckquand had opened his eye to the wide glade that led from the wooded hills of the Mohegan to the fish-pool of the Pocatuck, I was upon my back with my face to the warming sky. My lizard friend, frustrated by the fickle, changing shadows of our viny thicket, had gone to look for more constant shade beneath our stone, and I was lost in a daydream in which I swam with Aquinne in the still waters of Ashanduck pond.

A laugh. And I rose to toss a small stone back into the shelter of our hidden camp.

"Ow!" coughed Sawkunk. "What was that for?" he hissed.

"For laughing!" I whispered loudly through the thicket.

"We did not laugh," said Kuttowonk.

And I heard it again, from our south. But now our camp was murmuring against the stone I had thrown without reason.

"Be still!" I said once to the muttering Narragansett. "The laughter was not yours!" And the forest was quiet once more except for the birds and the beasts and the morning breeze that wandered through the treetops.

I sat up slowly and pushed my face to the edge of the thicket. Below me the hillside fell in rock and brush to the stony waters of the Shannuck. To my south beside the Shannuck, across a tangled field of berry bushes and tumbled white birch, rose a stand of great oak with small pines at its feet. Through the spreading upper trunks of the oak, I could see the open glade and the face of the sparkling waters of the fishpool. There were no deer standing in its shallows. A large snapping turtle lumbered from the reeds and slid into the pool. Someone was coming!

I saw them. Mohegan. Two men, two women, two boys. The braves were armed but not for battle. They had no clubs, only bows and arrows, knives, and poles and spears for fishing. Were there more? No—only the six. Easy prey for nine young warriors of the Narragansett.

I backed myself slowly into our pit. With signs and gestures I made my friends know the number and the gender and the years of the foe. Then we huddled our faces together to speak no louder than we breathed.

"Shall we descend?" asked Eatowock the first son of Eatawus.

"They have not settled at their fishing yet," I replied.

"It is my turn at the watch," said a younger of the sons of Eatawus, "let me rise to the watch-rock and see when they settle."

"I will go with you," said his brother the twin, for they went all places together.

"No," I said, "only one must take the watch. Sawkunk."

"If they see me?" he asked.

"They will not see you!" mumbled Kuttowonk.

"I would rather descend and watch them from our watch-tree," said Sawkunk. For we had a great elm that stood beneath us in the midst of the thicket. It was hollow on the north, with a break in its trunk that worked like a window to the south. A man could stand within its hollow and be hid from all eyes. Yet he could look out and see much.

"You wish to descend that you might first run if the foe should pursue us!" said Kuttowonk.

"Let us not argue," said the twins as one.

"Go to the watch-rock, Sawkunk," I ordered, "and come back to us when they have begun to catch fish.

"I will go down to the watch-tree," I said. "For it is not so safe a place as Kuttowonk says."

"But at least a man can stand in it!" complained Sawkunk, rubbing his cramped legs. And we all wished we could stand, but the moment was not yet.

"When Sawkunk comes back to the pit," I said, "let him and

the twins come down to me at the tree. The rest of you follow
Kuttowonk on the path that crosses the Shannuck to the pines.

"We will move in two bodies. My band will run to the woods-
edge at the east side of the Pocatuck facing the pool. Kuttowonk will cross the Shannuck and run to the opening of the
glade at the edge of the pines. I will wait for the sun to stand
over the glade. Then I will whoop and loose my arrows upon
the Mohegan. We will shoot as the Fool once shot, straight
and true. Then Kuttowonk will fall upon them from behind.

"Take no chances! If our first shafts take none of them and
they rise to fight, flee! Our mothers must not mourn tonight!"

The men of the Mohegan chattered and laughed as they
checked the strength of their lines and smeared fresh cornmeal
over their crusted plummet stones. One of them cursed as his
boned hook snapped in his fingers. It took him many moments
to secure another to his line. Then the fishermen jerked their
poles and flung their lazy lines into the still deeps.

The women waded out into the marshy shallows, squatted,
and thrust their arms into the soft sand beneath the green waters. With grins and quiet conversation, their muddy fingers
soon cast many a large clam upon the grassy shore.

Further out in the shallows stood the boys, spears in hand,
silently watching the wet and sun-splashed world beneath
them, chanting within themselves that the grandfather fish
might come within reach of their barbed, poised shafts.

I stared, barely blinking, from my hollow in the elm.

Behind me, the harsh rustle of leaves signaled the arrival of
my band. The twins came first to my tree, then Sawkunk. I put
my hand to my mouth to keep the men in silence, then slipped
from the elm and, bending to the earth, made my way through
the thorny berry patch to the twisted, vine-entangled birch.
Our way was harder in the thick growth, and we did not dare
to stand. At last we came forth in the oak, where we crawled
amid the new pine to the edge of the Pocatuck. Our prey were
before us, a short bow shot away, and we could hear their
words with ease.

I waved Sawkunk to my side and with some few signs made

him understand that he should crawl north along the river to spot out and report the progress of Kuttowonk. He stared for a breath at the fishing Mohegan, then started through the bushes as I bid him.

The women were done with their clamming and had cleared the grass for a small fire.

Perhaps they will also cook our lunch for us, I thought. And I wished that my father were here to take the meal with us, though his delight would have been in the appetizer—Mohegan blood—which pleased him more than fish these days.

The sun rose high, and the grasses of the marsh shimmered green in its light. *Where is Sawkunk?* I asked myself. The twins knelt still as stones, their shafts to their bows. *One must be a reflection of the other*, I mused of the two sons of Eatawus. Which is real?

I heard then new voices. More men of the Mohegan! Ten or twelve of them, walking freely from their wood into the glade. They hailed the fishers, and shouts of greeting flew between the bands. Did Kuttowonk hear? Did he see?

Turn back, my friend! I cried to Kuttowonk within my heart. *We will hunt Mohegan another day!*

To my right, upon the far bank of the Shannuck, another form moved, low and out of sight of both the fishers and the new warriors. Sawkunk! He had crossed the river! There he was, alone on the south bank, scrambling up toward the pines! Why? My eyes searched the wall of evergreens for Kuttowonk. I could not see him. Surely he was circling back to us by now. He would know not to fall upon so many of the enemy.

Sawkunk! As noisy as a racing moose! The Mohegan would hear him if he did not still himself soon! The twins read my thoughts and pulled their bows tight, their sights on the first of the Mohegan warriors. I did the same. If the foe detected our runaway moose, we would send quick rain upon them!

Sawkunk! What possessed the fool? Did the Terror or the spirits blind him and press him on? Did they chase him into the laps of the foe?

He made the rise of the bank at last and disappeared into the pines. Thank the gods! He was now on quiet ground and could run to his heart's content! But why did he cross the river?

A shout. Sawkunk called for Kuttowonk—curse him! Had he lost his head? The Mohegan turned their faces toward the pine. The glade sat in silence for a breath. Suddenly, as one, the foe lay themselves in the tall grasses, and I knew that our purpose was lost.

Just as suddenly, a feathered shaft buried itself in the oak by my head. Wary Mohegan eyes had turned once around their world and found us even here! The twins loosed their arrows across the wide river and into the vast, waving field of green.

"Hold!" I hissed. "We only add our arrows to the reeds of the pasture!

"Come!" I whispered, and I ran at once through the bushes where Sawkunk had crawled. The twins followed.

As we crashed through the thicket at river's edge, our view of the pines was clear. Directly across from us, entering the pine wood from the glasses of the glade, were several of the Mohegan, bows readied, feet flying. They had someone on the run.

"Dogs!" I cried to them. "Moose dung!" I shouted. But they did not turn from their chase. Instead, my shouts brought more arrows upon us from the rushes beside the clearing. The twins fired once upon the Mohegan in the woods, then took cover behind a great boulder.

"Come!" I cried again, and led the two brothers in a mad scramble back up our bank and onto the path that wandered north with the Shannuck toward the Quequatuck. "If Sawkunk follows Kuttowonk, they will cross at the Fallen Spruce. We will meet them there to keep the enemy at bay beyond the river! Then we may flee together toward home."

What if the fishers and the other warriors should cross the waters behind us? What if they hemmed us in as we had meant to do to them? Should we flee now? Should we leave our brothers to their own medicine and the watchcare of the gods?

No! This was my foray. I led us here. I must take us home.

My flying feet pummeled the stony trail. The twins were at my heels, their throaty gasps rising in a hard chorus of hot resolve. We would reach the spruce bridge soon! We would scream like men! Fight like men! Send our foes running back to their wigwams with empty quivers!

But the Terror pounded in my heart, louder as I ran. And I could not shake it though my medicine rose strong to call me to the rescue and the battle. *Down!* I cried to the Terror and my fears. *Down to stay down!* But they rose within me like the smoke of a hot fire to cloud my eyes.

The spruce. And none of our men!

I raised a great cry to call them to us, and I heard their answer from across the water. It came with the strong plea for help. Death flew upon their words, the Terror gripped me, and I could not move! The twins looked to me, wonder in their eyes.

"They call us!" they said. "Do we go to them?"

Go? To our graves?

Behind us the woods came suddenly alive with a terrible squall. Mohegan! They had crossed! They broke upon us shrieking. The twins loosed their bows once more, and two of the foe fell impaled. I threw the Terror from me and pulled my own bow to my chin. My shaft flew straight, passing full through the neck of a fast-flying brave. His legs buckled wildly, his hands flew up before him, and he plowed the earth at my feet.

With great cries we swung our warclubs about our heads, but we did not need to wail much, for the companions of the dead had fallen back behind some rocks. I turned at once to cross the bridge of spruce. Leaping like deer, the twins followed.

Our way was clear on the other side—only needles and twigs and a few rotted skeletons of ancient, fallen pine. I wailed once more as I ran, and the answer came. North!

The path was a blur.

A man upon the needled earth. Scalped. Kuttowonk! My feet flew. My head thundered. Blood for blood! Scalp for scalp! Kuttowonk my brother!

Another body. Arrows through the back. Tawhitch! Fire in my heart. Sweat like blood upon my brow. The mad cry of death upon my lips. It filled my being. It filled the air. It filled the forest.

Before me was a body of men, pulling red flesh from the heads of young warriors, scalps from the pates of the children of Eatawus. Dead on the pine floor, chests painted red with the blood of their own hearts! Great shrieks rose from their brothers the twins, and two shafts passed from behind me on either side. But the arrows fled widely into the wood, and we found ourselves facing four armed and ready warriors of the Mohegan.

Their clubs came up to meet ours, but our rush took the moment and we beat them back against a close stand of trees. With nowhere to run, they were cats in a cave. Their claws bit our flesh, and I saw one twin fall. *Not together!* my heart cried. But my fear was too true. The twins fell as one man to lie next to their brothers.

"Alone!" I cried aloud as I faced the leering Mohegan.

They lowered their weapons, panting loud like dogs, and laughed. They laughed! For what could I do but run and die?

If they took me alive? We had killed three of theirs—they would surely tie me to the pole of their torture. The Terror laughed with them.

I heard the zip of feathered ash, and the nearest warrior fell into the arms of his own, a Narragansett shaft firmly fixed in his shoulder. *Waumausu.* I was not alone.

"Run, Kattenanit!" cried Waumausu as he sent another arrow into the force of the foe. But the shaft merely splintered the pine bark at their backs. In a blur I saw my brother arm his bow again. Behind him rose the Mohegan who had come at last across the bridge.

I howled—once—as my legs flung me wildly through the brown shadowed forest. I prayed that Waumausu ran with me. His death wail followed instead.

I ran like the wind runs, like the moose runs, like the river runs in the Moon Of The Melting.

And the Mohegan ran always behind me. Sometimes shouting. Sometimes laughing. Sometimes silent. Would they never tire?

They ran me like we run the deer! They would follow me until I fell. They would haul me from the needled earth and walk me, with cruel jests and strong oaths, to their nearest city. They would give me meat and drink. They would let me sleep beside a warm fire. They would let their children come and gaze at me. They would ask me my name and the name of my father. They would admire my club and my bow and my arrows. Then they would decide if I was worth more as ransom or as entertainment at the pole of torture.

I would not tire! I would not fall!

I tumbled down out of the pine wood into a stand of maple and sycamore. Willows. The river.

Down the pebbled west bank of the Shannuck. Across the slippery waters. Up the far bank. Into the laurel. Up the great, rocky hillside.

Our watch-rock! One breath to turn and see my pursuers. They were crossing the river, but I was in Narragansett country. These were my trees. My paths. The Mohegan had to climb the tangled hill, but I could run.

I ran. Down the crooked path that led from our sad camp. Into the sunlit forest where familiar trails called me warmly, giving strength to my heart, my legs, my lungs.

Suddenly my foot caught beneath the rise of some roots, and I went down on my face in the ferns and the stones. In a breath, the Terror rose from the grasses and blew upon me.

Lie where you lay! it whispered foully. *Sleep in the safety of the tall ferns. If you rise, they will see you!*

No! my heart cried with the voice of my father. *Heed not the spirits! Spit upon the Terror! Rise! Run!*

I rose. I ran. But my foot was twisted sore in my fall, and I knew I could not race much further. But where was the cover to hide me?

The Hiding Place! The stone overhang along the Shannuck near the old chestnuts! If I could find it, my life was mine! It had hidden me well—Kuttowonk and Sawkunk, too—in our games of the last summer. *Kuttowonk my brother!* wailed my sorrowed soul.

And what of Sawkunk?

I turned from the path and headed for the Field Of Stone. If I could enter the thicket that lay about it, my trail would be hard to follow. Once I crossed the field, it would be harder still to pick up once more. Then for the river itself! It would carry me down to the Hiding Place, and surely none would find me there. In the light of a new dawn, I would take to the woods again for home.

My ankle pained me greatly, but I swallowed the pain and pushed myself on.

The thicket. Crawling through.

The Field Of Stone. Stumbling over.

The waters of the Shannuck. Plunging in.

Floating. Rolling. Riding south upon the waters. Aching. Tired.

Oh, great Cautantowwit, my brothers are dead!

Oh, merciful Jesus, their souls have all flown!

The cliffs. The caves. The Hiding Place! Dark beneath the pines. Cool beside the waters.

I pulled myself from the Shannuck and up the slippery wall of rock and rubble that fell into the river at the foot of the Hiding Place. My feet went out from under me twice, as my hands clawed the stone steeps for a firm hold. The gnarled roots of a grandfather pine were just beyond my reach, but I took them in hand at last, and with one final wearied effort vaulted myself into their arms. From there I stepped onto the rounded shelf that jutted out like a thick lip at the mouth of the Hiding Place. Safety!

Crawling back into the sheltered shadows of the rocky overhang, I lay upon my face on a hard mat of dried leaves and flat stone.

My tortured thoughts fought with one another in my aching head. My heart cried out in anger, in confusion, and in hard, dark disbelief. My soul wailed in anguished horror. My injured foot throbbed. My lips opened and closed in broken sobs and sharp gasps, and hot tears rose up to spill out from my darkened eyes. The world was gone from me in those moments, and all I knew was a suffocating flood of pain and despair.

At length the flood subsided, but the Terror remained—a living, breathing, pitiless presence that pressed me hard against my awful bed. It sang its dread song to my soul as I lay between waking and sleeping, a shadow of a man.

As my own breath slowed to a measured chant of wearied sighs and unconscious whispers, I heard the sound of something moving in my cave. A new wave of paralyzing fear walked up my back and into my head. The Terror grinned.

Katanaquat my father! I will die in this place! For I have swallowed the gods and they poison me!

The Terror.

What was it? Was it the Name?

Was it Chepi? Death? The Devil?

Was it in my cave? In my flesh? In my mind?

"Kattenanit," said the Terror with the strangled voice of Sawkunk.

I screamed. Something touched me on the shoulder. I rolled once and struck it. It cried out. It cursed. It took my head in its hands.

I punched it, clawed it, and rolled once more, against the wall of the cave, frantically wrenching my knife from my belt. The sharp English steel glinted strangely in the pale light.

"Kattenanit!" howled the beast. "I am Sawkunk. Do not kill me!"

We held each other for a long, long while, Sawkunk and I, and wept. The sun went down on our deep, deep sorrow. The moon came up on our lonely fears. We lay, exhausted, in our damp and darkened Hiding Place.

"Why did you cross the river to the pines?" I asked at last.

"Why did you bring us to this terrible day?" Sawkunk replied.

"Why did you cry out for Kuttowonk?" I asked.

"Why did you send me out alone to watch for him?" Sawkunk whined.

"You are a man!" I cried. "What is your fear?"

"I knew this would happen!" he said. "You knew this would happen!"

"You loosed your fear into the woods," I shouted, "and the Mohegan followed the smell of it!"

"You led us into the woods," said Sawkunk, "and the spirits fell upon us."

"The Mohegan fell upon us!" I spat. "It was your foolishness that called them into the pines!"

"I saw them scalp Kuttowonk," said Sawkunk.

"They should have scalped you!" I cried.

"You wanted scalps," he mumbled.

"Kuttowonk my brother!" I howled.

"They came running behind me after I entered . . ." he said.

"After you shouted!" I cried.

". . . after I shouted . . ."

"Why did you cross the river?"

". . . they ran swiftly, silently, but I saw them coming," he continued.

"Why did you cross the river?"

"What?" he asked.

"Why did you cross the river?"

"To find Kuttowonk."

"Why did you cry out to him?"

Sawkunk did not answer.

"Why did you cry out to him?" I said again.

"I was afraid, Kattenanit."

"You fool!" I spat.

"He was moving back toward the spruce bridge with our brothers. I was alone. He didn't see me. I called to him."

"Why did you cross the river?"

He sighed. He sobbed quietly.

"Why did you cross the river?" I repeated.

"Because it is easier to run beneath the pines," muttered Sawkunk.

"You fool!"

"I was afraid."

"You have killed us all!"

"You led us into the woods."

"Our blood is upon you, Sawkunk!"

"Our blood is upon you, Kattenanit."

"I will kill you," I said.

"I am dead already," he replied.

Long we lay in the stillness of the night, as the Shannuck sang its sad song beneath the chestnut and the pine.

He is dead already, said the Terror. *All that remains is for his blood to paint these rocks.*

Blood for blood, said my father and the father of my father and every father of all fathers of the ancient Narragansett.

Thou shalt not kill, said the preacher of Providence.

He is dead already, said the Terror. *You are dead already. Take your knives and carve each other's flesh. How can either of you ever go home?*

The murderer will go to Hell, where he shall ever lament, said Williams.

Kuttowonk my brother! cried my beaten, broken heart.

He is dead, whispered the Terror. *His soul is flown. They are all dead. They are all gone. Follow them.*

My knife was in my hands. My heart was in my bowels.

Sawkunk slept. *How can he sleep!?*

He is dead already, said the Terror.

You are dead already, said the Name to my soul, and my eyes opened wide with a start.

"Am I dead?" I said aloud.

You are dead, said the Terror.

You are dead, said the Name.

"Am I dead?" I asked again, setting my knife upon the stone and crawling out upon the shadowed ledge.

Nanepaushat yawned bright and full above the black leafy canopy that hung like a tent above my stone ceiling. The silver waters of the Shannuck winked and whispered as they walked south. A warm wind pushed great, grey clouds across the face of the moon.

My wall was ever weak, I said to the shimmering shadows and the shining Shannuck.

My shield is ever strong, sang the Name.

"You are not God!" I cried aloud.

He is not God! shouted the Terror.

"Shut up!" I said to the Terror. And it scraped its claws upon my wall, chuckling.

"The ransom," I said aloud to the memory of Williams, "does it buy me safety outside my wall?"

Your wall! laughed the Terror.

Your gods mock you, said Williams.

Your wall, said the Name, *stands between us.*

Build it strong! warned Katanaquat my father.

Your sins are a wall against God's love, said Williams.

The gods do not love men! said Father.
God loves you even now, Kattenanit, whispered Williams.
The Name is dead! cried the Terror.
You are dead in your sins, said the Name.
"Am I dead?" I asked.
The Blood is the Ransom, whispered the warm wind as it kissed my aching, opened eyes.
Our blood is upon you, Kattenanit, said Sawkunk.
"My wall was ever weak," I said.
It is much too strong, said the Name.
The Ransom, said Williams, *tears down the wall.*
Your wall! chuckled the Terror.
"Kuttowonk!" cried Sawkunk in his sleep.
"The fool!" I whispered.

The morning found us waking. But we had no heart with which to summon our legs to walk. For we were dead already.
"Can we go home?" I asked.
"Where is home?" he muttered.
"I should kill you," I said.
"Do not kill me," he pleaded.
"I will not," I replied.
We were hungry, but to think of fishing was to recall the horror of the day gone past. We sat without speaking as we watched the red dawn rise upon the Shannuck.
The sudden snap of a twig upon our roof.
The small patter of a single chestnut as it bounced and rolled down the hill of the cliff.
The muted sound of moccasins upon moss.
Low voices.
Mohegan!
Sawkunk gasped, and I clapped my hand upon his mouth. Had they heard us?
Slowly, so slowly—silently sliding—I pulled Sawkunk back into the narrow crack that lay in the deepest corner of our stony room. I listened with the ears of Noonatch for the sound of the foe. Was he still upon our roof? Had he moved back into the woods? Did he descend the cliffs to the Shannuck? If he

did, he would surely see my trail up the steep rocks. But how did he follow us here?

Sawkunk! He had not been so careful. His wild and blundering trail had led the Mohegan over the land and to this very Hiding Place. The fool!

I heard a soft splashing, and I knew that men were wading in the waters beneath us. My trail was plain from there. Soon we would be found. Soon we would face death once more. The Terror shrieked within, but a still, strong voice spoke through the loud wails:

I am your Shield and your Ransom, it said.

You are not God, I argued.

Then Sawkunk pulled his moccasins from his feet, my hand from his mouth.

"Do not move, do not so much as breathe," he whispered in my ear. Suddenly he slid from me and crawled toward the mouth of the cave. Frantically I reached for him, gesturing wildly, but he paid me no heed—the fool!

He moved out onto the lip, and stood. I heard the shouts of the Mohegan.

"I am alone," lied Sawkunk the fool, "but I am a dead man already."

"Not as dead as you shall be!" cried the mocking warriors.

"You cannot kill a dead man," said Sawkunk, and he stepped from the rock ledge to the roots of the grandfather pine. Where was he going?

"Why are you dead?" asked the wondering Mohegan.

"My cowardice has killed me, with all of my friends," he replied, and I heard him slide down the rock wall.

"All of your friends!" exclaimed the Mohegan.

"Their scalps are upon your belts," said the dead man. And many men began to speak at once.

"Here is my heart," said Sawkunk of the Narragansett. "Take it also." And there were many grunts of exclamation and strong wonder.

"Take his knife," I heard a Mohegan say. "But let him keep his heart for now."

"My heart is no longer my own," declared my brother, and

his medicine rose on the morning mist and entered my darkness to give strength to my own hard-beating heart.

"Swim!" commanded the Mohegan.

The sound of water splashing, men laughing, rocks rolling, branches scraping. Across the Shannuck and up its western banks. Faded voices. Far-off laughter, faint upon the wind, feebler still. Then gone.

Cautiously I crawled into the light. The Shannuck chuckled as it ran south. The courage of Sawkunk was heavy in the air.

I must follow.

Swiftly I rolled down the rock slide to the river. My foot! I had forgotten its pain. No matter. It was a small thing compared to the dreadful courage of Sawkunk on my behalf.

His trail was clear. I ran it with fire in my eyes.

Trodden grass. Thickets pushed aside. Last autumn's leaves kicked carelessly about.

The village of the Chicamug Niantic lay ahead of me. They would not go there—this was Narragansett country.

A deer path to the side. The bare prints of Sawkunk's feet beside the hoof marks of Noonatch. Water still settled in the heel.

A short whoop ahead I could hear them again. But I would not race so near that I might see them, for then they might see me.

The rocks of Ascoamoacot. We walked within ten whoops of the village of Nopatin my grandfather. Perhaps the Mohegan would blunder into his lap! But no, they turned again. Through Nopatin's hunting grounds and down to the bubbling Pocatuck. The border.

The river itself. Did they go up or down?

Wet stones on the southern side. Mud on the shore. The feet of Sawkunk again. *My brother sinks his heels low. Does he know that I will follow?*

The trail led out of the woods and into the cornfields of Wequatucket. The path was beaten here, a road much used, and it circled the wide fields to enter the Niantic town. I sank into the field. The ripe corn of late summer grew higher than my head, and I had no need to bow as I passed quietly amidst the thick stalks and the cat-tongued leaves. I would cross the corn in a straight walk, and come to its edge ahead of my brother and his captors. Then I would sit and wait upon the game of the gods. For what could else could I do?

In a tiny clearing in the midst of the field as the ground began to slope downward, I surprised some turkeys, but they ran off without tattling. Kaukant and his cousins circled overhead with rude shouts, but I knew that their racket was more on account of the walkers on the road.

The corn suddenly thinned, and I found myself at field's edge. There a tangled wall of red sumac, thorned blackcap, and viny red grapes rose within a sprawl of mossy boulders at the foot of the tall, rotted stump of an ancient willow. I crawled into the thicket and settled myself into a small hollow between a large rock and the old trunk. I could see the road clearly as it fell down onto the flats of the village of Wequatucket.

The smoke of many fires rose from the wigwams at the bottom of the hill. Women walked with wood and water. Men came out of their doors and blinked their eyes in the brightness of the new day, then sat beside their tents to smoke their pipes as Keesuckquand chased the mists of morning from the foggy lowlands. Dogs barked. Children ran and laughed. And the Mohegan came at last into my sight upon the road. Sawkunk walked in their midst, his head high.

My heart ran to him, but I did not stir one breath within my hollow.

Cries of greeting rose from the village below as the men of the Mohegan led their Narragansett captive down the steep path. Children ran in circles around the party, spitting cruel words at my brother. His face looked toward the morning clouds and the blue, eternal skies. Why did I wish that I were at his side?

The Terror was still. Had the medicine of Sawkunk sent it flying? Or did the Shield of the Name stand between me and the god of Death?

I am your Ransom, said the Strong Shield.

I am Narragansett, my heart replied. *The courage of my brother is my ransom and my strong shield.*

The sun rose high to the center of the sky before I spied Sawkunk again. I had taken a meal of grapes and raw corn which my stomach was not liking, and I almost slept for the weariness that pressed me as I lay in the hot sun within my hollow. But my heart woke me fully as I heard a sudden chanting from the town below.

Lifting my head as high as I dared beside my stump, I saw a great crowd gathered in a circle in the center of the stand of wigwams. Twenty tents. One hundred souls. They were not many or strong, but they were Uncas' Niantics, and they held my brother in strong arms. They tied him to their pole.

Not this! I cried within. *Not here! Not now!*

A fire shot up in their midst near the pole of Sawkunk, and a powwow began to dance. Men joined him. Sawkunk stood with his face to the sky, naked but for the paint upon his flesh which spoke his name. *I am Sawkunk of the Narragansett,* his colors declared. *I stand where I stand.*

I could no longer sit in the shadow of the dead willow. My own paint called up strong medicine to push me from my hiding.

Kattenanit the Night Wind, it cried, *though it is day, still you must blow!* Swiftly I crawled from the thicket into the tall grasses that grew beside the road. As I snaked down the steep hill, I could see nothing but the parting grass before me. I prayed none could see me.

For many moments I slid toward the loud chanting and the wild howling until my green cover thinned and I found myself at the edge of a bare table of flat stone, near a stand of young birch that stood poor guard at the very edge of the village. Beyond the birch were the first tents of the Niantic.

I flew over the stone table and dropped upon my stomach in the birch. Some small bushes made a weak attempt to hide me, yet I knew they could not. But neither could I see the circle from this spot, for the wigwams stood between us. I must blow on.

From the birch I ran to the nearest tent and looked inside. Empty. The next tent too, for all the town was about the fire and the pole. I saw them now. I must find my cover and hold it.

I entered a large wigwam. My entrance faced the hillside from which I came. The mats of a second door hung toward the center of the village. I peeked out. The backs of many of the Niantic were but two spits from my eyes. I saw the face of Sawkunk staring into the blue. "My ransom and my strong shield," I whispered aloud. None heard me. Even a loud shout from my lips would have been buried beneath the howling which rose from the circle of the torture!

I tied shut the mats of the second door, tightly to their poles—I did not want any guests. But I left the mat loose where I had entered, for I might need to leave by the same way—and swiftly.

I took hot coals from the morning's fire and scattered them just within the entrance—warm greetings to any who came home too soon!

Two English barrels sat against the wall. One I rolled onto its side just behind the coals. The other I stood at the back door.

A stock of fine arrows hung in a basket near the beds. I took them down and laid them against the upright barrel. Could they help me long against a siege?

Then standing upon the strong cask, I parted the mat a hair and looked out from the top of the door. From this position, above the heads of most, I could see my brother clearly. His eyes blazed like the fire that roared within the circle of his certain, slow death. My heart ran the distance.

Not this! I cried within. *Not here! Not now! Not Sawkunk my ransom and my strong shield!*

Here! said the Terror. *Now!* it hissed. And I stiffened coldly.

Begone from me! I commanded. But it would not.

He is dead already! it said.

I am dead with him! I declared. And I armed my bow. *Begone from me!* I said. But it would not.

Stay then, I said bitterly, *and watch how men die.* For men would surely die that day, and not my brother only!

But I could not hold the moment, for thoughts ran about in my head like frightened squirrels in a wigwam. And I wondered of a sudden why I'd come.

Sawkunk is a dead man, I said to my heart. *If I loose my arrows into the crowd, what will it buy him?*

And what will it buy me but my own dying upon the pole with him?

And shall I stand here like one who sits at the games to watch him die?

But I cannot leave him!

I must not leave him!

The crowd chanted loudly.

He is dead already, said the Terror.

An old squaw walked from the circle to the pole. Sawkunk did not look at her. She stroked his cheek with her hand and waved a large knife before his face. The crowd began to howl. The squaw smiled, bent low, and I lost her from my sight. Sawkunk bit his lip. The squaw rose again, her blade wet and bloodied. My heart fell. My eyes grew dark. The Terror held me strong.

Sawkunk began to sing, a strong song of the tales of the gods of the Narragansett. The squaw held the crimson blade high. The crowd wailed.

Another squaw left the circle to approach my brother, and the crowd laughed cruelly as the torture continued. Still he sang, though tears flowed like water from his eyes. Honor, strength, and medicine rose upon his chant and flew to my heart. I loved him in that moment more than I had ever loved a man. But I could not move, and I could not look away.

Men broke his teeth and tore at his hair. He sang while spitting blood, his thick, distorted words drifting on the tangled smoke of the near-burning fire. Great logs were added to the flames. The powwow danced.

My blood is upon you, Kattenanit, cried the dark memory of the night before.

"He gave himself up for me," I said aloud. "He dies for me."

The powwow took a burning brand and waved it in the air. A low wicked chant arose from the gathered Niantic. The Mohegan warriors joined the dance, each of them lifting fire from the torrid blaze.

I slid my knife across the ropes that held the door. The mat fell open. "He dies for me," I said.

He is dead already, said the Terror.

I armed my bow and raised it.

His blood is upon you, said the Terror.

The powwow swung his brand above his head in a wide arc, causing the Mohegan to fall back. With a great leap he bounded to the bloodied, broken face of the singing Narragansett. A touch of the sorcerer's torch, and my brother's hair went up in black and awful flame.

"It is finished!" I bellowed. I pulled my bow to my ear.

Sawkunk's dark eyes fell for one moment from the blazing sky—and found me. Fear burned within them stronger than the fire that swallowed their life. *Kattenanit!* they cried.

I loosed my shaft.

It leapt from my heart to his, and killed him in an instant. His head fell. His soul bounded free.

I armed my bow again.

One more, I said, and I let it go. It took the powwow in the back.

I jumped, howling like a demon, from the upright barrel through the opened door. My foes turned as one to face me.

"My ransom!" I cried to the clean skies and the flying soul of my perished brother. Then I ran. And a fire of great anger rose behind me. Hot and hard it followed up the hill.

"I live!" I shouted to the cursed Mohegan and the cruel Niantic, to the Terror and the Name, to the blood of my brothers and the heart of my father. And I flew toward home like the arrow from the bow of a great and mighty hunter.

"He died for me," I gasped, as I stumbled into the town of Nopatin my grandfather. And strong arms carried me through the wondering streets.

"My ransom," I moaned, as I lay in the tent of Nopatin my grandfather. And soft chants rose for me as I tossed within my dreams.

Part Two

THE
WORD

" Thus you see . . . that the
sound of the Word is spread a
great way—yea, farther
than I will speak of—
and it appears to me
that the Fields begin to look
white unto the Harvest."

—John Eliot

Chapter Eight

A Dark Dawning

Scalps held nothing for me anymore. Blood I despised. For where were the souls of my brothers? Heaven or Hell? Sowanniu or the Swamp of Chepi? Rolling upon the warm, free southwest wind or drifting outside my wigwam in the chill mists of morning?

The Terror remained.

Williams returned.

The Name wooed me.

Katanaquat my father grew dark like the cold storm of winter.

Silvermoon my mother grew quiet as the grave of our prince.

Nickeétem the powwow opposed me for adding the Name to my chanting and my dance.

Canonchet walked alone.

Aquinne slept in the bed of an older warrior and bore him a child.

Ohowauke, with Quanatik my sister and Winaponk my brother, left the tent of Katanaquat my father to live with her mother once more.

Canonicus our great and ancient sachem died upon his mats. Williams buried him in a new English coat while the city clothed itself in ashes and wept. Mixanno the son of our dead king rose to sit as sachem in his place.

Cutshamakin, Awawan, and Josias, sachems of the Massachusetts—with all the tribes from Tecticutt to the Merrimac— submitted themselves and their people to the English of the

Massachusetts Bay. The chiefs signed a covenant of peace and agreed to follow the Ten Words Of God in all that they did. An English God-preacher named John Eliot—a man with a clean heart and strong hands like Williams—ministered much good among them.

"See!" I said of the power of the Name toward the men of the Massachusetts. "The One God is a Strong God!" Nickeétem threatened me with sickness, and though my legs were weak, I stood where I stood.

An English war captain, Atherton by name, threatened to shoot the grand sachem Ninigret of the East Niantic. Though Williams intervened to quench the captain's anger, the dishonor of Atherton's violence stained the English with our scorn. Our powwows cried against the Name. The Narragansett spat upon the Ten Words.

But I could not hate the English. Should a man hate a tribe for the wickedness of few among many?

And I could not cry against the Name. For the Name had been crying out to me—with a clean voice and a strong heart— for most of the days of my life. Would that I could see His face! Even His shadow would lighten my eyes in the darkness of my days. But Williams said no man could see Him and live. Only the heart could see Him, the heart that believed in Him alone and cast all other gods aside.

Was Jesus the One Great God or was He not? I knew and then I didn't know. I declared it one day and denied it the next. Like the waves of the sea that are tossed by the winds, I rose and fell in the storm of my doubts.

I walked to Providence often to sit at the table of Williams, for his words were good meat and clean water. I walked much alone.

"Like your father, you are a man of strong heart and arms," said the preacher as we split maple together beside his wooden house. "But unlike your father, you do not war so hotly against the Lord Jesus."

"I would know Him," I said, "but He hides from me."

"I have told you many times, my dear friend, that it is your sin that hides Him," said Williams, wiping his sweated brow with the rolled sleeve of his white shirt.

"My sin," I mourned, "is ever with me. And thus God shall be ever hidden from the eyes of my heart."

"His blood can wash the stain of sin from your eyes," said Williams simply. He swung his axe swiftly and the blade bit the maple, cutting it in two. I picked up the pieces and laid them on the pile I had stacked against the house.

"I care not for blood these days," I replied.

"And in this you are hardly your father's son!" declared the preacher.

"So it would seem," I said, setting another log upon the splitting block, "and so I have been thinking."

"Would you come to live as a son in my house?" asked the preacher. I looked at him with wonder and fear. To live among the English! To dwell where the Great God dwelt! Did I dare?

He continued. "You know our tongue quite well from coming among us so often for so long," he said. "And your heart is for good and not evil. You could serve me in my trading with the tribes. You could help me with my cattle and my fields. And," he grinned warmly, "you could teach my sons to shoot the bow and arrow!"

"The bow and arrow!" I cried.

"Joseph is four," said Williams, "but he could bend a small bow of your making, and would love it! Daniel is six, and Providence Plantations has just made a law requiring every English male between the ages of seven and seventy to become skilled with the bow and arrow."

"But your guns!" I said. "They are the weapons of the gods! And our bows are . . ."

"Weapons of men," said Williams. "The English are men."

"What is this law?" I puzzled aloud.

"We live among archers," said Williams, touching my bow arm. "And what good would our guns do if we were deprived of our powder and shot? They are poor clubs indeed!"

"Do you fear us?" I asked.

"I do not," said Williams, "but a man is worse off than an infidel if he does not provide for the protection of his household in troubled times."

"An infidel?" I asked.

"A pagan," said Williams. "A worshiper of false gods."

"Am I a pagan?" I asked.

"You are," he answered. "But I love you nonetheless. And I would hire your arm to the task of arming my own."

"You shall have it," I said.

"And will you live in my house?" he asked.

"I cannot," I said suddenly, "for the Great God would fight against my spirits, and your house would be a field of battle."

"Your spirits?" frowned Williams. "Are you a powwow that you sleep with the spirits?"

"I am not," I declared. "For I stand where I stand, as my father has taught me. But . . ." I hesitated. "But the Terror . . ."

"The Terror?" asked Williams.

"It is a shadow or a god," I said, shaking my head in sorrow and confusion. "It follows me always, sometimes resting, sometimes waking, sometimes taunting. It is Fear. It is Death. I cannot loose it."

"Jesus can," declared the preacher.

"Will you pray that He does?" I pleaded.

"I will," the preacher promised, "but you must ask Him so yourself! And I want your bow arm still!" he added.

"It is yours," I said.

"You teach the English to bend the Narragansett bow?" challenged our powwow.

"Should not every child bend the ash and the oak?" I asked. "Have not our fathers bent it from the days of their creation at the hand of Cautantowwit?"

"And what if the English bend the bow against us?" he fired.

"Do you fear them?" I asked.

"I fear the gods!" he declared. "And they warn me against the English!"

"I teach the sons of Williams," I argued. "And they love us as their father does. They climb into our arms when we go to Providence to trade. They kiss our cheeks and run their hands through our hair. They blow their medicine in our faces and they strengthen our joy. Why would the spirits speak against them?"

"Because their father prays to the one-god!" shouted Nickeétem madly, and he swung his large arms around his head as if he were chasing mosquitoes.

"I pray to the One God," I said, my eyes upon the eyes of the powwow.

"Treason!" he shrieked.

"I pray to the One God for the good of the Narragansett," I said.

"This god is a deceiver!" shouted the powwow. "A liar and a lurker in shadows! He listens to you only to laugh in his loin clothes when your back is turned! You are a fool, Kattenanit son of Katanaquat, to treat with this god at all!"

"He is my Ransom and my Strong Shield," I heard myself say. And I saw Sawkunk my brother standing at the pole of his death. And I thought of Jesus giving Himself up to His foes. And I knew that blood could buy life. And I wondered that the Blood might buy mine.

"Fool!" wailed the powwow, pulling at his hair as if tearing it from his head might loose my foolishness to the wind.

"He died for me," I heard my lips whisper. And I saw the face of Sawkunk staring into the clear blue. And I heard his strong song. And I remembered my father humming the Song On The Wind. And I imagined the Name at the poles of His torture, looking toward Heaven, the song of His Father upon His lips.

"He died for me," I muttered as the powwow wailed.

"Assoko asks for you," said Williams.

"Is he well?" I wondered.

"Very well," replied the preacher.

"Did God give him a new soul?" I asked.

"It seems so," said the preacher.

It was a long ride by canoe to Capawack—the isle of the Vineyard of Martha—but I made the trip alone to see the Fool. The sea was high, and I thought myself lost more than once, but at last I made land.

"He is not here, but is gone upon the mainland," they said at the town where he lodged. "Perhaps if you stay with us a while, he will return."

"I cannot," I said, "for my people call me home." But it was not so, for the hand of my people was cold upon my skin. Yet I feared to stay upon this island, for I sensed strong war with the spirits. Too strong for me, for my wall was in ruins. The Terror blew in my ears like the wind of the storm at sea, and I had no club that could silence the gods.

"We will tell him you came," they said, and they treated me lovingly, giving me gifts for my father and his family.

These are men like me, and not English! I thought, *And yet they pray to the One God only. The bright sun shines warmly upon their strong island while I walk the forest with eyes that are dark amid days that are dim!*

How my heart longed to be one there among them! But the Terror would take me, the spirits would rend me! Oh, that the Name would rise up to defend me!

I could not see how to make Him my own.

"Call upon Him with your whole heart," said Williams. "Draw near to Him and He will draw near to you."

"Where does He dwell?"

"In all places! He is here even now."

"My heart cannot find Him!" I cried. "Give me to drink of the cup you gave Wequash."

"Your cup is the same," said Williams. "But your heart is your own."

"The Fool has a new soul," I said to Canonchet.

"Have you seen it?" he asked.

"Williams says it is so," I replied.

"Has he seen it?" he asked.

"He has seen the Fool," I said.

"Alive from the dead?" scoffed Nickeétem our powwow. "The English man lies!"

"The women saw Him first," said Williams, "on the day that He rose from His grave. But they did not know Him."

"Did He not look like Himself?" I asked.

"He did, but He was changed."

"Did His flesh sag upon His bones that they did not know Him?"

"It was changed into flesh that can never sag!"

"And does this flesh appear as the flesh of a man?"

"Yes, and more."

"As the flesh of a god?"

"The flesh of the Only God."

"For the spirits wear flesh that dies often," I said, thinking of the spirits of the birds and the beasts which gave themselves up again and again to our traps and shafts that we might have meat.

"And they are not God," said Williams.

"Only the Name?"

"Only the Name."

He is not God, said the Terror.

"You are not God!" I answered.

You are a dead man! said the Terror.

"Dead men rise!" I declared.

I will kill you, said the Terror.

"Jesus will save me!" I cried.

Shut up! shrieked the Terror, seizing me suddenly in a tangible grip that felt like the great hands of many strong men.

"God in Heaven, help me!" I cried. "Jesus, save me!"

Shut up! howled the Terror, throwing me upon the wigwam floor, rolling me toward the bright blaze of my father's fire.

"Jesus! Jesus! Jesus!" I cried. And the Terror shook me violently for a long moment—then all was still.

I lay upon my stomach with my face but a hand from the burning brands. The flames singed my brows. My breath fed the fire. My heart pounded loud within me. But a strange peace settled heavy on my soul. I wished to sleep.

"Kattenanit!" cried Silvermoon my mother as she entered the tent with kindling in her arms. I turned my back to the fire and stared into her troubled eyes.

"It is gone!" I said with quiet wonder. For the Fear had fully fled.

"When the evil spirit goes out of a man," said Williams, "he sometimes returns with seven wicked friends. If the house from which he fled has been cleaned and set in order but is empty still, the spirit may walk in the door as he first did. And then the state of that man is worse than it was before."

"Then I have no hope!" I cried. "For what good does it do to clean the wigwam and hang up all the baskets and bowls if the foe can enter so easily to kill and destroy?"

"Your hope is not in a wigwam that is set clean and in order," said Williams. "Your hope is in the Lord who promises to come in first and stand at the door."

I had to find Him. I had to have Him at my door. For what if the Terror returned to find me sleeping?

"I am walking to Cambridge of the English," I said to Canonchet as we fished together at Red Creek.

"Hold!" said the son of our dead prince, pointing to the far side of the laughing stream. "I think that great fish over there will take my hook. Let us sing to him."

"Come, grandfather, come," we chanted quietly, as the big fish circled lazily around the bait stone and the hook of Canonchet. It nibbled a bit at the stone.

"Stay, grandfather, stay," we sang, as the fish swam teasingly about the bent and sharpened bone. But either it was no grandfather or it didn't like our song, for it suddenly stirred up the mud with its tail and shot downstream.

"The spirits are troubled," muttered Canonchet, splashing his pole in the chuckling waters.

"Oh!" I said, as my own pole tightened in my hands. I let it into the creek a bit to play with my catch until I knew that my hook was swallowed. Then, with a steady tug, I hoisted my prey to the surface and snapped it back unto the shore. "The grandfather!" I said with a grin. "What were you saying about the spirits?"

"They are with you today and not with me," he declared grimly.

"No!" I countered with a laugh. "They are with us both, for we shall have lunch together."

As our grandfather fried above our fire, Canonchet sat back against Old Willow and sighed. "What is at Cambridge?" he asked, taking his pipe from his belt and pulling tobacco from his pouch.

the cold dawn?

This was a hard word indeed—*You shall not covet!*

"Your god asks too much," we said to our good friend the preacher. And we ate our stew and lit our pipes and remembered the Sabbath as we lay in our blankets and blew our smoke to the wandering wind that carried our daydreams upward and over the tallest pine to the god of the English who sat on his mats in a wigwam of blue near a path made of gold in the far-off country of Heaven.

We arrived safely in the English town of Hartford on the Connecticut, having seen none of the warriors of Uncas in our march. There had been rumors, we were told, that great numbers of the English had walked with us from our country. And the rumor had been as a wall and a shield to us, keeping the Pequot and the Mohegan at bay.

Governor Haynes greeted us well and gave us meat and drink. But Uncas sent a message that he was lame and could not come.

"A lame excuse!" said the governor, and he sent earnestly for the sachem again. At last the Mohegan came.

"What do you answer to the testimony of so many that your armies are robbing and pillaging among the Narragansett and the river tribes?" asked Haynes of the Mohegan king.

"I have been with my men in the hunt these many moons," said Uncas plainly. "We numbered no more than one hundred braves. I did not see any violence being done, nor fields being spoiled. We roasted some corn, that is all!"

"You promised to boil our prince in a pot!" cried Katanaquat my father.

"Not so!" said Uncas coolly, "For I am not welcomed at the table of the Narragansett."

And thus began much shouting between the men of Uncas and our own. While the Narragansett and the Mohegan traded threats and taunts and tales of trespass and treachery, Haynes drew Williams aside to counsel for a time. At last, they called Miantonomi to them.

"Will you sit with Uncas to talk of a peace between your people?" asked Haynes through Williams.

"I will," said our prince, "if the Mohegan will give up the Pequot who hide in his towns."

"We will speak to him of it," said Haynes.

Miantonomi returned to the fray and ordered us to withdraw from our arguments. "For we must speak of peace now," he said. He walked then into the ranks of the Mohegan, and the men of Uncas stood aside as he passed through them. Taller by a hand than most, our prince was like the oak, hard and strong and full of the deep medicine of the ancient earth.

"Uncas," said our prince as he stood before his cousin. "I would sup with you, if you will. For my hunters have killed some venison. Call some of your chief men together and we will dine."

"I am not welcomed at the table of the Narragansett," declared the Mohegan. He stood as the maple beside the oak, more broad but not so high, his boughs stretched wide about him. Beneath his powerful limbs the dark thicket spread, and none could see within it. His heart was as the clinging vine which rests by day and rises at night to creep about the forest, encircling and entangling all that sleeps within its path.

"You are welcomed at the table of the English," said Miantonomi. "And I would sit with you as in our youth. Come and join me at our venison. There is much we must speak of."

"I will speak to the governor if he wills it," said Uncas, "but I have no hunger for your venison. I am quite filled with corn at the moment."

Williams called Miantonomi to himself again, and together the two friends went into the house of the governor. There, in company with the English magistrates, our prince gave the names of the Pequot sachems and murderers of the English whom he knew to be among the Mohegan.

Then Uncas was called in, and was asked the names of any Pequot who might be among his people. He knew not their names, he said, but was sure that there were many on the Long Island, and some among Ninigret's Niantic. And he himself had only twenty.

A principal man of the English named Stanton, who knew well the Indian tongue, accused Uncas of dealing falsely. "We know that you have many more Pequot than twenty," said Stanton, "and that only lately you have fetched thirty or forty to yourself from the Long Island."

"Yes, I have thirty," said Uncas simply, "but I do not know their names." And he would speak no more.

"We'll give you ten days to bring in the exact number and names of your Pequots and any runaway servants of the English," said Haynes. "And if you don't deliver, we will come fetch them!"

And thus a kind of peace was struck in which the Narragansett and the Mohegan agreed to sheath their knives and bury their tomahawks. And if any quarrel should arise between the two tribes, neither side would begin war without first appealing to the English, whose decision would be binding. And the tribe in whose favor the decision was made would thereafter know the support and arms of the English.

Yet Uncas continued to breathe his lies against us. And he surrendered no Pequots, for he said that they were all gone to the wigwams of Canonicus and Miantonomi. But Haynes did not go to fetch them as he had said he would, for the English were busy with many things. And the wigwam dog made sure to wag its tail whenever it happened to wander the streets of Hartford.

Chapter Five

The Shield Of God

"**P**lease, send these gifts to Governor Winthrop at Boston," said Miantonomi as he laid a basket and a bundle of wampum upon the wooden table of Williams at Providence. "Here are ten fathom of wampum from Canonicus, twenty fathom from me, and a basket as a present from Wawaloam my wife to the wife of Winthrop."

The small daughters of Williams put drink upon the table for our prince and his braves. Our men took it thankfully, speaking many kind words to the little maidens.

"The governor will be very glad for this expression of your love," said the preacher, running his fingers through the strings of white and purple beads. "And what shall I tell him besides?"

"That we desire three things of him," said our prince. "His sure and constant friendship; the free use promised us, after the war against the Pequot, of the Pequot country for our hunting; and . . ." our sachem paused and looked for a moment toward the sun that peered brightly in through the English glass windows that faced south.

"There are many Pequot sachems and captains that have survived the war," said our prince grimly. "And this you know," he said, looking once more upon Williams his friend. "Many who murdered the English, and three who have slain some of our sachems, are still free in the forest and and in the tents of other tribes.

"Mr. Haynes has done nothing to take them captive, and Un-

81

cas lays the lie at our door that we gather them all to ourselves against the English. Yet I fear that the Pequots—and there are many hundreds of them—will do more mischief to us and to the English if they are not destroyed or made to bow the knee."

"And what do you desire of Winthrop in this?" asked Williams.

"That Winthrop and Haynes might agree together to allow me to pursue those Pequot princes and captains whom I named when we traveled to Hartford to treat of peace," said Miantonomi plainly. "And we shall not harm so much as a Mohegan or a Niantic in all of our business!"

"I will send Winthrop your gifts and your words," said Williams. "Is there nothing else you desire?" he added with a smile.

"Canonicus begs of Mr. Governor a little sugar," said our prince with a wide grin.

"You are no Narragansett!" shrieked Askug the powwow at Wequash the god-preacher. "You were born a Pequot serpent and you are yet a Pequot serpent. You say that you love us, but I look in your eyes and I see the poison of your heart that rises to your fangs whenever you open your mouth to speak of your 'great god'! I see the fork in your tongue! I see the rattle at your tail! You are the serpent who lies upon the rock, waiting for the careless traveler to take his rest beside you on his way!"

"I am none of this!" stuttered Wequash, his eyes red with the fire of his proud and angered heart. "And I have done you no wrong, bitter Askug! I have walked with your sachems in peace and brotherhood. I have taken wounds at their side in the wars of your people. I have laid many a Pequot relative dead in the dust. I have left my wife and children behind me in the tents of the Mohegan. And though I am nothing in the eyes of the Great God, still He loves me!"

"He loves you because you are as he is, a serpent who hisses in the shadows and strikes at the heels of men!" fired Askug.

"My words are not whispered in the night!" cried Wequash. "I speak true and openly of the one Son of God. It is you who are the serpent, you slippery snake! You are the slave of that devil the Great Serpent himself! Your evil spirits will choke you in your sleep one day, and you will wake only to wander in the utter black places forever. In the everlasting night your tortured soul will cry out in the dark fire that can never be quenched!"

The powwow rose up before the once-Pequot preacher like the great she-bear when it is cornered with its young. His eyes rolled wide in his reddened, maddened face, and his mouth hung open in a ghastly, growling gape. "May the four winds crush you in their arms together!" he howled. "May the sea rise up and take you in its icy limbs! May the beasts of the wild descend upon you as you walk your crooked path! May the warriors of Chepi sink their blades into your flesh and cut out your heart to cast it into the Great Swamp! Die in your dreams, Pequot dung! Die in your dreams!" wailed Askug. And Wequash stepped back from him in fear and amazement.

Would the once-Pequot burst into flame beneath the fiery curses of the powwow? Would the four winds rush upon him even now and crush him like the beetle that is ground beneath the heel of man? Would his skin slide off like the snake which sheds? Would his blood pour out like the cup that is spilled? Surely he could not stand before the great and bitter sorcery of Askug! Surely we would witness a terrible retribution this dark and awful day!

But the God of Wequash was a strong shield. And the preacher stood his ground.

"The Lord is my guard," he chanted. "I shall lack nothing.

"He makes me lie down in green grasses.

"He leads me beside the cool waters.

"He restores my soul.

"He leads me in the paths that are right for the sake of his own Great Name.

"And even when I walk through the Valley Of The Shadow Of Death, I will fear no evil, for He is with me.

"His club and His spear are my comfort and protection.

"He prepares my meat in the presence of my enemies.

"He blesses me for the battle.

"He fills my cup with water until it overflows.

"Surely goodness and mercy shall follow me all the days of my life, and I will dwell in the house of the Lord forever."

A knife appeared suddenly in the upraised hand of the powwow, and it flashed in the light of the fire of Katanaquat my father. *It is the lightning of the gods!* cried my heart. *And it will fall
upon Wequash!*

"Hold, powwow!" cried our prince, stepping between the lightning of the gods and the chanting servant of the Great Name.

"I will cut out his heart myself and eat it!" shrieked my great
grandfather as Miantonomi took the bladed arm in his own
strong hands.

"Hold, I say!" shouted our prince, and he bent the crooked
limb of Askug backward until the knife fell from its choked
and weakened fingers.

"You stand as a man who would take the charge of the bull
moose!" coughed the powwow to our prince. "For the anger of
the gods are against this Pequot pea!"

"My own anger would take you by the throat and rattle you
hard and long, you old gourd!" cried Miantonomi as he released Askug. The powwow crumpled in a brittle heap upon
my father's floor.

"Wequash may chant! He may preach!" thundered our prince,
and I thought I had never seen him so angry. "He may run with
my warriors on the hunt and in the battle! He may eat my soup
and sleep in my bed! He is as my brother and my son! He is under my tent and my protection! Canonicus has blessed him!
Our people owe him much! And you—you jealous and pitiful
old bag of spells and potions—you will cease in your curses and
your threats, or I will cast you from us like the carcass of the
dead dog that is thrown to the buzzards and the birds!"

Askug rose from the floor like a strange fire that has somehow awakened without fuel, blazing hot and strong in his
shame and in his wrath. His eyes lit up with a dark power that
filled his frail form with the illusion of a great and ancient
strength. A cold hiss blew from between his teeth as he gathered his robes about him. He bent to take up his knife, which
seemed a long claw that fitted his hand like a sharp talon on
the paw of Pussough the great cat. He shook his head, and his
tangled locks swung like the branches of a towering elm in the
midst of a summer storm. He stood tall for a breath, taller

than his own legs should ever raise him, and swept the door open with one swift motion of his shadowed arm. Like the wind when it turns in violent circles upon the sea, Askug whirled from our midst into the darkening night.

"Lift up your heads, oh you gates," chanted Wequash.

"Lift up your heads, you everlasting doors, and the King of Glory will come in.

"Who is the King of Glory?

"The Lord! Strong and mighty in battle!"

"Your words will lay you in your own blood one day," said Miantonomi to Wequash, sitting down hard upon my father's bed, wiping the sweat of his anger from his paling face. "I have made an enemy of my own powwow this day on your behalf, you Pequot pea! I hope you remember me to your god tonight when you chant yourself to sleep!"

Few gave any heed to the preaching of Wequash. For though we loved him for his heart toward us, we feared turning to his god because of the railings of our powwow, because of the teachings of our father's fathers, because of the terror of our own jealous gods. And who could say which god was the greatest of all gods? Did not Cautantowwit watch over us always? Did he not carve our first parents from the great oak that stood upon his mountain in the Southwest? Did he not breathe life into their forms and set them in this land? Did he not send our first corn, beans, and squash upon the wings of Kaukant the crow from his own great garden in Sowanniu? Did he not build many wigwams for us in his courts? And did he not wait for our souls to join him there when our days in this flesh were done? Could we turn our backs to him simply to please this strange god of the Ten Words and the Son Who Walks And Dies As A Man?

Perhaps Wequash was mad, said some. Perhaps the fire of the hill at Mystic had burned its way into his soul and he could no longer think as his fathers did, as the Mohegan do, as the Narragansett in their wisdom and their great and ancient traditions.

Perhaps the once-Pequot, once-Mohegan was now a once-

Narragansett. Perhaps he was an English and could no longer
hear the voices of the spirits of his people and their neighbors.

Perhaps he would burn down at last, like the fire without
wood, and be still.

Miantonomi asked fewer questions about the Name, and
Canonchet would not speak of Him at all. "I will follow no god
which sets the sachem against the powwow," he said. "For the
sachem and the powwow must walk as one or the spirits will
not bless our people. Wequash may speak his heart all that he
wishes, for Canonicus and Miantonomi my father have so declared. But I will not listen, for not every song is meant for
every ear. Does Katanaquat your father sing the same song to
you that he whispers to Silvermoon your mother?"

And I said he did not. But then no longer did he sing us any
song at all. And I wondered how the song of love could be
stilled in the heart of a man. Perhaps, in the same way, the
new song of Wequash might grow still one day. Yet though it
sang only for a time, still it was a strong song which rang with
a sure melody, like the arrow that leaves the bow to fly true to
its target. My own heart hummed its harmony, and it longed
for words with which to give the song wings that it might fly
beyond my wall to my anxious, waiting tongue.

But I could not sing the song aloud. It was not mine to sing.

"I do not know why you have ears for the words of this new
god," said Aquinne as she walked with me beside Red Creek.
The cold air was full of the drifting flakes of the First Moon Of
Snow. I put my hand upon the shoulder of my love, but it was
as cold as the day. Her eyes were deep grey like the dark,
clouded skies.

"My heart opens to the One God," I said simply. "My eyes
see His shadow when I wake. It is not my doing, Aquinne. I
am not running down strange paths to discover what lies there.
I am walking as ever I walked, yet there He is in all places that
my feet find me."

"But he asks things of you that our fathers have never asked!"
she said, tossing her head to chase the settling snow. "He asks
you to wait for my love! He asks you to love our enemies! He

asks you to let men strike you on your face without letting you save your own honor by striking them back! He asks you to be a woman, Kattenanit, and not a warrior!"

"I will be a warrior," I said. "But a warrior does not have to chase every dog that barks at him or kick every dog that nips at him. If someone were to strike you or another whom I loved, I would surely strike them in return! But my cheek can take the blow while my heart remains my own. I can stand where I stand. I will be the man."

"But this is not being the man!" cried Aquinne. "For strong medicine comes only by blood and much favor with the gods! And our gods oppose this English god. Askug says it is so. And I believe it is so. How can a brave protect his woman and his children if the gods are against him!"

I stopped and stood for a moment in the falling snow. The tall pines on the far side of Red Creek stood like blurred giants in the midst of the gentle storm. The gathering dusk cast blue shadows across the white carpet at our feet.

"I know men who stand against the gods and are still men," I said to the cold creek and the wondering woman. And I thought of my father. And I knew that a warrior could stand where he stands, even against the gods. "And the English are warriors and men," I said. "And do they not protect their women and children? And do they not shed the blood of their enemies when they must? And so a man may love his enemies in times of peace yet lift the warclub to protect his own in times of war."

"I do not know if I can be the wife of such a man," said Aquinne quietly, and her voice shook like the boughs of Old Willow in the cold winter wind.

"But I love you!" I cried, taking her in my arms and turning her to me. "I love you and I will always love you!"

"You are not the only one to say these words to me," she said, turning her tear-streaked face from mine.

"But we have spoken our love to each other," I stammered, "and we have spoken of our love to your parents and to mine. Many among our people know that you will be mine. Though others say they love you, it is not they who will have you!

"I will be your man! I will be your warrior! I will be the father of your children and the hunter of their meat! I will build your wigwam and fill it with plenty as the gods give me favor and the Great God gives me medicine!"

"But the great god will not let you have any other gods!" cried Aquinne as she pulled her shivering form from mine. "He will chase the others from you, says Wequash! And then he will be your only god. Who would we turn to if the great god closes his eyes to us? Who would we call upon if the great god turns his back to us? How would we live if he lowered his shield when all other gods opposed us?"

"He is faithful," I said, with the hope that arose from the echo of the words of Wequash and Williams. "He is good. He will not let His own fall that they cannot rise again. He will be their shield always."

"How do you know?" fired Aquinne.

"I—I just know," I said. "That is all."

"Askug says it is not so!" cried Aquinne. "And none can ask me to sleep in the tent of the man who will not shield his squaw from the anger of the gods!"

"I will shield you!" I declared. "My bow will be ready always! My tomahawk will be sharp! My eyes and ears will be open. My heart will be yours!"

"Mine?" asked the maiden of my soul's dreams. "Mine? How can your heart be mine if you must love this great god first?"

"I will have two hearts," I declared. "As Wequash does. One for the Great God and one for you, my love! Only for you!"

"It cannot be," she said to the paled, pleading form of the almost-warrior, myself.

I could not bear the warfare in my soul. The howling of the spirits of my fathers rose above the whisper of the fast-falling snow and rushed about my head like a swarm of summer bees. The song of Wequash rose above the howl and played upon the soft wind that sent the white sky tumbling down in small, wet pieces. My wall called my name. My father stared down upon me from the high faces of the dark pine across the waters. My heart cried out the name of Aquinne. And the evening grew still.

A cold and frozen piece of dreaming was this moment.

Aquinne stood before me, beautiful and chill, dark and inviting against the white wall of winter. Our quiet, rhythmic breathing slid from within us into the chilled air and hung like clouds between us. A dog barked, once, in the distance. My heart beat loud in my ears.

"I will love you first," I heard myself say, as my words turned to frost before my face and drifted away upon the north wind.

A new Dying came upon us, but it was not as the last Dying in which so many Narragansett slept without waking. Yet it took some to the grave and left many weak and weary from the fever and the pox.

"Wequash brings this upon us!" cried Askug to Canonicus our king. "The spirits are angry because of his preaching. They came to me in a vision, a pack of black wolves, and howled against the Pequot and his English god. I saw them chase him through a dark wood until he climbed a tree to escape them. They surrounded the tree, and one by one they began to climb it after him. He coughed at them, like our sick ones cough in the Dying, and they all of them fell from the tree as though dead.

"Then one rose up among his brothers and cursed the god of the English, at which Wequash lost his hold and fell from his perch into the midst of the slumbering wolves. They awoke as one and devoured the wicked Pequot. Praise them! They devoured him bones and all!"

"Why would Wequash send the plague among us?" asked our grand sachem as his fingers drummed absently upon the wooden lid of the small sugar box given him by Winthrop. It was long empty.

"Because we do not turn to his god!" replied the powwow, turning his head from side to side as though to read the shadows that danced within the wigwam of Canonicus. I watched his own shadow, which gestured and twitched with a life of its own. Perhaps it was its own.

Canonicus rubbed his thick hands across his greased chest. The firelight pulsed in his dark, thoughtful eyes.

"Williams often wonders that we turn not to this god," said

our king. "And I tell him always that no one god will hold my allegiance alone. For the sea is made up of many drops of water, and the forest is full of many kinds of trees. There cannot be one god above all, for then there is no *all.*"

"I do not doubt the love of Williams for our king and our prince and our people," said Askug, rolling his fingers over the fire, "but he loves his god more! And would not any man punish those who spurn the one he loves? Perhaps it is Williams who brings this upon us! But no! It must be Wequash," declared the powwow, for his hatred of the Pequot led him down this path anew.

"Williams told us long ago that the Dying was in the hands of this great god," said Canonicus, "so your words may be true. This is a sour grape! For I trusted Wequash as I trusted my sons."

"Never trust a Pequot!" sneered Askug, peering around upon the men who sat at the fires of their king. We loved not the Pequot, but neither did we hate them as our powwow did. His hatred was born of deep wounds, long since scarred but never healed for the powwow scratched at them daily.

Many seasons past, when Nopatin my grandfather was but a boy—and a Pequot boy at that!—his father and a small band of Pequot warriors crept one dawn into the city of Mascus and Canonicus. They came to murder the powwow of the Narragansett, but they slew his young son instead.

In vengeance, Askug and Mascus, with many warriors of the Narragansett, fell in battle upon the Pequot village, slaying some and capturing a boy-child named Waupi. The Pequot lad was adopted into the family of Askug and became Nopatin of the Narragansett, my grandfather and the father of Katanaquat my father. Thus my own blood was traced to that of the Pequot, and thus my heart rose up against the wrath of Askug.

I stood.

"Kattenanit the Night Wind," said Askug with a clumsy bow of his dark, matted head. He sat down awkwardly beside our king.

"Could not the plague be sent by our own gods?" I asked. "And if not, are they not strong enough to chase it from our doors? And if they will not, should we not call upon the God of Wequash and Williams to aid us in our sorrow and our need?" I had risen to defend Wequash, but my words fell out on the side of the Great God instead.

"Son of your father!" barked the powwow, leaping to his feet as swiftly as the dog who is poked with the sharp head of an arrow. "Should we call the wrath of the spirits upon us in concert with the plague of the English god? No! We will curse this English god and watch as Wequash falls from his tree! When he is devoured, then will the English god flee and the Dying with him!"

The Snake began to dance and coil himself around the central blaze, twisting his limbs about him in ways that astounded us all—for even the tree must break when it bends itself against itself! But the powwow was like the sea which could lift its waves high and push them low, over and under themselves forever.

A sudden chill came over me, and I thought for a moment that Askug had conjured the gods, but then I realized that someone had entered the house at my back. Miantonomi.

"My prince!" I blurted. "The powwow dances against Wequash and the One Great God!"

Then Wequash himself stepped into the tent. And Askug froze in midleap and glared at the once-Pequot god-preacher.

"Canonicus my uncle," said Miantonomi with a grim smile and a sincere bow of his head. "Do we dance against our brothers here tonight?"

"Against the Dying," answered the grand sachem with a troubled wave of his hand.

"Against the Pequot poison in our cup!" cried Askug, swinging his painted arms through the rising smoke of the fire of Canonicus.

Wequash stood for a breath in the door of the wigwam, one foot in the warm room, the other upon the white winter floor of the cold outdoors. His clean gaze walked the tent in an instant, and then fell sadly to the mats at his feet. He came fully in, but only by a step, and looked up once more at us all.

"I am Wequash of the Narragansett," he said quietly. "And my love for you is as the love of a child for its mother. What I

once was, I am no more. What I am, I will remain until the day
I close my eyes to open them in Heaven."

And he bowed his head to us and backed out the door into
the bitter night.

"We dance against the Dying," repeated Canonicus our king.
"And not against our brother," he said, looking hard at Askug.

"I will dance as the spirits bid me dance," said the powwow,
his eyes dulled in cruel resolve.

"But not against our brother," affirmed Miantonomi, standing still and tall before the jittering form of the medicine man.
"Wequash is my brother," said our prince. And then he too
passed out into the hard starlight.

"I am going home," said Wequash.

"Is this not home?" I asked.

"No longer," he answered. "For the spirits oppose me on
every side, and no man will hear the words of God. Askug
would have my scalp upon a pole, and Canonicus no longer
sees the love in my heart."

"Where is home?" I asked.

"Along the Connecticut, north of the Mohegan, where I was
born," he said. "I have lands there that were once under the sachemdom of my great grandfather. They are now hunting
grounds, fishing holes. I will build my wigwam, send for my
wife and children who are with Uncas, and raise young braves
and maidens who will call on the One Great God."

"Will you be safe?" I asked.

"God is my shield," he said.

"Will you not fear?" I asked.

"When I am afraid, I will throw myself on Him," said
Wequash.

Wequash left us, but Askug did not let him go within his
heart. For the hatred of the powwow was a master stronger
than our kings, harder than the gods.

Many moons waxed and waned, and Wequash raised his wigwam as he promised. I walked to him once, with Williams and
my father and Canonchet and our prince. His gardens were
full, his tobacco strong. His house was filled with children and

glad sounds. The song of the Name was strong upon his lips.

But the wolves followed him into the woods at last and found him up his tree. When he breathed upon them, they fell as in the dream of Askug.

The wolves were the warriors of Uncas and the powwows of the Long River. They opposed Wequash's claim to the land of his great grandfather, but he withstood them with the help of some neighboring tribes, and the Mohegan turned back bitterly in defeat.

But then the Snake of the mighty Narragansett rose up in the wake of the conquered wolves, and inwardly muttering oaths against the One Great God as he slithered up the trunk, he shook his rattle in the tree of the once-Pequot. When Wequash turned at the sound of the rattle, Askug spat poison in his face.

"Where has the Snake gone?" I asked.

"Westward into the woods," replied my great grandmother his squaw. "To visit Nopatin your grandfather."

But when he slithered home at last, the word had flown ahead of him that Wequash our friend had been bitten by the fangs of Askug.

"The shield of God has fallen," I said to Katanaquat my father with great and bitter sorrow in my heart.

"Even the gods must blink," said The Rain From God.

"It is murder," said our prince, with darkness in his eyes. "And it must be life for life."

"The powwow is our health and our strength with the spirits," said old Canonicus. "For all my days he has danced for our people. You would be dead yourself if not for his medicine and his magic!"

"It is murder," said our prince. "And it must be life for life. The poison was mixed in the tent of the powwow and poured into the cup of Wequash my brother. As they ate together at the table of Wequash! A bitter, wicked deed! Must I cover my own cup when I sit at meat with the powwow?"

"His hatred for the Pequot is buried now with Wequash be-

side the Connecticut," said Canonicus. "Askug will not spill his
wrath upon his own."

"Wequash was his own!" declared our prince. "For we made
him our own and he pledged to be our own. Did his battle
scars mean nothing? The blows he took on our behalf against
our foes? Did his bow in the hunt mean nothing? The meat he
laid upon our tables? He was our own! It is murder! And it
must be life for life!"

Canonicus laid his head in his heavy, gnarled hands, and a
deep sigh pushed itself from his thick, wrinkled lips.

"You are the man," said the chief sachem. "Do what must be
done."

And the man followed the snake into the woods one day and
did what must be done. For murder must not go unpunished.
Life for life.

"All men die," said Katanaquat my father, "no matter which
gods they bow to."

"All men die," I echoed, and my tears fell for Wequash my
friend. For he had loved me, and I had loved him.

But my heart grieved little for the powwow, the old gourd,
my great grandfather. For he had never loved me, as I knew
most fully now that his cold shadow no longer fell upon my
face. Worse, he had slain one dear to me! And thus I now
hated the name of the powwow.

Love your enemy, whispered the Name to my torn, embittered
soul.

Impossible!

The wolves rose up again, as in the dream of the now-dead
powwow, and fell upon the house of Wequash. They plundered
his gardens and dug up his grave. They cut up his body and
scattered his bones.

But his squaw and children were safe within the tent of
Miantonomi, for our prince brought them to us to live among
us as our own.

Chapter Six

The Terror

It was a time of tragedy and sorrows upon sorrows for my people. It was a time of terror in my soul.

Williams was gone across the Great Salt Sea to England of his birth, to speak with kings and princes, to ride horses across stone bridges and climb stairs in tall houses. I thought—when the Terror came upon me—that the Name had gone with him.

Miantonomi conspires against the English, said the old lie that Uncas loosed once more in the woods. The rumor was whispered in the ears of many, and it spread like fire in the leaves of autumn.

"With or without the consent of the English, I will take to the warpath against the Mohegan," declared our prince, "before his crooked tongue calls the soldiers of Boston to our shores!"

"I would not be so swift to paint for war against the mad dog," cautioned Canonicus. "For he will surely bark at the doors of the English at Hartford. And when they open to him, he will run inside. Then you will find yourself facing muskets instead of bows."

"I would rather chase him to their doors than have him lead them to ours!" said Miantonomi. "Yet I pray rather to catch him sleeping behind his own."

"You may find him lurking instead in the shadows along your path!"

"This also would please me," said our prince. "He has hidden

95

too long in the shadows! The hearts of my warriors have borne his taunts and lies for many seasons. Our quivers are filled with angry arrows. Much blood goes unavenged."

"Let vengeance rest awhile longer," counseled Canonicus, "for the English master may soon tire of the Mohegan dog who begs too often for too much. Then we may chase down the dog without fear."

But the dog ran unleashed in the woods. It stole more than it begged—and never from the English.

In the Moon Of Late Summer in my twenty-first year, Uncas crossed the Pocatuck and fell upon the village of Nopatin my grandfather. He plundered the harvest and burned many wig-wams. Eight of the warriors of Nopatin were killed in the first light of dawn. Many more were wounded. The cries of their mourning rose with the smoke of their fires and blew east upon the wind to our tents beside the Great Bay.

"I will dance tonight around the fire of war," said Mian-tonomi.

"I will dance with you," said Canonicus grimly. "Though my old legs are too weak to run straight on the warpath, I will dance. I will chant. The dog must be whipped!"

I had shed the blood of beasts from my seventh summer on-ward. I had beaten blood from my friends in the games, and had licked my own blood during the same. I had seen the foe die inch by inch upon the poles of torture, the red juice of life a thick puddle at his feet. I knew the stain of death that clings to the warrior who stumbles home from battles fought over the rivers and beyond the Bay. But though my sharp arrows had tasted the hearts of our enemies, the shafts had been sped by the hand of my father. War had not yet called me to the field of death myself.

But now I walked painted, burdened with vengeance, and armed with the long-crafted work of my own strong hands.

This was the end and the purpose of youth. This was the sure path of every young brave. This was the strength of the gods of our fathers. This was the medicine every boy dreamed for. This was the door into manhood and honor.

This was our hope and the day we all longed for—to walk with our fathers to war.

The day had only dawned as six hundred warriors of the Narragansett forded the Shetucket one whoop north of where it strikes hands with the Quinnibaug.

The birds and the beasts of the wood seemed to know that we hunted for something other than themselves, for they went about their chirping and their wandering and their grazing as if we were mere shadows upon the mists of morning. But the laurel on the hills sheltered watchmen of the Mohegan, and we heard them whisper, we saw them run. Uncas would soon be aware of our coming.

What would he do? Flee like the frightened hare? Take to the trees like the wary squirrel? Stand and coil like the angry rattlesnake? Strike like the hungry wolf?

And what would I do?

This was not the Great Hunt Before The Snow. This was not the Games Of Harvest. This was not the play of battle where arrows were dull and warclubs were rounded bats of white birch.

Katanaquat my father walked before me, his face painted red from the middle of his nose to his left ear, yellow from the middle of his nose to his right ear, with black circles around both eyes. Straight silver streaks fell from his chest to his loins, for this was the sign of The Rain From God. His hair was pulled back in a long braid, a single black feather of Kaukant tied at its end. Over his right shoulder hung his weapons belt, with his English knife under his left arm, his quiver and backbag behind him. His warclub hung at one side from the belt of his loin cloth. His oaken bow was armed and in his hands. Around his neck he wore a small bag of English gunpowder. He had no gun with which to use it, but "It is strong medicine against our foes," he said.

Katanaquat my father was my own strong medicine. How glad I was to set my moccasins in his step! He was the strength of my heart upon this path. Without him, I felt that I might have fled homeward at the first cough of the crow.

In front of Katanaquat and behind our prince walked Canonchet, a strong and confident reflection of his father. I wished that we were walking side by side, for that was always our way in the days before this long morning's trail to manhood.

Behind me walked the Fool, humming quietly in a constant pitch that sounded like the buzzing of a fly. *Today I will see the Fool fight!* I thought, for I had heard a thousand tales of his courage and his skill. None dared run into the enemy as our Fool—laughing, reeling, leaping, shooting, he was like a war-club with wings. His arrows always flew true. All foes feared our Fool, for they thought him a god or a man filled with ghosts. His scalp belt was the fullest of our tribe.

I will bring you the fresh scalp of a Mohegan warrior, I heard myself say to Aquinne. The memory, though new, seemed a far-distant dream as my feet fell in rhythm with twelve hundred more of the moccasined feet of the strong Narragansett. *And we shall be wed before autumn comes falling*—the thought gave me strength, cleared my eyes, stood me taller.

The Yantic was cold as we waded its waters. The hilltop above it was empty of life, but I felt that its trees were a door that, once entered, would lead to the contest at last.

As we topped the hill and walked out of its woods on the other side, a wide, level valley stretched out below us—the Great Plain of the Pequot. Here great herds of deer often grazed—but not on this morning.

Across the divide, in scattered clusters of tens and twenties, in the trees and along the treeline, stood the fighting men of the Mohegan. They were many, I could see, but we were many more. My heart beat loud enough within me that I thought it might be heard even across that great and terrible field.

All of my days had been walking toward this one. This was the high and one day of my first blood, the moment of manhood, the reason for living, the full cup of medicine—strong, red, and welcomed. My soul stretched its arms toward the heavens in anxious longing and fearful joy.

My hands moved unconsciously across my body. They found my weapons readied, my bow fitted with the straightest and best of my shafts.

My eyes moved intently from the ranks of the enemy to my

father, to Canonchet, to our prince, and back again to the grassy plain before me.

My ears keened themselves for the whisper of the sliding arrow, the thunder of the throaty warcry.

Hawks drifted, circling, high above the great divide.

A lone figure came forward from the line of the Mohegan, his palms held out in peace. A parley at the dawn of peril.

Our prince sent one of ours to meet him, and a message was relayed that Uncas would come to Miantonomi in the valley between us. The sachems would speak their hearts first. This was our way.

I watched our prince walk down the hill of my manhood. Tall and with grace in his step he moved onward. Uncas came forth from his forest of warriors and stood in the valley to treat with our prince.

You are a dog and a worm, declared my heart to Uncas, as it loudly spoke for Miantonomi my prince. *I have come to kill you. So fight as a man or run like the dog that you are. Either way, I will crush you beneath my foot as the heel crushes the worm.*

But nothing could be heard of the meeting in the field. The two men stood still as trees. Their tongues spoke to each alone. All eyes were upon them.

Suddenly Uncas threw himself upon the ground, and my heart cried, *Treachery!* In the same moment, the Terror came upon me, and I froze like the stone upon the hillside.

As in a dream, I saw the Mohegan warriors draw their readied bows as one. A blurred shower of sharp death leapt from their ranks and sped across the morning sky toward the astonished warriors of the Narragansett. I heard the great cries of my brothers as they reeled back into the trees. I heard the whistling descent of the dark storm of Mohegan shafts. They bit into the earth at my feet and rattled against the stone and wood behind my back. Still I could not move.

I saw Uncas roll forward and leap to his feet, his mouth open in an ugly gape. The sound of his cry came next upon the wind, its shrieking syllables calling for the bloody slaughter of the foe. In concert with that awful command, I saw the men of the Mohegan pour out into the field, their bows once more readied, their own mouths wide in a great, shrill cry of murder and war.

Miantonomi fled. Toward us he bounded like the deer that leaps before the racing hunter. We needed no cry to send us flying home!

Still I could not move! Though my heart shrieked to my feet to flee, they were rooted to the earth.

My prince raced past me. My father was gone. The Fool was nowhere to be seen. Not a shadow of Canonchet.

A painted, swirling flood of Mohegan demons rolled up the hill toward me. A feathered shaft passed by my face. Another glanced off the warclub that hung at my belt. A horrible roar— like the sound of the mighty sea storm when it comes ashore to shake the forest in its wrath—filled my ears and blackened my eyes. The scream of my heart burst forth from my lips as my feet tore themselves at last from the clinging soil. Before me was a charging monster of a thousand legs, a thousand eyes, five hundred gaping, howling mouths. I felt my fingers let go of my drawn bowstring. I saw my shaft sink into one eye of the thousand. I felt my form turn like the fallen leaf before the mighty storm. And I tumbled upon its awful winds into the wild wood.

The fire burned low within the wigwam of The Rain From God. I sat in numbed fear in the shadows behind our bed.

"The spirits have taken his heart," they said of me. And I did not doubt it. For my heart would not beat as it should, and my sleep was short and filled with dreams of death and terror.

"He brought home no scalp but his own," they said of me. Aquinne would not look upon me, and Silvermoon my mother could not comfort me.

The new powwow among us, Nickeétem by name, danced over me, but I would not rise from the shadows. Canonchet could not pull me up. The Terror held me there.

For where was my father? Our prince? Our Fool?

Twenty-three men were missing, besides the known dead who numbered nine. The city of Canonicus wailed with the loud mourning of two thousand angered, sorrowed souls. Ambassadors were sent from Canonicus to the country of Uncas to treat for peace, to bring home our dead, and to offer ransom for any who were captive.

While they were gone, others of our scattered warriors wandered home, mumbling tales of blood and slaughter. Miantonomi was a captive of the Mohegan, they said. We chanted and stomped for the safety of our prince.

Two men came last to the city of Canonicus, two dead men walking—the form of my father and Assoko our Fool. They too had been captive, but Uncas had finally set them free into the forest. My father, though not wounded, seemed a man without a heart. The Fool was a bloody and terrible sight to behold.

"He is gone from us!" we cried when we looked upon the Fool.

"The soul of Assoko is flown!" declared Nickeétem.

"It is gone with his scalp at the hands of Uncas," mumbled Katanaquat my father in the darkness of his own despair. For the Mohegan sachem had made the Fool race in the gauntlet. And when brave Assoko had mastered the run, Uncas met him man to man.

"The Fool fought as the wildcat fights," said my father to the shadows and the failing fire. "But Uncas slid his knife across his head. You see it for yourself! He lives—yet it is no longer him."

The great ghastly wound of the Fool stood gnarled and red upon his hairless forehead. We wept to behold it, for surely our Fool was now a man without a soul. For the soul is in the scalp! And when the soul has flown, is not the man dead?

"Not dead!" said the once-man firmly to his family and friends. But they wailed and wept and would not speak to him.

"I walk," said the once-man quietly to the children of our city as he wandered among them, his short, thick arms wagging like the wings of an English hen. But the children ran from him screaming.

"I am the Fool," he said sadly as we sat in the tent of Katanaquat my father. But I did not know how to speak to the once-man, and my father turned from us both to tend the fire. The Terror gnawed at my soul.

"Sawkunk fled first," said Kuttowonk.

"Our prince fled first!" Sawkunk declared. "And should we not follow his lead?"

"We followed your lead," said Kuttowonk. "For everyone was shouting, 'There goes Sawkunk. He knows the way home. Follow him!' "

"If Miantonomi had raised his hand against Uncas," argued Sawkunk, "I would have been first into the valley to aid him!"

"Had he raised his hand against Uncas," jabbed Waumausu, "you would have thought it first a signal to flee!"

"If our prince were here," cried Sawkunk, "he would speak for me!"

"He is not here," we said darkly, "and so none can say what he might speak."

"If Williams were here, he could plead for our prince!" I said.

"He is not here," we said sadly, "and so we must wait for word from the Mohegan."

"We have paid Uncas a great ransom!" declared Sawkunk.

"And if he will not take it?" wondered Tawhitch.

"He has taken it already!" I said. "But he makes no promises!"

"And if he harms our prince?" cried Kuttowonk.

"I will run first against the foe!" declared Sawkunk. "You will see."

"It was for his well-keeping while I had him among us," sneered Uncas concerning the ransom. "None ever spoke of release."

"He was arrogant and hard-set against us," said the Hartford English concerning our prince. "His friendship was feigned."

"He was given by the Mohegan into the hands of the English," said Katanaquat my father, "and they gave him back into the hands of Uncas. 'Kill him,' they told him. And gladly the dog took the bite for its master!"

"But our prince said he loved them!" I cried in confusion.

"They thought him a liar."

"The dog is the liar!"

"It bites when they bid him. It comes when they call."

Sachem's Plain we now call it, the place where the brother of Uncas buried his tomahawk in the head of our prince. The place where Uncas cut a piece of the dead sachem's shoulder and ate it, declaring, "It is the sweetest meat ever I tasted!"

Williams was over the Great Salt Sea when it happened. His eyes did not see. His ears did not hear. He could not run to the rescue. He could not plead for the life of his friend.

I wept upon the stones that covered the rude grave of our dead sachem. But my tears were as ashes compared to the storm that fell from the eyes of The Rain From God. My father had loved this great man from his childhood. Now he was gone. Forever and always. The forest was empty of light. My father was darkness itself.

Assoko would leave us, he said.

"Why?" I asked.

"To find a new soul," said the once-man who walked in the form of the Fool. And my father wept the more, for he knew in his heart that the once-man was still his Fool. He could not bear his leaving.

"Where will you go?" I asked the Assoko-man.

"To the English," said the once-man. "To Williams."

"But he is not home," I said. And our Fool did not know what to say or do.

"God gives a new soul!" he insisted at last, and would have walked north to search alone for the One God.

"We will go with you to Providence," said Katanaquat my father, and we walked him once more to the house of the preacher where Mary the wife of Williams took him in.

"He will be well with us until Roger's return," she said. And we left him sitting at that fine table before that fine fire with his scarred head in his hands, rocking to and fro, humming a quiet tune of his own making.

"Will the Great God give a new soul?" I asked of my father as we journeyed southward home.

"Does a man rise from the dead?" replied The Rain From God.

I woke in a cold, clammy sweat. The Terror slept. Beside me on the bed slept also Winaponk, my younger brother by Ohowauke. Shadows danced low in the warm wigwam. The midnight moon peaked in at our smoke hole. A fire burned outside. Men chanted softly. Women wept. Our prince was dead. It would be long seasons before our tears were done.

Where was the Name? Where was His shield upon the ones I loved?

Where was the Fire Of God upon our foes?

Where was the love of God in the hearts of the English?

Where was the Call that once woke me in wonder from my sleep?

Who gave the Terror such reign in my soul? And what was it? Why did it dog me? Where was my medicine against it?

Had my wall fallen? Had the spirits crept over it? Long I had left it untended, unfinished, unmanned.

Katanaquat my father moaned in his bed.

"Father?" I said. He rolled on his mat to face me.

"Hnggh . . ." he grunted.

"Are you awake?"

"I would not be but for your words!" he grumbled roughly.

"How does a man chase the spirits from him?" I asked.

"Two ways," he said absently, rubbing his fists in his eyes. "Either he dances and howls like the powwow, cutting himself with knives and throwing his best tobacco into the fire, or he hires the powwow to howl and cut himself and throw his best tobacco into the fire. Why do you wish to know?"

"My wall," I said.

The Rain From God sat up in his bed.

"Are you well?" asked Silvermoon my mother in her dreams.

"Your wall?" said Father.

"Something has crossed it," I said.

"I have seen the shadow of fear in your eyes," my father said.

"The Terror of Death," I said.

"Is it a god?" he asked.

"I do not know," I replied.

"Have you seen it?" he asked.

"No," I replied.

"Has it spoken?" he asked.

"Not with words," I said.

"Spit it out!" said the Rain From God.

"I would gladly!" I declared. "But I cannot force it."

"Blood will force it," said Father. "Blood of the Mohegan. Strong medicine will send it flying from you. The medicine of your own strong heart.

"Rise up in the battle, Kattenanit! Slay the foe! Be the man! The spirits cross your wall because you sit at it carving bowls!

"Rise up and cast this Terror from you with loud shouts of war. With the sharp edge of your knife at the scalp of the enemy. With the heartbeat of the warrior. Be the man. Show yourself my son!"

"I am a man, Father," I said in my pride. "I stood on the field of battle when all others fled! When you had fled! I loosed my bow upon the Mohegan! I am a man!"

The Terror opened its eyes within me. I felt its cold gaze upon my soul. Then I heard its voice!

You stayed in the field because I held you there! it hissed. *And you fled like the hare when I finally let you go! A man! Ha!*

"A man!" echoed Katanaquat my father mockingly. "Let me sleep," he said. And he lay down once more and pulled his mat over his head. "Our prince was a man!" I heard him whisper quietly, bitterly, and then he said no more.

It spoke! I said within myself, my heart beating wildly. But now it slept again, and all was still. I dared not close my eyes until the dawn.

Pessacus, the younger brother of our murdered prince, ruled now with ancient Canonicus, and the Narragansett plotted hard and hot against the murderous Mohegan.

"Let us call all our tributaries to us here at Narragansett," counseled Katanaquat my father in the wigwam of Canonicus. "And with our numbers as many as the trees of the wood, we will march once more into the country of Uncas as the English marched upon the Pequot. We will chase the foe onto some high hill and set fire to his bed!"

"No," said old Canonicus, shaking his wise and whitened head. "For the English would rise up against us. They will not sit still if we take to the warpath in force."

Many somber heads nodded assent to the words of our grand sachem.

Pessacus stood.

"If we cannot come against Uncas as the trees of the forest," said Pessacus our sachem, "then we shall sneak upon him as the vine that encircles the oak. We will be like the serpent that strikes him in the legs and then slides away in the grass to wait for another day to strike him anew. In this way our poison will weaken him little by little until at last he falls!"

We bit the dog's legs and it ran to its master. *A truce!* cried the master, his heel on the head of the serpent. We promised the peace for one year and no more. I was glad for the year, for the Terror did not wake within those days. *Sleep still!* I said.

The seasons walked on. I fished the Great Bay with Canonchet and Sawkunk. I tended the eel weirs on the Shewatuck and Matantuck. I hunted the forest for bird and beast. And I carved bowls and spoons for the further winning of Aquinne, for our marriage was put off by the cooling of her heart toward me. But my bowls did not impress her—she wanted warclubs instead.

"I have carved three already," I said.

"Where are your scalps?" she asked.

"Upon the heads of the Mohegan," I said, "waiting for my knife to kiss them."

"Will they wait forever?" she asked.

"They wait only for war," I replied.

"The truce is ended," she reminded me.

Though I longed for Aquinne, I had no heart for the war-path. But my father could think of nothing else. His days and nights were filled with dreams of vengeance against the Mohegan. He grew rough and rude with everyone, especially those within his own wigwam.

"Why do you not make new arrows?" he asked me one day as I sat at soup.

"I have many," I replied, "and more." Winaponk sat beside me. He was nine summers old.

"I have many arrows, too," said Winaponk, holding up the small shafts he had whittled with my English knife. Father ignored him.

"Why do you not take Aquinne as your wife?" he blurted at me, taking a bowl from Silvermoon my mother without thanks. "My tent grows crowded!" he growled.

"Would it not be still more crowded with Aquinne in my bed?" I said.

He looked at me darkly.

"You could have her love and a wigwam of your own if you'd wash your hands in Mohegan blood!"

"I saved your life from one Mohegan, Father, when I was not yet a man," I said, reminding him of his fight with Uncas those many summers past. "And I have blinded or killed another since."

"You have not the heart of the warrior!" snorted Katanaquat.

"I have not the heart of the killer!" I corrected him coldly, for my pride had risen against him.

He stood before me suddenly, his face dark with anger.

"Thou shalt not kill!" he scoffed. "Is that what your heart is chanting? Do you sing these empty words of the English god while you lie in the tent of your Narragansett father? Are you such a fool that you suck on the dry bones of the murderous English?

"They gave our prince over to the mad dog Mohegan!" he shouted. "They laid the highest and the best of the Narragansett beneath the butchering, black axe of Uncas!

"And you! My own son! You dare to sit in my house and carve spoons and chant *Thou shalt not kill."*

"Father," I said quietly. "I mean no dishonor to the name of our prince! I will take up my bow against the . . ."

"You will take up your bowls!" he shouted, tossing his own bowl aside while the soup splashed into the fire.

"Katanaquat, my lord!" cried Ohowauke. "The broth is rare! We have so little." And she took the soup pot from the fire to protect it from my father's rage.

He turned on her, and in the moments that followed, his anger gave vent to violence. He cursed at us all, scattering Winaponk's arrows and bow at our feet. My brother ran to stand behind his mother.

As my father moved toward the boy, Ohowauke stood in his way. Katanaquat struck her, and the boiling pot turned full upon her. It spilled upon her limbs, splashing the form of the crouching child.

"Aieyagh!" cried Winaponk my brother as the scalding liquid painted his small face.

"No! No! No!" cried his mother, flailing her pained arms in the smoky air, wailing for help for her wounded son.

Many came running, and the tent was soon filled with the busy hands of caring neighbors. Songs for healing rose from Silvermoon my mother, Quanatik my sister, and many of the squaws of the village.

I followed my father out into the night.

"Go back and wipe up the soup!" he said.

"Go wipe it up yourself!" I cried. "A man is not a man who strikes the doe for protecting the fawn!"

He swung his fist at me, and I caught it in mine. We were both men now. I held him fast.

"I am a warrior, Father," I said to The Rain From God. "Not a daughter!" And I pushed his hand from me. "I will run the warpath! I will take my scalps! But I will not drink blood as water!"

"You drink soup instead!" he spat. "And chant *Thou shalt not kill* to my children!"

"You are wrong, Father," I said, my heart cooling slowly with the chill night breeze. His eyes flashed hot, and he raised his hand to strike at me again. I turned my back against him.

"You mock me!" he cried.

"I do not mock you," I said with a heavy sigh. And I walked away alone to sit and think beside Red Creek.

Why did the Name call me to His words?

Why did His words turn my loved ones from me?

Why did I care for Him at all who would not show His face to me—or let me take my woman—or come into my heart to chase the Terror from my soul?

Was the Name a dream?

Did His Song die upon the cold lips of Wequash?

Would the Fool ever find Him?

Would He give the Fool a soul?

And who was the fool? I was the fool! For I sat beneath Old Willow in my sorrow and my pain while I could be lying in pleasure and peace in bed beside Aquinne!

Scalps—and only one at that! In my hands, warm and dripping! That was what I needed. Not the cold and distant twinkling of some far off Star!

"No," said Williams, "but I rejoice that I may walk with Him today!"

"I am now Joshua," I said to the English preacher. "For I walk with Him, too."

"There is so much to hear from you all!" said Williams, draining his drink and wiping his mouth upon his long sleeve. "But we are running down too many paths at once. Sassamon was telling us of his own path to the Lord. I think we should follow him to the end of it before we chase any other game."

"Where are your boys?" I asked, as the comment on game made me think of bows and arrows.

"Playing with the Harris children," Roger said. "They will be happy to see you. But first . . ." He turned his gaze upon the Wampanoag. "Your story, Sassamon?"

Sassamon rose and stood for a moment, looking out the windows that faced south and east toward the country of the Wampanoag of Massasoit. Keesuckquand had chased the morning's clouds completely, and his piercing gaze fell through the glass to bathe the form of Sassamon in its warm light.

The wife of Williams brought her man his pipe and tobacco. We reached into our bags for our own. Young Mary brought us fire from the hearth to start our smoke.

"When the Hatred and the Slaughter finally fled," said the Wampanoag, his broad back dark against the white light of the late-morning sun, "I went back once more to the wigwams of Massasoit. And though my sachem welcomed me, for I was the only son of his sister who died at my birth, yet many of my people did not know if I was any more an Indian. The powwows had poisoned my name among them." He turned from the window to pace the large room as he spoke. " 'But I am Sassamon the son of Sackwatuck,' I said to them, 'a Wampanoag by birth and by blood. My mother lies under this ground. My father, too. His brothers and sisters are many among us, and I have slept in their tents. My bow has put food upon your fires, and I have slain the foes of our people by the Slaughter and by my own hand. I wish only now to raise my wigwam among you as my father did and his father before him.' But the powwows danced against me, and the Hatred howled in my ears anew."

"The Hatred," I murmured.

"And so I rose from the bed of Massasoit," continued Sassamon, "and embraced the children of my sachem one last time. The youngest was a lad I loved the most. I took him outside the tent.

" 'Metacomet,' I said to the boy as we stood upon the hill of Montaup looking down upon the cities and the lands of Massasoit his father, upon the treetops that walked even unto the smoke of the chimneys of Plymouth and the bright waters of the Great Salt Sea beyond, 'this people may one day be yours to rule and love. Love them as the Great God loves all men.'

" 'And how does the Great God love all men?' asked the young prince.

" 'He lays down His life for them,' I said. And the boy laughed. For it is a weak god who dies. And no son of a sachem may be weak.

" 'I will take up my bow for them if I must,' declared the son of my sachem, 'but I will not lay down to die!'

" 'Take up your bow for them then,' I said.

" 'Will you come back among us soon?' he asked.

" 'Not soon,' I answered. 'Nor ever unless the powwows cease their wailing against me.'

" 'I will command them to cease when I am sachem!' the little warrior promised. 'And then you can come and live with me!'

"I held the lad tight and hid my tears from him. Then I bade my cousins farewell and walked from the Wampanoag country altogether."

"To Plymouth once more?" we asked.

"South and east to the country of the Nauset. And then out upon the Nantucket Sea to the Island of Capawack."

"Martha's Vineyard!" I cried. "Assoko!"

"The Fool of the Narragansett," said Sassamon fondly. "He speaks of you often, Kattenanit son of Katanaquat, and of your father and your people."

"I must go again to find him!" I declared. "Will you come with me, my brothers?"

Chapter Ten

Capawack

From the south shore's edge of the lands of the Nauset, at a point called Wood's Hole by the English, we pushed our canoe out into the great waters of the Nantucket Sea as the sky grew light to the east of Manamoick Bay. The wind was calm and the waves were low as we paddled toward the green isle that lay hidden upon the darkened horizon. Other canoes bobbed upon the great sea as fishers headed out in search of sea bass, bluefish, and sturgeon. One boat passed us close, coming in from a night beneath the bright, full gaze of Nanepaushat, its men singing loudly. They shook their harpoons high in declaration of good success. Their boat was filled with many fish. Gulls circled overhead, crying for meat. "Do your own fishing, brothers!" chanted the happy fishers to the begging birds.

The sun was rising from the sea as we spied the rocky shoreline of Capawack.

"The land of my New Heart," said Sassamon as we stared across the waters to the island that grew larger every breath.

"Is this where you bowed to the Name?" I asked.

"In the wigwam of Hiacoomes," declared the Wampanoag.

"A great man! A great preacher!" said the brothers Quannapohit. "Hiacoomes the First!"

"Hiacoomes," I echoed. *The first of what?* I wondered.

We could hear the sea against the rocks now, see the wind in the tall trees along the shore.

175

"And Assoko lives with Hiacoomes?" I asked.

"The two are neighbors in their own wigwams at Great Harbor," said Sassamon.

"I was in the town once," I said, recalling my first search for the Fool, the frustration of his absence and my hope deferred, the heartbeat of the Name within the men who bid me welcome, the warfare in my soul, and the fear—the Terror—that tore me from the shores of Capawack in sad and hopeless discontent.

The confusion of those days rose from its grave to haunt me. *Will Assoko know me? Will I know him?*

Is he still my Fool, or has he changed now that he has risen from the dead? Does his new soul grow upon his scalp to cover the wound that took his first soul? Does he still rock like my Fool? Cry like my Fool? Laugh like my Fool?

Our boat came into the surf. We rode it near the rocks and leapt into the waters to guide it to the land. We lifted it onto the shore and pulled it into the trees.

"Fear nothing," said Sassamon. "Here all things are safe from the hands of thieves."

"Why here?" I asked.

"God is sachem on Capawack!" laughed the Wampanoag.

But I was afraid anew. Afraid that the Terror lurked beside our path as we walked to Great Harbor. Afraid that Sassamon was leading us into an ambush where we all would die at the hands of vengeful powwows. Afraid that my hair was cut too short and the men of Capawack would laugh me to scorn. Afraid that God was truly sachem here—*how must I approach Him if He asks me into His wigwam?* Afraid that Assoko would again be gone, and that his people would smile as before and ask me to stay, and that I would speak falsely and say, *"Nickquennum;* I must go home." Afraid that my new life was but a dream and that I would suddenly wake in the tent of my childhood—my father snoring, my mother bent over the fire to make it rise, the Name calling mournfully, impossibly, upon the hard, cold Narragansett wind. Afraid, most of all, that Assoko would look upon me and say, "This is not Kattenanit," and "Why do you bring this bald fool to my tent?"

The smoke of the wigwams of Great Harbor met us before any man saw our coming. I heard children laughing, mothers calling, dogs barking. Where were the warriors? Waiting in ambush beside our path?

Here all things are safe . . . Why did I fear?

God, I said to the Spirit within, *stand at the door!*

I am your Strong Shield, said the One who stood at the door. Strength breathed upon my heart, but shame whispered too. I hung my head.

"Joshua," said James, "are you well?"

"My soul is weak," I said.

"Jesus is strong medicine!" said Sassamon. "The weaker you are, the stronger He will be within you."

"My Strong Shield," I muttered.

We crossed a small stream, scattering a band of ducks that rested in its waters, and came out of the woods into a large, cleared stand of rounded wigwams that stretched from the forest to the salt shores of the Great Harbor. A chorus of voices shouted greeting, as children came running and men pushed their heads out of tents.

"*Cowaunckamish, Netompaug!*" cried many, "Greetings, friends!"

"Where have you come from?" said some.

"How are you?" asked others.

"We salute you!" they cried. And I felt of a sudden that my fear was fully fled and I was home. The sun smiled brightly. I smiled with it weakly.

Children swarmed around us like so many ants upon maple sugar. Men's voices chanted the names of Sassamon, James, and Thomas. Friendly whoops filled the air as though it were the Games of Harvest.

A large, black dog pushed its way through the children and leapt upon my chest, tail wagging and tongue lolling. I laughed with sudden joy into its mangy, smiling, drooling face. "I wish you were a woman and my bride!" I declared to the lovable beast, as I danced in a circle with its paws at my shoulders.

"Get down, Shadow!" shouted a frowning maiden who had followed the bounding animal into the fray. She struck the great dog upon its back. With a yelp it dropped to all fours and, knocking several small children aside in its haste, sped off toward the tents with its tail between its legs.

"I am sorry for Shadow's naughtiness," said the maiden, her eyes lowered shyly to the earth, her black locks hanging in her face, hiding dark, embarrassed eyes.

"You must not be sorry for the welcoming love of a dumb beast!" I declared. "For every man longs for his dog to greet him warmly at his door."

The young woman did not look up. There was sorrow in her stance. Her face was blackened with the ashes of mourning. I searched my heart for words to cheer her, but James spoke instead in my ear.

"Here comes Jacob Takanash, sachem of these people, a wise man but not one who prays."

"He has a praying name?" I wondered aloud.

"An English name," said Sassamon as the sachem approached. "Jacob, Nétop!" cried the Wampanoag as he embraced the shoulders of the old king. "Jacob, friend!" he repeated.

"Welcome, John Sassamon," said the sachem. "Welcome, friend. What brings you here on this fine morning?"

"We come to see the good God-preacher Hiacoomes and his brother Assoko," declared the Wampanoag.

"Of course," said Jacob Takanash, "but come into my tent and sit awhile, for Hiacoomes and Assoko are with the rest of the men, and many of the women and older children, upon the southern shore. Paumpagussit the sea god has spat forth Potoppauog the whale upon the rocks. The people are cutting Potoppauog into much meat! We will eat well today. And for many days more!"

"God is good," said Sassamon as we entered the wigwam of Jacob.

"The gods are good," said Jacob.

"Has not Hiacoomes convinced you yet?" laughed the Wampanoag, and I wondered at his boldness.

"He has not," said old Jacob, folding himself stiffly upon his mats. "Sit down. Let us smoke. Tell me of your travels. And may I meet your friend who is a stranger to my eyes?" The sachem nodded his head toward me and looked me cleanly in the eyes. I felt a strange compassion rise within my heart. *Jacob does not know the Ransom and the Name,* my soul whispered sadly. And I wondered at this new sorrow that sang within so strongly.

"I am Joshua Kattenanit, the son of Katanaquat The Rain From God of the Narragansett," I said to the old sachem and his old heart.

"The Rain From God," chanted Jacob. "A great and hard warrior. Son of Nopatin of the Narragansett, another man of war and great wisdom and strong medicine. Adopted son of The Dead Snake of the Narragansett, a mighty powwow once feared by many. His spirits will look long before they find another like him.

"But your hair is shorn like the English, Joshua Kattenanit," said the sachem who knew many things, "and you walk to my town with Indians who pray. Are you no longer the son of your father?"

The son of my father? Who is my father? The man who shakes his fist at the heavens? Or the One who sits upon those heavens?

"I am the son of my father," I replied, fighting a shadowed shame that shook its own fists at both the man who raised me and the God who made me. And I wondered who it was that sat within my form before this ancient man of the ancient ways.

I looked upon my bare arms and there was no paint. I saw my dark chest, and it was clean of the grease of the bear. Neither tooth of any beast nor bone of any man hung about my neck. The chiseled image of the Name upon the cross of His torture dangled there instead. Trousers sewn at Boston covered my long legs. Upon my belt hung a blade of steel made in a land of dreams that lay far across the Great Salt Sea.

Who am I? I said within my waking pride. And I looked upon the old man who sat smoking before me, and I saw myself chanting with my grandfather the powwow. I glanced at the Wampanoag preacher, and I saw my father and my prince and Wequash and . . .

My vision blurred. A strong sickness washed suddenly over me and I heard a groan push itself past my lips. I held my head, blinking at the faces and the forms that swam before my eyes.

"Joshua! Are you well?" said the brothers Quannapohit, their troubled visages fading and changing, like a reflection upon the rippling waters of a dancing stream. I saw now the heads of the twins of Eatawus, hair cut short like the English, lips moving, eyes calling. Slowly their mouths stretched wide and still, their eyes fell shut. Blood ran from severed scalps into silent, parted lips. Fear blew strong upon my heart, and a cold familiar voice laughed in my ear.

"No!" I cried, scrambling blindly to my feet, staggering wildly about the wigwam. Strong arms took hold of me, but I flung them from me, prancing madly about the tent like a deer in a thicket that is caught in a snare.

"Katt!" howled a dog whose bark broke through my madness like a slap from my mother in the nights of my youth when my dreams held me trapped in a dark world of fear.

"Katt!" barked the dog once more. The bark was familiar. But who?

"Jesus!" I cried. "Help me!" And I doubled over upon the floor and wretched. Chants and prayers blew around me like leaves upon the winds of autumn. *Jesus. Jesus. Jesus.* The Name grew strong in my heart. I coughed up fear, hot and vaporous within my soul, until at last the madness fled, my senses stilled. I rose up, shaking, on my knees.

Tears choked my eyes. My breath came in gasps. My face was wet with cold sweat. But the fear was gone.

"Are you well?" asked the brothers Quannapohit.

"Jesus," whispered the Wampanoag.

"Manitoo!" declared the wide-eyed sachem.

"Katt?" said the old dog.

"Assoko!" I cried.

We sat about the fire of the Fool, and I wept.

"Who am I?" I blubbered.

"Josh Katt," said Assoko, stroking my shoulders with his strong, small hands. Those hands! My Fool.

"Where am I?" I stuttered.

"Soko's house," said Assoko, rocking beside me near the much-too-hot blaze. I thought I would burn, but I did not mind. My Fool was there.

"The Terror!" I stammered.

"Gone," said my Fool. Did he know? How could he know?

"My Strong Shield," I whispered, rocking with Assoko as though he were the wind and I the willow.

"Jesus," said Assoko.

"Jesus," I repeated.

"No fear," said Assoko. "Perfect love casts out fear."

"Perfect love," I echoed absently.

"Jesus," said Assoko.

"Satan is like the great cat of the mountain," said Sassamon. "He prowls about the forest in the darkness of the night, seeking someone to devour."

"But the Name said He would stand at my door!" I cried in desperation.

"And so He does," said the Wampanoag. "But sometimes He stands there only to call you to fight for yourself when He knows the foe approaches. For though He is the great warrior who protects His children, yet all His sons must learn to be warriors too."

"How can I stand against a foe no man can see?" I pleaded.

"By wielding weapons that no hand can hold," said Sassamon. "By standing strong in Jesus and speaking His name to the cold winds. By bathing your soul in the blood of the One who has ransomed you. Resist the Devil and he will flee from you."

"I have nothing to threaten him with!" I cried.

"You threaten him even as you sleep," said the Wampanoag grimly. "He fears you greatly. For even in your weakness, your shafts are stronger and straighter than his."

"My arrows cannot slay the wind!" I cried. "And though I loose them all into the swamp of Chepi, they will draw no blood there. They will sink into the mire and my quiver will be empty!"

"Your quiver hangs in Heaven," said Sassamon. "Draw your shafts from there in prayer. Your shield is Faith. Your belt is Truth. Your sword is the Word of God. Your club is the Love of God—the love that fills the New Heart.

"So throw your arms around the Great Invisible One, and when the Terror roars in your ears in the night, rise up and roar in his face instead. The Terror is but an ugly old cat snared to the shadows—he cannot stand the light. You are the cub of the Great Lion Of The Everlasting Mountain. The sun is upon your head. You need not fear the shadows. And you can never die.

"So do not fear. Fear is filled with torment.

"Embrace love instead! Love casts out all fear, covers many sins, lasts longer than the earth and the sky. God is love. Hide in His love! The Devil will flee."

"God loves Josh Katt," sang my wonderful Fool as we rocked by the much-too-hot fire.

"Who would have thought it of Hiacoomes?" said James.

"He was the First!" declared Thomas.

"Tell me more," I said.

And they opened the tale of Hiacoomes the First, as we sat in the tent of Assoko my brother, my friend and my Fool, on the isle of Capawack, Vineyard of Martha, where Jesus was sachem and love conquered fear.

"Hiacoomes lived here from his birth," James began. "His father was a brave of little account whose father was a cowardly man who begged more often than he hunted.

"Hiacoomes himself was, even as child, a boy whose speech was slow, whose countenance was marred by a thick nose and eyes that looked always as if to go to sleep. The people of his tribe thought little of him, and scarcely watched as he grew among them.

"But his heart was strong and his mind was good, so that he thought long on many things that others simply took from the hands of their fathers:

Who are the gods and where do they come from?

Why is the land water fresh and the sea water salt, and how is it that the waters of the sea stay in their place?

Why do men dream?

Why does not the great god Cautantowwit walk from Sowanniu to sit with us along the shore of the Great Salt Sea? And why should we not walk to see him?

Who are the English, and why have they come among us?
"Many questions did Hiacoomes put before the wise men of the town, but they thought him a fool and called upon the powwows to instruct him. The powwows soon ran dry of answers, and they cursed him.

"So he grew to be his own brave and his own warrior, and but for his family and a friend or two, only old Jacob loved him—and that for pity's sake. But the people thought him beneath themselves.

"He followed the tribe on the hunt and to the battle, but his shafts seldom found their prey, and no scalps adorned his poles. Yet he did not beg meat as his father had. Instead he fished, long and alone. And for this, at least, he was known, for the fish always came to his nets and his hooks. He shared the catch with such as had need, but few gave him thanks. He was under the curse, they said, and so their eyes would not look long upon him.

"At length he married, though none thought that any maiden would have him. But his heart held love, and all maidens want love though most settle for less. His love was like his nets and his hooks, and he caught himself a pretty little thing. They loved each other, and they warmed their bed together in the cold winter nights. Children were born. And this was during the time when the English first came to Capawack to settle, the first days of the tribe of Thomas Mayhew our English father and our great friend!"

"Great friend!" affirmed the Quannapohit who shared the name of Thomas. His brother continued the tale.

"Some houses were raised by the English upon the shores of the Great Harbor, and the English sometimes walked to the wigwams of their neighbors to visit. Hiacoomes, being of a larger mind than his people, gave better entertainment to the English. He welcomed them gladly and tried his best to hear and understand them as they spoke of their ways and their God.

"Hiacoomes began to walk to the houses of the English, and then to their Meetings. There he was the guest each Sabbath eve at the table of the younger Thomas Mayhew, God-preacher among the English of Capawack. In the kitchen of the preacher, Hiacoomes drank the milk of the Word of God even as he ate the meat of the house of Mayhew.

"But soon his people became alarmed that one of their own was so often conversing with and hearkening to the English, for some were jealous of Hiacoomes' favor with the English, and others were jealous for the ways of their fathers. Thus the Indians paid him more attention than ever they had, trying to discourage him from his friendship with the English.

"But all that they tried to say and do was to no avail, for God—who calls not many who are thought noble or mighty or wise after the flesh—called our humble Hiacoomes out of darkness and into His marvelous light. And now that he had tasted the goodness of God and the knowledge of Christ which is Life Everlasting, he was resolved that nothing should hinder him from laboring to know God better."

"And so he was the First!" declared Thomas happily.

"The First," I echoed.

"The First of all the Indian peoples to bow to the One God!" declared James.

"Though God knows there may have been others," added Sassamon.

"Quash," muttered Assoko almost to himself, running his thick fingers through his tangled hair.

"Wequash, perhaps," affirmed the Wampanoag. "Maybe more. God knows."

"But Hiacoomes we all know!" said James. "And he is called First among us, even by the Nipmuc who pray and the Massachusetts who pray, and many more upon the big land."

"Tell on," I encouraged the elder Quannapohit, for I longed to hear more of this story of the One God and His First.

And James told me more:

Of the time a powwow named Pahkepunnasoo struck Hiacoomes in the face, and would have struck him again if the English who were present had not prevented it. Afterward Hiacoomes said, "I had one hand for the injuries and another hand for God. While I held out one hand to receive the wrong done to me, I held more firmly to God with the other."

He told me of how Hiacoomes took it upon himself to learn to read. How he walked the island with a small book in hand, looking for those who might instruct him, until he had found enough help to read the whole volume. How his people laughed and scoffed at him when they saw him, saying, "Here comes the English man!" But he threw off their scorn, for it was a little thing to him who had borne it all his life!

And once, said James, Hiacoomes went to a house of his people in which slept Pahkepunnasoo, the one who had struck him in the face. This cruel enemy rose from his bed to taunt the Praying Indian. "I wonder why a young man with a wife and two children should love the English and their ways, and forsake the powwows!" said Pahkepunnasoo to Hiacoomes. "What will you do if any of you is sick? Where will you walk for help? If I were in your moccasins, nothing would draw me away from our gods and our powwows!"

And Hiacoomes held his tongue, James told us. But afterward, when Hiacoomes was from that place and among friends, he said, "God surely heard the evil words of Pahkepunnasoo. And God must sometimes answer for Himself."

Shortly after this, lightning fell from Heaven and smote Pahkepunnasoo, so that he fell down as though dead with one leg in his fire. And his leg was sorely burned before any of his people could pull him from the blaze. Yet he lived! And this proud Pahkepunnasoo then threw off the gods and became a worshiper of the only True God and His Son Jesus Christ.

And the tales were many more still, but the hour being late, and all but James and I being asleep, we called off our council till another day.

I met Hiacoomes the next morn, and he hung his head when I spoke of all I had heard of his courage and his love for the Great God.

"I love Him only because He loved me first," said the little man with the sleepy eyes and the pumpkin nose.

I met Pahkepunnasoo, too, in those days upon Capawack. The tales were true, he told me.

"And others of the powwows have turned from the gods to

the Lord," he said, "though many of their brothers hate them for it. Many strong sorcerers have declared war against the One God and His people. But the powwows only bleed themselves in vain effort to overthrow the One whom none can overcome."

"And what of the spirits?" I asked. "Satan and his demons? Do they not come against you?"

"Oh, yes!" replied the once-powwow. "But they are no more than mosquitoes before the Hand of God. Though they plagued me at the first, and made my nights a misery of sleepless fear, I have learned to simply hide behind the Hand—and laugh!"

"Your quiver is now in Heaven?" I asked.

"Sassamon has been instructing you," he noted.

"The Wampanoag is wise in these things, I perceive," I said.

"He is," affirmed the once-powwow.

The Lord's Day, the Sabbath. Hiacoomes had preached and the Meeting was ended. A few English had come to worship with us but by now had all gone home. Some of us gathered to smoke and take meat in the wigwam of Assoko, for it was quite large although he lived in it alone. "I built it to hold many children, for my squaw will come some day," he said, though his squaw was no longer his squaw. She had married again when Assoko the Dead Man had walked from the lands of the Narragansett to beg a new soul of the gods of the English. The Fool never knew, yet his tent was never empty. This day, the brothers Quannapohit were there, with Sassamon, Hiacoomes, Pahkepunnasoo, several of the praying men of the people of Great Harbor, and Assoko and myself.

We had raised a strong fire against the chill of the fall winds, and were smoking and laughing when the door was pulled back and an angry man entered the tent.

"I know all the Meeting Indians are liars!" shouted the tall warrior. He was Pamchuckit, a powwow of the island who hated the Name and any Indian who followed Him. I met him once at the weirs, where he shrieked against the Name as a dog that howls against the stranger who stands at the door of his wigwam.

"You say you are not afraid of the powwows?" cried Pamchuckit. "I say you are liars!" Assoko stumbled to his feet, for this was his home that the powwow was filling with such evil words. But the Fool stood only to listen.

"Sakatom! Hannawit! Janawummit!" hailed the powwow, pointing his yellow-painted fingers at three who sat near me. They bowed their heads and would not face him. "You are deceived, my brothers!" barked Pamchuckit. "For I tell you that the powwows could kill everyone of the Meeting Indians if we set ourselves to it. Who will save you from the spirits if we set them upon you? Who can stop our medicine if we send it against you? Can the waters of the sea stand as a rock wall against the hurricane? Can the proud birch stand tall against the great axe?"

Assoko shuffled toward the powwow, his palms held out in peace.

"I do not come in peace," said Pamchuckit through broken teeth. His face was painted crimson. His eyes were as black stones in a field of blood.

"But perhaps you should leave in peace," said our First One, still sitting. Assoko stiffened before the powwow, his face a mix of sorrow and surprise. Then his eyebrows rose and his mouth bent into the half-smile, half-frown that made his visage such a curious contradiction. He rocked a bit upon his feet, seemingly bowing again and again. A cough of a laugh escaped his lips, and then he sat back down and crossed his arms.

"I can kill you from my own wigwam!" declared the powwow. And Hiacoomes stood. A low grunt rolled through the wigwam.

"You cannot," said Hiacoomes quietly, looking into the black stones until they blinked and their gaze fell to the floor. "I believe in God and put my trust in Him. And therefore not all the powwows together can do me harm."

The black stones rose again to peer with strange fire into the eyes of our First One.

"He speaks true," said Pahkepunnasoo from beside the great blaze. "For I myself—though my god killed and wounded many at my bidding—could do nothing against this man! You know the power that was mine, Pamchuckit! Your uncle's son is lame for the biting of my snake! And you have placed stones upon the graves of others who will never wake from the poison of the spirit that I sent against them! But my god could do naught but rattle its head and wag its forked tongue against this Hiacoomes!"

Pamchuckit stood still as a pine stump, his eyes jumping rapidly from Hiacoomes to Pahkepunnasoo and back and forth again. *Is his body dead?* I wondered, *and are his eyes mere spirits that look out upon us like the English from the windows of their upper chambers?*

Pahkepunnasoo pulled his mats back from his scorched leg. The scars were great and ugly. "Can a man stand when lightning strikes him?" asked the once-powwow to the now-powwow. "And can a man lay his leg in the fire and not be burnt?"

"I have walked in the fire!" muttered Pamchuckit. "My legs are not burnt!"

"Can you stand forever in the fire that never goes out and not be burnt?" asked Hiacoomes. "For there you shall stand, weeping and mourning and grinding your teeth, if you do not turn from your false gods!

"Go in peace, bad Pamchuckit, and tell your powwow brothers that I will stand in the midst of them all. They may try their utmost against me if they will. And when they have flung the worst of their witchcraft in my face, I will set myself against them without fear. Jehovah will hear me. Fire will fall. We shall see who stands."

Pamchuckit went pale beneath his crimson mask.

"I put all the powwows under my heel," said our First One quietly, pointing to his foot.

And Pamchuckit turned on his own heel and fled into the darkening dusk.

With a great sigh Hiacoomes sat heavily back upon the mats.

"You are a Great One!" we cried, but he shook his head wearily and tossed his arms about him to shake off our praise.

"I am a small man who stands behind a Great Shield," he mumbled. "There is only one Great One."

And we hung our heads with his. But we marveled at his courage and the power of our God. Would the powwows take the challenge? Would the fire of God fall?

Pamchuckit probably never said a word about our meeting. Why should he shame himself? But whether he did or not, we know that the powwows continued to oppose this Wind of God that blew ever stronger among them. Yet none can stop the Wind, and one by one the powwows bowed before the Storm. One by one they let their gods be blown into the sea.

"Who does she mourn?" I said to Hiacoomes.

"Elizabeth was to be wed this autumn, but her man was drowned in fishing upon the Great Sea."

"I am sorry," I said. *She is beautiful*, my heart declared.

Elizabeth Whitewater. The maid who walked with blackened face and downcast eyes, her Shadow at her heels. How could I see beauty beneath the ashes? Why did I sense joy beyond the mourning?

"May I walk with you?" I asked. And she said I might. But we spoke no words together. Shadow followed.

Many days we walked thus, and my heart wept for her sorrow. But my joy grew strong as her head rose higher while our path stretched further.

Sassamon and the brothers Quannapohit went back across the waters. I would follow later, I said.

"Will you have us send your wigwam to you in an English boat?" asked James, his elbow at my ribs in jest.

"Yes, if you please," I replied in earnest.

Though the days were colder, my walking with Elizabeth grew longer and warmer, until one eve we stood upon the southern shore of Capawack and stared across the endless sea toward the setting sun. Shadow chased gulls and waded in the shifting surf.

"He cannot rise," she said of her once-love.

"He has risen in another place already," I said.

"He is with the One God," she replied.

The dark blue horizon was suddenly disturbed by a great band of porpoises, leaping and dancing like warriors who follow one another around the pole of war. Yet these braves of the sea are not warriors at all, but creatures of peace and great joy. It is as though they have always known the One God and

His ways, have never fallen beneath the curse or the shadow of sin. Their dance is not wild like the lusting warrior, nor does it cause the blood to rise. It is not attended with the confusion of many proud hearts and loose, prating tongues. It is one of ancient unity and deep and quiet strength, like the sea itself in its great eternal rolling.

Beauty.

Peace.

Eternity.

Love.

The things no hand can hold.

I took Elizabeth by the hand and watched the light of Keesuckquand fade low within the mysterious untouchable of the Great Salt Sea.

"He is buried," she said of her once-love. "Dead."

She turned to face me fully. Tears streaked her ashen cheeks. I wiped them with my fingers.

"Wash it all off," she said. And I bent to take the sea in my palms. Once, twice, thrice I gently rubbed the salt waters upon her proud forehead, her closed and fragile eyelids, her smooth cheeks, her soft lips and strong, rounded chin, until her face was clean of mourning. And when at last she raised her midnight eyes, they were clean too. *You are beautiful!* my heart sang.

"I am yours," she said.

Chapter Eleven

The Place Of The Hills

A *nno Domini* 1650. A strange way to mark the risings and the settings of the sun, to tell the numbers of the many seasons past.

Anno Domini. It sounded more like Indian than English to me. "It is neither," said Cochenoe the interpreter of Eliot. "It is Latin."

Anno Domini. It means "in the year of the Lord."

1650. Big numbers. One thousand, six hundred and fifty!

1650. It means one thousand, six hundred and fifty years since our Lord Jesus Christ was born as a baby to grow as a boy-child to walk as a man and to die upon the cross of His torture, our Ransom.

Anno Domini 1650, my twenty-eighth summer, Elizabeth Whitewater became Elizabeth Whitewater Kattenanit. She and Shadow came to live with me in my wigwam at Nonantum. And I thought I knew joy as none other could know.

"We are one," I said to my new love. "For John Eliot says that the two become one."

"I am yours," said my beautiful dream.

"And I am yours," I promised forever.

In that same year the English promised to purchase some land upon which we might start a new town, a Praying Indian town, which would be ours to build and plant and govern. A town where Indians could come to live and worship the One God. This is what Waban wanted more than anything. This is why we had made our laws. A town of our own like the English!

"I will not have it!" shouted Cutshamakin to Eliot. "If the Praying Indians have a town of their own, then they will not pay me the tribute that is mine by right and tradition! Already they say that their goods belong to God first and then to their families and their neighbors in need."

"But I have taught them that no king can rule without taxes and tribute," Eliot replied. "They know that they must give you the due that is yours, just as they give God His. They know that you must pay your emissaries and your traders. That you must equip your warriors. What has anyone withheld from you?"

The angry sachem swung his big arms about his head in protest. He did not answer Eliot directly, but carried his complaint further.

"The other sachems are growling against you, too," cried Cutshamakin. " 'Eliot turns our warriors into gardeners,' they say. And they point the finger at me. 'Cutshamakin goes to Meeting like an English woman,' they chant. 'He eats sugar out of the hand of Eliot.' "

"I don't recall giving you any sugar," said Eliot gently, a thin smile upon his straight face. "Nor any strong water either, though you manage to find plenty elsewhere!"

"My men buy it of the English!" argued the sachem. "And I take it from them so they will not be drunk and kill each other!"

"And you drink it yourself rather than let it go to waste," said Eliot.

"I drink it with my warriors, so that I can keep my eye upon them and keep them in hand!" spat hot Cutshamakin.

"And then you all fall down together in the forest and eat moss!" said Eliot.

"I will not have this new town!" roared the sachem.

"You smell like a barrel of strong water even now!" declared the preacher.

The sachem howled indignantly, but his eyes fled like guilty children to a wooden crate at the back of the wigwam.

"Who is not paying you tribute?" asked the preacher.

"I will not have this new town!" wailed the sachem.

"Are we wild beasts that we must howl?" asked the preacher.

And the sachem sat down with a glower and a sharp sigh. A great burp exploded from his throat. He raised a cough to cover it.

"The Praying Indians are paying you as much as they ever have, are they not?" asked the preacher at length.

"All the sachems are angry," insisted Cutshamakin.

"And the Praying Indians are doing much fishing for you, and clearing ground for you, and bringing you skins, are they not?" asked the preacher.

Cutshamakin turned his eyes darkly to the ceiling of his wigwam. A large wigwam it was, new and furnished with many fine things.

"And the Praying Indians built this new house in which we now speak, did they not?" asked the preacher.

The sachem dropped his face to the floor and mumbled something that could not be fully heard.

"Why do you growl against your friend?" asked Eliot. "I am your friend."

"I am sorry that I drink so much strong water," muttered Cutshamakin.

"Why do you not tell the truth to your friend?" asked Eliot.

"And I am paid well," admitted the sachem grumpily.

"Too well," said the preacher. "From now on, the Praying Indians among you and those at Nonantum will pay you a set amount. A tenth of their crops or their catch at fishing, or whatever that is worth in labor."

"A tenth," repeated the sachem gloomily.

"No more and no less," said the preacher. "It is all that God asks!"

"A tenth," said the sachem. "The same that God asks." he said. "It is fair."

"Will we see you at meeting on the Lord's Day?" asked Eliot. "Sober," he added.

"A tenth," muttered Cutshamakin. "The same as God. It is fair."

When the Sabbath arrived, the sachem was at Meeting in his English trousers and shirt, sober as an old owl.

"I am sorry, my people," he said to us all, "that I have opposed your town. I am sorry that I have once more let strong water be my master instead of the One Great God. I am sorry that I shouted at my friend as he stood in my great house, the wigwam that you built me yourselves.

"When I stand tall and look upon my brothers, I see myself a big man among little people. But when I look up to the heavens, I see that I am an ant before God and that all men are ants together.

"I will not stand like the stubborn oak in the path of your new town. I will not howl with the other sachems. I will not keep any of my own people from picking up their wigwams to move to this new town. I will help you in every way that I can."

And we marveled at his change, and we thanked the Lord God mightily.

"But where shall we build our new town?" we asked one another.

"We must pray the Lord shows us," said Eliot.

I saw him kneeling by the wide trail, his horse tied to a tree. *God will answer his prayer this day*, I said within myself.

Quietly I walked to him, until I stood beside him while he prayed. He had not heard me. When I set my hand upon his shoulder, his head flew up in a start.

"Joshua!" he coughed.

"Come with me," I said.

Eliot rose from the ground and untethered his horse. We walked in silence beneath the trees.

The birds of the new green were so many that their melody assailed our ears like a great wigwam full of singing children. So many whistling beaks, so many different songs, such joy and wild harmony! The hooves of Eliot's horse upon the beaten path were like a dull drumbeat in the midst of the laughing piping of the forest's feathered fliers.

"Where are we going?" asked the preacher at length.

"You will see," I said.

"Where are we now?" he asked.

"A place called Natick," I said.

"My house," mused Eliot.

"And a place of hills," I said.

The sound of the waters of the Charles grew stronger as we passed beneath the beech and the willow, the oak and the maple, the cherry and the chestnut.

"Here," I said, when at last we stood upon a slope of pine that walked gently down to the Charles.

"Here!" breathed Eliot strongly, his keen eyes growing bright with a vision none else could see.

Natick. My House. The Place Of The Hills.

It belonged at that day, in pieces and in certain places, to both the English at Dedham and the Nipmuc family of Speene. The people of Dedham gave it over to us in exchange for lands elsewhere. John Speene and his people gave it over to us also, gladly and freely, reserving only the right to the weir they had built on the Charles, and asking the privilege to trap fish there in season.

We began to clear the pines to lay out our streets and raise our wigwams, but our dull axes quickly wearied and our arms nearly fell off for swinging. We wondered how we might ever fell so much wood, and on both sides of the Charles!

"Where is Weetucks when we need him!" gasped James as we sat, discouraged, beneath a barely whittled trunk.

"Or some band of giant beaver!" I suggested.

But God heard our groanings and soon sent a great ship filled with English tools and iron and clothes from the churches in England.

"We have English brothers whom we have not seen!" I declared to James as our new axes splintered the trunk of the great pine. "They pray for us. They sing for us. They send us things that we could never purchase for ourselves. They love us!"

We felled and squared timbers to raise first a small English house in which to store furs, with a little room for Eliot to stay in when he came to be among us. We called it "the prophet's chamber" after a room once built at the top of a house for the ancient prophet Elijah. We had two Elijahs in our town already. So many names in the God-book! Not enough Praying Indians to name! "All in good time," said Waban.

Upon our shoulders we carried our timbers, singing like birds as we labored. Eliot directed us in all of this, and paid us for our work!

"I'll do this every day!" declared Thomas.

"Not on the Sabbath!" scolded James.

"Of course not on the Sabbath!" fired Thomas.

Our labors brought to my mind the past day when Providence was born and my father and I, with my prince and Canonchet and our Fool, had shoveled ground like women to help raise the house of Roger Williams. How long ago that seemed! And I wondered what each dawn brought to my father and my mother, to my brothers and my sisters and Canonchet the companion of my youth.

Our bridge was next, a mighty task and a torturous labor of pride and love. We waded in icy waters to set stone upon stone for a foundation that could stand against the spring meltings. The river was seventy-five of a man's foot wide, and we made our bridge ninety feet across and nine feet high. It was the best-built bridge upon the whole river, Eliot said when it was done, and better than any the English had yet made in the whole country round. When it was fully finished, Eliot brought his eldest son to celebrate with us. The boy's name was John like his father, and though he was nearly a young man of fourteen summers, we carried him about upon our shoulders as if he were a papoose. "John son of John!" we chanted. And he laughed with us long and loud.

Next we put up a fort, palisaded by twelve-foot-high tree trunks. We dug a deep ditch round it too—a "moat," Eliot called it. And he told us of great castles in England over the sea, castles made of great stone surrounded by great moats filled with water.

Then we set to raising our Meetinghouse. It too was larger

than many that the English had. Twenty-five feet wide by fifty in length and twelve feet high for each of its two stories. The bottom story was for our worship and preaching and all other meetings—and our school. The upper story was for storage and another room for John Eliot. An English carpenter helped us for two days when we raised the frame, but otherwise we built it all ourselves!

"Swinging this flat-faced tomahawk is easy enough," said James. "But knocking these little arrows into the wood is more pain than torture by the Mohawks!" His fingers were torn and sore bruised. We had never pounded nails before.

Then a few of us—myself for one—built houses like the English. But most preferred wigwams.

"My tent is warmer, Joshua!" said James as we sat at my table in midwinter.

"Bring your coat when you come to see me," I insisted. "And I will leave mine home when I go to visit you."

"Are we still Indians?" laughed my good friend, fingering my pewter mugs and scratching his close-cropped head.

"We are still Indians!" I declared. And we drew on our pipes as one, blowing rings of smoke toward the wooden-beamed ceiling.

"Nopatin!" I cried, dropping the kindling to the floor as I came in from the new-falling snow.

My grandfather rose from the table where he had been sipping the hot soup of Elizabeth my wife. In warm silence we embraced. Standing at the table was Mattachuk the youngest son of Nopatin. He was my uncle, but my elder by only five summers.

"It is like a joyful dream to see you both," I said as we sat upon piled mats in front of my fire—this was no time for stiff chairs! Shadow lay beside us, his face upon my lap. Elizabeth sat against the firewall, quietly puzzling over the words of an English book that she and I were learning together to read.

"The gods of the English favor you," said Nopatin as he looked about my house. "Though you walk the path of peace, you have many of the possessions of the great warrior."

"These are not the possessions of a warrior, my grandfather," I said sincerely, for I had no scalps nor the spoils of any battle. Neither did I own things taken from another's tent. "These are those things that any man can have if he commits his hands to work toward them," I said, "Yes, the Great God has blessed me, but I have labored hard for this house and this home."

"Your squaw is a fine wife," said Nopatin my grandfather, "and she served us well and plenty while you hunted wood for your fire. But are you not doing her work for her as you gather maple and push snow from your door?" Elizabeth swallowed heavily, but did not look from her book.

"I love her better than to make her old and ugly before her day," I replied. "And it is cold outside!"

"You are new-married, I have forgotten!" laughed Nopatin. "There are many more winters in which she may push snow."

"I hope to love her better still when next winter comes," I declared. "But tell me of your own squaw my grandmother. Of Silvermoon my mother. Of Katanaquat my father. Of Canonchet. Of Winaponk, and of my sisters. And I will tell you of Assoko and Hiacoomes and Sassamon the Wampanoag—he is my brother and not my foe!—and of James and John Quannapohit and of the new English whom I love."

Nopatin leaned back upon his crossed feet, pulled his pipe and his tobacco from his belt, and set himself ready to smoke. Mattachuk and I did the same. Elizabeth rose from her seat and brought fire from the hearth. Her eyes smiled as she lit each pipe. Then she sat down and lit her own.

"Taquattin your grandmother is well—but old and ugly," said Nopatin, blowing smoke from his nose like the warm breath of an English horse on a cold day. "Winaponk your brother carves arrows that he declares will one day be as straight and true as your own. Quanatik your sister looks much like your mother did as a young maiden. She will marry in the Moon Of The Melting, and she hopes you might come."

"I will come," I said. "And I will dance for her happiness. For I myself have never been so happy as in these days with my Elizabeth."

"Though our happiness is not the love of man and wife

alone," said Elizabeth quietly, face in her book.

"Truly she speaks," I said soberly. "For it is the love of the Great God that fills our own love to overflowing."

Nopatin said nothing. Mattachuk frowned.

"My uncle!" I said to the son of Nopatin. "Do you wish a mug of beer to cool down your smoke?" His frown lifted, and he grinned his glad assent. Elizabeth rose to bring mugs and drink.

"You take water like your father," said Mattachuk as he stared at my mug while emptying his own.

"I was bent toward water from my youth," I replied.

"I have bent myself the other way," chuckled Mattachuk.

"I prefer to be able to stand again after bending," I said.

Mattachuck coughed into his cup.

"Some old dogs have perished in the lands of the Narragansett," said Nopatin as he drained his own cup. "And so have some sachems, the son of Canonicus being one. Our wise men lay down and die, and they leave us foolish children in their place. Some are drunken beasts, some are proud squaws. The drunken beasts sell our land. The squaws declare themselves our queens.

"Quaiapen the widow of our recent-dead sachem has gathered men about herself and raised a palisaded town of her own. She has changed her name to Magnus—the old Squaw Sachem. The English call her town Queen's Fort. Her sons rise up and argue who should be chief over us all!

"And the English still hear the lies of Uncas! Though our prince is dead, the English believe that his spirit is in us to revenge his murder. We must pay Boston tribute to leave us alone. And when we have nothing with which to pay, they march into our towns like victorious warriors coming home to their own wigwams. Only last moon, soldiers from Boston came. Their warchief, an angry man who handles our tongue worse than a Dutch papoose, put a gun to the head of Pessacus. Roger Williams played the shield again and stepped between the two. One Englishman threatens to kill us. Another is set to protect us. But where is the strong medicine of the Narragansett? I have lived too long."

"May you stand tall still, Nopatin The Good Father Of My Own Father," I objected. "May your wind blow strong and long, for the Narragansett need men like you."

"They need men like you, Kattenanit son of Katanaquat," insisted my grandfather, "Men who drink cold water, think clearly, and can shoot straight." He pushed his mug toward my wife. I nodded. *One more*, I mouthed to Elizabeth my love.

"And old dogs?" I asked.

"Cold Tongue sleeps forever," said the old sagamore sadly. "And Coonbite my hound will never run again."

I scratched the shaggy ears of big Shadow. He slept also, but would wake and run soon enough when his tongue begged for water or his restless spirit called for play.

"Your mother," said Nopatin after taking a deep draught of his second mug, "is well. Her wigwam stands by mine, and she looks to the needs of young Metauhock your sister. How old is Metauhock?"

"Twelve summers," I said. "Is she near grown?"

"She is small," said Nopatin groggily. "Seems more to be ten summers than twelve. But I am an old buck and can hardly see well enough to tell a young maid from a young brave!" He tipped his mug again and emptied it with a satisfied sigh.

"Your father," he continued, "lives alone."

"Alone?" I said in surprise.

"Alone beneath the pines that sit thick between the Yawgod and the Shickasheen," he replied. "Just north of the Great Swamp."

"Alone?" I asked again.

"Alone," said Nopatin and Mattachuk together. And they pushed their emptied cups toward Elizabeth.

Alone beneath the pines. Alone in his darkness. Alone in his sin and his stubborn pride. Standing where he stands. Behind a useless wall that cannot be defended for a moment against the winds of any god or the smoke of any fire.

Alone in his hard heart. Alone in his calloused soul. Alone in his lonely chant, his private dreams, his precious war against the gods—against the One Great God.

I prayed for him much, and walked the Yawgod once in search of him. A palisade stood strong and sure within a stand of seven giant pines. My father's fort without a doubt. But he was absent, wandering perhaps upon some beasted path within a world that none could see but him alone.

I left no clue of my visit. I know now that he never knew I came.

But I sent him word by Nopatin from Assoko and myself. And I asked of him often to all who might know of his welfare.

Katanaquat. The Rain From God. Cold and hard he fell upon his friends and foes alike. And in the midst of his own storm, he could no longer hear the hearts of those who loved him and the One who loved him most.

Jesus, have mercy upon this my father Katanaquat.

Call to him strong like the Song you once sent to his ears and his heart on the wind of the night. Sing in his waking! Sing in his dreams!

And if he will not hear, if he stands where he stands in the clouds of his own rain, cast him down at last upon the earth where he cannot rise but to look unto You.

But have mercy, dear merciful Father, upon Katanaquat my father in the flesh.

In the name of Jesus I beg you. Amen.

Anno Domini 1651. The Moon Of New Green.

The geese came to our river in great numbers. The warm smile of Keesuckquand was joy to our hearts. We praised the Great God for the new life of the waking earth. More Indians came to raise their wigwams with ours, one hundred souls in all by now. Two hundred apple trees were planted in rows in the farthest clearing from the river.

We began to take the Good News of God to others beneath the trees and beside the rivers. My own heart lept whenever the chance arose to be part of the preaching of the Name.

"It is a strong joy and a strange medicine," I said to Elizabeth, "to sing of the Name to all who will hear."

Many heard, and some believed.

The Moon Of Mid-Summer.

Daniel Gookin, a strong man of good heart and much love for God and all the Indians, came with Eliot to preach and to pray and to sing psalms. We could hear his heart well, and we freely gave him ours. He promised us his friendship forever.

One Sabbath we held a Day Of Many Questions in which we could set forth anything that was upon their hearts. These days were favorites of mine, for often the questions of others were also deep questions of my own.

These are some of the puzzles that we laid before Eliot and Gookin:

How do I pray to Christ and the Spirit? I know a little how to pray to God.

Does the Devil dwell in us as we dwell in a house?

When the soul goes to Heaven, what does it say when it gets there? And what does a wicked soul say when it comes into Hell?

If a person sleeps at the Sabbath Meeting, and another wakes him, and the sleeping person is angry with the one who woke him, is this not a sin?

Why must we love our enemies, and how shall we do it?

When every day my heart thinks that I must die and go to Hell for my sins, what shall I do about it?

If a man thinks a prayer in his heart, does God know it? And will He bless him?

Should we trust in dreams?

If a wicked man prays, how can his prayer be good?

Why did God make Hell before Adam sinned?

If God promised Abraham so many children, as many as the stars in the night sky, then why did He give him so few?

Does not an Englishman spoil his soul to say that a thing cost him more than it did? Is this not the same as stealing?

You say our body is made of clay. What is the sun made of? And what about the moon?

If a young woman prays to God, may she marry one that

will not pray to God?

Is faith in my heart or in my mind?

And many more questions we asked on this day and on many other days and nights, and upon our walking in the woods and our fishing in the streams. And slowly the deep sea of truth became lighter in the sun of God's Word until at last I walked the sea bottom as if it were the forest floor.

The Moon Before Harvest.

"Call me Daniel," said Daniel Gookin as we sat together beneath the men's canopy upon Apple Hill. "For I am your brother."

The day was a dream in all ways.

The sun was at mid-morn, warm and full of strength. The sky was that blue that speaks peace to all who dwell beneath it, smoky white clouds sailing slowly across it. Eagles drifted high upon winds that barely kissed the earth. God was watching.

Three canopies were spread upon high poles in the glade that sat between the orchard and the first houses that topped the low hill on the south side of Natick on the Charles. One tent was for Eliot, Waban, Gookin, myself and the rest of the rulers and elders of the town. Another was for the men of Natick. The third for our women.

Today we were a Town!

Our government had been declared upon the pattern of Moses, who led his many people by letting them choose rulers over each ten of them, and then rulers over each fifty, and then a hundred, until the whole of the tribe of Israel was ruled in this way.

There were twenty-nine families in Natick, one hundred and forty-five persons.

Together we chose wise and ancient Totherswamp to be our ruler over all, the Ruler Of One Hundred. Though we numbered more than a hundred, Totherswamp would lead us all until we reached two hundred. Then half of us would be under Totherswamp and half would choose a new Ruler Of One Hundred.

Under Totherswamp we had three Rulers Of Fifty: Waban, Joseph Speene, and Jethro Shokaw.

Under these three we had fifteen Rulers Of Tens. James

Quannapohit my friend was one, and I was another. Monequassin, a bright young brave who could read much English, was also a Ruler Of Ten. I wished to know him better, for my own English needed much help, and I especially longed to read it and write it.

The way of this ruling worked thus: If any had a grievance that he could not settle with another, he took his complaint to his Ruler Of Ten. If the offense could not be settled there, the two—with the Ruler Of Ten—would go to speak to the Ruler Of Fifty who was over that Ruler Of Ten. And so forth. And if an argument went all the way to Totherswamp and still could not be settled—which seldom occurred—it would then be taken to Eliot or Gookin. And so was justice delivered after the pattern of God's wisdom as it was given to Moses. But this was for personal offenses only. We also had our laws.

We chose our good sagamore Waban to be our Keeper Of Laws, for he was zealous to enforce those laws that he had so greatly desired we make.

On this most beautiful of days, Waban sat soberly beside Eliot in the Tent Of The Elders. When Eliot had concluded our prayer, Waban stood to address us all.

Our Sagamore and Ruler Of Fifty, our Brother and Keeper Of Laws, our Comforter and Front-Walker Of God's Paths was not young, though his wrinkles did not show themselves except when he smiled—and then they spread across his face like the web of the spider! But he was strong and tall, and his short hair was dark about the ears of his sun-blackened face. He was not one to sit inside his wigwam and dream dreams. He turned the dark earth as we all had learned to do. Planted the seeds that his squaw once planted alone. Chased the birds—Kaukant, too! Hunted the forest. Fished the rivers and the sea. Dug for clams. And made chairs.

Rocking chairs. Only a few so far. And I myself was working hard toward buying the next that he made.

He squinted, though the sun fell only at his feet beneath the tent.

"Today we carve in stone what we have long drawn in the sand," he declared loudly, his head high and his broad chin pointed toward the tents of the men and the women. "Many times we have heard the words we will soon speak aloud as one. Our father John Eliot has brought us these words from Sabbath to Sabbath throughout the past moon. They are words of our hearts' desire, and today he will read them to us again.

"As the words come to our ears, we will take them into our hearts and raise them once more to our own lips before God and one another. Before our English brothers who sit with me here in this tent. Before the heavens that watch and listen. Before the birds that circle above us, the beasts that walk the forest. Before our children who sit at our feet. Before our fathers who know not the Great God. Before the wicked gods themselves who bound our souls these many dark years until the mercies of God came walking the woods in white men's shoes.

"Today we bind ourselves as a tribe of the Great Sachem in Heaven, to follow Him all of our days.

"Today we are His People In One Place.

"Today we are a Town. His Town."

Great chants rose from beneath the three tents. Loud warbles and unfettered cheers. Song leapt from heart to heart. And then just as suddenly we stilled ourselves to hear the words we longed so much to make our own.

Eliot stood. His mouth was still for many moments as his eyes walked the glade that lay in the shadows of the canopies of our rejoicing. His soft face, half-hid by the thin beard that encircled his lips and chin, twitched. Tears barely held themselves back from their falling. A calloused hand brushed back brown locks from his brow. And then for a breath he closed his eyes, squeezing water from them, and smiled a broad smile as he lifted his head to the blue skies above our still tents. We smiled with him. Some women cried.

"My friends," he began at last, leaning past the thin wooden pulpit behind which he stood. "My brothers," he declared. "My heart is full today, and words that I have practiced fail me. I will say only now that I love you and that God loves you. Let us stand together and repeat the covenant that is yours and yours alone before Almighty God and His Son the Lord Jesus Christ."

We stood. Taller than we had ever stood in the pride of our own hearts, the pride of our fathers, the pride of our gods and our ancient fallen darkness.

We stood in our newness. Upon the Rock Of Our Ransom. In the Day Of Our Promising.

And we turned our ears eagerly and hungrily toward our preacher, our brother, our friend. And as his lips moved with the tongue of our fathers, our hearts opened wide to drink in the sounds. We repeated these words after him:

We do give ourselves and our children to God to be His People.

He shall rule us in all our affairs.

He shall rule us in our worship.

He shall rule us in all affairs of the Church—for we desire to be a Church as soon as we can and as soon as God wills.

He shall rule over us in all our works and affairs of this world.

The Lord is our Judge. The Lord is our Lawgiver. The Lord is our Sachem and our King.

He will save us.

The Wisdom which God has taught us in His Book will guide us and direct us in the Way.

Oh Jehovah! Give us wisdom to find out Your Wisdom in Your Book. Let the Grace of Christ help us, because Christ is the Wisdom of God.

Send your Spirit into our hearts, and let Him teach us.

Lord, take us to be Your People, and let us take You to be our God.

Men with hoes, mattocks and rakes, standing and kneeling in their gardens.

Spinning wheels visible through the doorways of wigwams and wooden houses.

Children wearing clothes.

The school bell ringing.

Young braves and old warriors with short hair.

Rocking chairs.

This did not look to be an Indian town.

This was Natick.

My Home.

The Place Of The Hills.

Chapter Twelve

The Praying Indians

A nno Domini 1652.
January: The first of twelve seasons of time, called *months*, that fit together to make one year. February is the second month, then March, then April—I was probably born in April—and then seven more until December. The year is then done and January begins again. It is much like the Moons.

The English also cut these months into *weeks* (with no names) which are made up of seven *days* (which have names). "Because God made the world in six days and then rested on the seventh," Cochenoe told me. "But we rest on the first day of each week instead of the seventh."

"Because we are not God?" I asked.

"No," said the Montauk. "Because the Lord Jesus rose on the first day, called Sunday."

"Then should we not rise with Him instead of resting?" I asked.

"You must ask Eliot," said Cochenoe.

Sunday, Monday, Tuesday, Wednesday . . . seven days all, with names, in each week. But each month has not the same number of days! It gave me a headache to think of such things!

"Cochenoe is going back to his people on the Long Island," said Eliot to me as we walked the white path that circled the small snow-covered trees of Apple Hill. "And I am looking for another to help me as he did."

"But I do not know your words as he does," I said. "I could not turn them so quickly into ours at Meeting. And even the tongue we speak in Natick is not really mine, though it is close. My heart still speaks Narragansett, and so it makes my tongue trip!"

Eliot laughed. He did not mock me. His laughter was clean and it lifted my heart. But I could not laugh with him, for he seemed to be asking a heavy thing.

"I am not looking for a new tongue at Meeting," said the preacher. "Monequassin can help me there."

"He has helped me much as well, but mostly with the words that are in the pages," I said. "I find that my eyes do better than my ears when it comes to the English tongue."

"That is why I asked you to walk with me today," said Eliot.

Our path lay in snow, well-trodden though deep, and the world around us lay carpeted in white. The trees to our south and over the river to the north wore sloppy, dripping hats. The Charles was frozen still, though wet and slick to walk upon. I thought it might break open any day. The streets of Natick sat below us, dark and muddy. Many shovels had cleared the straight ways. Warmer days had thawed the naked earth.

"Monequassin tells me that you are very quick in hearing the words on paper," Eliot continued. "That you have already read every book on his shelves! That you were the first to understand the catechism that I had written in your own language."

My eyes brightened, not for the praise of Monequassin but for the joy that burned within at seeing the tongue of the Indian scratched upon the parchment of the English.

"They are not chicken scratches to me!" I exclaimed. "They come alive to my mind so cleanly and strongly. I—" I hesitated for a moment—was it pride or shame?—but then I pushed through. "I have even written some of my own thoughts on paper. Even some words that were not in your book. I don't know if they are right—for you know all these things, not I—but after I write them and leave them alone, I can come back and they are the same as before and I know them right away! As surely as the prints of any beast of the woods I know them. There they are on the paper—my own thoughts again!—and I can speak them out loud exactly as I thought them and wrote them."

"Excellent, Joshua!" said Eliot, picking up his pace as we circled the trees again. "And I am no magician when it comes to these things," he added with a fling of his hand.

"I wrote a song last week . . ." I said to myself and the Great God above us.

"A song!" said Eliot.

"A song," I repeated, embarrassed.

"I would see it," said Eliot. "I would hear it."

"Oh no, Master Eliot," I cried. "It is a papoose that can hardly speak. I must look at it and listen to it again many times before another can hear it. And then I must sing it to only one."

"He hears it already within your heart," Eliot declared, "and He loves it much. That is all that matters."

I wished to tell him that the song was not to God, but he stopped of a sudden and we turned to walk around the trees the other way.

"The God-book," said Eliot. "The Bible. The Holy Scriptures. In the tongue of the Indian. This is what I most desire to put in your hands, Joshua. In your hands and the hands of all our brothers here at Natick and in all places that we preach among the Indians. This is the work that Cochenoe has helped me begin and which you can help me complete. The Bible in the tongue of the Indian."

"Not chicken scratches!" I shouted excitedly.

"Nor English words that few among you know," said the preacher.

"But *wussuckwheke enapwáuwwaw*—'words that speak Indian'!" I cried. And I lifted my eyes to the sky and let fly a whoop of joy.

"*Wussuckwheke enapwáuwwaw*," Eliot repeated quietly many times as we packed the snow harder in our glorious, dizzying march.

One among us split a piece of wood on a cold Sabbath. Someone saw him. Someone told Waban. The criminal paid a fine.

Another among us got drunk and fell in the mud near the

Meetinghouse. Waban had him tied up and whipped, along with another who had supplied him with drink.

The wife of Thomas Quannapohit spoke an evil word about the wife of James Quannapohit. She had to sit in the stocks for an afternoon. It was not like her to speak such evil, I knew, but after her time in the stocks she would not speak to the wife of James at all for two weeks! Then the brothers got their women together and they made things right. Elizabeth had prayed they would love one another as they once did.

Oh, it was hard to keep all the laws! But we had to walk straight with God. We had to walk right as the English did. Even our leaders could not stand taller than the laws!

Jude the son of Totherswamp was gotten drunk by three naughty Indians who came to visit. They thought they might escape punishment if they invited the son of Totherswamp into their crime. "How can your father punish us," they said to Jude after filling him with strong water, "since you are drunk too?" But our Ruler Of One Hundred said that he had warned his son against such things and that all four were guilty alike! The next day the three were put in the stocks and then given thirty lashes each at the pole. We wondered what would become of Jude. Would he be let off after all? But no! The boy was put in the stocks for a short time as well, and then taken to the schoolroom where he was whipped before the whole school!

"Foolishness is bound up in the heart of a child," said Totherswamp with the words of the God-book. "And the rod will drive it from him!"

Even Waban was not above the law. One Sabbath he ordered a young man to shoot a raccoon for him to supply food for an unexpected guest. Someone heard the gun, saw the beast fall, saw who picked it up, and noticed where it was taken. Waban had to pay a fine in his own court!

The laws were good, for they made us see our sins. And they showed our sins before all, that we might hold each other to the straight paths. They kept us like a fence that keeps the English cows from wandering and losing their way in the swamps. And I knew God was pleased.

"I do not believe a man should be whipped for breaking the Sabbath," said Roger Williams as I sat with him at Providence.

"But the Ten Commandments declare we must keep the Sabbath!" I cried.

"It is a commandment of God," affirmed Williams. "But not one that any man can hold another to."

"Then how can God bless a people who do not keep His commandments?" I asked. "And how can we say that we love our brother if we let him trespass against God?"

"We must encourage one another to keep the laws of God—those of us who know God. But in some things God alone can judge each man," said Williams.

"Shall I not take a man to court if he steals my axe and will not return it?" I argued. "And should he be allowed to go unpunished for stealing?"

Williams screwed up his mouth in a puzzling way. His brow wrinkled deeply for a moment, and then he relaxed.

"Here is what I have thought of the matter for many years now, Joshua," he said. "The first four of the Commandments of God are those things that speak of a man's relationship to God: having no other gods but the One God, making no idols to bow down to, not making God's name an empty thing, keeping His Sabbath. These I wish all men would keep—but only if they know God! For the laws of God will not save a man who does not know God."

"They will not save a man," I said, "but surely they please God."

"Only faith pleases God, Joshua," said the preacher of Providence. "And holding men to anything less than faith only makes them think they are good men and safe men before God. This is a terrible sin, and many burn in Hell for thinking themselves good when they were not. If I neither steal from my neighbor, nor lay with his wife, nor say anything evil against him, I break no law. But if I hate him, even though I do him no harm, my sin is not less for keeping the law."

"Then should we not punish men for hating as well?" I asked.

"No," said Williams, "and that is my point. Hatred is in the heart. No punishment can make it leave. Only the heart can make it leave. Only if something else fills the heart will it leave. Only if love takes its place. Only if God turns the heart of stone into the heart of flesh.

"Men can punish crimes against men, but none but God can punish the crimes of the heart. He alone is Judge of the soul."

"Then why do we have laws?" I asked.

"To keep me from stealing from my neighbor. To punish me if I steal from him. For peace and justice among men!"

"Natick is a Town," I said with my eyes to the floor. "We have laws like the English. This is pleasing to God. We cannot let our people break the Sabbath or speak against God's Name and His Commandments. He would be angry with us. Are you not angry when someone speaks against your name?" I challenged.

"I am quite used to it by now," laughed the gentle preacher. "And our Lord tells me to turn the other cheek when someone strikes me. To never return evil for evil.

"Can anyone strike the cheek of God or wound His pride by speaking against His Name? We wound only ourselves by making little of the One who fills all things.

"Faith, Joshua, is the only thing that pleases God. Faith and the love that grows up from it."

"I have faith, Roger Williams," I declared, holding my head up once more. "But my faith is a dead thing if I do not obey the Commandments of God."

"You speak true," said the preacher.

"Then what is this stone that you throw in my path?" I cried.

"I wish I could move it for you," said Williams sadly, and he put his strong hand upon mine. "Do not be troubled by my words, Joshua, and let me try once more to make them clear.

"If you and I were to lie upon my lawn and look up at the clouds," continued the preacher, "you might imagine that you see the shape of a great whale within the clouds. I might see the head of a horse. Should I cast you in the stocks for not seeing my horse's head? Should you whip me at the post for not seeing your whale?"

"Of course not!" I declared. "It is a hard thing to see what another sees in the clouds. Canonchet and I saw different things always!"

"And so it is with God," said the preacher. "Men do not see Him alike, though His Word is the same for all." He slumped back in his chair and stared out the window at the crimson setting sun.

"But must we not call all men to obey that Word, for we know He is the True God and His Word the True Word?" I wondered.

"What are they teaching these boys in that Town?" mumbled the preacher as he fingered the ends of his shirt sleeves.

"We are raising apples," I remarked.

"Did I ever drag you to court for picking one of my apples on the Sabbath?" asked Williams, sitting up suddenly to his full height. "No, I did not, because you didn't know God or love Him, and so you could neither honor nor dishonor His Sabbath. Besides, I told you to help yourself to an apple any time.

"And would I rebuke you even now if you picked an apple on the Sabbath? No, because that is a matter between you and God alone! Even our Lord healed on the Sabbath. And His disciples picked grain as they walked in the fields. The Sabbath was made for man, not man for the Sabbath. Rest if you will—it is good! But do not condemn the man who does not. God is his judge."

Williams pushed back his chair and reached behind him into a small crate. He pulled out an apple and set it on the table. "Eat it," he offered with a smile. I took it nervously. "Eat it!" he said again. "It is a Jonathan. Very good. Cleans the teeth, too."

He selected another for himself.

"But if you come with a basket and empty my trees while I am away, taking what is not yours to take, then I will demand just pay when I find you out," said Williams, taking a large bite of his Jonathan. He chewed it slowly, talking all the while. "And if you will not pay, then I will take you to court in a breath! For thievery is a crime against your neighbor, and one that should be punished so that all may know that this kind of behavior will not be allowed among civilized men."

I bit into the sweet fruit. I chewed it. I swallowed. I sighed. I thought I could see, though as in a fog. "So you say that the Sabbath is a thing between the heart and God, and that God will judge such things at the Final Court," I said.

"Yes, and if the heart has loved God, such things will not even be written in the books that God keeps of the deeds of men," said Williams.

"But those who pray must come together to pray," I said. "And they must do so on the Lord's Day, mustn't they?"

"Yes, we must come together to pray," said Williams. "And the Lord's Day is a fine day to do so. But so is any other. Or as many days as any might choose."

"But what if my heart hates, as you spoke before," I asked, "will this not be written in God's books of the deeds of men?"

"If your heart hates, you do not love God," said Williams. "For if a man says, 'I love God' and hates his brother, then he is a liar. For if he doesn't love his brother who he sees with his eyes, then how can he love God whom he has never seen?"

"So it is written in the first letter of John, chapter four, verse twenty," I said, for I had written it myself in my own tongue while working with Eliot only two days before.

"So may it be written on your heart," laughed Williams, amazed. And he took two more apples from his crate.

Elizabeth was pregnant—praise the Great God of Light and Life! And I told everyone I knew who might be passing south through the pines where my father sat alone, and south still further to the towns of the Narragansett and the wigwams of Nopatin.

I prayed Father might come when the child was born. Mother would come surely if she could. Nopatin, too. Perhaps Assoko if I sent him word. Canonchet? I hoped so. Why not? The Great God made all things work good for those who loved Him. And I loved Him more each day.

A wife. An English house. A town with straight streets and a bridge no flood could carry away. A child of my own. Friends among the English and the Indians alike. Laws I could take in my hands.

Peace. Love. Hope. Faith. Joy. Strong medicine in my soul. Medicine that no powwow could sell and no man could steal. And the Name at my door.

A strange new life of unwaking dreams this was!

"Now we have a Town like the English," said Waban to Eliot. "So let us have a Church like the English." For though we met often, on the Sabbath and at other times for preaching and prayer, we were not baptized as the Lord commands us, nor were we gathered as a Church with a minister and elders. Neither had we yet been allowed to eat and drink of the Lord's Supper as the friends of Christ Jesus had done on the night He was betrayed to the men who would put Him upon the Cross of His Torture, our Ransom.

"I will sit with you all," said Eliot, "and hear your confessions of faith. Joshua will write them down for me. Then he and I, with Monequassin and Job Nesutan to help us, will write them again in English to send to the ministers of the colony. If these men accept your hearts, we will meet again, all of us and all of them together, that they might hear your confessions anew and question you further if need be.

"But you must have patience as the Lord desires," he cautioned. "For patience will work hope. And hope will not disappoint you even if the days are longer than you wish before you are a Church yourselves."

And so we gathered in our Meetinghouse on the twentieth day of August, and one by one we stood to tell all that was in our hearts concerning our love and our knowledge of God.

Totherswamp was first speak.

"I confess in the presence of the Lord," he said. "That before I prayed, my sins were many. Not one good word did I speak. Not one good thought did I think. Not one good action did I do.

"I sinned all sins, and my heart was full of evil thoughts.

"I confess I deserve Hell. And I cannot deliver myself! But I give my soul and my flesh to Christ, and I trust my soul with Him for He is my Redeemer. And I desire to call upon Him while I live."

Waban was next.

"Before I heard of God, and before the English came into this country, many evil things my heart did work. I wished for riches. I wished to be a powwow. I wished to be a sachem.

"When the English taught me, I was angry with them. But

then the Great Sickness came, and I saw how the English cared for all. I thought that perhaps I could be as they are, a man who did good works for others. I saw also how they worked and how they prospered in their work, and I began to work as they work, and not to dream idle dreams.

"I have done all as I see the English do, and my Town has made laws that we might walk as the English walk. I make sure the laws are kept, and I punish those who break them.

"But I do not know how to confess, for though I know a little of Christ and that He can carry all my sins, I feel there is little good in me. And my heart does not know grace."

Was this our great Waban, doubting the grace of Christ in his own heart? How could this be?

"I tell others to believe," he continued, shaking noticeably, "and I tell them the stories of Jesus. I comfort them in their grief, and I give great speeches about the love of God. But I am ashamed of all that I do, and I do not repent of my own sins."

"This is not so!" we cried. "You must be ill to say such things of yourself," we shouted, "Look how you shake! Do you have a fever?" But he quieted us with upraised arms and hung his head.

"Hear my confession, my brothers," he choked.

"We will hear you," we muttered.

"I hate my sins!" he moaned. "Yet I do not truly pray to God in my heart!"

"But you must pray to God in your heart!" we exhorted our beloved. "For He will surely hear you and pardon all your sins."

"I can do nothing," said Waban, his arms hanging limp at his sides, his head slumped low upon his breast. "I pray loud at Meeting, but the words are words my mind makes up from the prayers of others. My heart is hard. I deserve damnation. I judge I am a sinner who cannot repent."

"No!" we cried. "All men can repent if they will but bow before the Great God and tell Him their sins. All men may find mercy if they will but bathe in the Blood of Christ."

But Waban would not be comforted, though many followed him from the room with tears.

Only faith can please God, Joshua, said the words of Williams.

And I knew of a sudden that not all the laws in the world could help Waban. *God, give him faith!* I prayed.

Monequassin our schoolmaster confessed next that when he first heard the teachings of Eliot, he laughed at them and scorned praying to God. Later, when he thought more about it, he wished to learn to pray. But he did not want at all to come to Natick, he said. And cutting his hair off was hardest of all, though he had finally done that too.

Robin Speene then told us of his shame, still upon him, because he did not pray to God when first he heard of it. "I see my sin now," he said, "and I know I need Christ. But will you please answer me this question: What is Redemption?"

Ephraim Wannesum said that sometimes still he thought the Word of God was false.

Peter Wannesum, a Ruler Of Ten, confessed that he once followed after many women, but that now he had but one. And that he used to hunt and shoot and play upon the Sabbath Day, but that now he would rest and not work. And that many other sins had long been his, but that now he would cast them away.

Many more—James and Thomas Quannapohit among them—stood to share many things, and many were the tears that we shed as our hearts were lifted up for all to see. And some of us were strong in Christ, and some of us were weak in our sins. And some of us could see Him well, and some of us groped about like blind men.

I stood last of all, and found my tongue only after I had prayed within, *Jesus my Ransom and my Strong Shield, show me my own heart that I may find it to give to these my brothers. For this day is a strange, misty day in my soul.*

"When I first heard of the One God and the Name, my heart was like the child in the crowd of its elders," I began. "It wanted to be lifted up to see and to hear and to know. But none could lift me, and so I stood upon my toes. I climbed the trees. I walked to the top of the hills. But still I could not see.

"Yet like the one whoop of the hunter in the woods, or the signal of the bird from the lips of the warrior, the Name called me in my dreams, so that I stopped to listen. But I could find no footprints in the mud, no turned leaf, no path beneath the trees.

"What was the Call like? Like the mother who gently touches her sleeping child to wake him from something less than life, to open his eyes to the morning light. But I could not wake and I did not wake. Always I turned in my dreaming. Always my eyes were in shadows.

"But I whispered the Name in my heart and with my lips, and I felt Him near—beside me, behind me, before me out of sight upon my path. It was a strange and troubling, hopeful, awful thing.

"My father thought me mad to chant the Name, to strain my eyes to see Him. For my father fought the gods with all his might. He stood where he stood. He stands there still.

"My powwow hated the Name and cursed Him. The gods had swallowed him. They cast him all about in their bowels whenever they heard the Name. They loosed him upon the earth and then swallowed him anew. It made him uglier still. It made him hate all who loved the Name.

"Roger Williams taught me much about the One God, and I heard the God-preacher gladly. I felt the hand of God upon me in those days, upon my soul, upon my mind. But His grip was such that I could not see past His palms to His face. Instead I felt the weight of His hand upon my conscience. I saw my sin, but I did not wish to know it.

"Wequash the once-Pequot bowed to the Name, and I thought I might stand upon the head of Wequash and see Heaven. But the evil eyes of my powwow caused Wequash to flee the city of Canonicus. And then that Snake, for Askug was his name, slid after the Praying once-Pequot and bit him and slew him while he sat at his own table in peace. And I wondered why the Name had let him die.

"Then my prince Miantonomi—I may say his name now, for many years have passed—was captured and killed by that black and wicked Uncas who still lives and whom God has still not stricken dead for his foul deeds! And the Terror came upon me at this time, stronger than my longings, louder than the Name. And I thought I might die for the fear. And I doubted the Name again, though I could not shake His Call.

"And then, for the love of a maiden, I pulled myself from the Strong Hand, closed my ears to the Still Small Voice, and led my brothers to the river of death. Their blood . . . the blood of my brothers . . . the stain . . ." I looked at my hands. They shook. "The stain . . ." I coughed. My eyes welled up with water and I could not speak. I stood with my face to the wooden floor. My heart cried, *Kuttowonk!* And then I closed my eyes.

The bodies of my brothers lie dead upon the pine floor. The last cry of Waumausu shakes the forest, chills my soul. My feet fly—never fast enough!—beneath the terrible trees. Cold and merciless, stinking and close, the Terror breathes in my face, laughs in my ears.

Horror burns in the eyes of Sawkunk as the flames claw his head. My bow is in my hands. The string is to my ear. The shaft leaps. The feathers whisper a brief prayer. The sharpened stone bites the flesh of my brother, kisses his heart, drinks his blood.

My ransom! My ransom! My ransom!

I moaned aloud and great tears rolled down my face. I thought I might faint as I lowered myself to my knees before the rising, grunting, shuffling congregation. Many prayers rose about me. Many caring hands were laid upon my shoulders. I sobbed with my face between my knees.

"Thou shalt not kill. Thou shalt not kill. Thou shalt not kill." I muttered again and again until I could mutter no more.

Then I was emptied. My brothers helped me to stand. Their words of comfort and concern buzzed in my ears like so many flies upon the windows of the Meetinghouse.

"Thank you," I whispered. "Please . . . please let me finish. I am almost done."

Eliot brought us to order once more, and once more I held my heart before our faces.

"The stain," I said, breathing loudly, wearily. "The stain is still upon me. Though I knelt in the woods of Nonantum and laid my sin at the feet of my Ransom, still the stain is upon me.

"Though the Blood of Christ has covered my sin, still the blood of my brothers is upon my hands," I cried.

"Though my soul is free to fly to the Heaven of God, still my

heart lies bleeding upon the bloody needles beside the Shannuck!" I cried.

"Though your sins be as scarlet, Joshua," blurted James my
brother, "they shall be white as snow!"

"I must know the grace of God more fully," I said quietly.
"We must be a Church so that I may be baptized for the washing away of the blood of my brothers," I said, raising my head
to look about the room more fully. "We must be a Church so
that I may drink of the cup of my Ransom's love," I declared
with growing strength.

"We must have the Word of God in our own tongue so that I
may open it and know the forgiveness of my sins more fully," I
cried.

"We must walk the woods to tell others of Christ Jesus so
that He may gather us all into One Tribe," I boldly declared to
the Praying Indians of Natick on the Charles, to the women at
their spinning wheels, to the spirits who trembled in the trees
beyond Apple Hill. "For He is Sachem over all the earth! And
His is the kingdom, and His is the power, and His is the glory
forever!"

"Amen," said the short-haired, teary-eyed, dark-skinned
saints.

I took my seat and hung my head. Eliot put his hand on my
shoulder. I took his hand in mine.

There were now two hundred eighty-three Praying Indians
upon the Vineyard of Martha, said Sassamon as he ate at my
table in October, the Moon Of The Fall.

"I am going back over to help in the work," he said.

"It is a great work," I declared. "And I would love to return to
the island myself. For I brought home from there the most
beautiful thing that eyes can see upon the earth."

"It is a beautiful land," said Elizabeth from behind me as she
took the bread from the fire. She was baiting me.

"Did you think that I meant the island itself?" I asked, turning to look upon her shining face. I was baiting her.

"Of course!" she declared, a mock frown upon her precious
brow. "For there is no island like it upon the earth!"

"I suppose you are right," I said, letting the bait lie.

She set the bread and board upon the table rather heavily and without a word, then turned to the fire to stir the stew. But I held her dress and pulled her to me.

"You are rude when guests are here," she said coldly.

"You are beautiful at all times," I said simply.

Her frown turned up into a smile, and the room warmed all the more for it. Her hands moved to her full-rounded stomach.

"The child kicks!" she said.

"He practices heel ball," I replied.

"He will play no such vain games!" declared my wife. "For he will be a Christian. He will not run naked and make a fool of himself at the Games of Harvest!"

"He practices swimming, then," I offered.

"He may not be a 'he' at all!" said Elizabeth, turning once more to her stew. "Perhaps 'she' practices kicking you out of bed in the morning."

"Impossible!" I laughed.

We walked in October to pour our confessions into the cups of the English ministers. Many were gathered to hear us and question us, and we spent near all of one day in our Meeting. But though our tears for our sins were as many as when we shed them first before Eliot, and though our joy in knowing Christ was stronger than ever it had been, the magistrates of the English did not think us ready yet to be a Church.

"Does not Jesus say that if two or more are gathered in His Name, there He will be?" I asked with the wisdom of Williams as we walked the path back to Natick.

"Yes," said Eliot. "And it is so."

"And is that not a Church?" I questioned. "For some say it is."

"Some who wish Church to be anything at all say it is," said Eliot. "But the Bible says a Church must have a minister and a teacher who is ordained by other ministers. And ruling elders who are chosen from among the people."

"Do the men of Natick not have teachers, and are there not many elders among us already who know and love God?" I argued.

"We must wait on God," sighed Eliot.
"We must wait on the English," I muttered.

The world turned to Spring in the middle of Winter. Or at least it tried to for a time.

Warm winds blew from the southwest. The deep snow slid from the rocks and the pines. The Charles yawned and woke, sending great melting chunks of ice down its wide path. We feared for our bridge, for the icy river assailed it mercilessly. Still it stood.

A fog, like none I had ever seen, covered the earth from dawn to dusk. The nights were in cloud and the days were dim. Even our great, black dog Shadow was invisible beyond the kick of a stick. We stayed inside.

Then Nanúmmatin came whispering from the north, and the heavens were joined in battle. Winter fought to claim its own as Spring retreated in defeat. Thunder rocked the forest and lightning lit the night as cold rains fell.

In the midst of this battle, on a Sabbath morn, we gathered in out of the rain and sang our psalms and prayed. Daniel Gookin was among us to preach. As we rose from our seats to sing, I caught Elizabeth's eye as she stood in the women's place. She pretended not to see me, for our eyes should have been upon God. But I knew she saw me, and we looked upon each other for a long moment. *You are beautiful*, said my lips without words. And she turned her eyes to the ceiling with a satisfied smile.

I lifted my head then as well and lent my tongue to the chorus of the psalmist. The room lit suddenly as God sent His flaming arrows into the forest. Very near! His cannon roared. Some of the women were frightened. Some of the men could not sing.

Another flash and another crash tore into our worship, and the singing ceased altogether as we left our places to crowd at the windows in awe of the war of the winds of the seasons.

All tongues were silent as our eyes traced the lightning and the wild, wet rain. All lips were still as we listened to the rumble of the thunder and the rattle of the sleet upon the roof, against the windows and the walls.

The Rain From God, I mused within my wondering heart. *Katanaquat!* the thunder seemed to howl. *He stands where he stands*, I whispered sadly. *Katanaquat*, echoed the elements, with the voice of my father. *It is him!* my heart cried. *God sends his name upon the wind from his lonely shelter beneath the pines!*

"Do you hear it?" asked James.

"The voice of one crying!" said many.

"Katanaquat!" cried the phantom in the storm. And we wondered in fear. And the women began to weep.

"It is my father," I said, for I saw his proud form when the world flashed white. Standing with his hard face to the pummeling heavens, arms raised in defiance, hands clenched against the gods. "It is my father."

I pushed my way to the door, shoved the latch up, and wrenched the door open wide. The rain flung itself in as I flung myself out. Other men followed me into the storm.

"Father?" I whispered as I stared at the dark, wet, painted shadow of the man whom my heart knew was blood of my blood.

"Father!" I choked, though none else could hear it, as I walked out into the mud-rutted streams that filled the wide street between the phantom and me.

"Father!" I cried, as I reeled toward him at a run, mud splashing my Sabbath pants, cold rain mixing with my hot tears.

"I have no vine to throw you!" howled The Rain From God, as the sky lit up to show me eyes wide in fear. Eyes that were dark and empty and hungry and longing—and hard.

He turned on his heel—like Noonatch at the sound of the hunter—and leapt in fearful flight into the greyed winter torrent.

"Father!" I cried, following hard behind him. But he ran like the wind, like a man without weapons who flees from the foe. Like a dog who fears whipping. A child who fears lashing. He ran, and I followed until all my breath was gone. Till all my strength was gone. Till all my tears were gone. Then I lay down in the cold, pelting winter and pounded my fists on the fast-freezing floor of the wide, lonely forest.

Slowly I walked down the hill into Natick. Back to my warm house, my pretty Elizabeth. Back to my dream among Eliot's Indians. Back to my God and my laws and my rocking chair. Back to my Town with its bridge on the Charles. Spring would soon come, and the apple would blossom.

But why had he come to me? Why had he come?

"Your father is a ghost," said Nopatin my grandfather. "When I speak to him, all that he says in return sounds like the whistling of the wind."

"Why did he come to me?" I asked as we smoked at my hearth.

"Ask the wind," said Nopatin my grandfather.

I desired to walk south with my grandfather, but the winter returned very strong, and Elizabeth felt sick at her stomach because of the child within.

"When the baby is born," I said to my love. "I will walk to Silvermoon my mother if she cannot walk to us."

"Once the baby is born, I will walk with you," she promised. "For my heart is lonely to know at last the mother of my man, the grandmother of my child."

"She was once beautiful," I said, fingering the black locks that hung upon the dark cheeks of my love. "But never so beautiful as you."

"Sing me my song," she sighed.

The snow was heavy, but our fire was warm.

Chapter Thirteen

Words That Speak Indian

*A*nno *Domini* 1653.
My thirty-first year.
Moses Kattenanit was born. He kicked both his father and his mother out of bed! We carried him to the town of Nopatin.

My mother was well. My brother was tall. My sisters were shy—but they pulled Moses from us and showed him up and down the streets and in every tent!

We then took the path to the city of Pessacus and Cojonoquant. I slept and smoked in the wigwam of Canonchet my friend. We talked of Uncas the mad dog. Of the Dutch Governor who was trying to stir up the Mohegan, the Niantic, and the Narragansett against the English. Of the lands now fenced that once were free. Of the days of childhood past and the seasons unseen that lay ahead. Of the Name and how none among the Narragansett cared to hear any more of Him. Of Sassamon the Wampanoag preacher. Of Massasoit our old enemy. Of Hiacoomes the First. Of Cutshamakin and the Ten Commandments. Of Natick. And of my short hair, which Canonchet said was silly. Some came to join us and to hear of my life among the Praying Indians. Nickeétem stayed in his tent.

"The spring starts small at the foot of the hill," I said to Elizabeth as we walked again north to Natick. "And then it runs to find more small streams like itself. Hand in hand the streams run to the river. And the river walks to the sea. But where does the sea go?"

Moses was quiet, eyes opened to the wide world around him.

Tied to his board and covered quite warmly, he rode upon his mother's back. She did not answer me, but waited for my thoughts to find themselves.

"It goes to England of course!" I said. "And so the brook that is born at Acuntaug becomes at last the great river that flows through London and under the bridge that is covered with houses where Williams walked when he was a boy."

Elizabeth smiled. Moses stared.

"And don't you see, my love," I said, "that we are like the brook at Acuntaug? For our lives began as Indians at the foot of a wooded hill, and then we ran into the woods to find others like us. And then we walked together until we came to the River of God where we heard about Christ Jesus. And the river took us to the sea where all the Praying Indians were sailing toward Heaven. And then we came to England and built our London and our bridge. And now . . ." I stopped to watch a turtle cross our path. "So slow it goes!" I said to the winds and the winding vines that spread their arms above our heads.

"Are we not still Indians?" asked Elizabeth.

"I don't know," I answered. "I never knew I was an Indian until an English man told me so."

"What do you mean?" she asked.

"I thought I was Narragansett! And Williams says I am Narragansett. But he calls me Indian also, because the English once thought our country to be called India." I laughed. "It does not matter what we call ourselves, my love, so long as God is our Ransom and our Shield! For He calls us His Children, and that is what we are!"

"I wish to be your woman, Joshua," said Elizabeth. "To be the mother of your children. Little else matters."

" 'Bible' means 'book,' " said Eliot. "Nothing more."

"We have no word for 'book,' " I said.

"Shall we try 'leaves-with-much-painting-on-them'?" suggested Job Nesutan.

"It is too much for our people to learn new words as we make them up," said Monequassin.

"I do not think so," I said. "For if I am lost in the forest, still I may find my way home if one comes to guide me. You are a good teacher, Monequassin. You can tread the path first. We will follow."

"Leaves-with-much-painting-on-them is too much!" he insisted.

" 'Biblum' then," I suggested.

"Biblum!" said the others. "Good!"

Eliot laughed.

"Why do you laugh?" we asked.

"I am happy," he replied.

I woke in a cold sweat. What a strange dream!

The pines. Where Katanaquat my father lived alone within his fort. It was surely the pines.

Giant red ants as large as foxes had come into the pines and surrounded one tree in which an old dog had a house. A dog in a house in a tree!

The dog barked and clawed at the ants as they climbed up to his house. Some of the ants were killed by the dog and fell at the foot of the tree. The rest of the ants ran from the tree and sat in counsel at a distance to determine what they might do next.

The dog then grew wings and flew from his tree to circle like a hawk above the ants. Barking loudly, he dropped a great pinecone on one of the red beasts, crushing it. The others fled the forest.

Then the dog, as it flew back to its tree, lost its wings altogether and fell violently to the forest floor. There it lay, broken and wounded near unto death.

Then I came into the forest myself and saw it lying there. It was Cold Tongue! But when I tried to help the old beast, it bit me.

Why do you bite the hand of one who loves you? I cried.

You are not my son! it growled with the tongue of Katanaquat my father. And I woke.

"We must pray for my father," I said, shaking Elizabeth out of her sleep.

"Why do you wake me to pray just now?" she asked. And I told her my dream.

"What does it mean?" she asked.

"That we must pray," was all that I knew.

The dog was indeed my father, said Nopatin my grandfather

when next he came to Natick. And the ants were Uncas and some of his worst.

"Did Uncas die?" I asked.

No. The red beast still lived. Untouched. Unscratched. Unbroken.

"And the dog?" I wondered anxiously.

"He fell from a high and ancient pine," said my grandfather, "and lay many days within the woods. But the Great God strengthened him when his life was almost gone from him."

"The Great God! Does the dog follow the Great God?" I cried.

"You would not say so," said Nopatin the father of the dog.

"And do you say so?" I asked.

"I would not say so," said Nopatin.

"But the dog says the Great God gave him strength and life?" I asked.

"The dog says so," replied my grandfather.

"My prayers!" I exclaimed.

"Your God has good ears and much medicine," said Nopatin.

"Where is the dog now?" I asked.

"He limps the forest alone."

"Alone?"

"Alone."

Assoko walked the woods with me, on many paths that only beasts had trod. We stood at the doors of the English. We entered the towns and villages of the Nipmuc and the Narragansett, the Niantic and the Coweset, the Wampanoag and the Nauset. We crossed into the Mohegan country and passed by the city of Uncas to walk beside the Connecticut.

"He was among us for two nights just last moon," said some.

"We have not seen him in four summers," said others.

"I would kill him if he came to me," said one.

"I have heard he sleeps in trees," said another.

"Are you not the Fool of the Narragansett?" said a sagamore to Assoko.

"Soko Fool of Christ," answered my great friend with a wide grin and arched brow.

But we did not find the dog. Though his trail was sometimes

clear upon the forest floor, it would disappear completely at the next step. Did he have wings indeed?

We went back to Natick disappointed.

Assoko returned to the Vineyard.

"There were giants in the earth!" I cried as I read the English words of the Genesis book.

"But they were not good ones like Weetucks," said Monequassin. "Do you not remember the story that Eliot told us of Goliath the wicked giant?"

"And of good David who slew him though he was but a young boy," I said. "Of course I remember."

"And when will we set that story on paper?" asked Monequassin of Eliot.

"Not for quite some time!" said the preacher. "We must finish Genesis and then move next to Matthew."

"I cannot think of a word for this beast you call a donkey," I said.

"We will simply call it a donkey, Joshua," said Eliot.

"A-horse-with-long-ears," suggested Job Nesutan.

"Donkey," Eliot insisted.

"We have no word for horse, anyway!" argued Monequassin.

"We call a horse *naynayoumewot* among the Narragansett," I said, "for the sound of its whinnying."

"Write it down under 'N' in this book," said Eliot, pushing the Indian word-book toward me, "with the English meaning after it. And then write it down under 'H' in this book," he said, handing me the English journal.

"*Naynay*-what?" asked Monequassin curiously.

"*Naynayoumewot*," I repeated as I dipped my quill into the ink.

Rumors walked the woods that the Praying Indians were taking guns from the Dutch in order to rise against the English. Armed men came from Boston to talk with Waban and Totherswamp. Gookin was with us at the time.

"These men are Christians," said Gookin to the English soldiers. "They are more your friends than you know, and better Christians than some of your neighbors!"

"My neighbors are English like I am," said one of the soldiers. "Not simply Indians dressed like English!"

"Our love is true," said Waban. "We are English also. We keep the Ten Commandments. We plant our gardens and build our own houses of wood. We love God. We do not love the Dutch."

"These Indians would fight for Boston before they would ever fight against it," insisted Gookin. "They have no relationship with the Dutch at all. And the poor guns these men own are English guns, for they bought them of the English."

"I think it's a black rat who sells them!" said one of the armed men, a big, red-bearded fellow with thick dark eyebrows. "Who knows but these Injins might fire them in the wrong direction when nobody's looking." It was against the law for the English to sell us their guns, but some did so anyway.

Gookin took the English aside and spoke to them strongly. Some hung their heads at his words. In a few moments they returned.

"I apologize for saying those things a bit ago," said the red-beard meekly. "My uncle was wounded in the Pequot war. And he don't say much good about any Injin."

"I have many cousins who were killed in the Pequot war," said Waban, "and they don't say anything about anyone anymore."

"My father fought with the English in that war," I said. The soldiers shook their heads. I saw shame in their eyes.

"Reckon we should head home, boys," said the red-beard at last to his band of English.

"Eat with us first!" said Waban. "Venison, corn, raisin pie, and cider!"

"I can always eat!" shouted the red-beard strongly, and he set his gun down to follow Waban into the house. With a sudden burst of embarrassed laughter, the rest of the English did the same.

Anno Domini 1654.

My thirty-second year.

Elizabeth gave birth a second time. Mercy Kattenanit looked like her mother. Joy filled our hearts and our home.

Great Cutshamakin of the Massachusetts, second Ruler Of One Hundred at Natick, grand sachem and mighty warrior, fought his last battle upon the bed of his death.

We did not throw ourselves upon the ash heap. We did not paint our faces black and wail to the four winds. For though our hearts mourned that our brother was gone from us, we hoped that his soul flew ahead of us to God. The Indians who did not pray had no such hope. Some marveled at our peace. Some scorned us for having hard hearts. Some looked into our eyes and saw that our tears were as real as theirs.

Josias Chickataubut, nephew of Cutshamakin, became sachem at his passing.

"Waban will like these stories about the Judges," I said, for we were now done with Matthew.

"Does our Law-Keeper rest any better in the grace of God?" asked Eliot.

"He rests quite well at his desk," said Monéquassin.

"He works hard!" I argued.

"Harder than Job Nesutan, anyway," said Monequassin.

I said nothing, but waited for Eliot. The preacher said nothing. We knew that Job must be drinking again.

"I have found the word that we are looking for," I offered.

"Which word is that?" asked Eliot, pushing his chair back from the table.

"We need a word for 'lattice,' " I said. "For the English Bible says, *The mother of Sisera looked out through a window, and cried though the lattice . . .*"

"Yes, I remember we needed that word," said Eliot. "And Job Nesutan wondered why she was weeping."

"But she was not weeping, she was shouting," said Monequassin proudly. "Shouting through the eel trap!"

"Through the what?" asked Eliot, rising from his chair in wonder.

"The eel trap," repeated Monequassin less enthusiastically. For we could see that our word might not work.

"*Mishanttooan papashspe,*" I said, pointing to my chicken scratches.

"It means eel trap?" asked Eliot gently.

"Did you not say that a lattice was made of narrow, thin pieces of wood, and that it was a barrier?" I asked, puzzled.

"Yes, yes," said Eliot wearily. "But it is not an eel trap. We cannot say that the mother of Sisera cried through the eel trap."

"Nor wept through it, either, I guess," mumbled Monequassin.

Eliot sat down and threw his head back in laughter.

"He is happy," I said to Monequassin.

"Just call it a 'lattice,' " laughed Eliot. "Eel trap, indeed!"

"My first!" I said to my cousins from the city of Canonchet. And I let them sit upon the chair and rock it to and fro.

"May we take it home with us?" they asked.

"It is for Elizabeth," I whispered. "That she might rock our children to sleep. Do not tell her so, for she thinks I made it to trade for a new plane to shave more wood and make more chairs."

"Canonchet should have a chair like this!" said the youngest cousin.

"Perhaps I will make him one," I said. "But not until my next one buys me that new plane!"

"I am going to college," said Sassamon, "with Caleb Cheeshateaumuck of Martha's Vineyard. Caleb and I have been chosen as two of the first students for the Indian College at Harvard in Cambridge."

"What is the Indian College?" I asked.

"Hasn't Eliot told you about it?" asked the Wampanoag. "It is a big school that you go to after you have learned all you can in the smaller schools."

"Smaller schools," I said, wondering.

"The smaller schools are the ones like yours here at Natick, or the school that Elijah Corlet has at Cambridge, or the one that Daniel Welde teaches at Roxbury where John Eliot has his English Church."

"There is more to learn than the things that are taught in the school of Monequassin?" I asked.

"There is always more to learn," sighed Sassamon.

"I do not think I could possibly learn any more!" I said, for my head was too full now with English words and Indian words and chicken scratchings and giants and chariots and donkeys. How could there be more? Why would anyone want more? Did the Great Salt Sea ever beg for rain?

"I will be learning two new tongues: Greek and Hebrew," Sassamon declared. "Although Eliot tells me nobody speaks those tongues anymore."

"What foolishness!" I cried.

"But the tongues are still alive in books!" said Sassamon. "And so I can learn things that were written in Greek and Hebrew, as the Bible was written."

"The Bible was written in English!" I proudly declared, for surely I knew more about this than Sassamon.

"The Bible was written first in Greek and Hebrew," said the Wampanoag. "The English then made it speak in their own tongue."

I was stunned. Did not God speak English?

"God speaks all tongues," said the Wampanoag preacher. "Even the tongues of angels. English is but one tongue that He speaks. And He doesn't like it any better than another."

"Does He speak Narragansett?" I asked.

"Of course," said Sassamon.

"Then why did He not write the Bible in Narragansett?" I asked angrily. "For it would be much easier for Him to do so than I!"

Once again we gathered with the English ministers that they might hear our confessions and grant us our Church.

"Surely their hearts will hear yours this day," said Eliot, for his heart heard ours always. "But trust in God who knows best," the preacher exhorted. "And lean on patience in the matter."

We walked to Roxbury where Eliot lived, for that was a friendly place and full of friends to the Praying Indian. The good preacher Thomas Mayhew, who shared the same name as his father the governor of Martha's Vineyard, came also, with many who could help the Indian to hear the English—and to help the English hear the Indian.

But those at Natick who knew both tongues could not come on

that day, for Monequassin fell ill and could not walk, and Job Nesutan—scoundrel that he was at times!—got soaking drunk with two of the worst of us. This was a sour plate of grapes to set before the ministers and the magistrates, and though Eliot dropped Nesutan from the Bible work at once—yet only for at time—still our examiners had their teeth set on edge. Only eight of us stood to testify. God shook his head, No. And we limped home leaning hard on the staffs of patience.

"We are blessed! For we believe in Jesus even though we have not seen Him!" I announced upon reading the words that were spoken by Christ to Thomas His friend in the Gospel of John.

"Thomas!" said Eliot, looking up suddenly from his writing. "*Didymus!* Do we yet have a word for *didymus*?"

"*Didymus* means 'twin'!" barked Monequassin the schoolmaster. "Thomas was a twin," he instructed.

"Yes, yes," said Eliot, waving his hand impatiently before his eyes. "But *didymus* is Greek and not Indian. Have we an Indian word for twin?" asked the preacher.

"We wrote it already last week," I said, turning the pages of our word-journals. "It is *tackqiuwock*," I said, pointing to the word I had entered under "T." "Had you forgotten?"

Eliot laid his hand upon his cheek and stroked his beard. His eyes were red and tired. He pushed a weary sigh from thin-pressed lips.

"I had forgotten," he admitted.

"*Tackqiuwock* is a word whose face even a child among us knows," I chided. "But I am lost now and walking around the same bush looking for a word for 'hypocrite.' "

"That is simple," said our schoolmaster. "*Nesutan*."

Eliot stood. "Monequassin son of Nanequassin, your tongue is too loose! But it betrays your heart! Judge not or you will be judged! And with the measure that you give out, so will it be given back to you!"

"I am sorry, Master Eliot," said Monequassin quickly. "Perhaps I should have said that *Monequassin* is a good word for 'hypocrite.' "

"Confession is more Christian than judgment," hammered the English preacher.

"But," offered the schoolmaster, brightening, "if Job Nesutan were here he would surely find the word."

"Does he know the word?" I asked, wondering if Eliot might call Job back to us soon. For the poor man had repented of his drunkenness with many tears.

"I know his heart so well that I can hear the word he would suggest," declared Monequassin confidently. "It would be *Nnín-nnínnnuog cowwawwunâunchim ewowem matintiantásampáwwa.* 'The-man-who-tells-false-news but says, "I-am-no-lying-fellow." ' "

Eliot stared blankly at the schoolmaster. Then he laid his head upon the table and began to chortle.

"*Tawhitch ahánean?*" I said. "Why do you laugh?"

"*Ahánuock,*" chuckled Eliot. "I am happy."

And Monequassin and I burst into merriment. Eliot looked up in amused surprise.

"*Tawhitch ahánean?*" he asked.

"Because you said *ahánuock,*" bellowed Monequassin mirthfully. "Because you said, 'They are happy'!"

We all laughed then. We all had red eyes. We all were weary. We all were happy.

Chapter Fourteen

Some Years That Walked Swiftly

It is hard to say how my heart fully saw the days that it loved so well yet could not understand. For the world of my father's fathers stood as always about me, tall and green and eternal in the memory of my people, in the memory of all the peoples that the English call Indian.

But the door that I walked to when I bid farewell to the lands of the Narragansett was a door that opened—as it seemed—into a dream beyond the skies. It was a dream and a world that no magician could conjure, for no man could have imagined it, but now it was here. Yet though it was real to the touch, and any eye with wonder could behold it, still the fear walked near me that this dream might one day wake itself. Might open up its eyes and shake its head and see itself as but a dream. A mist departed. A world between worlds that lives only in the tales of two men who make that world real as they sit by the fire and dream it together aloud. But when they sleep to wake again, they say to each other, "What was that dream we conjured last night around the fire?" And they cannot remember, so they rise to go about their day. And all is as it always was.

Daniel Gookin was made Superintendent over the Praying Indians by the English of the Massachusetts Bay Colony, and we were very glad, for he loved us much and we loved him.

"I am not your sachem," he said to us as we gathered at Natick to hear him. "I am not your king. I am not your Governor or your Mayor or your Law-Keeper. I am your friend and your brother, and my ruling will be no more than the caring eye of a brother, the strong hand of a father, the protecting arm of one who knows your hearts and can take your hearts to our brothers the English."

More Indians bowed to the One God, and a second Town was made at Punkapaog, fourteen English miles south of Boston and the same-and-a-mile more from Natick, southeast and below the Neponset. The Praying Indians of Punkapaog farmed as we did, and they also had cattle and pigs. There was a great cedar swamp within their lands, and they made shingles and clapboards of the trees to sell to the English.

Hassamanasitt—which means Place Of Small Stones—was next laid out about halfway between Nipmuc Pond and Manchaug Pond, and about five miles north of both. The people there, having removed many of those small stones, farmed better than any of the other towns. They had many cattle and swine, and orchards of several kinds—but mostly of apple like at Natick.

James Quannapohit moved to Hassamanasitt, for his father's brothers and sisters had always lived by there, and now his father and mother were there, too, though they still did not pray.

"I will ask God to help you much with the Bible words," James said to me when he departed.

"I wish you would be here to help us yourself," I said, "for Job Nesutan has gone back to drink and has left Natick altogether."

"My prayers and my hammer would be of better help," said James. "For my heart and my hands have taken to the English ways much quicker than my tongue."

"You no longer hit your fingers when you swing your hammer," I noted, seeing his hands were sound and strong.

"I have learned all that I can," said Sassamon as we smoked at my table after meat. He had returned from Harvard earlier than he thought or than Eliot had hoped.

"But is there not always more to learn?" I asked. "You said that there is!"

"In other places, in other books, and in other ways there is much yet to learn," said Sassamon. "I know I shall never know all until I see Him who knows all. Then I shall know as He knows, for I will see Him face-to-face. His eyes will burn all the filthiness from my soul and I shall be like Him—without sin!"

"We shall never be like God," I scolded. "Nor should you say so!"

"Have you not read it yourself in the Bible?" he wondered.

"There is only One God!" I declared.

"Of course," said the Wampanoag preacher. "And I did not say that we should be God. Only that we shall be like Him. I do not know what it all means, for it stands higher than my eyes can see, but I know it is true because God cannot lie."

"God cannot lie," I repeated.

Sassamon tapped his pipe against the stone above my fire. His ashes fell into the flames. "Eliot has asked me, since I will have no more of hard Harvard, to teach at Punkapaog. So there I will go."

"Was Harvard hard?" I asked.

"Only the chairs," winked the Wampanoag.

Anno Domini 1660.

The year that Natick was given a Church.

Our joy was too much to contain in one barrel. The staves burst and the joy flowed into the streets and into the Charles. Our fasting became feasting, and all peoples marveled. But the day itself was as solemn as is possible for children who have awaited a gift for so long from their Father.

We gathered at the Meetinghouse, with prayer and preaching as always, but we stood tall upon the hill of our faith and stretched our arms toward Heaven as we read aloud the covenant that made us Church.

"Church!" cried Assoko, beaming like a fool as he sat next to Hiacoomes. Mayhew the Father was there. Cotton also, with others of the English ministers. John Eliot, father and son, were present at the front of the room with Gookin. Elder

Heath of Roxbury was present to rejoice with us, as were some of our closest English neighbors. James and Sassamon had come from their Towns and were seated beside Hiacoomes and Assoko. I saw envy in the eyes of James, for had he stayed in Natick he could have been chanting the covenant with the rest of us.

Fourteen of us stood as members, fourteen who had finally passed the test of the ministers and magistrates of the Bay Colony. Monequassin and Thomas Quannapohit, Tother-swamp, Joshua Kattenanit, and ten others—good Waban included, for his faith had grown real and strong under the sun and the rain of the Word of God.

Eliot stood before us all and read, with our own tongue, the words that he had written for our covenant, our promise, our confession unto God and one another. We each had this covenant in our hands. The words of both the Indian and the English tongue were side by side upon each stiff, white leaf. James Quannapohit had pressed them there himself, with a marvelous English machine called a printing press. His hands, if not his tongue, had indeed been a great help. "Printer James is my new name," he said. And as I looked upon him from where I stood, I saw pride in his eyes that was stronger than envy—good pride, warm pride—and black printing ink upon his hands.

Eliot read each line, and we returned the words in unison.

"I believe with my heart and confess with my mouth," we chanted, "that there is but one only, living and True God, but that He is Father, Son, and Holy Spirit.

"In the beginning God made Heaven and Earth very good. He made Adam to rule this lower world, he being made perfectly righteous.

"Adam quickly sinned and was punished.

"Adam conveyed to us his sin and also his guilt and his punishment, and for this cause we are all born in sin . . ." Our voices were lifted strong and solemn.

At last we came to the part that we had never spoken aloud before. The part that our hearts had long cried for:

"For these causes, we that dwell in this Town called Natick

are gladly willing to bind ourselves to God, to remember the Sabbath Day to keep it holy so long as we live.

"And also to bind ourselves to each other, to meet together every Sabbath Day (when it is possible) to do all our Sabbath Day services, prayers, etc., according to the Word of God, the Holy Spirit helping us.

"By this Gospel covenant we do give ourselves and our children to Jesus Christ to walk with Him in Church Order so long as we live.

"Oh, Lord Jesus Christ, by Thy pardoning free grace and mercy gracious, receive us!

"Amen."

Then we said one thing more in unison as we looked upon all who stood within the Meeting. "We force this on no one, but do meekly say to all, 'Let us join together to do all this!' "

And then we whooped so loud that the rafters rattled.

At the meeting of the Merrimac and the Concord, there is excellent fishing to this day. But it was more excellent in the days of which I now write. At that place was a town of Indians called Wamesitt. Many of the people of the town prayed to God.

At the season of the Salmon, men from all places came to fish the river, and powwows mixed with Praying Indians as the waters gave freely to all. Sassamon was there one day when a band of Mohawk came among them.

The Mohawk are a fierce and wicked people, and they seem to honor no one but themselves. Thus the band that came to Wamesitt fished by themselves, for nobody wished to speak with them, being afraid. But Sassamon, who saw all men alike, joined himself to them.

"Nipmuc?" they asked him.

"Sometime," he replied, fingering his spear nimbly, eyeing the waters for the fins of his prey. The Mohawk held their heads high, their harpoons loose.

"What is the name of your sachem?" they asked.

"Jesus Christ," replied the Indian preacher.

"Hawgh!" coughed the Mohawk. "Praying Indian!"

Sassamon's shaft slid into the river in a blink, and he pulled it back with the finest, fattest salmon of the day.

"Oough!" cried the Mohawk with admiration.

"I pray," said Sassamon with a slight smile.

"Sometime Nipmuc Praying Indian of Jesus Christ," said the largest of the Mohawk, a warrior with thick red paint from cheek to cheek and black around his eyes, "do you not fear the powwows?"

"Does the flea fear the dog?" asked the Indian preacher.

"He calls himself a flea!" they laughed.

Sassamon's shaft flashed once more into the frothy waters. It came back out with a catch nearly as large as the first. "This is for you," he said, handing the wild-flapping fish to the black-eyed Mohawk. "I can stick more."

"Do you not fear the Mohawk?" challenged the big man as the salmon slapped his bared arms.

"Does the birch tree fear the pine?" said Sassamon. His gaze sunk once again beneath the waters. He stepped further into the river.

"He speaks in riddles," said the big Mohawk, though the tall warrior probably liked the thought of himself as an ancient spruce whose head stood closer to the sun than all the trees.

Sassamon's spear bit the waters a third time. It came up with salmon in its jaws. The Wampanoag cast the fish upon the shore where the Mohawk chased it.

"When the great winds blow, which trees fall most often in the forest?" asked Sassamon.

Pine, of course. Which the Mohawk knew, but would not say.

"And when the great snows bend the boughs of the giants of the woods, which break most often beneath the weight?"

Pine, of course. This riddle was an insult and a taunt, the Mohawk surely thought, but still they did not speak.

"And the winds and the snows both come from the hand of God," said Sassamon, standing in the midst of the river with one hand upon his spear and the other pointed toward the sky. "Thus both the birch and the pine should fear God and not one another," he said, smiling.

"Do you mock the Mohawk?" cried the big warrior angrily.

"I do not," said the preacher sternly, sincerely, strongly. "And you must not mock God who plants each tree where He will and knocks each down as it pleases Him." With a quick kick of his leg, the Wampanoag lifted another salmon from the laughing waters. As the fish thrashed about like a bird without wings, Sassamon's shaft struck it through the head.

"Woogh!" coughed the Mohawk fishermen.

"Good morning!" said the Wampanoag, "and good fishing to you, too." And he came out of the river to join his brothers just a whoop to the south.

"Much medicine!" he heard the big Mohawk say. "Sometime Nipmuc!"

Massasoit of the Wampanoag. Nobody thought he could die. But no man lives forever. The old king was buried, for his flesh would rot without his soul. And his soul was flown.

The forest was still but for the sounds of the birds as they flew from tree to tree, the patter of the woodpecker as he hunted for his breakfast, and the chatter of the squirrel as he cursed some porcupine which ambled near the foot of his perch. But we knew that Noonatch was near. He cannot hide his prints as the Indian can. And he follows the same path always from his bath to his bed.

Canonchet sat beside me, his musket at his chin. He didn't blink. I had an arrow at my string, but it was not pulled. I was not so sure as my brother that the beast would show its face.

For long moments we sat, still as the stones at our backs, and then I turned my head to the right. Canonchet let his breath out quietly through his nose. He nodded.

We moved like shadows from our cover and slid into the thicket to our right. I thought I heard our prey before us in the laurel. Or was it just the wind? No. A quiet crunch of heavy hooves upon the dry forest floor. A crackling rustle of antlers amidst the thick web of branches.

Canonchet raised his gun again. I pulled my bow tight. But we still had not seen the beast.

The wind was behind the buck, and we smelled him now. *Come closer, brother,* we chanted within. The beast had left his path for some berry or bush that caught his eye, but his breakfast would soon be done.

There! Great antlers and a fine face! Food for Elizabeth and the children. Food for the house of Canonchet, too. We were in the hunt together.

I heard the musket bellow at the same breath in which my fingers loosed my arrow. Smoke stung my eyes as I leapt from the thicket to follow my shaft. Canonchet was beside me.

Noonatch lay dying in the laurel, his proud eyes fading as they stared in sad defiance at the men who knelt beside his head.

"I am sorry, my brother," we chanted quietly. I stroked the cheek of the great beast. It snorted in sharp resignation of its coming long sleep, and died.

"Your shaft was true," remarked Canonchet.

"Your ball was true, too," I said.

The bullet had taken the heart. The arrow had taken the lung.

Canonchet had come at the birth of my third child, my second son. Elizabeth named him Daniel, for he would stand strong against that Lion the Devil.

"Wamsutta is king in his father's place," said Canonchet of the oldest son of Massasoit. "The English call him Alexander, after a great king who once lived across the Great Salt Sea. Metacomet, the next oldest, they call Philip."

"Is Wamsutta wise like his father?" I asked.

"Wise enough for a young warrior," said my old friend.

"Does he love the English as his father did?" I asked.

"The English have not killed any of his people," said Canonchet grimly. And I knew that he thought of Miantonomi his father, and of the English who looked the other way when Uncas slew our prince beneath the trees.

Moses and Mercy came bursting through the door. They had seen Noonatch strung high behind the house. "Meat for supper!" they shouted.

Mercy climbed into my lap. Canonchet caught Moses and wrestled him to the mats that lay before the fire.

"Fetch us some water," I said to Mercy, and the child was quick to bring us cups and drink. "Thank you, little love," I said. "Now climb the ladder to your mother and see if she needs anything. Your tiny brother is crying."

"I am fine!" said Elizabeth from the loft. "And every baby cries!"

"Are you well enough to cook venison?" I asked.

"Well enough!" she said. "And hungry enough to eat it all myself!" She came down from the chamber, and handed the tiny infant to the great warrior of the Narragansett. He took the boy in his arms, gently but firmly.

"Sit here," said my love to the friend of my youth, and she pointed to the moving chair that I had given her. "It rocks," she said.

"Like the Fool," I said.

And Canonchet sat rocking, his face all aglow, cooing like a dove to the newborn son of Kattenanit.

Did the English poison him? Some said so.

Or did his own pride stab his heart when they dragged him to court?

"He was sick with the fever already," said some, "and why should the son of Winslow slay the son of Massasoit?"

"It will be war!" said others. "For Winslow and the English came to his fishing hole and took him at gunpoint."

"Did they shoot him?"

"No. But he is dead just the same!"

"And why did they take him? What was his crime?"

"Selling land to the English."

"But the English wanted his land!"

"They have it already all the way to the foot of the Montaup!"

"He was selling some land to Williams. Plymouth does not love Williams."

"Can a sachem not sell to whom he will?"

"Plymouth says, No."

"It will be war."

"Not war! For the brother of the dead sachem has renewed his father's long promise of peace."

"Philip asks for peace? At what price?"

"The Wampanoag must give up their guns."

"They will not!"

"Alexander is dead," said Sassamon. "I stood with my people as we laid him in the ground."

"And Metacomet his brother is now king," I said soberly.

"King Philip," said Sassamon.

Mamusse Wunneetupanatamw Up-Biblum God. The Bible. It was complete!

Many copies were brought into Natick in a cart pulled by *naynayoumewot.* Printer James ran through the streets shouting and passing out the books to everyone he met. Eliot tried to calm him, for he dropped as many books as he gave away. Every house received one copy. Every Indian praised God greatly that day. From kitchen to kitchen we raced, reading to those who could not read. Tears of great joy filled many eyes.

I wept, too, and hugged my brother Monequassin tight to my breast.

Job Nesutan put down his bottle long enough to clutch a volume in his shaking hands. He set the bottle aside long enough to read. He came back to Meeting, mourning for his sins, and cast aside his drunkenness for all time.

Copies of the book went to all the Praying Towns and to all the English ministers of all the colonies of New England. To Connecticut and New Haven, to Massachusetts and Rhode Island. I took a copy to Providence myself. Williams barely held his tears back. He blessed God abundantly. "The Bible! In your own tongue, Joshua Kattenanit," he said. "This is the first Bible ever printed in this great, wild country of America! God must be laughing in Heaven for joy!"

Even the Great King who sat upon his velvet chair in London across the Great Salt Sea received a copy. Though how he could read it, I do not know.

Oh, happy day—that day in my forty-first summer in the year of the Lord 1663. And my children danced around my wooden table singing psalms!

I woke in the cold mist of morning, and a strange question rattled around inside my head: *What was that dream we conjured last night around the fire?*

Chapter Fifteen

Ashes and Tears

I do not know how it began. A spark from the hearth or a brand that fell loose and then rolled. A candle? Mercy loved to hold candles. Oh God! I do not know how it began, but I know how it ended.

They are in Heaven now. I heard my Elizabeth singing just yesterday, high in the clouds. As I prayed. As I walked this awful path anew. To write it here. To write it now for you.

I hate to write it.

There was nothing left. Just ashes. And tears.

I cried for so long that I could have filled the Charles—I do not jest! Please do not think I jest!—so long that I thought I would die. And I wished I would die. For what was my life without blessed Elizabeth? Where was my joy without Moses and Mercy and Daniel and . . . God! Where was God?

But I could not curse Him. He was my Ransom. He would some day lead me into His mansion. There would my wife be, with my children beside her.

I could not curse Him. My Savior. My Ransom.

Job. I was now Job and no longer Joshua.

Job in my mourning. Job in my wailing. Job in my walking, my waking, my nightmares.

Joshua died when the flames took my loved ones.

I was now Job.

I could not stay at Natick. I thought of Silvermoon my

mother and of Nopatin my grandfather. But that was impossible. How can a man climb back into his mother's womb?

James. James Quannapohit my brother and friend. Printer James, good Printer James. He called me to his house at Hassanamasitt. He let me soak his shirts in my tears. He prayed with me. Wept with me. Clothed me and fed me.

"My house is your house, Joshua."

"Job."

I carried the ashes in a bag.
I spread them on my face.
I walked in shadows.
I could not be comforted.
Jesus wept. Should I not weep?

Naked I came from my mother's womb, and naked I shall return.
The Lord gave and the Lord has taken away.
Blessed be the name of the Lord.

Even the rain clouds of the heavens must empty themselves before they can be filled anew.

The Spirit of the Lord God is upon me, because the Lord has anointed me to preach good tidings unto the meek.
He has sent me to bind up the brokenhearted,
To proclaim liberty to the captives,
And the opening of the prison to those who are bound.
To proclaim the acceptable year of the Lord,
And the day of vengeance of our God.
To comfort all that mourn,
To appoint unto those that mourn in Zion,
To give unto them beauty for ashes,
The oil of joy for mourning,
The garment of praise for the spirit of heaviness,
That they might be called trees of righteousness,
The planting of the Lord,
That He might be glorified.

But when the darkness finally lifted, I did not care to see the sun.

Chapter Sixteen

Strong Water

It was against English law for an Englishman to sell strong water and hard liquor to an Indian. For strong water in the Indian's belly is like a gun in the hands of a little child.

Roger Williams, even before such laws were made, would not sell strong water to the Narragansett, or to any Indian who came to his trading house to buy or barter. "Shall I sell you poison and say it is milk?" he argued. He knew how the strong water addled our senses, maddened our hearts, reddened our eyes, boiled our blood. He loved us too much to send such fire into our tents.

"Strong water is filled with the spirits," said Katanaquat my father. For he saw much evil come to men who drank from the glass bottle of the English.

But the English drank. Every day. Before breakfast. Even the children. Though most did not drink unto drunkenness. For drunkenness was sin, and punished sorely.

Yet when an Englishman—some of the baser sort—wanted to buy some ground from an Indian, he often invited that Indian to sit at his table for meat and drink. And he might just fill that Indian's cup more than once, and with cider that is strong and hard. And of course the Indian was very happy to get happy drinking the Englishman's cider. But he was not happy in the morning when his head felt like a cow had kicked it, and he had sold his mother's wigwam and his father's hunting grounds without knowing it!

I drank. Not because I wished to sin. But because the sun was too bright outside, and I did not wish to look upon that awful path that led back to Natick.

I was drunk sometimes, but not always. And I repented before my brothers many times at Meeting. Many more times than any man should have to repent of such a sin. James was ashamed for me more than I was ashamed for myself.

"I do not know where he gets it," he said. But he lied, for he often helped me buy some when I could not find it for myself. And so my sin caused my brother to stumble.

And the drink finally made my heart drunk, so that I could hardly see my sin, and I repented less. And the wise words of Solomon came true in my life:

Wine is a mocker, strong drink is raging, and whoever is deceived by it is not wise.

Who has woe? Who has sorrows? Who has contentions? Who has babblings? Who has wounds without cause? Who has redness of eyes? They that tarry long at the wine, they that go seek strong water.

It bites like a serpent and stings like a spider.

Your eyes will behold strange things, and your heart will utter perverse things. Yes, you will be like he that lies down in the midst of the sea or he that lies upon a canoe that is lost upon the great waters.

"They have stricken me," you will say, "and I did not feel it.

"I was sick," you will say, "and I did not know it.

"When shall I awake? I will seek it yet again!"

It was against English law for an Englishman to sell guns to an Indian. For guns were power, and the English did not want to lose the power that was theirs. Guns were death in the hands of a foe, and the English did not want to die. No man wants to die.

But to sell a gun was to make much money, and the English liked money. So the Massachusetts Bay Colony made a new law, not so wise as their first one but to better profit for their pocketbooks and their storage houses.

They determined to sell guns to any Indian or any tribe that was not hostile toward the Bay or toward any of the English of

New England. Many Indians came with their wampum and their skins and their various goods to declare their love of the English and to buy a gun.

Thus I bought a musket, as did many of my brothers among the Praying Indians. And we set our thunder loose in the woods. My, how the beasts fell! But still I slung my bow, for my gun was yet a stranger in my arms.

Then Connecticut changed its laws as well, and Plymouth also, for all the Indians who wanted guns had been walking to Massachusetts!

And so the colonies counted their coins. And so the country was armed—King Philip, too.

I was drunk. *If only my old father could see me now! The Rain From God would fall and beat me for my foolishness!*

What matter? Nothing matters.

I walked to see a woman that I knew. Esther Talltrees. She was shorter than my chin, but pretty. Not like my Elizabeth! None like my Elizabeth. Still, she liked me. And I was lonely.

I shared my drink with her. We lay in the woods.

"Job! Job! You old sinner, you! Where is your head?"

Upon a canoe in the storm at sea.

"Job! Job! You old fool, you! Where is your heart?"

Lost. Lost in the darkness of my sin.

"Call upon the Lord while He may be found! You are not so lost that He cannot see you. Even in darkness."

Esther Talltrees was pregnant, and I was the man.

We were whipped through Hassanamasitt at the tail end of a cart.

But it made me see my sin. And I cast aside the bottle—the Lord Jesus helped me to! And I bowed with tears at Meeting and called upon my brothers to have mercy upon me.

And Eliot came to see me much, Assoko twice too, and their love for me was tender.

And I scratched a small house of my own upon paper, and my brothers helped me raise it.

And I married Esther Talltrees.

And I made her a rocking chair.

And on March 10, 1667, in the Moon Of The Melting, in the forty-fifth year of my life, my new wife gave birth to a daughter we named Joy.

And I looked to the sun once more, though it hurt my eyes much, and I squinted through tears.

Katanaquat my father. Was he alive or did his spirit claw the clouds of winter and howl in the storms of summer? He was alive, said many, but the old dog still ran fast. And none could keep his tracks!

Silvermoon my mother was an old bent squaw, but to look in her eyes was to peer at the stars eternal, shining without sleeping in the night.

Nopatin my grandfather slept in his grave by the Pocatuck. Would I ever see his face again? Could the Great God have mercy on a bloody warrior who never turned his heart toward Heaven?

Winaponk my brother was a warrior and a brave, the husband of two wives and the father of eight children. His arrows were straight and he shot them true.

"Do you remember this?" he asked once, pulling an old shaft from his quiver.

"It looks like one of mine," I said, "Though I don't use those markings anymore."

"It is yours," he said, "I have it with me always."

Quanatik and Metauhock my sisters had wigwams full of children. Grandchildren, too!

Canonchet my friend was now a sachem of the Narragansett. He could now consider the things of God as he once had promised. He could now counsel his people to look to Christ Jesus. But he did not counsel them so, and none of them looked. None of them prayed.

Among the Nipmuc and the Massachusetts, there were more Praying Towns each year, and perhaps a thousand Indians now prayed. The Son rose higher over this New England, and my own eyes grew strong again upon the path of God.

I loved my wife, though never with the same heart as Elizabeth my lost. Esther was grumpy often, and it took me pains to cheer her. Her faith was not as Elizabeth's had been, nor her eye for the beauty of the world God has made. She didn't laugh much, and life was hard for both of us. Still, I loved her, for this was the commandment of God: *Husbands, love your wives, as Christ loved the Church and gave Himself up for her, that He might make her holy and cleanse her with the washing of water by His Word.* And sometimes we were happy.

A son was born, John, in the summer of my forty-sixth year. And another, Jacob, in the summer following. The children were a light to my eyes like none other.

Then in the year of our Lord 1670, on a cold night in November, a third son was born. And his name was Ezekiel, but he would never speak his name, for he died before the dawn. And Esther took ill.

I prayed. I asked the Good God to have mercy on my Esther Talltrees. But I really wanted mercy more for me, for how can a man stand under such sorrow? A physician came to my house. Gookin came too, and many friends. They sat with me long by the fire.

Then they carried Esther—though it was cold they said they must, for otherwise there was no hope—to an ancient and skilled woman at Woburn named Goodwife Brooks, and the mother of my children grew stronger under Goodwife's care.

But her strength was only as the sun that finds a crack in the clouds of the storm. And in very few days I was left with the children alone.

I could not cry. Perhaps all my tears had been lent to Elizabeth. Somewhere in Heaven they filled many bowls.

Chapter Seventeen

Sassamon's Song

"**I** am going home," said Sassamon as we walked beside the Charles.

"Where is home?" I asked, for the preacher moved his wigwam more than any man I knew.

The sky was grey and the day was damp and cool. The birds were fewer in the trees, for God had warned them that cold nights were coming. Naked arms of elm and oak stretched bony fingers upward toward the muted light of dawn. A great arrowhead of squawking geese flew swiftly south above the shivering boughs. I pulled my hat close down around my ears.

"Where is home?" echoed Sassamon, throwing the question sadly to the winds that tossed his hair about his shoulders. "Home is somewhere I have never been," he said at last.

We took a less-beaten path into the woods and away from the river. A large black bear stood up amid the yellow ferns and stared for one long moment as we stopped to pay it our respects. With an offended blink of its wondering eyes, it dropped to all fours and ambled off into the rocks.

"Go home, big black," said Sassamon.

Squirrels chased dim shadows up the ladders of great maples. A lonesome turkey fled, embarrassed, as we crossed a small clearing where lightning had slain an ancient chestnut. A confused and fallen tangle of thin brown thorny vines threatened to block our way. We made our own path now.

"I am going to Montaup," explained the Wampanoag.

"Philip," I said, "Metacomet."

"The king calls," said Sassamon, "but he does not know that it is the King of Heaven who lays this call upon his heart. In fact, he does not know the King of Heaven at all. And that is why I go."

"What does Philip want?" I asked.

"Justice," sighed the Wampanoag, "but I cannot give him that. He wants an Indian with an English tongue and an English mind to help him in his councils with Plymouth. He needs an interpreter, a counselor, a secretary to put his words on paper so that the governor of Plymouth doesn't think him a dirty, brutish savage who picks his teeth with men's bones!"

"Does Philip wish to hear the Gospel?" I asked.

"By the Footstool Of God, no!" swore the Wampanoag. "He would rather hear his own death-rattle. Which is why I must sit in his wigwam and write him his letters. For the man is as bound for Hell as any man I know. For after all, he is in fact a dirty, brutish savage. He has never liked soap."

"I did not like it either, at first," I said.

"The moon is red at night," said Sassamon, his mood a strange and distant thing.

"There is a fence just beyond Swansea," continued the preacher, "at the neck of Montaup. The English put it up at Metacomet's request, for the cows and the pigs of the English wandered like lost children in the Wampanoag fields, knocking down the corn, trampling the squash. The fence will keep the dumb beasts out of Philip's garden.

"But as you stand upon the God-blessed hill at Montaup, or Mount Hope as the English call it," said Sassamon, a troubled light upon his dark brow, "if you are an Indian, a Wampanoag—if ever once you were an Indian!—and you look at that fence from the throne of Montaup, it changes, it grows, it moves before your eyes. It is not a fence—it is a wall! And though the English is allowed—in his own simple arrogance—to cross it, the Wampanoag is not."

"It is just a fence," I said absently, troubled by the fire in Sassamon's eyes. "And surely Philip may cross it."

"It is a wall!" shot the Wampanoag. And we walked on in silence.

"I am a shadow," said Sassamon, "which walks in shadows. The light of a darker, simpler day lies behind me. It is darkness eternal, ignorant and foolish, but there is comfort in its dark rays. Even the Devil remembers Heaven.

"I am man without clothes," he continued, "for I don't know what to wear when I wander in these shadows. Who might see me? Who might wonder if my paint means peace or war, my hair means friend or foe? And so I go naked, and let all men clothe me as they will. God sees the heart. God sees the soul. It is a lonely world.

"And why cannot men see that all men are only men! Williams sees! Though he still combs his hair as the English, he sees. But who else?

"Eliot? Yes, Eliot sees. At least he strains his eyes to see. He walks the path with both eyes open. His heart sees.

"Gookin? He carries an English gun. And he will use it. But he loves. He loves. God is love, Jacob—Job—Kattenenit! God is love. Gookin sees, but he carries an English gun.

"Waban? Waban forgets. He spits on his fathers. Don't throw me his mud about 'pride is in the hair'! My hair is long because God makes it grow. Waban's hair is short because he loves the English more than he loves the grace of God! There's more pride upon that man's head than hair upon mine! Do I judge him? Do I misread the Scriptures? God forgive me! But no one walks to Heaven just because his boots are English!

"And you, my friend! Do you see? Not at all. Your eyes are closed. But your heart is good. You stumble through the forest like a child chasing after its father. Follow the Father, Kattenanit! He will never lead you wrong.

"Ah, what strange beasts we are! What a strange woods we walk in!"

We had wandered into a stand of great spruce. It was warmer there, for the spruce kept their coats on all the year round. It was darker, too.

"Shadows," Sassamon said.

"When do you walk to Montaup?" I asked, afraid of the shadows.

"Philip is angry," said the Wampanoag. "I hope to stroke his shoulders, to whisper peace in his ears. But his is a full cup. I must go soon."

"What angers the sachem?" I asked, afraid of the answer.

"Would you like to be called to court for entertaining friends?" queried the preacher. "Would you like to be told you are a naughty boy for dancing in your own kitchen? Would you like to be mocked behind your back because your clothes are out of style?"

"I do not know your riddles," I said impatiently. The wind whistled mournfully above our heads.

"Plymouth doesn't like that the fires burn late upon the hill at Montaup, that Indians come in great canoes, that men dance, that kings wear rings in their ears and feathers in their hair and paint their faces like women," said Sassamon. "Plymouth doesn't like a king who can't read English or stamp his grand seal in wax. Plymouth wants a king who sits on gilded satin pillows—far away! And Plymouth doesn't want to see heathen smoke rising from Mount Hope. It reminds them too much of Hell!

"They forget. Like Waban, they forget. Their fathers are dead and they forget.

"Bradford, Winslow, even Standish—they were good men, humbled men. Men who knew that they were saplings at the edge of a terrible tall forest. They feared Massasoit then. Massasoit feared them. But God took that fear and made it love. My people—the people of Massasoit—they speak of it still: the friendship, the love, the First Feast at harvest—three days they ate together, laughed together, played together. Played together! We speak of it still. The English have forgotten.

"It was fine for the first English fathers, when the English were starving, to invite the Indian to bring a bit of corn from their hard-hoed gardens to lay upon the wooden tables of Plymouth. It was fine, when the English were lost, to ask an Indian to show them the way home. It was fine, when the beaver were plenty, to pay the Indian to go kill every flat-tailed one of them that he could find. It was fine, when the forest went on forever, to speak of sharing the 'King's Land' with the wandering savage.

"But now the trees are fallen along the eastern shore of the Great Salt Sea, and the children of Bradford and Winslow look lustfully to the last, lone hill of Massasoit where naked, painted half-men huddle around a dying fire.

"And as the poor children of Massasoit look down upon the world that was once theirs, they see English houses and English horses and English roads and English fields, and English smoke rising from English towns where English ships sit at English harbors with their wide white sails blowing in the wind like strange clouds that have blown from another world beyond the skies. And do you know?—they do not hate these things! But these things are like another man's goods upon their beds. What do you do when you are tired and you wish to sleep?"

The grove grew light as we approached a clearing.

"There is a wall at the foot of Montaup. Philip is angry," said Sassamon.

We came out of the spruce at a small pond filled with cattails.

"Look at this water," said Sassamon, walking to the edge of the brown-bristled marsh. "Can a man drink at it? Can he swim? Does he dare to walk into it? No, for God set this pond here for another reason. This is the home of the snake and the frog, the snapping turtle, and the long-leg heron.

"But man will make this mirk his own. He will cut the tail from the cat, pull the reed from the mud, take the frog and the turtle home for soup and meat, and chase the serpent. And should he not? For he is Adam, and the earth is his.

"But the children of Massasoit are the children of Adam too. Williams sees, Eliot and Gookin—but who will hear them that the Indian is no beast? And that the earth is no less Metacomet's than it is the English King's!"

I pulled a tail from the mud and picked at its snowy seeds. They drifted past our faces and blew into the woods.

"Do you suppose that God would prefer to live in an English house instead of a wigwam?" Sassamon asked.

"I do not know," I said, though I thought He might prefer the house.

"Jesus had nowhere to lay His head!" declared the preacher, as we circled round the pond, pushing a trail through the high, dry grasses.

"Will there be war?" I asked.

"Let us not talk of war," said the weary Wampanoag. "Let us talk of peace and the Prince of Peace. Let us talk of all that God is doing instead of what men suppose they should be doing in His Name."

Some winter ducks rose from the marsh as we walked, scolding us loudly, scattering wildly.

"A preacher named Fitch brings the Word to the Mohegan," Sassamon declared, his eyes brightening. "At first Uncas let him wander, let him speak, let him pass out blankets and fruit and nuts among his people. I was there. I wondered that the mad dog had such patience for the presence of an English preacher in his midst. Surely the powwows counseled against it. Then I saw the sachem gather many of those blankets for himself. And he sent men with baskets to take half the fruit and half the nuts. He could stand a bit of preaching if it put blankets on his bed and food in his stomach!"

"Eliot too has walked along the river of Mohegan, on the Massachussetts side," I said. "The Word has been sown, and so another Praying Town has grown there."

"Wabquissit," said Sassamon knowingly, "They grow much corn there—as well as Christians—for the soil is very rich."

We entered the forest anew while the day grew lighter as the grey gloom above us retreated before the battering rays of the autumn sun. Soon there would be blue, I thought, and all would be well.

"How are your children?" asked the Wampanoag.

"They are well," I said gladly, squinting as the sun came suddenly through the trees. "Joy is as her name, full of sunlight and smiles; she is seven years now. John is a bullock, happy and always running; he is six. The youngest, Jacob, is five and full of fun—but he sits at times and stares forever into the fullness of a world that is his own." I laughed. "They are life itself to me." The sun fell back again behind grey clouds. "Why have you never married?" I suddenly asked of the shadow who walks as a man.

"How could I beg another to walk naked with me in the woods?" he answered. A dark shadow. A strange beast.

"I might not marry again," I said to the bare trees and the fallen leaves. "The children have many mothers to watch them at Town. They love the house and wife of James. They are safe within the walls."

"There are no walls that keep men safe," said the shadow with the voice of the autumn wind. "No walls. No laws. No towns. No preachers. No bows. No shields. No guns. Only God. And only so long as He thinks our safety suits His ways and purposes.

"He works all things together for the good of those who love Him, but His good is not to be nailed up in boxes or written down in covenants. His good is wild like Pussough and Noonatch. It runs where it will at His bidding. There are no walls that keep men safe."

"You trouble me with riddles!" I cried. "You break the windows of my faith and let in the birds of doubt! What good are your words?"

"Heaven alone has windows that won't break, Kattenanit," said the preacher.

"But Heaven is not yet!" I argued, "and so God gives His Word and His Church and His Laws and His Towns."

"His Word is the whisper of His own tongue," said Sassamon, bending his dark eyes into mine, "and so it is true—always true—for God cannot lie.

"His Church is the fruit of His Word, alive with the seed that cannot die. His Church is flesh and spirit, you and me! It is not wood or paper or stone. It is not covenants or creeds.

"And His Laws! They are righteous and holy. But they are not living and they cannot give life. Oh, Kattenanit!—can you see the wind? Do you know where it comes from or where it goes? You cannot follow it. You cannot hold its softness in your hands. Yet it is hard enough to lay this forest to the earth in its wrath!

"The Spirit of God is like the wind. He blows and no man can hold Him. But we can open our mouths and breathe Him into our souls. Open our hearts and let Him do whatever He wills to do. Let Him lay us to the earth if He will! But we cannot hold Him in our hands."

"Riddles! Dark riddles!" I moaned. "Worse than the riddles of Williams. Let me be!"

"Kattenanit," pleaded the preacher, "we are Indians who pray. We can pray right here beneath these naked oaks, and God will hear us, will He not? Surely He will, for He pushed these oaks into the earth Himself. This is His garden. He walks here with us. He cannot do otherwise.

"And He does not dwell in houses made by man. His Word tells us this. He cannot lie. And where then does He dwell? You know where He dwells! In hearts that say, Yes! to His love. In souls that kiss the Son. No house will keep us safe. No Town. No Meeting. No guns. Only Christ. *The warrior may be armed for the battle, but safety is from the Lord."*

"Safety is from the Lord," I echoed weakly.

"When I was child and a servant in the house of Hennicut at Plymouth," said John Sassamon quietly, "a small bird had found its way into the house somehow. I was alone, and I tried to catch it so that it might go free. But it flew about the house in such terror that it knocked itself into all sorts of things. At last it was so tired that it sat upon the floor and merely shook. I felt so bad for the little creature.

" 'You will be safe in my hands, little brother,' I said to the bird as I caught it in my palms. For a moment I could feel it shaking for weariness and fear, and then at last it calmed.

"Holding it gently, I opened the door and took it outside. But when I spread my hands to let it fly, it fell to the ground. Dead. It had died of fear in my hands.

"Had I opened my door first to let the little thing find its own way out, instead of chasing it around to save it myself, it would have flown out at last into the winds of God. Alive. Free. Rising toward Heaven on the wings that God gave it.

"The hands of man, dear Kattenanit, no matter how loving, are not the hands of God. They will kill you if you fear them. Fear God alone."

"I do not fear your hand," I said.

"That is because it rests in yours as we walk this path together. But if it threatened you, you would fear it. And if it promised to keep you safe, you would trust it.

"Walk in love with your brothers who pray. But fear God alone. Trust God alone."

"You walk too much alone," I said.

A chickadee whistled in the thicket. A cardinal sang. The one was early, I thought, the other late.

"I have a song!" declared Sassamon, his countenance lightening, "Though it is all in English. Would you listen to it?"

"I will listen," I said.

The Indian preacher changed his step to take on the show of the warrior who stands to tell tales at the campfire. His face grew solemn, and his back went straight. His chest came out a bit—that strong chest covered with English wool, deep red wool, which covered that strong heart which beat with the strong love of God—and his chin was lifted so that his eyes could take in the world a bit higher. He pulled his long locks absently behind his ears and said, "I will speak it as a poem, for it does not have a tune yet. I have no ear for tunes:

The world doth turn, the English say, as a wheel upon a cart.
And God sits on the wagon and He sees each human heart."

"That is it?" I asked, for the song I had once written for Elizabeth was much longer, and had a tune besides.

"If you sing it, of course, solemnly and with a tune that fits it, it will grow in length," said Sassamon, coming down to his normal height and starting off again upon our walk.

"It is a riddle?" I offered, not knowing quite what to say of it.

"The world turns," said the preacher, serious once more, "like the wheel of a cart. And the wheel of a cart only turns when the cart is going somewhere. From Boston to Dedham, from Concord to Natick.

"God made this world to go somewhere—not somewhere like from one town to another, or from my tent to your tent—but somewhere from darkness to light. From bad to good. From sin to righteousness. From Satan to God. From earth to Heaven.

"Life has purpose beyond what we can lay up in our tents for ourselves and our children. There is more. There is Heaven—in our hearts first by the grace of Christ, and then evermore beyond our dying. And we must be moving there or we are stuck in the mire. Sinking. Dying. Dead in our sins. Destined for darkness and Hell.

"God sits upon the wagon, turning His horse where He will, watching the sons of Adam as their faces go down in the mud and come up again to blink at the clear sky. He calls to our hearts. He cries for our hearts. He sends His Son to die for our hearts. And He sees our hearts as they open or close their eyes to the Son. He sees what none other can see. And what He sees is all that matters. That is the riddle. That is the song."

"It is very good," I said.

"Of lesser length than some of the poems of Williams, " said the Indian who went to Harvard, "but deeper. Yet I will not judge! *Let another praise thee and not thine own lips.* What do I know? And I have no ear for a tune."

Part Three

THE
BLOOD

"The Lord mercifully
cleanse the land from blood,
and make the blood
of His son Jesus
more precious in all our eyes."

—Roger Williams

Chapter Eighteen

A Solitary Sound

Home. Safe. Free. Dancing like a grasshopper within the Garden Of God. Evermore alive. Nevermore alone.

"Beneath the ice at Assawomset Pond?"

"Drowned."

"No, no! Oh Great God, no! This cannot be!"

"It is a dream—an awful dream! Wake us, wake us, Great God!"

"Some say the spirits broke the ice beneath him."

"Liars! For the gods could never hurt him!"

"Some say a great fish pulled him in."

"No, for he was mighty!"

"Was it murder? Was it theft?"

"It could not have been, for I heard that his coat and his gun were upon the shore. Many fish, too."

"Drowned, drowned! At Assawomset Pond!"

"And who found him?"

"Two men of the Nipmuc of Nanosack pulled him out. One said he saw him go in."

"He saw him fall? He heard him cry out?"

"He saw him killed!"

"Killed!"

"But his gun . . . his hat . . . his fish."

"To make it appear as no murder at all."

"Who has done this?"

"They must pay!"

"Blood for blood!"

"They came to sit by him in peace, said the one who saw. They smoked by him and spoke to him and laughed with him, said the one who saw for he watched from the hill where he was hiding in hunting. They waited until he had a fish upon his hook, said the one who saw, and then they fell upon him, hit him much, took his head in their hands and twisted it violently until he died."

"I will kill them!"

"Get my gun!"

"Vengeance is not ours, brothers!"

"Who has done this?"

"Three men."

"English men?"

"Indian men. Wicked men. Philip's men."

"Why? For they are his people!"

"*Nipwi mâw!* He is gone!"

"Our brother!"

"*Mauchúhom!* The dead man!"

"Our love!"

"*Michemashâwi!* He is gone forever!"

"Sassamon, Sassamon! Light Of The Dark Wood! Fire In The Black Night! Song Of The One God! Walker With The Word!"

Dead. Gone. Killed. Beneath the ice at Assawomset.

Assawomset is in Plymouth country. The murder was done on English lands. The killers would be tried by English law. Their names were given by the one who said he saw, and three men of the Wampanoag were led to Plymouth, pled innocent, were tried by a jury of English and Indians, found guilty, and were hung by the neck until dead. One at last confessed when the rope was over his head. May God have mercy on his soul.

Philip was angry. His cup was full.

In Boston, a great gun that none could see was fired in the air, bullets whistled overhead, phantom armies marched through the woods to the beat of a ghostly drum.

In Plymouth, invisible horses raced to and fro in the streets, whinnying, snorting. Men arose from their sleep to see what

was the matter, their eyes could see nothing. Children cried—
their mothers held them close.

The moon was red at night.

"I have warned the English once—a month ago now. I have
told Boston twice," mourned Waban. "But they do not believe
it can be so.

"Our cousins among the Wampanoag say it is so, I tell them.
But the English think it is just women's fables!

" 'He is not strong enough to war against us,' they say. 'But
then why did he kill Sassamon?' I ask. For we know that Sassamon went to the governor at Plymouth to tell them the very
same thing: 'Philip makes ready for war!' "

The broad-shouldered, short-haired Ruler Of Fifty paced about
my kitchen as if he were an anxious dog upon a staked leash.

"He followed the Wind into the dark cave of the sleeping
hungry wolf," I said grimly of Sassamon the Lonely. "The wolf
woke, his hunger gnawed, he growled of his schemes for the
midnight hunt and the blood of the prey. And when Sassamon
heard the plans of the wolf, our sometime Nipmuc had to
choose whose children should live and whose should die. He
went to Winslow. Then he went fishing. Does not God see all?
The wheel turns and our faces are in the mud."

"Boston scoffs! Plymouth sleeps! Philip sends wampum and
runners to gather an army from among the Indians of New England! And Sassamon's riddles are now yours!" cried the sagamore.

"I would rather his faith," I said.

"We must buy more powder," said Printer James, "and further fortify the Towns. If Philip comes, we can be ready."

"We are too few!" cried Waban. "We are not used to war, for
God has called us to peace. Our children hardly know how to
pull the bow, for God has filled our rivers with fish and our gardens have fed us too well. I haven't shot a man in twenty years!"

"Perhaps God will fight," I said. "Perhaps He will send fire
from Heaven. Perhaps he will burn Montaup as He burned
the hill at Mystic when he punished the Pequot."

"Yes!" cried Job Nesutan. "Or perhaps He will send an angel
of death into the camp of Philip and the Wampanoag will all
die in the night!"

"The Dying! Remember what our fathers told us of the Great Dying?" I said. "It killed so many thousands. And the English said that it was God who sent the Dying to clear the forest for the coming of the great ships and the English people. Perhaps God will send the Dying upon the Wampanoag. Can we pray that it will be so?"

"No," said Monequassin, "we cannot pray for such things. Do you not recall that Jesus rebuked his friends when they wanted to call down fire upon the towns that scoffed at the Word? Do you not know that our Lord commands that we love our enemies and bless them?"

"Surely we cannot kneel in our streets praying for Philip while his Wampanoag drag our women off to their wigwams!" cried James. "Surely we cannot open our doors to Philip and say, 'Come in, neighbor, and eat'! For he would start a fire with the logs of our own houses and cook and eat our children upon them!"

"God is our Fortress," said Monequassin. "He is our Strong Shield. We can trust in Him and be safe."

"Safe?" I asked.

Fires burned high at Montaup in the Moon Of The New Green. Many canoes crossed the waters to spit armed warriors upon great Metacomet's shores. Warriors drank late and danced long and laughed loud atop the torch-lit mountain. Plymouth woke with the noise, and begged God to quiet the heathen.

Men walked from Rhode Island to counsel peace. But Philip was painted for war. His heart was set. "When the English first came to this country," said the Wampanoag warrior to the peddlers of peace, "they were only poor children, forlorn, distressed, and lost beneath the great trees.

"My father opened his arms to serve them, to feed them, to hold them as the father holds his ailing child to his breast.

"They did not die but grew strong, like children who have much to eat, children who have much medicine in their souls and many strong dreams yet to dream.

"The wise men and the powwows of the Wampanoag feared these strong children. 'They will soon be men,' they counseled, 'and they will bind us to their laws and take away our lands.

We must kill them while they are small, or they will rule us when they are big.'

"But my father was also the father to the English. He loved them. He remained their friend.

"But who was right, my father or the powwows? For my father is gone and his trees have fallen, while the English grow mighty and many and tall. They stand over us and wag their heads. They take our guns. They make us walk paths that are not ours, and they punish us when we run in the woods as our fathers once did.

"Their cows eat my corn, and do they pay me? No, they put up a fence instead. To keep the cows out or to keep the Indian in? And if my cows eat their corn, they call me to court. Then I must sell another hill, another pond, another stand of trees to pay for the corn and the damage to their fields.

"Tree by tree I lose the country of Massasoit. Rock by rock I give up what has always been my father's but can never be my children's. I stand now on Montaup, and it is still mine. I will not stand to see the English boot upon this neck.

"I have sworn not to live until I have no country."

Swansea lay closest to Mount Hope of all the English towns. Philip had many friends among the English there. He warned them that they ought to leave their houses and go elsewhere, for his warriors were hot for battle and he might not be able to hold them much longer around the fires of Montaup. He might not desire to hold them much longer. Philip was angry. His cup was full.

"The spirits tell us that the victory is ours," said the Wampanoag powwows, "if the English fire first."

On Sabbath Day, June 20, 1675, while most of the English of Swansea prayed at Meeting, a musket barked in the distance, only once.

Was someone hunting on a Sunday?

Did someone drop or kick a weapon and it discharged by itself? Or was it war?

Awaun necáwni aum píasha? Who shot first?

On Montaup, Philip wept.

Chapter Nineteen

Chickaúta Wêtu
(House On Fire)

Péskcunck. A gun.
Mechimúash. Load it.
"Blessed be the Lord my Strength, who teaches my hands to
war and my fingers to fight."
Machíppog. A quiver.
Caúquatash. Arrows.
"Bow the heavens, O Lord, and come down. Cast forth light-
ning and scatter them. Shoot out your arrows and destroy them."
Quaquawtatatteâug matwaûog. They train for war.
Mecauntítea. Let us fight.
"To every thing there is a season and a time to every pur-
pose under heaven: a time to be born and a time to die . . . a
time to get and a time to lose . . . a time to love . . . and a
time to war . . ."
Jûhettítea. Let us fight.

On the eve of Thursday June 24, 1675, after an anxious day
of fasting and prayer, the people of Swansea walked home
from Meeting. The fragile, hopeful silence of their fearful
meditations was suddenly shattered when bushes exploded
with the loud roar of guns. Women and children were
wounded, one man died, and the English fled to lock themselves in at four stronghouses in their sad, beleaguered town.

English horsemen thundered to Plymouth to cry for help. The plea galloped north to Duxbury, Braintree, and Boston. A messenger ran to Natick to ask for Praying Indian guides to lead English soldiers onto Montaup. Waban sent couriers to Hassanamasitt. Houses burned in Swansea.

"I will go," said Printer James.

"And I, too," said Thomas his brother.

"I have made paint," said Zachary Abram Pohoput. And the three of them raced to Boston where horses carried them south to Taunton and south more to Swansea where Captain Prentice gave them guns and sent them into the woods to scout against the enemy.

"You must not stand so tall in the forest," said James to the English, "for your faces are targets as white as the sun!"

But the English thought his words small and stood themselves tall in their pride and their purpose. They fell all the harder when the darts and the bullets of Metacomet flew from behind the black rock and from within the thorny thicket.

"We must not walk together as though we were walking to Meeting," warned Thomas to the soldiers of the Colonies. "For then we are as easy to shoot as an English house!"

But the English knew how to war, they said, and there was safety in numbers. They fell all the more before the sudden thunder of Philip's guns and the deadly whisper of his feathered shafts. The Wampanoag warriors painted themselves like the shadows of the forest and clothed themselves in shirts of green boughs. They rose against the English in ambush and then melted into the dark wood like Pussough who leaps upon her prey and then slinks away silent to her shadowed lair.

"Your shoes squawk like birds," scolded James as he led the English on the darkened path. "Yet they are not birds—as any Indian ear will tell! Take them off! Here are my moccasins instead." He carried an English man's shoes at his back and went barefoot himself.

"Your trousers rustle like leaves as you walk!" said Thomas to another man whose dry, leather breeches announced themselves with whistling whoops at every step. "But they are not leaves and we are not the wind—as any Indian ear can tell!

Take them off, or wet them at our next crossing of water!" The Englishman waded to his waist in the Kickemuit, and his trousers ceased their prattle.

"We must walk in silence as the sunlight walks," counseled Zachary Abram Pohoput, "for our wagging tongues will either call death upon our heads or cause the foe to flee. The trees have ears," he cautioned. "So close your lips, quiet your hearts, open your eyes—and pray."

In the first days of July, 1675, Major Daniel Gookin—given command of a portion of the English army—came to my house at Hassanamasitt. He carried a gun.

"Job, my brother," said Daniel my friend, "I pray that the days will soon come when we sit once again at this table to laugh and to smoke. When we look back upon this storm of war and thank our Faithful God for His watchcare and His mercy. When the only fires that burn within our towns are those that burn within our hearths to warm our families and our neighbors.

"But today we must arm our hands for battle. We must run in the woods against the wolf. We must track him to his very lair and flush him out. For he rages and howls and tears and kills, and none of us is safe while he lives."

The summer sun fell strangely uninvited through my windows. It smiled upon my floor, upon my mats. But the smile hid a mocking heart that burned hot against a hardhearted ancient people and the contrary children of King Charles the Second from over the Great Salt Sea. Keesuckquand had always been a bright, deceitful god.

"I have no heart for blood," I said.

My precious Joy laid bread and cider on our boards. Nine summers she was mine now, and oh! she was a joy indeed. But her own warm smile hid sorrow that was borrowed from my cup of mourning. She climbed the ladder to the loft and sang quietly upon her bed. I would have raised a ladder to Heaven for her if I could!

"I am asking for one-third of our able Praying Indians to join me in the fight," said Gookin. "I have almost fifty already. We will meet with our English brothers near Sowams. If we strike Philip now, we may trap the wolf upon his mountain, set a fence of flesh about him, and drive him either to surrender . . . or to death.

"But we must not tarry!" said the major and his gun.

"I have no heart for blood," I said.

Young Jacob and John sat together upon our rocking chair and made it move. It was their great friend Horse, and they rode it hard over the wide roads of their imagination.

"The Quannapohits are with me," said Gookin. "Job Nesutan, too. And others of your brothers and mine. We will travel to Taunton first, with a good troop of horse, and join with Captain Johnson. Johnson will take the men from there and deliver them to Major Savage, commander of the English army camped at the foot of Mount Hope. Savage will order the whole affair. He is a good soldier and a man who fears God. By God's mercy, we are safe with Savage."

"Safe?" I asked.

Keesuckquand grinned. My soul squirmed against his brilliant grimace. Jacob pushed John from Horse.

"I have no heart for blood, Daniel," I said.

"Pray for us, Job," said the good major with the English gun.

"I will pray for the peace of Jerusalem," I said. "Night and day."

"Why do we leave our house, Father?" asked my little Joy, as we loaded some few goods upon a wagon bound for the Praying Town of Okkokonimesit.

"We will return when God has stilled the present storm," I said.

Okkokonimesit was at English Marlborough, further from Philip, closer to Natick and closer to Boston. Shielded to the northwest by English Lancaster and to the northeast by English Sudbury, it was a town that could be held against the foe. It was "safe."

"Can we take Horse?" asked John, pointing back into the house at the lonely chair. "And who will feed it if we leave it?" pleaded Jacob.

"It eats little," I assured them. "And you have nearly ridden it to death! It will no doubt enjoy a bit of rest and quiet. And when we return, it will be strong and refreshed and ready to carry you on new and long adventures."

"Goodbye, Horse!" cried the little fellows as we closed and locked the door.

"Goodbye, house!" shouted my Joy as we walked behind the wagon on the road out of Town.

The wolf fled his den, tumbled down his mountain, and ran with his pack beside the Chauchacuit. The hunters of Savage followed, but many were lost in the woods. Some battle was held, and good men died with the bad. The blood of both ran red upon the forest floor.

Job Nesutan lay in the ferns with his back against the chestnut—a Wampanoag bullet in his breast—and whispered his last prayers. Whether his words were English or Indian I do not know. But God heard him. God called him. God took his soul to the Safe Fort and the House Of Peace. There he sings the Word of God in tongues of men and angels. I will listen for him when my own feet walk that last path.

Thomas Quannapohit shot his own hand to pieces. He was on his horse, his gun upon its butt upon the ground. He leaned upon the muzzle of the musket with his left hand. The weather was hot. The horse was troubled by flies. It pawed the gun. The gun was charged—the cock half-turned already, foolish Thomas!—and it went off with a roar. The hand has since healed, and the man is since wiser in the use of such terrible tools.

"Some of the English laughed when Thomas shot himself!" James told me. "Others said the Praying Indians were cowards who hid behind trees in the battle. They say that we whooped to warn our foes, that we fired over the heads of our enemies, that we were all one with Philip!

"It is hard to make myself fight with men who hate us when they ought to love us! Are we not brothers? But I did not skulk. I did not shoot high. And I ran like the wind to chase the foe! I saw Philip, and he saw that I saw him. Yet he did not move, but stood still as the trees that rose about him. He glared at me. I fired at him twice and missed—somehow, I missed—

though we were close! *Is he a god?* I wondered for a moment.
Then suddenly he was not there, gone into the shadows as
though he were a shadow himself! And Nesutan was beside
me in the battle. He was no coward! His blood sings his own
strong song, God knows!"

The wolf and all his pack—men, women, and children, some
five hundred in all—trotted the tangled trail beyond Rehobah.

The horse of the English followed, with some of the men of
Natick under Captain Henchman, and fifty warriors of the
Mohegan who had come from Uncas to assist the English
against Metacomet. They fell upon the rear of the enemy late
in the morning of August the first—a Sabbath—killing fourteen braves of the Wampanoag. Nimrod Woonashum, a great
captain and counselor to Philip, was among the slain. And
though the wolf now limped, he fled all the faster, leaving
much booty behind him. The Mohegan loaded themselves
with the spoils and let the wolf run.

"We can chase him down still!" said James Quannapohit to
Captain Henchman. "Let the Mohegan lie down with their
feet in Philip's rum! But we shall run like Moosoog! Though
we are not many, Philip is weary. His warriors have spent
much shot. He is laden with old men, tired women, and barefoot children. Let us chase him down and take him by the tail!"

But Henchman didn't think it wise to run so fast and so far
with so few. "Captain Mosely has fresh troops from Boston,"
said Henchman. "I will let him run this race for now."

So the wolf still howled, still prowled, still fell upon the English where he could and when he would. Other wolves joined
him: Queen Awashonks of the Sakonnets with her three hundred warriors, Wetamoo the widow of Alexander and her Po-
cassets, the sachems of the Quabaug, and many of our
neighbors among the pagan Nipmuc. Taunton burned. White
men lay scalped upon the narrow, winding path and in the
wide, straight road. The smoldering ashes of Brook field rolled
about the smoky streets with the midsummer wind.

"And what of the Narragansett?" I asked old Roger Williams
as I sat at his old oaken table upon an old chair of hickory and
ash.

"Canonchet has risen to the top of the cup," said the preacher as his strong callused fingers drummed an uneven beat upon the time-scarred tabletop. "He tells me that he will not fight with Philip. Perhaps it is good—for the English at least, if not for the souls of your people—that the Narragansett have not forgiven their foes!

"And Ninigret?" I asked.

"The sachem of the West Niantic says he will fight for no one," said Williams, "though some of his men have already left him to run with Philip. But Ninigret guards his wigwams well. The former town of Nopatin your grandfather has been palisaded. Niantic warriors walk the borders of their lands always. Ninigret will wait out this storm."

"And Katanaquat my father?" I asked at last.

"The old dog has come home, or nearly so," said the English preacher with a sad smile. "He sleeps in a tent at the edge of the city of Canonchet. Alone. He limps to Providence and back. His arm is still strong—stronger than mine—and he'd fight a wildcat if it looked at him sideways!

"Silvermoon your mother is well. Her tent is her own. Winaponk your brother brings me news." The old Englishman sighed sharply and pulled himself up in his chair. "The Lord declares that those who wait on Him will rise up with the wings of an eagle, run and not grow weary, walk and not faint. But the promise was meant for the spirit of a man and not his flesh," he said. With a slight groan, he bent himself beneath the table and came back up with a neatly carved staff in his hands. "This is my third leg," he said, brandishing the oaken cane. "Without it, I can't even walk!"

"I will come again soon to see you, the Lord willing," I said to Roger Williams as I tied on my quiver and pulled on my hat.

"Will you fight?" asked the old peacemaker as he stood at his door to watch me walk.

"I will pray," I promised.

Chapter Twenty

Love Waxed Cold

Indian. We were Indian. Brute beasts and hopelessly heathen sons of the Devil. False in our hearts, bent in our souls, destined for the black pit and the horrid fires of Hell, damned and delivered to darkness forever. Our fathers were Indian, their fathers before them. As the tree is bent, so it grows. And if the fruit is bad, cut it down.

But no one was looking at the fruit!

It didn't matter that we spoke English, read English, wrote English, thought English. That we cut our hair, wore trousers and dresses, went to school, planted orchards, hoed our gardens, built bridges and houses, worked with our hands, loved our neighbor, kept the Sabbath.

It didn't matter that we swore allegiance to the laws of the English, the laws of God's Word, the laws of our Towns. That we went to Meeting, gathered at Church, read our Bibles, tithed our earnings, prayed to God.

Few heard our hearts that we loved the English. Few could trust that we promised to scout for them, fight for them, die for them, arm our families, and make our Towns a wall and a fortress of defense against the common enemy.

We were Indian.

Our fathers were Indian.

Once an Indian, always an Indian.

The enemy was Indian.

We were Indian.

We were the enemy.

"I once thought that Eliot was a god," said James, "but I know now that he is a man like me. He is my brother, he loves me, and I thank God for him. But if he were a god, then Captain Mosely would surely be a devil."

Ruth Quannapohit clucked her tongue at her husband's words. "Printer James!" she scolded, "The ink of God's Word once stained your fingers! So how can you speak of the English Captain in such a way? Didn't Jesus warn us of the danger of Hellfire if we curse our brother?"

James shot his wife a sharp glance, but his eyes softened when he saw her distress.

"Darling Missus Printer James," he said, pulling her to him. "Jesus said that we should not be angry with our brother without cause. But I have cause, and plenty! And I judge righteous judgment. I do not sin!

"Nor is Mosely a brother as Eliot and Gookin. That is why I said what I said. For Eliot loves us, but Mosely hates us. The Devil is in the man, or I don't know the Devil!"

"You are my husband," said Ruth, "and you may speak as you will. I only fear for your soul if you speak as you should not!" She turned from her man to our supper which was cooking in the pot within the fire.

"They could not have done the murder," I said, "no matter what Mosely says. For they are not murderers. They are Christians!"

"Mosely sees dark skin and says 'murderer,' " said James. "He sees the blood of Noonatch upon their shirts and spent guns in their hands and he says, 'English blood and stolen weapons!' "

"Gookin is at Boston with them," I said. "He will argue for them at court. They were not even near Lancaster when the murders were done!"

"Oh, but they were!" declared the Printer. "For Noonatch took them a merry chase through the woods!"

"Their hunt was on Saturday, and the murders were done on the Sabbath!" I cried. "They were here—with us—at Meeting, praying and singing and hearing the sermon, all the Sabbath Day!" I cried.

"We must pray much and talk less," said Missus Printer James from her station at the supper pot.

"I am sorry, my brothers," said Daniel Gookin from the pulpit of our Meetinghouse, "but God is covering the eyes of the English to your love. They do not see Christ among you or within you. Their fear and their anger have quenched their compassion. Their reason is darkened. Their love waxes cold. Too many have wakened from their sleep to hear the shrill cry of death at dawn. Death from the arrow and the tomahawk. Death from the smoke and the fire. Even death from the hands of Indian neighbors we once thought were peaceable friends.

"I am sorry, my brothers," said the good man who carried a gun, "but God has called us all to suffer. He is not done with this war, to punish us for our sins and to squeeze out blood for His own just purpose. Yet if we suffer for His Name's sake, we shall also reign with Him. If we are persecuted for His Name's sake, our reward shall be great in Heaven."

"What of our brothers in prison at Boston?" we asked.

"They will not hang," said Gookin, "for there is much proof of their innocence, and truth will win it with the jury. But Boston is angry. Even some among the best give ear to the worst. They want blood. Indian blood. Even the blood of an innocent Indian. And they are angry with me for taking your side. They say I am Indian, too."

"You love us!" we cried.

"My life is in danger on the streets of Boston for that love!" said Gookin, "Yet that is a cross I gladly bear. For you are my brothers.

"But I am sorry, my brothers," he continued, soberly and sadly, "for these days are a trial not only to our friends who sit in prison but also to our souls and to all that we have built together over these past thirty years. Yet even if God should knock down these Praying Towns that were built with men's hands, we are not forsaken, for we look for a City eternal and unshakable whose Builder and Maker is God."

"Our Towns will stand!" we declared.

"For we shall trust in the Lord and do good," said Joseph Tuckappawill our preacher. "And as it says in the Psalms, *So shall we dwell in the land, and truly we shall be fed.*"

Gookin wept.

"I am sorry, my brothers," he said, his voice quivering, "but you must move from this place."

"We must move?" we cried loudly, rising as one man from our benches.

"Where do we go?" asked John.

"Why do we go?" asked Jacob.

"When do we go?" asked Joy as she sat at the door of the wigwam, for we had no English house in Okkokonimesit.

"We are going back home," I said.

"To Horse and our house?" cried the boys.

"To Hassanamasitt, Father?" asked Joy.

"Yes," I replied, gathering all three of the little English Indians into my arms. "All of the Praying Indians, no matter where they now live, are going to one of five of our Towns. The English have asked us to do so."

"I am so glad they love us!" cried the children.

But it was not love that moved the governor and his council to herd us into the five Towns. It was fear on top of fear. The first fear was that which ruled in men's hearts and which cried out the lie that every Indian was false and wicked, and that the English were in danger on all sides, even from those Indians which prayed. The second fear was that which the council conceived in regards to our safety, that those who harbored the first fear might rise up against the Praying Indians and slay them. And so to quiet the hearts of the fearful, and also to protect the Indians who prayed, the Christian Indians were ordered to find a home at Natick, Punkapaog, Nashobah, Wamesitt, or Hassanamasitt. We were to set our wigwams close together to better afford our own protection. And once we had done so, we were not to walk more than a mile from our Towns in any direction unless an Englishman walked with us, upon peril of our lives. For if we were found alone in the woods, it was now the law that any English could command us to surrender. And if we did not, it was the law that they could kill us. For if we did not hearken or surrender, were we not enemies indeed?

And this was hard, very hard, for though my Joy could cook our meals once more at the hearth that had long been home, and my boys could ride their Horse to their heart's content, yet I could not walk the woods in search of meat for our table. I could not run to Dedham or Newton or Watertown to cut wood for the English or to trade my chairs for clothes.

And our cattle, our swine, and our crops were ofttimes outside the mile limit, on lands and in fields that we could not reach if the English walked not with us. And so we often walked alone and in fear, and sometimes we were caught, and sometimes our guns were taken and never returned, and sometimes we were led to prison where we sat anxious and hungry and sorrowed until someone let us go at night or walked us to our Towns by day.

And then a new law was made, and one that was meant for our good and our better protection. Two or three Englishmen were to live among us in each of our Towns, to watch how we walked and to look to our needs, to make sure that none took wicked advantage of us. This was good, and we said so. But few of the English wanted to come to us, and only at Natick did any come to live. John Watson the elder and Henry Prentiss of Cambridge set up a wigwam by the house of Waban. They were good men, and we thanked them for their love. At Punkapaog, too, a few came among us in turns of one week, but none stayed any longer.

"Are we lepers or do we have the plague that our English brothers fear to walk our streets or stay in our houses?" complained Thomas bitterly.

"God does not forsake us," said Joseph Tuckappawill. "For as the Psalmist wrote, *Though we fall, we shall not be utterly cast down, for the Lord upholds us with His Hand. I have been young, and now am old, yet I have not seen the righteous forsaken, nor his seed begging bread.*"

"Our bread is scarce, good preacher!" said Thomas.

"Then we must pray to the Father as the Son has taught us

to pray," said the Man Of The Word, *"Give us this day our daily bread."*

"Roger Williams wishes you to walk with him to Narragansett," said Daniel Gookin as he stood at my door under the tired gaze of the late October sun. "Canonchet has taken many women and children of the Wampanoag into his tents. The English wish to know his heart. Williams says you may be of some service to the peace in all this. And indeed, Job, I believe that you may."

"Peace?" I asked. "Where is the peace?"

I walked with Daniel and the brothers Quannapohit from Hassanamasitt to the beginning of the waters of the Sneechteconet. Gookin and Thomas departed from us there to take the path north and east toward the Charles and Natick. James and I headed south along the Sneechteconet toward Pawtucket and Providence.

"The rivers sing as they did in the days of my youth," I said to my brother as we trod the leafy trail, "and yet their song is one my ears have never heard."

"When you were a child, you spoke and thought as a child," said James, "and the rivers hummed a lullabye and not a song of war."

Our feet held to the well-worn path as our eyes and our thoughts wandered the ancient woods that once had been my world and my home. Birds bickered in the branches and squirrels scampered among the lately-fallen leaves besides the sliding, silver waters of the mournful Moshassuck. I smelled the dark, damp sweetness of the numberless seasons that lay in settled, soft decay upon the forest floor. I wished to close my eyes and dream. But I could not close my eyes, for the rivers sang of war.

The smoke of Providence hailed us as the woods thinned around us and the path grew wider.

"Job Kattenanit and James Quannapohit!" announced the aged preacher as he opened wide his door to usher us in.

The wigwams at Narragansett were many more and packed

much tighter than my eyes were used to seeing. There were many strange and sobered faces sitting at the many tents. Many bent and aged forms walked sadly through the grass-bared streets. Many old men, wrinkled squaws, and naked, dirty children played round the smoky fires. There were fewer warriors, I thought. Fewer greetings from faces I thought would have lightened at the sight of mine. And fewer dogs. Food was scarce for such a hungered multitude.

I smelled anger, suspicion, and fear upon the drifting smoke of the many dull fires that lit our road as Williams and James and I made our way to the wigwam of Canonchet of the Narragansett.

"Greetings, Nétop!" I said, as I beheld the face of my old friend.

"Greetings, Kattenanit," said the sachem grimly, taking me in a hopeful, strong, and sad embrace. "But are we friends?" he added.

"Forever, my brother," I said, my eyes declaring to his the truth that my heart had raised to my lips.

"Or until the earth swallows our flesh," he added. "Sit down."

We inclined upon his mats at one end of his great tent, and his squaws brought us water and pipes. He pulled some tobacco from his pouch and passed it to James without comment.

The wigwam was warm with the glow of three fires and filled with the low chatter and busy clatter of women and children. Sometimes young braves or old warriors stuck their heads in at the doors, but the women sent them away, saying, "The sachem is in council. Come again."

"Your children, Kattenanit, are they well?" asked Canonchet.

"They are well," I said, "and they ask that I bring you their love. For Nonatic and Mentonomou, they send this," I said, pulling from my back bag a small gift that Jacob and John had made for the young sons of the Narragansett king. Canonchet leaned forward and took it from my outstretched hand.

"It is a tiny chair that rocks!" he said, his lined face widening in a weary smile. "But my boys dare not ride it!"

"Perhaps they will let their sister set this on it," I said, removing another gift from my bag.

"A doll!" said Canonchet. "An Indian maiden!" he laughed. "And did Joy sew this with her needles and her thread?"

"Yes," I beamed. "For young Quiopitic. She asked me to give the little dear a kiss for her, but I cannot tell which one she is," I said, scanning the far end of the tent for the young girl.

"She is the one whose face is painted yellow," said the sachem, pointing his pipe to aid my search. "That is her mother at the soup—my last bride, I will take no more. And you may kiss my Quiopitic after meat. But for now, we must talk."

Roger Williams rocked beside the fire as though he had been taking lessons from old Assoko.

"Are you thinking deep thoughts like the Fool?" asked Canonchet of the preacher.

"I was thinking of the Fool," said Williams, somewhat surprised, and then he saw himself rocking. "Oh!" he said. "Of course." he laughed. "But yes, I was lost a bit below the surface. Perhaps I should come up now and see to the matters at hand."

"The English wish to know why my city is filled with Wampanoag," offered the sachem. "And they wish to know if I am now in league with Philip. They wish to know if I mean to fight with him. And if I still say that I truly love the English, then they wish me to surrender these poor refugees to them, and also to give some small token of my faithfulness: my guns, or my wampum, or my promise to pay them fifty skins of the beaver and ten skins of the wolf each season for the next ten summers." Canonchet drew deeply from his pipe and then blew out the smoke through pursed lips. "Are these not the matters at hand?" he asked stiffly.

His heart is set, I thought. *His feet are planted. His eyes are fixed. His cup, like Philip's, is full.*

"You are wise, Nétop," said Williams cleanly. "And these are the matters at hand."

Canonchet stood beside his angry blaze. His eyes held fire of their own. I saw Miantonomi his father stand within him. I saw Canonicus his uncle. Askug. Nopatin. Katanaquat The Rain From God my father.

Canonchet's hair waved gently with the pressing heat of the pulsing fire and glistened upon his strong, set brow. His face and arms were painted with crossed streaks of red and black. His wrists were encircled with woven bands of many colors, set with shell and bone. A deerskin vest, embroidered with the faces of many beasts, was open at his chest. A long belt of wompompeague hung about his neck and to his belly. His loin clothes were girded with an English belt upon which hung an English knife in a red leather sheath. His feet were bare.

"These wretched Wampanoag who sit at their ragged tents within my city are here by honor and tradition," said the Narragansett prince, his eyes upon the shadowed ceiling of his wigwam. "Though they are the people of my enemy, it is on a deeper trust that I hold them in my care while their men are upon the warpath. The men of Philip brought them here for safekeeping and begged that I set my hand over them to watch them and feed them while they could not. I said that I would, for how can a king let women and children starve while their warriors run the woods in war?

"And some of these whom you saw as you came to my tent are those that I took with force from Uncas only a few settings of the sun ago. For the mad dog had laid his hands upon some squaws and old men and would have held them as captives and slaves in his own tents. This I could not allow as long as it was in my hand to set them free. And so they, too, have lit their fires among mine. Is this a sin? Is this a betrayal of love and peace with the English?" Canonchet glared. He did not look us in the eyes.

"And I shall not bend the bow against the English or run with Philip in this sad storm," continued the sachem, lowering his stare to peer upon the dancing flames that cracked and spat and whispered their own hard words to the wind that sucked their smoke through the roof of Canonchet of the Narragansett. "I will not fight against any who does not first raise his fist against me. I do not wish for the blood of any man to stain these lands. Do you?" he asked, looking upon us straight.

"We do not," said Williams.

"We do not," I repeated. James was silent beside me.

"And do the Praying Indians not rise up with the English against the Wampanoag?" asked the strong sachem.

"Some take up their weapons to fight against the wolf," I said. "But none cries for blood. And all lay themselves upon their faces to ask the Great God to hold back His wrath from those whom He loves."

"And does he not love all? Have you not said so all these many years, Kattenanit? Williams? Quannapohit of the Praying Nipmuc?" flared the angry king. "And have not the English always declared their love for the Narragansett? And have they not said that their god commands them to love even their enemies?

"Light words! They fly away like the dandelion upon the first whisper of anything that will not bow before the English and their Laws!

"False words! For Miantonomi my father was faithful in all things to the English, and they gave him up to Uncas to be slain beneath the trees!

"Words like water! For any man can see through them to the hearts that speak more truly than the crooked lips!" The sachem stamped his bare feet upon his mats. The tent was quiet of all but the crackling fires.

"Love! Never speak again to me of love, Kattenanit son of Katanaquat, for though you have love for me in your heart, yet your hands work for another people!

"Love! Do you think that your wooden boxes hold love, Roger Williams? When the sugar has been eaten, the box feeds the fire! Canonicus the Great is dead. The love that you shared died with him!

"Love! Is it love to call me to Boston again and again to make me agree to promises that I have already made or to force me to put my sign to treaties that I cannot read? To treat me like a naughty servant and a dirty dog? To hunt the woods in search of some small sagamore or distant cousin of mine who will agree to sell my lands out from under me for a bottle of rum?

"Love! Do not speak to me of love!"

He turned his back to us and stood still as stone for many moments. Then his form relaxed and he swung slowly round to face us—to face me first—again.

"Kattenanit?" he pleaded of a sudden. "Can the tree that is fallen ever stand again?"

I could not answer, for his heart was surely asking more than his words.

"Williams?" he begged of the preacher. "Can the house that is burned spring up whole from its ashes?"

"Quannapohit?" he asked of the Praying Nipmuc. "Will Weetucks ever walk these lands again?"

He paced before us, stopping once to lay another log upon the waning fire. It thanked him, licking the dried bark with its hot, splintered tongue.

"I have no skins to give the English," continued Canonchet, "nor wampum to spare. And if I had, what should I get in return? Guns? Never!—they say I have too many now. Axes? The English need them to build forts along my rivers. Rum? No—for their laws will not allow me the pleasure unless they wish to get me drunk so they can stick their hands in my baskets. Sugar? Williams will give it to me free." The sachem glanced at Williams. "I would like some sugar, and your love besides, old man," he said softly. "I wish you no ill, good preacher. You have always done me good. Do not take my anger into your own heart. It is my anger alone, and it is not aimed at you.

"But as for these helpless Wampanoag who are under my hand," said the king of the mighty Narragansett, halting in his pacing and straightening himself again before us, "I will not give them up." His eyes were hard as stone, but great pain sat behind the stone. "Not one Wampanoag," he declared, "nor even the paring of a Wampanoag's nail!"

I went to see Silvermoon my mother. She wept as I sat on her bed. I showed her the amulet about my neck. I told her I thought of her, prayed for her, often. I gave her a small bracelet from Joy, and kissed both her cheeks from Jacob and John. Katanaquat my father was gone, she said, on the hunt, alone.

We walked to the house of Williams—the ancient English preacher and the two troubled Indians who prayed—and we did not speak much. From Providence, James and I cautiously, hurriedly wound our way past rock and tree, over hill and water, toward Hassanamasitt our home.

On October 26th, a poor old house not worth a basket of corn was set aflame at Dedham. The Praying Indians were blamed by those who hated us. It was laid at the door of the people of Natick, and this time the Court passed an order that pulled our roots loose from all but our Great God's strong and unseen hand.

I heard the news and wrapped my coat about me. Gathering the children, I bundled them to the house of Printer James and cast them upon the good wife of Quannapohit. My printer friend I took in arm and—slapping his hat upon his head myself—pulled him out the door.

"When will you be back?" cried Missus Printer James as we ran the street toward the stable.

"Before the dawn, two days hence!" shouted James to the wind. We found one horse only. It was being fed and groomed by Tahattawin the horse-holder. We told him our need and he saddled the old mare at once.

"She may not like to carry you both," warned Tahattawin. "Perhaps one should run while one rides, in turns."

"We'll try her with two first!" I said, pulling James up behind me on the pawing mount. And we rode off together as the afternoon sun began its descent toward the dusk and the dark night.

The mare tired quickly under her load, and we took our turns as Tahattawin had counseled. Though the horse was thirsty and slowed at every crossing of water, we spurred her on through the thick woods. Sometimes we came upon small bands of wandering hunters, and the fear of an enemy caused us all to run wide of each other. Sometimes we chased Noonatch out of his dreams or sent a band of skinny turkeys stampeding loudly. Sometimes we passed out of the trees into small villages and shouted words of peace as we ran the road through. Once we heard gunfire in the distance. And the sun sank slowly toward the western hills.

Magunkaquog, so recently a Praying Town filled with laughing children, working men, and singing women, was empty and still but for some strangers who were poking around the latched houses and cutting corn in the golden fields. We passed through without stopping.

The Charles twisted beneath the elm as we pushed our way toward Natick. The closer we came, the more our legs wearied and our mount slowed beneath us. Some Nipmuc women ran from a grove of bushes as we finally crested the low ridge that led out of the forest onto Apple Hill.

Natick. Spread out beneath us on both sides of the Charles, her strong, stone bridge a proud buckle on the wide-belted road that ran from east to west across the river.

Natick. My House. Place Of The Hills. Home of my New Heart. Elizabeth my love. Moses, Mercy, Daniel. Waban. The brothers Quannapohit. Eliot and the Words of God. Totherswamp. Monequassin. Job Nesutan.

Natick. Wood and stone to our eyes. Ashes and tears to my heart.

Keesuckquand, though stretching his arms toward the horizon and casting his eye upon his bed, still yawned bright upon the lonely town. The doors of the Meetinghouse were swung open inwards, and they moved slightly in the early evening breeze, like great praying lips. James climbed from the horse, for he had been riding the last length while I ran, and we tied the tottering thing to an apple tree and gave her some shriveled fruit that still hung from the leaf-bared branches.

We walked down the street in silence, for silence pressed us all about. Horses had been here only hours ago, their tracks told us. The streets were full-trodden with the feet of our brothers, some bare, some in shoes, some in moccasins. Small goods were strewn here and there. Printer James knelt in the mud to lift a tattered Bible, laid open at First Kings, the black tracks of a cart wheel blotting out the words that had come from the press at his own hands. No fire burned in any house or wigwam. No candle flickered at any window. A lone dog greeted us shyly at the opened doors of the Meetinghouse.

"I can't run any more," I said. "Nor can our mare."

"We must follow our brothers," said James, "Though our legs break beneath us and our hearts burst within us, we must follow them." He wiped his white shirt against the mud-soaked pages of First Kings in a vain attempt to make them come clean. "Oh, I cannot bear this day!" he moaned, as he stuffed the wounded book into his back bag.

"Ho, friends!" came the cry from behind us, and we spun to see the dark form of a man and his mount at the top of the hill from which we had descended.

"Friend!" we answered hastily. But was he friend or foe? We stood to see. The horse and its rider came slowly down the hill.

It was John Hoare of Concord!—a good friend to the Praying Indians, and one who loved to come among us to pray and to sing and to exhort us to follow the Lord God.

"God has sent you," I declared.

"And your horse with you!" cried James.

"I saw your worn animal on Apple Hill," said Hoare. "And I wondered whose it was, the poor thing! Where has it dragged you from?"

"From Hassanamasitt since noon," I said, "for we heard that Natick was being removed to The Pines On The Charles and then to Deer Island in the Boston Harbor. And it must be so, for all are gone—near two hundred of them—though not long since. We must follow them! Can we ride your mount? Can we run in turns with you? Our legs are near lost, but God may grant us more strength to finish the race."

"I cannot run," said Hoare, "for I am neither an Indian nor a young man! But if you will take my good stallion—and he has plenty of fire left in him for the run—you may have him for the journey. I will sleep here tonight in Eliot's room and take your old mare with me back to Concord in the morning. Meet me there when your business is through."

"God bless you, good Master Hoare!" we cried, and I took to the saddle to let James run.

"Get you both up on the beast!" prodded Hoare. "He's stronger than a wagon and will not even notice. Besides," laughed the Praying Englishman, "I think I weigh near as much as the two of you! Ride! Ride! And carry my prayers with you!"

We rode, and the trail of our brothers was a clear one even in the gathering dusk. Now and then we stopped to pick up some small thing that must have fallen from the hands or the bags or the wagons of the sad people of Natick. As darkening night spread its wide arms over the sorrowful world, a thin, cold piece of the white moon rose to walk above the tall, full heads of a thick stand of evergreens. The Pines On The Charles.

As we entered the black woods that walled the northern shore of the wide Charles, we heard the heartbreaking sounds of mourning and weeping, the jostle of horses upon stone and earth, the creak of wagons heavy-laden though at rest, the voices of men—both Indian and English—speaking earnestly, fully, cleanly. Babies cried. Children wailed. A dog barked.

We could see fire, several fires, beyond the pines. And many people, standing, sitting, pacing. On the rocks by the shore. Upon horseback. In the wagons.

We heard voices that we knew. Waban. Totherswamp. Monequassin.

And Eliot!

In a breath we were in their midst, and great cries arose as our stallion danced beside the horsemen of Captain Thomas Prentiss.

"Job!" shouted Monequassin. "James!" And we were suddenly surrounded by the crying faces and groping arms of a hundred of our suffering brothers and sisters.

"Have you come to take us home?"

"Are there more with you?"

"We die!"

"God is taking us away!"

"Job! James!"

"We are not hurt."

"Have you any food?"

"Where do you run from?"

"Is the enemy around?"

"We have no guns!"

"Eliot is here!"

"God is with us!"

We climbed from our mount and waded into the sea of outstretched hearts and arms. Eliot found me.

"That is John Hoare's stallion," said the preacher. "Is he well?"

"Very well," I gasped, out of breath and near full with tears that wished to fall. "He lent us his mount so that we might find you before . . ."

"Oh, Job," cried the preacher, nearly weeping in my arms. "This is a hard river to cross! But God is with us even now. He will draw near to us as we draw near to Him. He will never forsake us. It is through many tribulations that we must enter into the Kingdom of Heaven."

"Where are they going?" I asked, as we stood in the midst of the sobbing sea.

"To Deer Island," said Eliot. And suddenly a great shout arose from the multitude, and the crowd moved as one toward the shore. "The boats," said Eliot, "they are here."

I found James' hand and we walked with Eliot to the lapping waters of the moon-shadowed Charles. The dark boats heaved toward land, as lithe phantoms leapt their sides to pull thick ropes upon the rocks. For a few eternal breaths, the only sounds that found my ears were the slapping of waves against the wooden ships and the splashing of English boots at the riverside. Then the weeping rose, raucous and renewed, with the strong song of Eliot lifted loud above the mournful tide.

The wind came warm from the south of a sudden, and the song of Eliot quieted our hearts before God. Sobbings continued, but now the men of Natick girded themselves with truth and called us to prayer. Encouragement walked the shoreline. Prayer swam the Charles. Angels hovered in The Pines. The Name spread His tortured hands above us in a great embrace of Peace. I took off my shirt and gave it to Waban, for I saw that he had given his shirt to two small girls to keep them warm together. I hid behind a rock to give my trousers to Joseph son of Monequassin, for I saw that he wore only a loin cloth, having to leave his home in such a hurry. James took the mud-encrusted Bible from his back bag and gave it to Totherswamp. And slowly, ten by ten, and twelve by twelve, the Praying Indians of Natick boarded rowboats and were ferried to the waiting ships. At last no Indians stood upon the shore but Printer James and I.

At midnight, as bitter winds returned from the north, the tides finally willing to carry themselves east to the sea, three ships set loose in the Charles toward the salty Massachusetts Bay. Natick sailed with them. My heart was an anchor that dragged hard behind it, clawing the sea in a violent, great vain attempt to hold back the hand of God.

Eliot sat upon the rocks beside the lonesome fires. Others sat with him. I walked to them, empty and lonely and naked and scared. They put their coats over me. Their arms and their prayers held me tight through the cold October night.

Chapter Twenty-one

I Would Be Joshua Again

Grey skies lay over the earth. Cold winds rattled the treetops. Hassanamasitt cut its corn upon the sloping hills that lay outside the Town beyond the maples and the birch grove.

In two bands we worked the fields, laying the stalks low, pulling the dried ears from their severed trunks. The cobs were packed tight into baskets and hollow logs we had cut into sections of two or three feet in length. Wrapped in mats, we buried the harvest in our sandy pit-barns that were dug into the hills as deep as a man stands tall. Perhaps the corn would last the winter. The stalks were fine kindling for our fires.

Wuttasacomponom our chief Ruler Of One Hundred—whom we all called Captain Tom—worked the south fields with nearly two hundred of our people. This land had hardly been cut, for most of Hassanamasitt had been at Marlborough when the harvest grew ripe.

The north fields were near bare. Some had been worked by our neighbors in our absence. Some had been cut by our enemies. Some had been burned by the English who thought they were hampering Philip from taking food where he might find it. But some still stood and was good to be laid up for the lean, cold months ahead. Printer James and I, with some few squaws and children, gleaned the north fields. My children were with Missus Printer James upon the south fields.

"We might build us an English barn next summer," I said to James as we toppled the tall stalks with our long knives. "And then we would not have to dig up so many pits. For we dig them and cover them, dig them and cover them. An English barn would let our corn sit handy all the time."

"Some might too easily take it," said James, "especially in this war."

"I was thinking without the war upon my mind," I said, swinging all the harder at a stalk that bent but would not break.

"Your blade is dull," James remarked, as his stalks fell swiftly with his blows. "How can it gut Noonatch?"

"I have one for corn and cattails and brush," I said, "and one for the hunt. But they both are dull! Who do we have who can make them sharp now that Andrew Sharpstone digs clams at Deer Island?"

The winds of the sunless day fell low from the trees and suddenly took my hat from my head. It bounded across the field as I chased it over the stalk-stubbled earth. Like a scared rabbit it tumbled before me, first one way and then the other, until it leapt at last into a bared and briared blackberry bush at the edge of the woods that sank to the south fields. And there it stuck.

I looked back at James where he stood at the top of the hill. I saw his mouth hang open in mirth, but I could not hear his merriment. The whistling winds took his laughter and flung it to the skies. He shook his head with a great grin, and then turned back to his work among the waving stalks.

As I brushed the dirt from my naughty cap, I heard instead the garbled words of women and men in the south fields below. Their voices rose upon the winds and walked the woods. But something was not right in the sound of it all.

I sank without thought into the thickest of the bushes and made my way swiftly and silently through the birch trees and the maple. When yet I could not see the fields but knew that ten more paces would be all my eyes required, I dropped upon my knees and crawled beneath a tangle of tall yellow grasses and vine-shrouded sumacs. In a breath I was in sight of the wide, golden garden.

Warriors! Nipmuc! Fifty and many fifties more, maybe three hundred in all, well-armed and standing as a wall of painted flesh about the huddled mass of my humbled people.

"We cannot come with you," said Captain Tom to a sa-gamore of the Nipmuc. "For this harvest is our chief food for winter, and we must pack it in against the cold. But take some if you will, and leave us in peace."

The enemy sagamore held his head high above our captain, staring hard upon him with eyes encircled by blood-red paint and midnight temples. He snorted like a mocking buck, and shook his head like the rattle of a powwow. His one, thick braid was tied at its end with a leather band that passed through smooth, round stone. It swung upon his proud head like a strong arm wielding a warclub.

"If you do not come with us," warned the war-captain, "we will take all of your corn and then all of your people will starve."

Murmurs and mourning arose from the Praying Indians. Some of our men stood tall in their anger. Some were upon their knees in prayer. I saw Joseph Tuckappawill our preacher hold his father in his arms. The old man's eyes were a toma-hawk, but they could not strike the foe. The eyes of Joseph Tuckappawill were rimmed with cold tears. The children were gathered in the cloaks of the women. The women whispered, whimpered, prayed, and stood strong guard about the little ones. Where were my own? There! Under the coat of Missus Printer James.

"Then take it all," said Captain Tom, "but leave us in peace, for you found us in peace."

"You are women!" scorned the war-captain. "Peace is all you know!"

Captain Tom turned his threshing knife in his strong, dark hand. He walked closer to the armed sagamore, who stepped back a bit with both hands upon his musket.

"Peace is my choice," said the Ruler Of One Hundred to the face of the painted Nipmuc. "But it is not all I know." He pulled himself swiftly back, spun about with his knife above his head, and then flung it blade first into the earth at the sa-gamore's feet. The war-captain stumbled backward and raised his rifle, but he did not fire.

"My knife has tasted the blood of men," said Captain Tom, his wide shoulders heaving in emotion, "but my heart has since tasted the Blood Of God. And the Blood Of God has wiped clean the blood of men from my blade and from my soul. I am no woman, Tattahammock of the Nipmuc, as you well know! I am a man. I stand where I stand. Peace is my choice!"

The sagamore lowered his weapon as loud mutterings passed among his warriors.

"Kill him, Tattahammock!" said some.

"Let him have his peace!" said some.

"Let us take but a few women and a little corn," said others.

"Come with me in peace, Wuttasacomponom," said Tattahammock, "and you will all live. The fields we will leave alone."

"Will you not leave us alone as well?" asked Captain Tom once more.

"If we leave you alone, will not the English come for you anyway?" argued the sagamore. "Will they not put you on boats and send you to some island to starve you with cold and hunger as they did to the people of Natick? And in the end will they not pick the strongest among you and sell you out of the country as slaves? Come with me in peace, and you will all live."

Captain Tom looked upon the people of Hassanamasitt. Their eyes pleaded, but for life or for liberty he did not know, I did not know. And I wanted to rise from my hiding and cry out the name of Jesus upon the bitter winds. I wanted to stand like Weetucks and sweep the field clean of the enemy with the heel of my foot. I wanted to take a tall birch tree in my hands and bend it like a great bow to send a mighty arrow flying that would lay every Nipmuc warrior on his startled back beneath the scattered stalks. But I could not stand, for a Hand held me low within the grasses. A voice told me, *Stay*.

Captain Tom put his foot upon the hilt of his knife and pushed it full beneath the dusty earth. The warriors of the Nipmuc murmured. Some moved forward toward our captain with cruel mischief in their eyes. Tattahammock held his arms out against his men.

"We will come," said Captain Tom to the strong sagamore and the wall of painted Nipmuc.

I felt faint, but the Hand was upon me both to hold me in my hiding and to keep my heart from failing. Great weeping rose from the Praying Indians as the Nipmuc gathered our knives, our hatchets, and our hoes. They tossed the hoes aside.

The men of Hassanamasitt stood like a palisade about the women and the children as together they were herded toward the western woods. I saw my little John search the fields and the trees with his bright, black eyes. They ran the stalks quickly and climbed the wooded hills. *Father!* they cried silently, and my heart heard, but I could not answer. My own eyes spilled over with tears and the Hand held me firmly as the light of my life walked in small English shoes into the shadows of the lands of the Nipmuc.

I rose at last, and ran. "James!" I hollered as I burst forth from the forest into the north fields. "James!" I shouted as I stumbled up the dusty hill. "James!" I croaked between gasps and great sighs, as my good friend rose from his work to gaze upon me in astonishment. The women and the children who were gathering the fallen stalks stopped to stare. "James! The Nipmuc have taken us captive!"

Captain Henchmen and Captain Syll came at our call, with two companies of English soldiers. We led them into the western woods, and though we found signs of the exodus, we met only scattered small bands of the enemy which ran from us always on paths that held no promise for our search.

Once, we came upon seven of the foe leading a captive youth. The enemy fled, pushing their prisoner ahead of them through the trees. James ran swiftly and fired upon the man who led the youth, forcing him to leave the prisoner and flee into a swamp. We rescued the boy, but he was not of Hassanamasitt. He was a poor English boy who had been seized at Peter Bent's Mill in Marlborough.

John! Jacob! Joy! My lights and my loves! Where are you?

Our search took us further toward Packachooge, about ten miles from Hassanamasitt to the northwest. Thomas now was with us, for he was a favorite of Henchman who trusted him always on the trail. We found great fields of corn, much of it newly gathered, and expected to find some camp of the enemy. But only two wigwams stood upon a hill near the fields.

"The enemy was here in great numbers," we told our English brothers, for the signs were clear. "But they knew we were coming, and they have taken to the swamps in hiding." It rained that night, and Captain Henchman slept in one of the wigwams. The next morning, after a new and futile search of the fields and the hills, we marched back to Hassanamasitt.

But as we neared our Town, Henchman discovered that his letter-case was missing, in which his writings and his orders were, and so he sent Thomas and two English back to the wigwams on horseback to see if his case had been left there.

When they climbed the tall hill upon which the wigwams stood, being only a whoop from the tents, Thomas saw two Indians standing at one of the doors, and four more sitting around a fire within.

Thomas quickly looked behind him, shouting down into the woods as if a great troop of soldiers followed him. "Surround the hill!" he cried. "Encompass the enemy!"

One of the two who stood at the door raised his gun at Thomas, but it misfired for the dampness of the last night's rain. The Indians within the tent leapt up in fear and came tumbling out against their own. Then they all ran as fast as they could—like mad hares—into the cedars and the swamp.

"And then we ran, too," Thomas told me, "to our horses and back to Hassanamasitt. For I had only one pistol. Peter Whitbridge had a gun with no flint. And the third one among us had no gun at all!"

Henchman's letter-case was not lost after all. He found it wrapped in his blankets in a bundle he had tied upon his horse's back.

"I would be Joshua again," I said as I stood in the house of Daniel Gookin at Cambridge.

"Yet God had made you Job," said Daniel my friend.

"He has made me Job in my sufferings," I said, "and I will not curse Him for it. But I would be Joshua again for a season. My children need Joshua. The Praying Indians need Joshua. You need Joshua."

The major stood from his chair where he was seated by his writing desk. "I need Joshua?" he asked.

"Joshua went forth into the lands of the enemy," I said, "and saw what could be seen. He spied out all the towns of the foe, their strength and their numbers. He brought back a report of all things. He gave good counsel to Moses and to the children of Israel. And had they followed it, victory would have been theirs."

"And how would you be Joshua?" asked Gookin, leaning up against the great stones of his warm fireplace.

"My children, Daniel!" I suddenly gushed, sitting myself in the rocking chair I had made with my own hands. "I am willing to risk my life among the enemy to find my children and secure their freedom! What else have I upon this earth? I am widowed twice! My first wife and children wait for me in Heaven, and Esther Talltrees stands tall within the Eternal City. I sit alone in my house at Hassanamassit while my neighbors weep in the tents of the Nipmuc. My brothers of Natick dream of meat on an island where the deer have long been slain. My ancient mother sits like a ghost in a world that I no longer know. My father is a lame, old dog who hides alone in caves. The English have declared war against Canonchet and the Narragansett for protecting old hunters and children and squaws. Eliot is thought a fool and a traitor for his working among us. You cannot walk the streets of Boston in peace because of your love of the Christian Indian. And my children, Daniel, I do not wish to live without them!

"If I am Joshua, I can spy out the enemy. I can rescue my children, God willing. I can find out Philip's plans and his paths. I can help to bring down the wolf in the woods. And this storm of war will cease its bitter blowing in the faces of the English and the Indians who pray."

Gookin put his hand upon my shoulder. "You shall be Joshua," he said.

I ran beneath the spruce along the Quaboag west of Wickaboag Pond, my bow and quiver at my back. Snow drifted gently from the frowning skies above the dark green boughs. I prayed.

Make my feet swift, Lord, and my eyes keen. Make my ears to hear the hearts of my children as You hear the hearts of all men. Open the path before me to the camp of those I love. And deliver us all from the mouth of the wolf.

I stopped to inspect a cold fire. Four men had sat there. Three days ago at most. They had cooked no meat, for there was no fat among the ashes. They had eaten no fish—though the river ran beside the camp—for there were no bones amid the spruce needles. Nokehick, perhaps, had been their meal. And maybe bread or beans.

I ran on, out of the spruce and into a mix of elm and oak that locked arms in battle for the mastery of these ancient lands. The oak stood most and tallest, but the elm had many young warriors gathered about upon the forest floor. Two paths crossed each other beneath these great wrestlers. I chose the narrow path that turned north toward a great swamp of cedar and serpents and mud. Both man and beast had walked it not many days past.

A moose guarded the trail where the woods opened suddenly into a wet glade that ran like a thin icy road to the edge of the swamp. I clapped my hands as I galloped toward the startled creature, and it leapt from the path, wildly splashing through the stiff, grassy mire.

Into the swamp I followed the path, and out again upon the other side. A horse-road lay here, running east to west from Brookfield to Springfield on the Connecticut. I stopped to listen to the breathing of the forest and the heartbeat of the earth. The beat was loud. Horse? Yes. Eight or ten. From the east. Very close. Should I run or should I stand? I had nothing to fear. I was Joshua. I stood in the road as soldiered horses came round the rocks at a saunter. They pulled up short as they saw me, and rifles leapt from English saddles into English hands.

"Let us kill him," said some of the men as they rode to where I stood.

"He is alone," said others. "Kill him not! But take his weapons and carry him to the captain."

"I run the woods by order of Major Gookin," I declared with their tongue, and I reached for my bag to find the paper that

Gookin had written for my safe pass through the trees.

"Take him!" shouted one of the English, for they thought I was going for my weapon. They fell on me from their mounts and held my arms. I did not struggle.

"I have a pass . . ." I shouted as they stripped me of my bow, my knife, my quiver, and my axe. "From Gookin!" I coughed as they pushed me to the ground and put their feet upon my stomach and my neck.

"Gookin!" spat one who still sat mounted. "Gookin is an Indian!"

"Nice coat, Darkskin!" said one whose foot was at my neck. I could not speak, for his boot made me choke and cough. "Who did you take it from?" And several pairs of strong arms pulled me roughly to my feet again. They stripped my English coat from me and threw it to the one who sat upon his horse. He laughed, and spread it over his shoulders. "Fits you well, Brockleboon!" shouted the men who held me. Then they saw the stone about my neck. "A crucifix!" cried one, taking it in his hands and holding it to his face. "This heathen must have wandered north and scalped some monk and took his crucifix! Maybe we got us a Praying Injin here! But which God does he pray to? The one what Rome's got nailed to their cathedrals, or the One what reigns in Heaven?" They laughed coarsely, pushing me toward their horse. "Which do you pray to, Cross Boy?" they asked.

God! I cried within. *I pray to You!*

"Which gods do you dance to, Cross Boy?" they asked, as they bound my arms behind my back with rope.

My heart rose to my lips and I found my voice.

"To the Lord Jesus Christ who has come in the flesh to shed His blood for the sins of the world and to rise from His grave that we might have life that is New and Eternal!" I shouted to the white-falling snow and the black-hearted English.

They were silent for a breath as their horses pawed the fast-freezing roadway.

"Let's go!" said the one who commanded them. "The captain can figure him out!"

"This may certify that the bearer hereof, Job of Hassanamesitt, is a trusty Indian, and therefore if any Englishman meet him, it is desired they will not misuse him, but secure him, and convey him to the Governor or myself, and they shall be satisfied for their pains," read the sergeant to his captain.

"That's what the paper says?" asked Mosely.

"Dated the 13th day of the 9th month, 1675, and signed by Daniel Gookin, Senior," said the sergeant.

"Daniel Gookin, Senior," sneered the captain. "Our honorable major and principal Indian lover." He looked at me with eyes that held contempt. I tried to look on him with love, but my heart rose up to declare him a foul and wicked man. "Hassanamassit, huh?" he said. "Your kind isn't supposed to crawl one inch past the mile line of your towns, don't you know?"

I did not reply, but nodded to the paper that the sergeant held.

"Spying for Gookin?" asked the captain.

"Yes," I said.

"And who's Gookin spying for?" coughed Mosely. "The English or the Indians?"

"The English," I replied for the honor of the major.

"Job of Hassanamasitt is a trusty Indian," said the Captain mockingly. "And he runs alone in the Nipmuc country, sergeant."

"Alone," agreed the sergeant.

"With God," I said for the honor of the Name.

Mosely glared at me, then turned to stare out his window at the falling snow. "As much as I would love to misuse this trusty Indian," he muttered. "I think we must send him to the governor, sergeant. For the governor can best determine what to do with Gookin's Suffering Servant. And of course the governor will satisfy you for your pains, sergeant."

"I am Joshua," I said to the black shadows of my brothers the English.

"What?" shot Mosely, turning from the window to stare at my face.

"I am Job," I replied.

Chapter Twenty-two

Deer Island

The governor read my paper. He asked for my story and my purpose. He treated me kindly. He told me Gookin would be called to come and see me. Then he let me be led to the prison where I sat cold and hungry in the midst of many others of my people who sat cold and hungry. And we endured the railings and the murmurings of the English of Boston who howled like angry dogs outside our walls. For the dogs wished to put us to death, though they had no cause, and they barked that I was a spy for the enemy and that Gookin was a false friend to the English. I prayed much. A few prayed with me.

"Job, my brother," said Daniel my friend as he came to sit with me in the shadows of my sorrow. "There are few but God who believe you or me in this matter, and I give myself constantly to convince the rest. God hears from me always, and I can only hope that His will is for a quick ending of this brutal war and a sure release for you and your brothers."

"Why do they hold me?" I cried. "I ran the woods for them! This is not justice, Daniel. This is not righteousness! Where is the love of God in their hearts? Are they hypocrites all? And why does God allow this suffering of His people?"

"There are many hypocrites among the English," declared Gookin, loudly enough that any ear could hear that might be straining to catch our words, "as there are among the Indians. This war is a rod upon the backs of all. And it is a fire that will bring forth gold to the glory of the Father and His Son."

311

"I will not murmur," I declared, "as Israel did at Massah and Meribah. I will not say, 'Is the Lord among us or is He not?' I do not want to look upon Heaven but never walk beneath its trees. I will not murmur.

"But my children, Daniel," I pleaded. "Will you pray all the more for them?"

"I do and I will," said the good major who carried a gun.

For many days and nights I lingered in the Boston jail. Gookin came often, Eliot too, with news of the war but no word of my children.

Another fire was set. A barn of hay and corn was burned that belonged to Lieutenant Richardson at Chelmsford. The lieutenant, who was our friend, spoke against blaming the Christian Indians, but again the mobs howled for blood. Some fourteen armed men from Chelmsford, pretending to scout the woods for the enemy, walked to Wamesitt and called our people from their tents. The poor Indians obeyed, both men, women, and children, not suspecting any harm from the English. But two of the Chelmsford men, their guns loaded with pistol shot, fired upon the Indians, wounding five women and children, and slaying outright a lad of twelve years whose mother was a good and godly widow named Sarah.

When the other Chelmsford English saw the Indians fall, God held back their hands from firing, and they went home. The murderers were taken and tried, but the jury would not find them guilty, saying that none could tell them the truth of the matter. And so the wicked men walked free.

Then the people of Wamesitt fled north, Eliot told me, for they feared for their lives if men could come and kill them without punishment.

"The angels saw the murders done," I said. "They know and will not keep silent when the Great Jury sits at the Last Day. There will be another Judgment where the truth will win."

At the end of three weeks, I was taken from my cell to stand at court. I could go at last again among my people, said the court, but I could not walk free.

"Where must I go?" I asked.

Deer Island.

The winds of winter swept from the Great Salt Sea and from the Massachusetts Bay across the bleak, rocky land where few trees stood and few deer roamed. The snows lay heavy upon the earth, and the wigwams—poor and mean—shivered even in the brightest day beneath the winter sun. Firewood was scarce, food scarcer still. Some corn and beans were shipped little by little across the waters from the stores around our Towns upon the mainland. But shellfish and clams were our breakfast and supper more often than not. We dug our meals out of the sand when the tides were low. It was a cold and hungry world which only love and brotherhood could hope to warm.

There were five hundred Praying Indians upon the island, and we worked hard to help one another in the constant struggle to live each day with our hands in the Hands of God.

Many of our preachers were among us, and the Word of God was our meat as much as the clams and the fish of the sea. Everyone prayed. Everyone sang. Everyone passed round their Bibles to those who could read. The precious pages that were pressed by Printer James grew thin and worn. They fell from their bindings. They were carried around as scraps. They were gathered in bundles and brought to Meeting wrapped in thin clothes.

Our own flesh was wrapped in thin clothes, and some of us were naked and could not go out from the fires at all. Many of our aged died. Children grew ill and faded fast. Many souls flew singing upon the salt sea winds to the Island Eternal.

And though we passed our days in a hard, cold place because of the cruel darkness of other men's hearts, we did not complain against the English for our sufferings. For we knew that many loved us still, and that God had blinded the eyes of others to our love.

God is our Safe Place and our Strong Medicine, a very present help in trouble.

Therefore we will not fear, though the earth be removed, and though the mountains be carried into the midst of the sea, though the waters roar and be troubled, though the mountains shake with the swelling thereof.

There is a River, a stream which makes glad the City of God, the Holy Place of the Throne of the Most High. God is in the midst of her, she shall not be moved. God shall help her, and very quickly.

The heathen raged, the tribes were moved, God uttered his voice and the earth melted. The Lord Of Armies is with us, the God Of Jacob is our Safe Place.

Come, behold the works of the Lord, what destruction He has made in the Earth. He makes wars to cease unto the ends of the Earth. He breaks the bow and cuts the spear in half. He burns the wagons of war in the fire.

Be still and know that I am God. I will be great in the Earth.

The Lord Of Armies is with us, the God Of Jacob is our Safe Place.

"James! Thomas! Is this a dream?" I cried as my waking eyes beheld the smiling faces of the brothers Quannapohit. I sat up and shook my head hard to see if the vision might stay fast or fade.

"We are flesh and bone," Thomas declared, rolling his strong, scarred fist in my face. "And you must get up at once."

I gathered my blankets about me and set my bare feet upon the chilled mats of my earthen floor. My fire was up and awake before me, for the brothers had fed it quietly and well before they had jostled my bed.

"When did you come?" I asked. "Why are you here? Is the war done? Have you found Joy and John and Jacob? Is Eliot with you?"

"We came last night," said Printer James, the smile fading from his dark and tired face. "With our wives and our children and many of our brothers."

"You are prisoners!" I said, my face falling. "And the storm still howls."

My brothers sat beside me on my hard bed. Their faces mirrored mine, weary walls of dark flesh upon which the flames of morning painted bright moving colors and sad shifting shadows. We stared together at the meager, burning logs.

"I would not have used those logs until the day was done," I said, "for it took me half the day yesterday to find that wood upon the shore. But it is good to sit in its heat with you."

"We are well," said Thomas. "And we brought some clothes and some corn with us from Gookin and Eliot and the churches at Cambridge and Roxbury."

"Waban will be glad to see you," I said.

"We saw him at dawn," grinned Thomas, "for we woke him first today."

"My children?" I asked to the brothers Quannapohit and the bright morning fire.

"They are well, too," said James, leaning into the blaze and turning to face me. "They are somewhere in the northern Nipmuc country, in the wigwams of the sachem Mautampe, we are told. He treats them kindly, with all the people of Hassanamasitt. Our preacher Joseph Tuckappawill, with his family and his ancient father Naoas, have a tent near the wigwam of Mautampe. Your children were with Joseph, but are now under the care of Mary Widowed-Once, a captive Praying Indian from Punkapaog. She has a small child of her own, a girl or a boy—I do not recall which. But she has been mother to your children since Hassanamasitt has been among the tents of Mautampe."

I closed my eyes and sighed a grateful prayer.

"But what of your own children and their mother?" I asked James suddenly. "For did you not say that your wives and children were with you here?"

"My own children and my precious Missus Printer James, with Old Black John our Leader Of Ten, came home two weeks ago," beamed James Quannapohit. "Old Black John has a brother among the Nipmuc of Mautampe. The brother, Old Black Andrew Shickenauq, is one of the chief counselors of the sachem. One night John's brother and the sachem were drinking and gambling and Shickenauq won the sachem's goods, wigwam and all!

"Well, what can one old counselor do with the wigwam of a sachem? And if the drunken sachem wakes up the next morning with a headache and a swimming stomach in the poor counselor's cold wigwam instead of beside the fires of his own great tent, he may decide he wants a new counselor—and his great tent back besides!

"So Old Black Andrew thought to barter all of Mautampe's goods for the release of Old Black John and a few of the Indians of Hassanamasitt. Mautampe, whose rummy head was howling like Nanúmmatin the North Wind, thought that was a pretty good trade, and said that Old John could go, and also anyone who lived in his tent. My missus and our children were in the tent of Old John, because Old John's ailing wife had died upon the forced march and he had none to care for him. You know my Missus Printer James, always caring for those who need care!

"They came into Hassanamasitt on the Sabbath, two weeks past, over the snows. I thought I'd jump to Heaven with joy! And that's how we know how your own children are, for Missus told me so herself."

The tent grew lighter as the waking sun rose higher from the sea.

"But why have the English sent you here?" I asked.

"Captain Mosely thought we missed you all so much that he'd help us to get together," said Thomas. "So he came to offer us a ride to court because of some new fire set by some old skunks who wish to set the English and the Praying Indians at odds. And here we are. What's for breakfast?"

"Clams," I said, pointing to a cold pot of water filled with small shells.

"And corn," said James pulling a bag of dried kernels from beneath his coat.

"The little that a righteous man has is better than the riches of the many wicked," said Thomas.

"From the Psalms," said James.

"Could you hand me my shoes?" I asked, for my feet were very cold.

I woke before dawn and the tent was black as a pine woods at new moon, cold as the midwinter wind upon the ice of Ashanduck Pond. But my face dripped with sweat from a fire behind my eyes as a vivid, frightful vision hung before me on a great and ghostly, bright, embroidered mat.

"Katanaquat my father," I whispered to the scene that played upon the wall between the worlds.

I could not see him, but I knew that he was there. Somewhere in the fire. The bloody, black, and brightly burning fire that roared before me in the air. Wigwams, a mountain of them, stacked side by side in a great inferno of screaming flames. The torrid hill was surrounded by ice that would not melt. "God!" I cried aloud. "Merciful Father! Pull that old dog Katanaquat from these awful flames! Do not let him die in his sins to be lost forever in the fires of Hell! Save him, Jesus! Save him!"

And I heard the laughter, strong and mad and purposeful, riding on the winds of a love unconquerable. Assoko! Standing like Weetucks on the moat of ice, reaching his stubby, wrinkled hands into the torturous blaze. Laughing. Playing in the fire like a child that plays in mud, searching for something, for someone. And suddenly his hands came forth from the ghostly flames. He held them aloft to the howling winds which wrenched from his palms some wriggling creature, sending it flying up into the shimmering blue. Was it a bird?

It was a man. Katanaquat The Rain From God! And he flew to the clouds where he scattered them widely, laughing— laughing like the Fool! And then the rains fell. Soft at first and steady. Then hard and pounding. And the mountain of flaming wigwams was quenched by the drenching Rain From God.

The vision ceased. The tent was black again and still as the clay caverns below Moose Rock.

My heart beat within me like the English drums of war. I wiped the sweat from my face.

"Katanaquat my father," I whispered.

The war had not gone well for our brothers the English, for though they had fallen upon the Narragansett in the Great Swamp, burning the wigwams like they had the tents of the Pequot upon Mystic Hill those many years past, now they had stuck their boot in the nest of the hornet! For Canonchet declared it was blood for blood and he razed the country like a ravenous wolf, burning and killing and howling in the dark of the long, cold night.

None knew if Katanaquat my father was alive or dead. Nor had we any news of Silvermoon my mother, of Winaponk my brother, of my sisters or my nephews or my nieces.

"I saw him fly," I said to James. "The wind took him from the hands of Assoko! What does it mean?"

"I am no reader of dreams," said James.

And my heart nearly broke for the weight of the war and the ache of my never-sleeping loneliness.

Daniel Gookin came to walk among us. His heart was sad, his eyes were dim. But his hair was combed, his smile was good medicine, his hands were warm, and his words were strong.

He did not come this time to sing psalms, but to resurrect Joshua, to recruit Caleb.

"I will go," said Job with the heart of Joshua.

"And I will go with him," said James with the soul of Caleb.

Gookin sat at my small fire and fed it with dried dung from the droppings of his horse that had clung to his boots.

"I can hardly believe your love," said the good major, shaking his head. "After all that has befallen you falsely, you still stand up for the English. I wish they could sit here now and hear your hearts! For your love would heap hot coals upon their heads and they would either fall in repentance upon their knees or be damned on the instant! I can hardly believe your love."

"God has poured His love out in our hearts by the Holy Spirit," I said quietly, "and so how can we not love?"

"Yes," said Gookin. "How can we not love? And how can anyone repay you for this great service of love? Five pounds each? That is what the Governor's Council promises you to hike a hundred miles through the snows of winter and into the jaws of the enemy—five pounds each! It is pennies for gold! But I say that your reward is great in Heaven, my brothers!"

"If I can but hold my little ones in my arms one last time, my reward is full!" I declared. "And if I can discover some secret of the enemy that will shorten this terrible storm of war—and bring that secret back safe to your door, Daniel Gookin—my reward will spill over the top to bless many!"

"Back safe to my door," echoed the Major.

"Now tell me, Daniel," I said, "when do we leave this wind-blasted rock?"

Chapter Twenty-three

The Camp of Mautampe

Before the dawn of day on December 30th, 1676, having spent several days in prayer at Gookin's house in Cambridge, James and I followed an Englishman through the trees to the Falls of the Charles River. The stars sunk into the heavens as the morn woke dim and grey and weary in the east. No man had seen us on our path, and when our guide at last turned back toward Cambridge, we were two lone Indians treading north and west in the cold wood of winter.

Snow drifted softly from the lightening heavens, dressing the world in a new clean coat without color. Nothing moved—no bird, no beast, no branch or breeze—other than the finely falling flakes and the trudging, silent, praying spies.

It was bitter—cold enough to freeze the Falls themselves— and the Charles ran silent and deep beneath a thick ceiling of snow-encrusted ice. Keesuckquand rose slowly, bright but hidden, above the gentle avalanche that tumbled from the skies. Our eyes blinked sore against the growing brilliance of a world washed white.

We carried little—some food and water for our journey, a bit of fire in a punk-shell, a small metal pot, our bows and our quivers, our knives and our hatchets. Woolen caps covered the hair that had grown longer in our imprisonment. English coats covered English shirts. Indian breeches were tucked into Indian boots and pulled up over Indian loin clothes. Under it all we wore English wool. Thin leather gloves let us use our fingers while keeping our hands from the frost, and the hard march made us warm in spite of the winter.

"I feel like flinging this coat off!" said James as we tread the wide, icy surface of Wachuset Pond.

"When we sit down for supper or lie down to sleep, we will be very thankful for our heavy skins!" I said.

"There is no wind to cool us!" James remarked.

"The snow is plenty," I said. "Wash your face in it if you need a cooling!"

My companion turned squinty eyes toward the blinding skies. He gritted his teeth and sucked cold air into his strong lungs. He opened wide his mouth to let the loosed and falling heavens kiss his lips and tongue.

"Tastes good," he said with a wet grin, "but not as good as Missus Printer James' iced apple cider!"

The Woods of Waushaccum stood before us in the soft storm like a great ghostly wall. We entered its trees and discovered a deer path through the frozen ferns and the snow-carpeted rocks. The tall black oaks pushed their great spreading toes deep beneath the cold earth and the cover of winter. A cardinal flitted cross our trail, a startling crimson blur before our white-wearied eyes.

We crossed the Stillwater—stiller than I had ever seen it—and walked the long, weary woods to the pines beside Asnocomet Pond. There we rested beneath the cover of the evergreens, starting a small fire to dry our boots and our gloves. In some places amid the ancient, tall trees, the snows had not yet found their way to the dry, needled floor. We melted a bit of the fallen winter in our pot, stirred in some nokehick, and ate a small meal.

"God is good," said James to the still pines and the chuckling blaze.

Smoothing our fire over with a heap of snow, we left our camp and headed west toward the Great Lake of Quabbin. We hoped to find the enemy—and our brothers of Hassanamasitt—upon those frozen shores.

At the Swift River—a wide, slow road of ice and snow—we found a path trod by men.

"Indians," said James quietly, as the winter winds began to wake, "mostly walking toward the Great Lake. Some walking south. A few heading north. A town must be near." His hands found his bow and his string. He bent and looped it, shook his shafts loose within his quiver and brushed the snow from their feathers. I fingered my knife and loosened my tomahawk at my belt.

We followed the largest body of tracks toward the Quabbin shores. Our eyes walked ahead of us, beside us, behind us. Our ears woke fully. The winds whispered a chill tune above the chattering boughs of the frozen oaks.

Smoke. We could smell it on the winds. From the north.

We left the trail, pushing our way through wet brush and snow-bent birch, making our own path toward the fires that burned at camp or town not many whoops away.

More smoke. We could see it wafting through the trees, thin and wispy upon the winter winds, then thick and hanging low like the mists of summer morning.

Voices. Children, women, men. Not a hunting camp, but a town for certain. Whose?

We crept into sight of the wigwams from a grove of ash and maple. The trail we had abandoned lay close at hand upon our left. I took James by the hand, and his eyes found mine.

"God in Heaven, watch over Joshua," he whispered to our Strong Shield on my behalf. "Mighty Father, keep Caleb safe," I quietly prayed for Printer James Quannapohit. And we stepped back onto the trail.

"Men!" cried a squaw who was carrying wood, and she dropped the fuel and fled wailing into a tent.

"Men!" shouted a small group of children who were playing snowsnake beside an outdoor fire.

"Warriors!"

"Strangers!"

"Take arms! Take arms!"

And we were soon surrounded by a scowling, burly band of armed and painted Nipmuc.

"Why do you come?" asked the grand sachem Mautampe, as we sat beside his fine fire within his great tent. A well-raised wigwam is warmer at winter than the thickest-walled house at Natick or Boston or Cambridge or Hassanamasitt!

"Our people are here," I said. "My children are here. And oh! how I long to sit at the fire and hear their hearts and hold their hands."

The sachem nodded grimly.

"Quannapohit," said Mautampe to my brother, "are you English now or Indian still? For your hair is not long, but neither is it short. Do you pray to God? Or do you take up the warclub against the English?" For the sachem knew James from fighting beside him in the Mohawk war and from running the warpath together many years past.

"I am Indian," said Quannapohit. "And I have come to be with my brother Indians to see how things go with you in strength and numbers and unity. For we have been prisoners of the English upon Deer Island, and we have suffered much in that cold and barren place. But Kattenanit and I found our way off the island to walk our way to you. For we wish to know how the war goes against the English, that we might better advise our friends at Deer Island and elsewhere, that they might better know what path to run when Keesuckquand rises on the morrow."

"Your children are here?" the sachem asked me.

"Among those who lived at Hassanamasitt," I replied.

"Did you live at Hassanamasitt?" he asked, turning his pipe in his hands.

"I once lived there," I said. "But whether I shall ever return I do not know."

"And do you pray to God?" he asked, staring through my eyes into my heart.

God! I will not lie against your Name! Help me! Be my Strong Shield! I pleaded within.

"I have prayed to many gods," I said, "though my father, Katanaquat The Rain From God, thinks me a fool to lean toward any spirit."

"You are the son of The Rain From God?" fired the sachem, leaning toward me while his dark eyes walked my face amazed. "Yes," he said to the anxious fire and the listening winds. "Yes,

I see him in your form, your features. Katanaquat The Rain From God. I see him in your face." And the strong king sat back with a great sigh and stared at me. He smiled. He shook his head. "Katanaquat The Rain From God. His son."

"Father!" cried Joy, nearly falling over herself to run into my arms.

"Father, oh Father!" cried John and Jacob as they crushed their sister in a dual embrace that wrapped small arms around us all.

We wept. We laughed. We sat hugging, rocking, kissing, stroking hair and arms by the happy fire.

We prayed. We sang psalms. We danced. We told stories. We prayed the more. We wept and laughed anew. And then we slept soundly—more soundly than I'd slept in a mess of moons—in one tight, bundled heap beside the low blaze of Mary Widowed-Once and her young Patience.

The good woman took her small daughter to the wigwam of Joseph Tuckappawill for the night, and left us alone to our great peace and joy.

"Two more warriors for our war!" Mautampe announced, and we were warily but surely welcomed to the tribe, Quannapohit and I.

James enjoyed the special attention of the rugged sachem, for old war brothers have many tales to share, many scars to show and boast of, many songs to sing together of blood and battle, of danger and death, of vanity and victory. James could sing as well as any, and better than most.

My father's fame walked before me into every wigwam that opened its door to me. And that I was a Narragansett added honor to my own head, for—since the Great Swamp Fight— the Nipmuc were looking to make a pact of war against the English with the people of Canonchet. There was much talk of this joining of hands, for if the Nipmuc and the Narragansett were united, they could raise many warriors for Philip and his wandering Wampanoag.

At many fires I told many stories of the Narragansett might, of our wars against the Pequot and the Mohegan, of our once-

kingship over Massasoit himself. Empty boastings and vain re-
membrances, but meat for the stomachs of those who make
war.

"The Great Miantonomi was a strong prince," I said, "and
Canonchet his son is my brother and friend, whose tent has
been as my own—and mine as his—since we were both pa-
pooses."

"But you later lived at Hassanamasitt?" some would sometimes ask. "And you cut your hair to pray to God?"

"I did," I said, my eyes filled with a shame that all could see.
And they thought that I was ashamed of my praying and my
taking up of English ways. But the shame was for the shame
that I lived while I was Joshua among the Nipmuc, not for the
Name who was my Strong Shield even in the presence of my
enemies. And the longer I sat at the fires of the foe, the more
God gave me favor among them.

The snows fell heavy and were piled deep upon the lands of
both the Indian and the English. But though the war was
slowed by the weight of winter, it was not stilled. It boiled hot
within the pot at the fires of Philip, Canonchet, Weetamo,
Quannopin, Mautampe, and many another scheming sagamore and sachem beneath the white-cloaked trees of the
Great Eastern Forest.

While Mautampe and his counselors plotted an alliance with
the Narragansett and a great meeting of all the enemies of the
English for the spring of the year, James and I listened to every
word of war. The Nipmuc boasted of how they would fall upon
the English in the Moon Of The Melting, how they would burn
English towns and cut off English heads, how they would stop
all Indians from praying to the English god, how their victories
would be many and great and glorious, and how—like a merciless, raging storm—they would push all their foes to the shores
of the Great Salt Sea where the English would huddle in fear
upon their wooden ships and set themselves out upon the waters to sail away forever and never return.

Guns and powder and shot would be supplied against the
English by the French, for the French hated the English. The

hunting Indians who walked north to Canada would purchase the weapons for Metacomet's war.

How could Philip lose? For he and his allies were strong and many. They had blazed a bloody, smoky trail through much of New England already, and had lost few men upon the warpath. They were wintered safely in many scattered places, with plenty of corn and venison in store. Their fires were warm. Their powwows danced for victory. The spirits were with them. How could Philip lose?

We held a council of our own, James and I, with Joseph Tuckappawill and his wise old father Naoas. My children and Patience played quietly at one end of the preacher's poor wigwam, while Mary Widowed-Once and Faith Tuckappawill tended to a late supper of stew and bread. Outside the tent, the winter lay cold and quiet upon the slumbering earth.

Joseph played with his hands and thumbed his worn Bible as he laid some news before us.

"Some women of Mautampe came to ask for prayer today," said the preacher. "These are those who have been coming to ask about God when their men are away on the hunt. They are very close to bowing to the Lord, but they are still filled with many questions and many doubts.

"They hate this war and wish to see it ended, for they do not want their men to die, and they think they cannot win it.

"One of these women is Passakitawny wife of Old Black Andrew, and she is a good and quiet friend to the English. She told me today two things that we must pray to God about. Two things that we must act upon in any way that God gives us strength and wisdom."

The wide-faced preacher sighed through his nose and opened his Bible. He turned the frayed pages for a few long moments, but whatever he was searching for eluded him. He closed the book again.

"Two things," he said, his brow bent hard between his clean, dark eyes. "One is news that Mautampe—perhaps with some of the Narragansett—purposes to fall upon English Lancaster within three weeks."

"Three weeks," I muttered, my gaze lost deep in the hot fire before me.

"They will cut off the bridge when they've crossed it," Joseph continued, "to keep any other English from running the road to assist the town. Then they will burn and destroy as they are able, and fall back across the river near The Stones. And this will be the beginning of greater war and much blood at their hands."

"Three weeks," said James nervously. "We must begin to plan our return. We must take this news to Gookin."

"Not at the word of one woman," I said. "We must hear how this news grows, and whether the Narragansett will fight with the Nipmuc. We must know exactly when Mautampe will run the warpath. We must know if any are joining him—Philip perhaps—and where they will run from. We must know more. We must be spies still. We cannot escape so soon."

"Job is right," said old Naoas. "for Solomon said, *Go not forth hastily to battle, or you will not know what to do in the end when your enemy has put you to shame.*"

"I am afraid, my brothers," said James wearily, "for Mautampe pulls me closer to his side each day. He thinks I am his brother in all things, and that my arm will fall with his upon the heads of the English. I am afraid, my brothers, that he will find out that my heart is not as he thinks, and that he will kill me."

"Your fear has a strong face," said Joseph, "and I pray for you often as the sun rises and the sun sets. It is a hard and dangerous thing to be Caleb. And the second news will not ease your heart, James, but perhaps it will throw you more surely upon the Strong Hand of God."

"Tell us," sighed James sharply, pulling himself closer to the comfort of the fire.

"Philip has given strict orders to his warriors that they capture certain of the Praying Indians—the most valiant of our brothers who have run with the English against him—and deliver them to him alive. The wolf wishes to put them to death himself, cruelly and with torment. Your name, James Quannapohit, is one which Philip has given to his men. Thomas Quannapohit your brother is another."

James drew his lips tight upon his anxious face. His eyes grew narrow and cold. He sat without moving or speaking for many long moments.

"Does Mautampe know of this?" I asked.

"No," replied the preacher.

"The Lord is my watcher," said Caleb Quannapohit at last. "I shall lack nothing. He prepares my food for me in the camp of my enemies. Though I walk through the valley of the shadow of death, I will fear no evil. God's weapons protect me.

"Oh God!" he cried aloud. "You must protect me! For my own arms are weakened by this long, frightful winter of war. My own heart is melted within me.

"But I will not run like a whipped dog, Job!" he said to me. "I will be Caleb as long as the Lord calls me to be Caleb. But He must deliver me—He must!—for I cannot deliver myself."

"Let us pray to God," said Joseph.

"Father?" said a quiet voice in the cold of the black night.

"Yes, my Joy," I answered. My hands found her bony shoulders and I hugged her gently beneath the thin mats. Jacob groaned and rolled, his arm falling across my chest. John snored. We kept each other warm.

"What shall become of us?" Joy asked, her breath rising like a dim, grey cloud in the darkened tent. Our fire was little more than red coals and thin smoke. I would have to get up and tend it in a moment.

"We shall all be well one day," I said.

"One day before we die?" she asked. "Or afterward?"

"Both now and then," I said. "For God holds us in His hands here, and we shall throw our arms around Him there."

"What is Mother doing now?" asked the wondering daughter of Esther Talltrees. And I wondered, too.

"She is puzzling why you are still awake though the hour is so late," I said. "She is thinking, 'Job Kattenanit, that fire will die if you don't feed it soon. Now don't be lazy just because your feet will get cold upon the floor!' "

"Oh, Father!" whispered Joy. "Does she see us?"

"She sees so many things that you and I have never even dreamed of," I murmured sleepily.

"Well, I will sleep now," said Joy, "and I will dream of the many things that Mother sees. And when I wake, if I remember my dream, I will tell you what she sees." And my little maid rolled on her side and sank very fast to sleep.

"God never sleeps," I said to my snoring sons and my dreaming daughter. "And I guess I must get my feet cold or the fire will die."

"My troubles give birth to troubles!" James declared with great distress. "Mautampe says to me, 'I will give you one of my guns, and we will walk in the hunt together.'

"And I must say, 'Not today, my great friend, for my stomach aches and I must lie down.' But how many days can a man have a stomachache?

"Or I say, 'Thank you so much, dear friend. I would love to walk the woods with you, but today I have promised to take the sons of Kattenanit fishing through the ice of the Great Lake.' But how many times can I make such excuses?

"For I can't tell Mautampe that Philip's men hunt the woods looking for James Quannapohit, and thus James Quannapohit cannot hunt the woods with the sachem of the Nipmuc!"

He walked many circles around the warm fire, first one way, then the other, again and again until I was dizzy just from watching him.

"And now Mautampe asks me something that is far worse than walking the woods in the hunt!" he said. "He wants to take me with him—but four days hence!—to visit Philip himself! He wants to present me to the Wampanoag king that I might inform him on affairs in Boston, and on the breach between the English and the Narragansett!

"I said to him, 'Thank you, my brother, for the honor of sitting at this inner council and for the great trust you place in me. But would not Kattenanit be better able to speak of the English and the Narragansett?'"

"You said that?" I exclaimed, leaping to my feet.

"I am sorry!" pleaded James. "I do not wish to throw you into the lap of the enemy! I was frightened! And anyway, Mautampe would not hear of it—I am his darling, not you! He loves my strong songs of war and my heady tales of battles and blood! No, he would not hear of it, but insisted that I come with him.

" 'Thank you, dear sachem,' I said, 'And I hope to be worthy of the great cause of helping Metacomet in his plans against the English, but,' I said, 'Philip knows me, for I fought against him last summer with the English at Montaup. I fired upon him—twice! He will not believe that I am really turned to his side.'

"And Mautampe was surprised that I fought against Philip, and that I had turned my gun upon the sachem and shot twice. And he sat down to think about my words. But only for a moment did he sit, and then he leapt up with laughter and slapped me on the back.

" 'Quannapohit!' he shouted. 'You are telling me a false story! And it is very funny. But I wish to take you with me, and I will not be talked out of it! Shot at him twice and missed! Ha! You never miss!' "

"And so I said to him again, 'Please, dear friend and great sachem, I am telling you the truth. Perhaps the gun was not straight. Perhaps the spirits kept me from killing him. But I tell you the truth.

" 'I will go with you, but let me first do some great exploit that will convince Philip of my allegiance. Let me go and kill some Englishmen, and we will bring their heads to the Wampanoag sachem. Let me do such a thing, and then I will go to Philip.'

"And he frowned and muttered and waddled about his tent like a child who may not go out on a warm summer day because he is sick. 'There is no time to go kill Englishmen,' he said. 'I will tell Philip that your heart has changed and that you love him now. And then you will tell him so yourself. That is what we will do. Let us not talk of it anymore today.'

"And now I must run away for sure, Job!" cried James, "For I can't walk into Philip's camp and shout, 'Here I am! It is Printer James Quannapohit, scout and soldier and spy of the English!' "

He sat upon my bed and sank his head between his knees.

"Will you come with me?" James pleaded. "For if I go alone, Mautampe will think I was a spy all along, and your life will be in great danger. He may kill you."

"You must go, as you said," I replied, "but I cannot go with you. Not yet. We still do not know the full plans of the attack on Lancaster. And I must find a way to bring the children out. Joseph and his family and his father too. And Mary Widowed-Once and Patience, for they have been life and a family to my little ones while I was in prison and upon Deer Island.

"I will not be in danger, James, for your story is true concerning Philip and the war of last summer. And when you are gone, I will tell Mautampe the same that you have told him already, and that you knew in your heart that you could not face Philip without the heads or the scalps of some English. He will believe me, for he trusts you. And these words are true."

We went out the next day on pretense of hunting, and killed three deer quickly. But we thought that some Nipmuc dogged us, and so we crossed an iced pond and hid deep in a swamp until the sun went down. A small, sheltered fire kept us warm through the night. I hoped that my children did not cry much for my absence. We slept in shifts, and early before the dawn we rose and prayed together. Then James ran away into the wild white woods, and I walked back to the camp of Mautampe dragging three dead deer behind me over the snow-encrusted earth.

"Where the two trails meet near the Black Rocks, in the glade by the backwater of Assabet River, there we shall meet in two or three weeks of my escape," I said. "There is shelter under the Rocks on the south side of the cliff. There is a spring upon the hillside within sight of the shelter, and surely you can break the ice to it with a little effort. Keep your fire low and under the Rocks. I will come in the second week if I can, and no later than the third."

The children's eyes were wide. They barely understood the things we counseled. "Father will take care of us," they thought, "no matter where he is." They little knew the danger or the hardship of the plans we made. "Adventure!" thought the boys. "Home!" hoped Joy. Joseph and Naoas leaned intently into my words, and they asked me to speak them three and four times over, so that they knew for sure what it was they were to do.

"But if I do not come by the third week," I said. "Leave your camp and strike for Natick or Hassanamasitt. But beware of all men in the woods, English or Indian, and send word immediately—by trusty messenger—to Gookin or Eliot when you have come at last to any of our Towns. They will find me if I can be found, and they will take care of you if I cannot.

"God will watch over you as He has until now. But let us talk no more of being apart until the Lord Himself separates us. For the Nipmuc are not yet dancing for war."

Naoas drew a deep breath and sat back against the mats of his bed.

"The wife of Black Andrew will help us in our own escape," said the old man, "but I am afraid I will slow us all up more than an oaken canoe upon dry ground!"

"God will carry you, Father, if He must," said Joseph the preacher.

"Mary," I said, turning to the woman who had cared for my little ones as though they were her own. "I cannot say how much your love has meant to my children. I feared for them so in the cruel days and nights I lay at Boston prison, and in the bitter loneliness of my dreams upon Deer Island. I feared for their well-being, for their hearts and souls among the enemy, and for their very lives. And even when at last I saw their lovely faces here within your wigwam, I feared that their hearts might have turned cold with the winter and the pain of their captivity. I feared that Satan might have snatched them from me. That they might be prisoners to sorrow or terror or bitterness or the deadly tears of unbelief.

"But my fears were foolish. For God gave them you. And you took them in your arms and kept them safe from all their enemies. You kept them warm. You comforted them. You held them and fed them and sang to them and told them strong tales from the Bible. You prayed with them and for them—and for me whom you had never seen! You have been as a mother

to them even since my coming with James to the camp of
Mautampe.

"I . . . " and I found that I did not quite know what to say to
this woman whose love had covered my children in a warm
cloak of summer.

Mary Widowed-Once and Patience. I hardly knew them,
though they were constant warm shadows in the tents of the
captive people of Hassanamasitt. Mother and daughter, dark
and handsome, small and strong, gentle and quiet, full of good
works and constant song, giving and never asking in return. I
had hardly spoken with either in all the long months we had
passed in the tents of the Nipmuc. A word here and there. A
please and a thank you.

And soon these two angels would be creeping out into the
frozen forest with Joseph and Naoas and Jacob and John and
my Joy, to run the woods and sit beneath the Black Rocks—
and wait. For me. They would wait for me, this quiet woman
and her precious little echo. When I finally ran the path to
meet my children at the Black Rocks, Mary Widowed-Once
would be there too. Waiting. For me. And where would she go
then?

"Thank you," I said to the woman who waited. "Thank you
for all you have done."

Chapter Twenty-four

A Long Run

"**K**attenanit!" I heard my name and turned. Who called? Was I caught? But I saw no one. I plunged on into the deep forest, pushing my way past snow-bent birches, climbing awkwardly over high drifts. My snowshoes were clumsy, but they let me walk the white path without miring myself hopelessly in the wet snow.

"Kattenanit!"

I spun around again and swept the still trees with my gaze. A dark form approached. But could it be him? A phantom, perhaps, a spirit or an Angel Of The Lord—but not him!

"Kattenanit!" it said once more. And I stayed my place and waited.

"Canonchet," I said to the shadow that walked like a sachem.

"Where do you go?" he asked, as he stood before me, his breath falling on my face like the mists of the Narragansett Bay on an autumn morn.

"To a far place," I replied. Was he alone? Did the Nipmuc follow? Why did he chase me into the woods? How could he know?

"I saw you leave the war dance last night, and I left it myself not long after," said the man who once danced as a child round the fire of Katanaquat my father. "I wished to talk with you, for Mautampe said that the English were now your enemies and that you would join in the battle with Philip. I did not question him, but I knew it was not so. And when you did not sit with me at the council of Mautampe, or join him in the dance of war, I knew that you were not the friend of Philip that he thought you to be."

"I did not know you were coming to Mautampe's camp," I said. "And when I saw you, my heart was afraid to sit with you. For there are many things that I could not—that I cannot—tell you."

"My heart was also afraid," said the dark sachem, "but not for myself. I was afraid for Job Kattenanit the spy of the English in the camp of the Nipmuc. And so I followed you to your tent. But there were men and children in the wigwam with you, and so I did not enter. Instead I laid myself upon the ground and listened. And I heard. And thus I discovered your purpose and I knew that you would run before day.

"I returned to the tent of Mautampe, but I said nothing to anyone, nor did I sleep. At last I rose when I knew the time was at hand for your escape, and I left the tent—to relieve myself, I told the young son of Mautampe who woke as I rose. I fast found your trail. Your tracks are like those of the moose! Though the moose runs more quickly."

"I cannot stand and talk, Canonchet, for the hours move swiftly toward blood, and I must race to sound the alarm," I said. "Have you come to stop me?" My eyes were upon his in the dim light of dawn.

"I cannot stop you, Night Wind of the Narragansett," said the man who once wrestled the Fool with me as we lay and laughed beside Red Creek in the distant land of summer. "But I cannot save you, either, if the Nipmuc find you running to spoil their game! We no longer walk in the same day, Kattenanit. Nothing will ever be the same. We cannot be brothers again."

"I am your brother forever!" I declared, strange grief and cold anger rising in my heart. "No sun or moon rises that will ever see me hate you. No war can separate your heart from mine. You are my brother. And I will be your brother forever."

Canonchet stamped his wet boots in the soft snow. The slush slapped our faces. "You are an English Indian!" cried the man who could not be my brother. "And I am an Indian at war with the English! They slaughtered us at the Great Swamp, Kattenanit! Slaughtered your cousins and brothers and sisters—and mine! Old men and children!

"I did not want this war! I told them so. I told Williams often. All I wanted was to walk as my father in the lands that are mine, to hunt the hills and fish the streams, to wade the shores and ride the waters. I am no friend to Philip! I took his squaws and his children into my tents to save them from death while their sachem set fire to the world, but I am not his friend!

"I am no man's friend anymore, Kattenanit, and no man's brother. I am a wolf who must protect his pack, that is all. I can never love the English again, for they killed my father and now they would kill his children and all his people—your people! How can you walk in their path?"

I had no answer.

"Kattenanit! You were born in the tents of the Narragansett. You grew beside me as a Narragansett. You are the Night Wind of the Narragansett. How can you blow for the English? How can you fight for them against your own? We cannot be brothers again!"

"I do not fight against my own!" I declared. "I walk with God!"

"Where is God?" cried the man who once chanted with me by the fire of Askug the powwow my grandfather. "And why does he fight against the Narragansett? You say that he loves us, but he burns our children alive in his fire! And then he throws them forever into a lake that burns without ending! This is love? This is God? And you walk with him? I spit on his path! I spit on your path, Kattenanit son of Katanaquat!" And he spat at my feet and flung his arms wildly about his head in great anger and distress. My eyes were dim. My heart was blackened. Confusion and sorrow and passion and pride fought within me. I stood where I stood.

"The English walk a wide path where the trees are fallen," whispered Canonchet to his never-again-brother and the waking dawn, "and they make their paths wider as they walk. They scatter the old shadows and trample the old ways. They do not know the hearts of the Indian or the ancient paths that lie hidden under our trees and in our souls, and they do not wish to know. They wish only to open the forest to the sun and to their god, so that they can better see what their greedy hands are grasping for among the ferns. Land—more land—always more land! And never a foot of it for the Indian who walked it forever! If the Indian says, 'This is mine!' then the English calls him naughty and a rebel to their king across the sea. And they put on helmets and pick up guns and march to punish the naughty savage!

"But now I am their enemy. Now I will war against them with every breath I breathe. For our lands and our lives are never our own again until the English surrender or lie dead upon the shoreline of the Great Salt Sea. I have no home, Kattenanit. Like you, I am a prisoner of this war. I must wander from wigwam to wigwam until the peace is won by blood. I cannot sit and smoke with my brothers. I cannot laugh with my children. I must run the warpath like that mad wolf Philip. I must howl like a beast. I must shoot and kill and burn. For there is no other way, now. No other way."

"I must go," I said quietly.

"Go," said Canonchet. "I will say nothing of our meeting or of where you are running. I will not be at Lancaster with Mautampe. I have other towns to burn."

I wanted to say something, anything, that would lift this black moment to the light. But no words found me, and the moment lay heavy and cold upon the earth of winter.

"Run," said Canonchet, wiping his painted forehead with the hand that once pulled a bow at my side in the hunts of our youth, "for the hours move swiftly toward blood."

We stood silently for a long moment, peering into one another's eyes, and then the Narragansett sachem turned upon our path and walked slowly back the way we both had come.

I ran as fast as a man in snowshoes can run. And I took them off at times where the snow was not deep or where it had barely settled beneath the evergreens. I loped and I stumbled. I ran and I fell. My hands and my face and my feet were raw from the soaking cold drifts and the breath of the bitter north wind. I did not stop to light a fire to warm my boots or boil a meal. There was no time to rest. The day would run more swiftly than I could ever race, and the night would find me only too close to the blood of the next morn. I must not stop. I must not sit for even a breath. For Mautampe and his warriors were running the warpath even now. They would fall on Lancaster at dawn tomorrow!

I chewed on nokehick as I forged through the forest. I swallowed melted snow to quench my thirst. I prayed to God for strength and speed and sight and breath.

Once, I came upon a small band of Quabaug Indians fishing at a pond. They scrambled for their weapons, but I cried "Nétop!" as I ran across the ice. They took up guns and held them ready, but they did not aim or fire, and they watched in troubled silence as I galloped across the frozen waters and into the woods again.

My lungs ached. My legs cried out for mercy. My eyes grew blurred as tree after tree slid by upon an endless path of slipping, sliding winter white. My side felt often as if a knife had been pushed into it. But I ran on.

The sun rose high above me in a cloudless sky, and fell again toward its waiting bed. *He rejoices as a Strong Man to run a race,* said the psalmist of great Keesuckquand. Who would win this race? The Strong Man or the Praying Indian?

I run with God, Canonchet my brother, I run with God! The people of God are my people—the English who pray, the Indians who pray.

They watch me, the people of God who have run this race before me. They watch me from the Hills of Heaven. They cheer me on as I run this bitter gauntlet. They send medicine into my heart as the boughs of the forest seek to beat me down, as the spirits of darkness seek to fell me to my face upon the earth.

I will lay aside every weight and the sin that so easily ambushes me, and I will run with patience the race that is set before me.

I will look unto Jesus, the beginner and the finisher of my faith. For He did not fall from His own race, but looked ahead through the trees to the joy that awaited Him. Despising the shame of His torture, He ran to the cross, and now is set down at the Right Hand of the Throne of God.

I will lift up the hands that hang down. I will strengthen the feeble knees. I will make a straight path for my feet. I will look diligently before me for the Fire of the Grace Of God. I will not let any root of bitterness trip me up.

I will trust in the Lord with all of my heart. I will not lie down in my own understanding. I will acknowledge my God on this long path I run. And He will direct my steps.

Assabet River, cracked and cold. Concord Road, trodden by horse and rutted by wagon. Stony Brook, frozen and tangled with fallen spruce and scattered vine—dusk painted the world grey. Nonantum, bitter and barren. The Charles, welcome and wide. The road to Cambridge, dark and dangerous.

Horse and riders! I flung myself over the side of the road and lay in the snow-wrapped brush. I climbed out hurriedly again when the horse had passed.

The night was deep upon me and my weariness weighed as heavy as death as I followed the road into the town of English Cambridge. Houses were lit with fires of oil and wax and wood. I stumbled down the shadowed streets in a mad and desperate search for the door that would open into warmth and rest and merciful deliverance.

"Who goes there?" cried a voice from a lit porch.

"Joshua!" I croaked, as I reeled past the man who hailed me.

"Indian in the street!" he howled.

"Friend!" I coughed, as I wildly hauled my legs toward the house of Major Gookin.

"Indian in the street!" rose the cry behind me from doorstep and alley, and I heard men running. There was the house! Ten steps, five steps, two steps more.

My fists pounded wood. My heart pounded louder. My eyes rolled in a dizzying spin.

"Indian in the street!" my pulsing head echoed.

The door opened. I saw the face of Daniel my brother. My mouth spread wide in a rasping, wordless greeting, and I tumbled in a useless heap into the major's arms.

Chapter Twenty-five

Rendezvous

It was near midnight when Daniel opened his door. Four hundred Indians under Mautampe would fall on Lancaster by dawn of the morrow.

James had given the very same date upon his return to Cambridge some weeks before. Though Gookin wrote it all down and went with James to the Governor and his council, little had been done to act upon his words. "I was an Indian!" James later said, "and though I told them my *Yea* was *Yea* as Jesus has commanded us, they were slow to take the word of an Indian against an Indian."

But here was Joshua at last, wearied from a marathon run for the life of the English and telling the same tale as Caleb had. Gookin sent the alarm by horsemen to Marlborough, Concord, and Lancaster, ordering men to take up their arms and surround Lancaster with all speed. The alarm reached Marlborough by the break of day, and Captain Wadsworth ran with forty soldiers the ten miles to the beleaguered town.

Mautampe was there ahead of him, and had burned the bridge and the stockaded house of the preacher Rowlandson. Forty of the English had already died, men, women and children—shot, clubbed, scalped, and stripped as they fled their burning house—and a few were made captive. The family of the preacher at Lancaster—Mary Rowlandson and several of her children—were led away by the warriors of Mautampe. A two-year-old maiden, the youngest Rowlandson, was shot through the stomach in the battle and died later in the camp of Philip where the preacher's wife was taken. But Wadsworth was able to enter the town by a secret way other than the common road and thus avoided ambush. His men, though few compared to the Indians, beat off the enemy and saved another full and garrisoned house from the fire and the tomahawk.

Medfield, Groton, and Marlborough would also shortly be attacked, I told Gookin as I lay in exhaustion upon his mats by his great stone fire, for the Nipmuc, the Narragansett, and others of the forest Indians were joining with Philip to fall upon the English in all places where they might cut them off from their cities upon the shore.

"Your children?" asked my friend, though I hardly could hear him for the buzzing of bees within my brain.

The warmth of the fire nearly laid me to sleep against my own will. I pulled myself up to sit. My head swam. "My children will flee from the camp of their captors—with Joseph Tuckapawill—seven days from now. I must meet them within a certain time at a certain place," I said weakly. "But I will need papers again, and I will not stand in the road this time if horses approach!"

"You will have your papers, good Joshua Job," said the voice of Gookin from a world far away. And then I remember no more.

Deer Island. I had prayed to see it never again, but God was not done with his work in my heart. I chafed at the walls of deep water that held me from the mainland and my children.

"It is not time for you to seek them yet," said Waban. "And God will preserve them if you cannot."

"Why do the English pen me here when I risk my life for them over and again?" I murmured. "Why does God allow this?"

"Count it all joy that God sends this trial from His Hand," counseled Waban with the wisdom of the Word. "For God's trials test your faith and work patience in your heart. But let patience have her full work that you may be a full-grown man of God, lacking nothing."

"The letter of James, chapter one, verses two through four!" declared Monequassin from his sickbed.

"A good letter," said James from beside the fire.

"Why didn't Thomas write any such letters for the Bible?" queried Thomas from beside his brother.

"I wish God would write a letter to the English to take us off this cold rock!" I muttered.

"He has written to them already," said Waban, "in the pages of their own Bibles. But when they read its words, they do not see Praying Indian written there."

"They read with their eyes closed!" I declared.

"They read with their hearts closed," said Waban.

"The mobs cry against me," I said darkly. "They cry against me! Though the governor and some of his wise men thank me for hazarding my life, the people howl their reproaches, saying that I slept in the tents of the enemy sachems and told the enemy all the secrets of the English. Otherwise how could I have come home safe and alive? they growl. Do they not know that God can preserve His own?

"And they paint Gookin false and black for trusting in me, for sending me to Mautampe. They say that my words about the enemy are all lies, and that James and I led Philip to burn Mendon. The town was deserted—I don't know who burned it!"

"You trip over the roots of bitterness, my brother," said Waban gently. "Cast your cares upon God, for He cares for you. Do not let the Devil set his foot within this tent, or this bitterness will defile you and many more of us besides."

I stared into the meager fire. Its small flames licked the tangle of log and brush that fed its hunger. Its weak light chased the shadows at my feet. And this was in the second week of the second month of 1676, my fifty-fourth year.

Gookin came upon the island, for the judgment of God was thus far against the English in the war. Unless they had the help of the Praying Indians, said Gookin, they would surely lose and all of us might die. Some of the captains of the English armies, who trusted well in the former service of the Christian Indians as scouts, would no longer go against the enemy unless they were given guides from among the men of Deer Island.

James and Thomas stood up to serve, with Andrew Pitimee, John Magus, and William Nahaton. "And will you be Joshua again?" pled my great friend who carried a gun, endeavoring to sever the bonds of my despondency. For he knew my distress and that my heart had fallen from those who had used me so sorely.

"I am Job," I said.

"Come, Job!" Thomas shouted. "Rise up and fight for God. Philip hates the Name, and your brother Canonchet spits upon The Path. Rise up and fight with the English against the wolves who devour our country and our people."

"I would rise up, yes," I said, "from this pit of desperate helplessness. But to what end? To run the woods first into the guns and arrows of Philip? To spill his blood now so that the rivers will run clean of it one day through the towns of the ungrateful English? And to return to the governor to be mocked by the crowds and blamed for every barn that has burned since this war began? Let me lie in this pit! It is better to sleep here and dream of Heaven than to run the woods and witness Hell."

Gookin bent over my bed. His strong eyes found mine and sank behind them to my heart. "If you cannot run the woods, at least rise from your sin and your pride, and pray to God for those who run on your behalf whether you believe that they love you or not," he said. "There is still time to meet your children at the Black Rocks."

I sat up, my lips pulled thin with hard distrust. "How do you know of the Black Rocks?" I asked, for I thought I had spoken of the rendezvous in vague words and no more.

"When you slept your well-deserved sleep after your long and cruel race to warn us of the attack at Lancaster, you mumbled much in your troubled dreams," said the major. "I have ever since kept in mind the time and the place of your rendezvous, and have been doing my best to obtain your release that you might run to meet them as you had planned."

I stood from my bed, my heart a battlefield of shame and anger, gratitude and disbelief. "I will come," said the words that tore themselves from the battle and ran to my lips.

Armed and fitted to fight with the English, six Praying Indians of Deer Island took to the forested highway under Major Thomas Savage and six hundred English soldiers. We marched to Marlborough first, and there Major Savage gave me leave— as I had permission of the governor's council at the request of Major Gookin—to run to my rendezvous at the Black Rocks some twelve miles distant of Hassanamasitt. But the great enemy of the Christian Indians among the English, Captain Mosely of the Black Heart, caused a mighty stir among the commanders of the army when they met in council at William Ward's house in Marlborough.

"It's ill enough that these sons of the Devil walk ahead of us to warn the enemy that we come," Mosely spat, as Gookin was later told. "But to send this one dog off into the country by himself is like sending Judas to the house of the High Priest! He will inform the enemy of the army's motion and frustrate our entire design."

"Job is a faithful man, I am assured," said Savage in my defense. "And his closest companions, the Quannapohit brothers, have served me well in the past and have run after and fired upon the enemy to great effect. These Indians are our ears and our eyes upon this campaign, and I trust them with my life and the lives of all our men. Would you like to run the woods in their place, Mosely?"

"You're a blasted fool, Savage!" roared Mosely, rising from his chair. "And there are other men in this room who would tell you the same if they had the guts!"

Savage remained seated and calm, and if he was shaken by this rattle of mutiny he did not betray it.

"The governor's council has given Job leave to meet his own children and their pastor in the woods," said Savage. "And I daresay that if your dear Johnny and Suzie were huddled under some icy crag with the minister of your church, you would let nothing on earth stop you from going to their rescue. Why don't you go with Job yourself and see to it that he goes where he says he will go and does what he says he must do? Take Jack Curtis with you, and some men on horse if you will—two or three of your own choice—so long as they aren't mean men and Indian haters."

"God hates all Indians!" declared the Black Heart. "So I'll hate them too! For we should love what God loves and hate what He hates!"

"God loves all men," said Savage quietly, "and hates all hatred against any man."

"Indians ain't men!" muttered a sergeant who sat near the door. And there arose a general argument among the leaders in the room.

"Sit down, men, sit down," ordered the major firmly. "I do intend, because of the suspicions of Mosely and others among us here, to send someone out to apprehend Job Kattenenit. But this is against my better judgment, for the man has the permission of the governor himself. And he has served us often and patiently and with little pay for his pains and his suffering. To hold him back from this meeting with his family is a cruel device. But I shall send others of our men to secure the safety of his children on his behalf. Mosely? Will you go to the rescue of this despised dog's poor litter?"

Mosely said nothing, his dark frown and set lips speaking for themselves.

"Who will go?" asked the major to the divided room.

"I will take James Quannapohit and ride with Wadsworth to overtake Job and explain things to him," offered Captain Syll.

"I will take a few good friends of the Christian Indians from among our men and run to the Black Rocks," volunteered another.

"Mosely?" said the major as the men began to file out the door. The Black Heart turned to stare at his commander. "No army can march together when its captains are divided," Savage said. "There is a chain of command among us, as there must be in all of life, and we must not chisel against the links that hold us to one purpose.

"Please hold your temper and your tongue when your thoughts run opposite of the counsel and orders of your superiors, or I may advise your removal as captain in the army."

Mosely coughed and nodded disdainfully. Then he turned and walked into the winter, closing the planked door roughly behind him.

James led the horsemen purposefully west of the Black Rocks. They never suspected his ploy, and I never saw them.

The men who rode to find my children became bogged upon the path by swamps and snow, and they didn't arrive at the Rocks until the children and their father had already come and gone.

But their father did not find his lost and loved ones as his heart had so yearned and hoped and believed beyond belief. For the time of their waiting was passed, and they had walked on—to where?

The fire that had warmed them was covered and cold. The spring that had refreshed them was thawed and running strong. Its banks spoke loudly of their recent presence: small prints of children, the tracks of the men, and the feet of the wife of the preacher and Mary Widowed-Once. I dug up the droppings of their bowels from beneath a heap of snow at the end of a short path. I searched the rocks for any sign they might have left me, but finding none, I took up their east-running trail until new snow covered all hope of running them down. The soft-falling skies covered the world anew in a blanket of peace which belied the war that raged within my soul and upon the scorched and bloody earth. But a psalm rose up in spite of myself, and I sat down upon a great, white rock and bowed my head between my knees.

"*Unto Thee will I cry, Oh Lord my Rock!*" I chanted. "*Be not silent to me.*

"*If You are silent to me, I become as one who goes down into the pit.*

"*Hear the voice of my pleading when I cry unto You, when I lift up my hands toward Your Holy House!*"

I shuffled to my knees upon the hard, wet stone, and raised my arms to the white, falling heavens.

"*Draw me not away with the wicked and with the workers of wickedness,*" I cried, "*who speak peace to their neighbors when mischief is in their hearts.*

"*Give them according to their deeds and according to the wickedness of their words. Give them the poison that they mix with their own hands, and render to them what they deserve.*

"Because they scoff at the works of the Lord and the works of His Hands, He shall destroy them and never build them up."

My hands fell to my side, and my own heart cried for mercy for my own sins and my own scoffing and my own blackness and wickedness against my neighbors and my enemies. For I did not love those who persecuted me. I did not pray for them. I did not do them good. I prayed instead with King David that the judgment of God would fall upon their heads so that they would never stand again in the land of the living. I wept.

"Blessed be the Lord, because He has heard the voice of my pleading," I sobbed to the white world and the One Who Hears All Things.

"The Lord is my Strength and my Shield. My heart trusts in Him and I am helped. Therefore my heart greatly rejoices, and with my song I will praise Him."

I stood upon the slippery rock and sang for my children. For my brother Joseph and his father Naoas. For Mary Widowed-Once and her little Patience.

"The Lord is their strength," I chanted to the silent spirits and the Black Hearts of all men. *"The Lord is the saving Strength of His chosen people.*

"Save your people, Lord, and bless all your children. Feed them also, and lift them up forever."

Thus, by the aid of the Holy Spirit within me, I cast my children into the care of the Great God and turned upon the path toward the army which waited at Marlborough.

Chapter Twenty-six

Reunion

U pon meeting the army again, I reported the disappoint-
ment of my short search and offered myself back into
the services of the English. My return and my submission
shut the muttering mouths of many against me, and proved
me faithful to many more. Even Mosely himself did not
grumble so much. But I could not bear to walk long in the
woods as scout against the enemy, for though I considered
Philip a wolf to be slain, I could not forget my Joy and my
John and my Jacob. My waking walking and my storm-
tossed sleeping were filled with dreams of my wandering
children. Were they well? Were they safe? Were they fed?
Were they warm? Were they alive or were they dead?

They were not dead, I knew within my heart, for a hope not
born of my own understanding spoke strong within my soul
that all would be well one day. *One day before we die?* argued
my heart in the words of my little Joy. *Or afterward?* My
dreams were a sorry distraction. My scouting was poor.

"I wish to return to Deer Island," I said to Captain Savage, "for
I am no good to anyone here. I will lead us all into an ambush or
get killed myself as I blunder into the camp of the enemy. My
heart is sick for my children, and I cannot make it well."

Savage sighed as he sat beside his fire at our rough camp. He
played with the quill in his hands, and set a page of parchment
aside upon his writing box.

"Some sick among us are riding back to Boston in the morning," said the captain at last, "and you may go with them. I will write you a letter of good service and commendation. And I will pray that your children be restored to you before many days."

He rose from his seat of saddle and blankets. "God be with you, Job Kattenanit," he said, reaching his right hand to embrace mine. "Great is your reward in Heaven."

I took his strong hand in mine. I could think of no words, but my soul sang a song of love for all English who walked with the Name. I could only shake my head in gratitude and squeeze back my tears.

Upon the morrow, a horse was found for me that I might ride with those who were ill. Captain Brattle rode at our head, and a few armed men came up behind. I bid James and Thomas farewell as our mounts moved us east upon the road from Marlborough to Sudbury and then toward Charlestown and Boston.

As we came to the snowed-over path that veered south to Natick, I felt a great urge to turn. The nudge would not leave me alone, and finally—though several miles further on our march—I rode forward a bit to talk with Captain Brattle.

"Please, dear brother, hear me a moment," I said as we walked our mounts side by side. "For I have a request that I know you should not answer in my favor, but I would ask it just the same."

Brattle nodded solemnly.

"When we passed the road to Natick, and ever since, I have felt that I should ride to the Town and see if my family is there," I said fearfully. "And I know I have asked much of the English in this war, but might I beg you for leave to ride back and see. And if they are not there, I will meet you in Boston as soon as my search is ended. And if they are, I will bring them to Cambridge to Major Daniel Gookin—and then I will report to you wherever I may find you."

The captain sighed through clenched teeth and looked straight ahead upon our snowy way. Then he turned his face to me and said, "I trust you as my own brother, Job, for I know your life among the Christian Indians and your service in this war. And I would let you go if it were not for these men who ride sick behind us. Many of them hate you and all Indians, for their hearts are hard to the love that is ours. If I send you back to Natick, they will cry out against both you and me when we reach Boston, and the mobs will taunt and threaten to riot. To let you go would only further divide the army and give men like Mosely reason to rant and rave."

My head fell as we rode.

"But," said the captain quietly, a slight gleam in his eye. "We will stop to rest shortly at Watertown, and if you were to excuse yourself from our company for a moment after meat, in order to feed your horse some bit of oats or sugar, I think you might take your mount for a little ride at your own will. I will tell our men some fine tales after dinner to keep their minds occupied in your first absence. After that, you are on your own."

"Will you send men to find me?" I asked.

"I will have none to spare for chasing down a lone Indian in the woods," I said. "And if the sick men who hate you wish to chase you themselves, I will be very surprised! Even if they should attempt it, which I will forbid, they could not ride fast or far in their weak condition. I will inform Major Gookin myself of your purpose."

That evening, after meat at the house of Peter Hunter in Watertown, I took some sugar to the stable—and rode out into the night.

Natick was deserted. No sign that anyone had been there for weeks. *Should I return to Boston?* I troubled. *No,* the Spirit answered. I rode to Hassanamasitt, but none there had seen my children or any of their company. I rode the next day as far as Woonsocket, then left my tired mount at the house of George Turner who had a barn with many horses. He said he would send it to the army with some of his own before long.

From there I crossed the Sneechteconet by foot into the lands that had been given by the Narragansett into the hands of Roger Williams. Near Woonsocket Hill, I came upon an Englishman with his cart stuck in the mud. I helped him get it loose, and he let me ride with him to North Smithfield. I begged him a horse to ride to Providence, and he gave me one on my word that Roger Williams would return it soon. I gave him my crucifix in trade until his horse came back, and though he called it a papish device, he knew it meant much to me and said that he would keep it in a safe place.

Near the Absolute Swamp above Providence, my new mount twisted its leg upon the slippery, rutted path, and I was forced to lead it slowly from there to the house of Williams.

"Kattenanit!" cried the bent preacher as he opened his door to let out the warmth of my youth and the bright shining light of the eternal things that dwelt always by the good, old man. "Come in this minute, you lost dog! Mary, Mary! See who is here! And do we have news for this haggard son of Adam! Come in, you weary traveler, do you think I can entertain you upon my doorstep?"

I laid myself wearily in the rocking chair that my own hands had crafted. I rocked before the fire. I sighed and closed my tired eyes.

"I will send the servant for my son Daniel. And Freeborn is in town and will want to see you," said the good preacher. "Take off those boots, you winter-beaten beast, and warm your feet at the fire. In fact, get up to the loft and take off everything! I will toss you some warm clothes and Mary will dry those rags that are clinging to you now. Go on, before you start snoring in that idle rocker you made for an old man. Go on!"

When I was fully clothed in dry garments, we sat at meat with Daniel and his children and Freeborn and her family. Laughter rose around me. More meat and drink was set at my hand each time my board was emptied. The infant daughter of Freeborn was placed in my lap, and she played with my hair which was now grown long again. Did I dream? Or was I dead and this was Heaven?

"Canonchet roams the woods," said Williams as we sat after meat, and smoked before the fire. "And he threatens to burn even Providence."

"He would not," I declared, "for he loves this town and many who are in it."

"His warriors do not love it as he does, and we have no defense against them if they should come," said Williams, "for though we have men who can shoot, we also have those addle-brained Quakers who refuse to pick up a gun to save even house or home."

"Can you not order them to prepare for war?" I asked, surprised that any should be allowed to let his neighbor die.

"I am king only of my own castle," winked the old preacher at his faithful Mary, "and even here I give few orders."

"That is because your subjects know your heart and trust your love," I said.

"We are subject one to another within these walls," said Roger Williams, "though I still stand first at the door and eat first at the table.

"But this town is now governed by those who heed only the 'inner voice' of their darkened and befuddled reason, and if their conscience calls them to lay their heads before the tomahawk, so they say they shall do!" puzzled the wrinkled Father of Providence. "And perhaps," he mumbled, "we would be better off with a new set of heads in their place."

"But Canonchet . . ." I began to say, and then I remembered our parting in the woods outside the camp of Mautampe. "Surely not the house of Williams," I murmured to the fire and the children and the grandchildren of the ancient God-preacher.

"Perhaps not," said Roger Williams, sitting suddenly higher in his chair, "for his uncle Canonicus once commanded him never to allow any to so much as harm the hair upon my hallowed English head!" He combed his thinned locks with his bent fingers. "But let us tell you the good news that everyone here already knows but yourself," said the preacher, leaning toward me with a fine light in his clean eyes.

I looked around the table. All eyes were upon me. I felt my face flush, and I lowered my gaze to my empty cup. Mary filled it anew with cold water.

"Your father is well and alive upon Martha's Vineyard," said Roger quietly.

"Alive and well!" I echoed sharply, rising from my seat and upsetting my cup.

"And your mother, too," said Mary Williams as she wiped up the spill with a large napkin.

I sat back down, and nothing could hold in the tears that rolled shamelessly over my cheeks and soaked the table anew.

The sails caught the northwest wind which pushed my boat down from the shores of Tuncawoden into the wide mouth that led to the Great Bay of the Narragansett. The long shore of the isle of Acquidneck stretched to the east as I passed Quinunicut upon my west and slid out past the neck of Cajacet into the Great Sea. But a storm rose from the sea and pushed me back into safe harbor behind Acquidneck where I waited two days for the skies to clear. From there, when the sea was once more willing, the winds drove me over the waves toward the isle of Capawack—the Vineyard of Martha.

My landing brought Indian and Englishman alike, both armed but unalarmed, to the shore to welcome me and help me disembark. The sun shone warm and bright, though the air was cold with the winter, and I felt again the strong smile of God that seemed to rest upon this isle no matter what the season or the state of peace or war elsewhere in the wide, wicked world. *God is sachem on Capawack,* I heard Sassamon laugh from beyond the clear skies.

I walked to Christiantown where a Church of Indians was in meeting, for it was the Sabbath, and I joined my brothers in song and prayer.

There I saw men and women I knew, but I could not find my father or my mother or my Fool or Hiacoomes among those who worshiped.

"There are two more Churches upon the island," declared some who knew me, "with six services in all each Sabbath! We have ten Indian preachers now, and several smaller Meetings that are not yet Churches. Come, let us introduce you to our minister, Wunnanauhkomun. He is a very good man among us, and his children all walk with God."

I met good Wunnanauhkomun, and he had heard of me.

"Assoko prays for you whenever he is among us," said the preacher. "And surely his prayers have been heard in the Halls of the King Of Heaven, for here you are!"

"Where may I find my father and my mother?" I pleaded.

"At the town where Hiacoomes and Assoko now dwell," he said, "where the younger Mayhew and Hiacoomes first preached to us about God."

I saw him sitting at the table, my father The Rain From God. Sitting still as death beside the rocking Fool. Sitting with his face in his meat, staring at it as if it should walk to his mouth on its own. Sitting like an ancient phantom in a near-forgotten legend of a ˙ dream once dreamed beyond remembrance. Ghostly in his sitting, but of flesh and blood and bone before my eyes. The flesh was mine, the blood was mine, the bone my own, no doubt, no dream. His hair was black, no touch of grey, and it hung upon his back unbraided, bent where his own bones curved beneath his years. He did not see me, but the Fool looked up with grinning eyes and gaped as though an angel caught his gaze.

"Father?" I said, and the sound of the word hit Katanaquat like the blow of a warclub upon his bent neck. He turned in a breath to face me, and his eyes filled with light as though the sun rose within him.

Staggering to his feet like a blind man, he stumbled toward me like a dog who runs to the call of his master, and his arms flew around me in a crushing grip that made a lie of his weeping, wrinkled face and his sad and sagging flesh.

He fell to his knees with his arms around my legs, and I could not speak for the great gasping sobs that arose from his lips and filled the room, the house—the island itself it seemed—and the very heavens that reached to touch and kiss the air we breathed.

Is this Katanaquat? my heart cried in wonder.

Chapter Twenty-seven

The Blood Of God

I lingered upon the Isle Of Dreams And Peace, upon the City Of God Upon Earth, for it called strongly to my war-weary soul. And it captured at last even that old Dog of War, Katanaquat. For there upon Capawack, where Silvermoon my mother combed her long, silver locks and sang a New Song to the One God, The Rain From God flung himself at last into the Ocean of God's Mercy and declared himself a conquered man and a Christian Indian. He prayed. In his own way, he prayed, and who could ask any more of him? For he stood where he stood until his last day some many seasons hence. But his feet were now upon the Rock of The Ransom and he stood with his face to the Light Of Grace and let the Son Of Righteousness flow through his old, tired eyes into his strong New Heart.

Though the smoke of battle never crossed the waters to cloud the clean skies over Capawack, the news of war came to us often.

Providence was burned—fully one hundred of its one hundred twenty-three houses—as its preacher had feared. Canonchet himself set fire to the home of the great old friend of the Narragansett, though the sachem threatened his own men with death if any should touch the good preacher. Only one Englishman died that day.

A Praying Indian on Deer Island volunteered to run an ad-

venture to the camp of Philip to beg the release of Mrs. Rowlandson, who was captive there since the attack of Lancaster.
This Indian ambassador, Tom Neppanit by name, went back
and forth between Philip and the English until Philip finally let
the woman and her children go. And this was a turning in the
hearts of the English toward the Praying Indians, and a cause
of dissension among the ranks of the enemy. Philip and most
of the Narragansett separated from the Quabaug and the Nipmuc and went down to their own country. The Nipmuc and
their friends remained in the north around Wachusett Mountain.

Then two-score Christian Indians were loosed from Deer Island and were armed to fight the enemy under Captain Hunting and Lieutenant Richardson, who both were well-
acquainted with their new and eager troops. The Praying Indians had guns of their own before their imprisonment, but the
English had taken them all and squandered them away. The
newly armed Indians took to the warpath to defend Sudbury,
which was then under attack by the enemy. Our Indians
proved themselves so well, and wept so at the sight of the English dead in the streets at Sudbury, that the English saw our
love for them at last. A ship arrived with fresh arms from England, and more men were let off Deer Island to fight. Captain
Hunting now had eighty Praying Indians in his army, and the
dim dawn of victory rose at last upon the English.

At Weshakum, at Mendon, at Montaup, at Wachusett, at all
places where the English marched to fight, the Praying Indians
ran as scouts and fought with the regular troops. Scalps were
brought back from the forest by the Christian Indians, and by
the end of the summer my praying brothers had killed fully
four hundred of the enemy.

By July, one hundred fifty of the men of Mautampe surrendered themselves to the government of Massachusetts, saying
they had seen enough of war. Several more bands of the enemy gave themselves up at Plymouth and Hartford. But the
blood was not done, and many barbarous acts were still com-
mitted against all sides and in many places. Innocent Praying
Indians were slain by both English and the heathen Indian.

The Squaw Sachem, Old Magnus of the Narragansett, was trapped in a swamp and killed along with most of her men. Quaiapen was captured at Bridgewater, tried at court, and shot.

But Canonchet my brother?

In April, after I had left the Vineyard and returned again with my family whole—a tale I shall tell in a moment if you will patiently await it—and before some of the events I have already told, Canonchet my brother was camped near Pawtucket in the country of the Narragansett. I have this mournful tale from Winaponk my brother, who was not in the Great Swamp when it burned, and who has since come to live by me in the place I now call home. He was at Pawtucket with Canonchet, and was with him to the bitter end.

There were only seven men with the son of Miantonomi, upon a small hill with no blaze among them. Suddenly a warning came from one who stood watch, but the alarm was too late, for a body of some eighty soldiers under Captain George Denison, with some of the men of Uncas as scouts, were climbing the hill before any defense could be made. Canonchet was forced to flee, but not before the Mohegan recognized him.

"It is Canonchet!" they cried, and they flew ahead of the English in pursuit of the sachem of the Narragansett.

Winaponk turned to send a shaft flying at the Mohegan, but his foot twisted as he pulled his bow, and he fell to the ground and lay there with his weapons readied. The men of Uncas fled past him, and he rose behind them in the pursuit.

Canonchet was desperate, for the wolves were at his heels, and he threw off his blanket and his silver-laced coat in an effort to make more speed. He stripped away his belt of wompompeague and took to the Pawtucket like a bounding deer. But his foot slipped on the stones, so that he stumbled and his gun went into the river. He stood still of a sudden, his back to the on-running world, and held his head high to the trees that grew green by the singing waters. Winaponk ran to the shore of the river, and yelled to his sachem, "Fly like a bird, Canon-

chet my prince!" But the sachem did not move. Several of the
Mohegan leapt upon Winaponk and stripped him of his arms.
The Mohegan sagamore Monopoide strode into the water and
seized Canonchet by the shoulder. The mighty sachem was a
prisoner of war.

Soon the English arrived, said Winaponk, and a man named
Robert Stanton spoke first with Canonchet. Stanton was no
hater of Indians, nor a hater of any man—even an enemy—and
he asked many clean questions of Canonchet my brother,
carefully, respectfully. But the sachem stood silent. At last he
turned to Stanton and said, "You are a little child, and do not
understand matters of war. Let your big brother or your sachem come, and him I will answer."

"Why did you not fly?" cried the captive Winaponk to his
proud prince.

And Canonchet looked into the eyes of Winaponk and said,
"When my gun fell under the waters, my heart and bowels
turned within me so that my bones were weakened like rotten
sticks."

When Captain Denison arrived, Canonchet was calm in the
face of the foe. When he was threatened with death, he said,
"The war will not end when my blood feeds the earth."

When chided about tales of his famous, boastful speeches of
slaughter and battle, he replied, "Others were as forward about
the war as myself, and I desire to hear no more about it."

When many of the soldiers continued to question him, he
said, "I was born a prince and the son of a prince. If any prince
among you comes to speak with me, I shall answer. But since I
see none here today, I must in honor hold my tongue."

When told at last that he would in a short while be put to
death, Canonchet said, "I like it well. For I shall die before my
heart is soft or I have said anything unworthy of myself."

When asked how he might wish to die, he said, "Let Oneco,
the son of Uncas, who stands there among you, lay me to the
earth. For his father killed my father, and there is none among
us here of equal rank to me besides Oneco."

They walked the prince to Stonington, Winaponk in tow, and
there the sachem died. The Pequot shot him. The Mohegan

cut off his head and quartered his body. The Niantic built a fire and burned his quartered flesh. His head was sent to Hartford as a trophy of war and a token of love and fidelity from the men of Uncas. Oneco watched. He would not even afford our prince the pleasure of an honorable death.

And so my people—my first people, the people of my father and my father's father—staggered and stumbled and finally fell, a man without a head.

But my children—to return to my first week upon Martha's Vineyard—where were they? News came swiftly across the waves, and I heard—to my heart's unfettered joy and unbounded gratitude to God—that they were safe within the tents of Waban on Deer Island.

A ship set sail to Boston and I was aboard.

When we came into Boston Harbor, I was surprised to see my great friends at the moor. Eliot was there, Gookin too, and the Quannapohit brothers, looking a bit more ragged for the war than since I'd seen them only a few weeks before.

"Job!" cried James from the shore when he saw my face at shipside. "Praise the Lord, it's Job!"

And when we all embraced, I thought that the war was surely done.

"Not nearly done," said Thomas soberly, rubbing the old scars that his own gun had painted on his poor hand. "For though we are not so out of favor among the English as we were, still the wolves run loose in the woods, and smoke rises everywhere from fires set at dawn!"

"Let us go over now," I begged, "for I never thought I'd want to set foot upon Deer Island again, but my loves are there waiting. Waiting. And I cannot wait another moment myself. Let us go over!"

We hired a boat—my two English brothers, my two Indian brothers, and I—and we rowed the still harbor to the bleak island.

Waban met us, for many had spied us while clamming in the shallows, and a shout had arisen announcing our approach. The hardy Ruler helped us pull our boat upon the rocks, chattering like a squirrel about Joseph and Naoas, about my children and their mother.

"Their mother?" I asked.

"Mary, your woman, their mother!" shot the impatient Waban, pulling me toward the path that led to the hill where the wigwams stood in a small grove of willow and ash. And I smiled, for good Mary Widowed-Once still played the mother to my little ones—so much so that even old Waban thought she was my wife.

Mary your woman, their mother, I said to my soul. And I found that I walked in a dream toward the poor tent of Waban.

As the sagamore swept his door open to usher me in, I saw the gay and eager faces of my little Joy, my rascal John, my darling Jacob. I heard their precious voices and I felt their sweet kisses. I ran my hands through their long hair, held them tight in my longing arms, spoke words of love and comfort to their young souls. But all this was in a fog, for the eyes of my heart led the eyes in my head to search the room for another.

She stood beside the fire, her Patience smiling shyly at her side, her own head bent a bit toward her feet. Her eyes found mine.

Who are you, Mary Widowed-Once? my heart asked.

I am Widowed-Once-But-No-More, her heart answered.

I am Widowed-Twice, my heart replied. *I am Job.*

You are my Joshua, her heart declared.

You are my woman! my heart admitted fearfully, joyfully, troubled and sure and amazed. *You are the mother of my children!*

I pulled my gaze away from her, shaken and shamed, and threw myself under the frantic, full affections of my joyous little ones. I picked them up as one in a great hug like that of the bear, and dropped them all as one upon the mats of Waban's bed.

"Father is home!" they cried, dancing shamelessly like little Indians around the laughing fire. "Father is well and home! God is good to us! Father is home!"

I sailed back to the Vineyard, and the children went with me. The governor said we could go.

Mary Widowed-Once stayed upon Deer Island to help the wife of Tuckapawill look after the ailing Naoas, for the old man had taken ill with his wanderings. The fugitives from Mautampe had waited as long as they could at the Black Rocks, and then had walked toward Hassanamasitt. They did not get far when Captain Benjamin Gibbs and a party of horsemen met them in the woods. The soldiers seized them and took what few things the escapees had smuggled with them from the camp of their captors: two rugs, two brass kettles, some dishes, and a pewter cup that the preacher had saved which Eliot had given him to use in the serving of the Lord's Supper. None of these things were ever returned. But the company was not harmed.

They were led by Gibbs to Captain Savage, who upon understanding that they were my children and my people, treated them well and sent them under guard to Marlborough. While they were there, they were lodged in the house of Captain Nicholas Page and his wife, who fed them and clothed them and comforted them much.

Then they were taken to Boston and kept there a night or two before they were ferried to Deer Island. There the Christian Indians of the desolate isle took them under wing, and with prayers and much love preserved them until my coming.

But now we sailed for Capawack, my children and I, for Katanaquat my father longed to see the grandchildren he had never known. And when the old dog saw them, they ran to him like a pack of puppies. They hugged him and kissed him and told him tales until his tears of joy and laughter had soaked their clothes. Then they spoiled him the more, walking the peaceful shores with him, telling him how much they loved him, thanking God aloud for the Grandfather Rain From God, and running around his limping legs until he couldn't even walk for their dizzying play.

Silvermoon my mother sat with smiles all the while, humming old familiar tunes and new ones she had heard at Meeting. If I closed my eyes, I could see her young and beautiful upon her bed, weaving baskets of reeds and rushes, combing the hair of Quanatik my sister. But when I opened my eyes and looked into hers, I saw something much older yet forever-young and never-dying deep within her soul. It sang in harmony with the peaceful hum that rose from her happy heart to her smiling lips.

Assoko our Fool, that great friend and gentle warrior of the Mighty Faith, rocked in his great rocking chair—or anywhere without it—speaking his soft, slow wisdom, wrinkling his strange face like a child's leather ball within a man's nervous hands, his ancient scar turning crimson upon his wide head when he laughed, and white when he cried.

And the dream of the fiery mountain of wigwams, with Assoko The Giant pulling Katanaquat The Bird from the burning nest? When I told the Fool of the vision one day, he explained it very simply.

"God told Soko, 'Go get Kat.' I said to God, 'Where is he?' And God said, 'Great Swamp. Much trouble. Go now.' Soko called three young braves, 'cause Soko is not so young and so brave! And we sailed over the waters. And we walked the white woods—lots of snow, Jobee—and we came to Great Swamp." The Fool threw his hands in the air as he began to tell this next part, waving them about with a wild look upon his face. His eyes rolled in circles and his tongue hung out. "Fire! Great Swamp was on fire like the meat of the Pequot when Soko was a young warrior and Jobee was a small Katnit. Fire everywhere!

" 'How we getting in there?' asked one of my braves.

" 'Run fast, I guess,' I said. And we ran fast.

"The smoke was so much that I could not see, and I said, 'Good! Now God will lead me, 'cause I can't lead myself.' And His Hand moved me to the tent of Kat and Silmoon. I laughed like a fool—'cause I am a fool, Jobee—and threw open the door.

"Silmoon tried to shoot me, but God blew smoke in her eyes. My braves picked the old dogs up and God took us out of the fire." He blinked and grinned and blew out his cheeks several times. "Then we ran as quick as we could to the shore and the ship. And home again."

He sat still and smiled.

"It was easy," he said, smiling, his old rotted teeth sticking at odd angles from wide lips. "Any more dreams?"

"No more," I said, "but that does not explain the end of the dream, where my father makes the rain fall upon the flaming mountain."

Assoko rocked more quickly, his brow bent in an unusual

contradiction of pain and joy and simple confusion.

"Ask me next year," he said at last, smiling once again. I didn't need to ask him next year, for my father told me the end of it himself. I have written this tale in the book about Katanaquat. You can read it there if you will.*

Philip fell near Mauntop. The bullet flew from the musket of a Praying Wampanoag. Metacomet's powwows had said that no English would kill him. They were right in this at least. Sassamon's body turned in its grave, moaning for his prince, some said. Blood for blood, chanted the Indians who do not pray. Blow for blow. Bullet for bullet.

If a man digs a pit to catch his brother, he shall fall in it himself, says Solomon of Israel.

The war was over. The wolf was dead. Only a few small fires still burned, and they were soon quenched.

"The blood of men covers the earth," said Hiacoomes at Meeting, "and we weep and mourn for our brothers who are fallen. We weep for their wives and their children. We weep for the trees that must live with the memory of all of the violence and the savagery of man that has run the paths at their feet.

"But the Blood Of God covers the sins of the world," said the preacher, "and we rejoice that our hearts are made clean by the tears of God as He sees His Son die for us, the Ransom for our souls.

"And the love of God rules in our hearts," said the Praying Indian, "as we lift up our faces to the Son who is risen and reigns on high to come again some day at the Last Battle and the Great Shout.

"And we shall rise with Him," said the First One of Capawack, "for He shall take us up in the air and we shall ever be with Him to sing in His presence with all of our brothers who have gone on before us. Amen."

We sang a psalm and then went out.

---

* See the first book in *The Cross and the Tomahawk* series, *The Rain From God*, Chapter 20: "Is This Katanaquat?"

Chapter Twenty-eight

Breakfast with Williams

"This is for you," I said as I placed the small book in the outstretched, shaking hand of the first preacher of Providence. "Our Printer James has proudly scratched his name on the inside after scratching your own. He dated it there as well, '*Anno Domini* 1680,' with a small prayer for you and your family."

Williams thumbed the book open to James' blessing. Then smiling warmly, his face a web of thin wrinkles, he turned the pages at random.

"It was the second to be bound after the pressing," I said. "James gave the first to Eliot himself. We have London to thank for the paper and ink and the funds for this new printing, but Eliot is disappointed still, for he wished for the entire Bible again and not just the New Testament."

Roger Williams reached for his worn staff and leaned on it hard as he forced himself from the wooden bench beneath the apple tree that spread its fruited boughs beyond the small fence that kept it from the horses and the cattle.

"It is a fine gift," said Williams of the book, "and my great thanks to Printer James when next you see him." Williams put his hand upon my shoulder, partly to support himself and partly to usher me down the path and onto the road where the sun shone unshadowed. We walked slowly together. "It is a great work, this Indian Bible," he said, tucking the volume into the pocket of his cloak. "God has used it—and will use it still—

to His own glory and the betterment of your people, Job Kattenanit. It is a far better work than my own feeble efforts, so
long ago, to put your language on paper for others to read and
learn. My book was for the English to understand the Indian—
something that we still need help with—but this book is for the
Indian to understand God! And the latter is the better—
though God will hold us to the former as well, for we walk this
world together."

The wide, dusty street was busy with men and horses and
carts hauling produce, children playing, women carrying baskets of apples and buckets of water. A donkey was tied to a
sapling oak in the front yard of a house that was only half-
raised—I thought it a humorous-looking beast and I said so to
Williams.

"God used an ass to speak to a man once, Job," Williams replied. "Do you remember the story from the Scriptures?"

I said that I did, and that Eliot and Job Nesutan and Monequassin and I had been stuck at one point in Genesis trying to
conjure an Indian word for "donkey."

"And what word did you come up with?" asked the old
preacher.

I said that I could not recall at the moment, though I
thought it was something simple. It is strange how words
sometimes blow from the memory like dried leaves in the
wind.

"Ah, well," said Williams as he waved to some men who were
hammering at boards to build a porch. "We will someday know
all things and remember all things that are worth to remember.
In the meantime, if there is something that we cannot recall,
or something that God wants us to know but we are too deaf
to hear Him say, He can always use a jackass to get our attention."

" 'Morning, Master Williams," said a young lad who was running by with a small puppy.

"Good morning," said Williams to the sun of early autumn
and the sounds of the busy city and the leaping lad who was
long past us when the preacher finally recalled his name, "Master Underhill."

Providence was slowly rising from the ashes of the war. New houses lined the furrowed street, some complete, but many only on their way.

"The cost of building has doubled, even tripled, since the war," said Williams. Charred timbers lay overgrown with brush and thorn in several empty lots where cold, stone chimneys rose as hard, stark monuments to the vengeance of Canonchet.

"How many years?" asked the preacher, as he stopped in front of an old house that had escaped the war pyre.

"Thirty-five," said a voice from beside the clapboard home. "Thirty-five years ago I raised this shack, Roger Williams," said a thin, little man with tangled white hair as he hobbled into his front yard and up to his fence to greet us. "You made thet door yerself, you old moose!" said the wiry Englishman. "Boasted it would stand against an Indian attack, if it ever came to that. And you were right!"

"Good morning, Mr. Harris," I said, extending my hand over the fence to clasp the strong, bony fingers of the old neighbor of Williams.

"Good day to you, Job," said Harris cordially. "Some Indians ain't so bad once they get the gospel and get civilized," he smiled, winking at me. " 'Course, some English ain't never got civilized, Gospel or no!" he added, frowning at Williams in jest.

Williams set his staff against the fence and leaned upon the rails. "I meant, how many years since that attack I sadly prophesied?" said the old preacher.

"Four," said Harris immediately. Then he cocked his hoary head and looked at Williams with a straight gaze. "You losing your recollectness, Roger?" he asked.

"Too many miles and too many memories packed into one tiny brain, Benjamin," grinned the preacher. "But you're still as sharp as a new-whetted knife on an old, worn haft!"

"That's because I lay my head on stones at night, instead of goosedown pillows!" jested the old man. "I got to get cutting some wood, so I'll talk to you men some other time. Good day!" And he waddled back to his work.

"My Mary and yours will be wondering if we wish to eat their breakfast," said Williams suddenly. "Let's get up to that new 'shack' of mine, Kattenanit, and let the women feed their old men!"

We made our way slowly back through the bustling street. The fires of many morning meals filled the air with the odors of crisping bacon and frying ham.

"And your Towns?" asked my ancient friend.

I sighed as I stared into the clean blue of the sun-kissed skies. "We've only four left of the fourteen that God raised up before the war," I said. "And only Natick looks itself. I returned to Hassanmasitt after I married my precious Widowed-Once, but it was mostly deserted for fear of the Mohawk. We live at Natick now. James and Thomas dwell at Cambridge among the English."

"And your people?" asked the old preacher. "The Praying Indians?" queried the old skeptic who never believed that a Praying Town could make a Christian.

"Some of us have fallen away," I said sadly. "Mostly those who fought with the English during the last days of the war. They drink and curse. They gamble and make themselves filthy with loose women. They sit often in prison bemoaning their sins—yet when they get out, they run like dogs right back to their own vomit."

"You went through a drunken spell yourself," Williams reminded me, "so don't go throwing stones at your poor, weak brothers!"

I lowered my eyes to the stones upon our path.

"Some of us are dead," I continued. "Mostly the eldest who could not bear the hardships of Deer Island and the wanderings in winter that were forced upon us by fear and by our enemies, both Indian and English, during the war. But these dead now live in the light of a long day where no peril or prison can ever darken their eyes."

"I look to that day!" declared Williams, stopping short and turning his strong eyes upon me. He shook his staff vigorously in the warm air, tottering a bit in the act. "I will fling this staff into the sea as I fly!" he declared. And we resumed our walk. "But I thank God for it in the meantime," he muttered, clutching the stick tightly.

"And many of us are gathered gratefully in our Churches once again," I said. "And many more are coming to pray and to trust in Jesus."

"And old Waban?" asked Williams.

"He is hale and well at last, though he fell ill near unto death when he was left off the Island," I said. "Yet only last Sabbath, when Eliot came to preach—Eliot is more lame than you, Roger, but he rides his horse still—our good Waban rose to give a speech. Gookin was there and several other English as well, and Waban wished to tell them of our love." I halted in the road, and gathered myself to look as much like Waban as I could. Williams stood patiently, smiling, as I mimicked sincerely the old sagamore's speech and actions.

"We do, with all thankfulness," I began in the deep tones of the ancient Ruler at Natick, swinging my arms up to frame my face, "acknowledge God's great goodness to us in preserving us alive to this day. Formerly, in our beginning to pray to God, we received much encouragement from many godly English, both here and in England." I swung my right arm straight before me to point eastward beyond the hills and the Great Salt Sea.

"Since the war began between the English and the wicked Indians," I continued, "we expected to be all cut off, not only by the enemy Indians who we know hated us, but also by many English who were much exasperated and very angry with us. In this case we cried to God in prayer for help." I lifted my hands and my face to the shining heavens.

"Then God stirred up the Governor and Magistrates to send us to the Island, which was grievous to us for we were forced to leave all our substance behind us, and we expected nothing else at the Island but famine and nakedness. But behold God's goodness to us," I declared in the excited tones of Waban the exhorter, flinging my arms wide to embrace the whole of God's creation, "and to our poor families in stirring up the hearts of many godly persons in England, who never saw us yet showed us kindness and much love and gave us some corn and clothing, together with other provision of clams that God provided for us." I looked about the street as though the curious passersby were a rapt congregation at Meeting. And indeed they were beginning to gather and to give me at least their amused attention.

"Also, in due time," I continued. "God again stirred up the hearts of the Governor and Magistrates to . . ."

"Father!" came the sharp cry that interrupted my Waban speech. "Meat is on the table!" Heads turned toward the sound, and many among my standing flock chuckled out loud.

"Let us go," said Williams, "for I know the end of the speech anyway." And he tugged at my sleeve to pull me up the hill.

"How do you know it?" I asked.

"It is always the same with such speeches," explained the old speech-master. "The speaker summarizes those events which are already good knowledge to everyone present at the meeting, then he acknowledges his love to any present who might in any way doubt that love, then he pledges full loyalty and love to any present who might in any way be due that loyalty and love, and then he gives all the glory to God—and sits down."

"You were not there, were you?" I asked amazed.

"No," said Williams.

"It was a good speech," I said.

"Thank God, it's over!" proclaimed the preacher suddenly. "The war, Kattenanit, I mean the war!" he explained as we walked. "Thank God the whole dreadful affair is done! The wolves are dead, the seas are calmed, the proud are humbled, the heathen are chastised, and I praise the Lord daily that He has preserved you and your family as He has me and mine. His purposes are many and His own, and they will ever be fulfilled to the amazement and confoundment—is that a word?—of all men. Especially old men. Let us eat." We were once again beneath the spreading apple tree and standing nearly at the door of the house that had been raised upon the cold ashes of its recently reduced ancestor.

"Father, I called you many times," scolded Joy as she opened the door to us. The sweet face of my little lady—for she was now all of thirteen years and nearly a woman—scowled impatiently. The bacon was getting cold.

"Daniel!" I exclaimed, looking past my daughter to the grown son of Roger Williams. "I did not expect to see you here!"

The tall, pale son of his father leaned past my flustered Joy and pulled me into the house. We embraced. "Your family is growing like a young pine grove!" Daniel Williams declared. "And these boys say you have barely taught them how to bend a bow!" John and Jacob sat sheepishly at the long table, avoiding my eyes.

"They have guns," I said, "and little use for the bow and the arrow anymore. I wouldn't trade my own bow for a dozen English guns, but these boys must learn to shoot as New England shoots. There are fewer deer in our woods, Daniel—as your father well knows—than when Roger Williams felled his first trees on this very spot."

"I still hunt with the bent oak myself," said Daniel, tipping his head toward a fine bow that leaned against the chimney. "And my family eats well."

"Let us all eat well, then," said the king of the castle, thumping his dusty staff upon the wooden floor.

When our meal was done, the preacher and I sat at the fire to smoke. Daniel and my boys fled the dim house for the warm sun of autumn. Mercy and Joy and our Marys found such things to do and rattle about as women will always find time to do while their men sit and smoke.

"Your father is well?" asked Williams.

"Well enough to sail to and from the Mohegan country with Assoko," I said.

"Oh?" nodded the preacher.

"To seek Uncas and tell him to his face that The Rain From God forgives him for his long, black years of wickedness."

"Oh?"

"And Uncas heard him, but did not repent of his deeds."

"The old fox is a vicious, willful, drunken beast," said Williams, "and perhaps he can never repent. Perhaps he is one who is chosen for iniquity and the fires of Hell. Have your forgiven him, Kattenanit son of Katanaquat?"

"I have, though my dreams yet rise against him in the night."

"Your dreams will not be judged upon the Final Day," said the preacher.

"I had another vision not long ago," I said to the old man who rocked beside me. "Do you wish to hear it?"

"Your young men shall dream dreams," quoted Williams, *"and your old men shall see visions.* I am ancient now, and have never seen a vision. I suspect mine await me in Heaven. Tell me yours."

"I was praying, alone and in the woods as I walked," I said. "And suddenly a great moose stood before me, larger than any I had ever encountered. At first I stood still, and considered walking back the way I had come. But then the trees around me began to wave like the tall grasses of a marsh beneath a breeze, and I shook my head in dizzied disbelief. The trees faded as a colored mist rose up like a giant mat before my face, and I knew then that this was a vision and nothing for my flesh to fear.

"The moose was now a horse, saddled and fierce, and I could see many warriors upon its back at once, some English, some Indian, some dressed as we dress, some in costumes of crimson with tall pointed hats, some in coats of white and others of blue, with swords and very long guns. They fought one another upon the great beast, and its coat and its mane were stained with their blood.

"At last the stallion reared upon its hind legs, tossing its riders to the misty ground. Then it galloped west through the trees, with two Indians upon its back. One held a bloody tomahawk high in his hands, the other a bloody wooden cross.

"On the ground, the warriors and soldiers wrestled and rolled, becoming one English man who stood at last and walked slowly west in the path of the fleeing horse. As I looked to see where the rider and the walker had gone, the path opened to a grassy plain that stretched toward mountains higher than any I have ever seen or dreamed of. The heads of the hills were white like snow, and palisaded in drifting dark clouds. Lightning flashed and blood rained from the heavens.

"I heard a loud snort at my side, and when I turned at the sound, an antlered buck—of flesh and bone and no dream!—

darted into a thicket and was soon gone from sight. The vision too was gone, and the forest now stood tall and still as always."

Williams rocked slowly at his fire.

"What can this mean?" I asked the crackling flames and the twisting smoke that rose from our clay pipes.

"I am not Joseph son of Jacob that I can interpret men's dreams," said the old man. "But I am glad that my lifetime in the great forest has been undisturbed by such omens and mysteries!"

"What shall I do with it?" I asked.

"Write it down, Kattenanit," said the man whose quill had walked more miles than some men's legs. "Write it down, for like the words of Daniel the prophet, it may be a mystery that God now hides but will someday open to the eyes of another generation."

"When shall He return?" I wondered aloud.

"Very soon, I wouldn't doubt," said Roger Williams.

"Job Kattenanit!" came the shout of Daniel Williams from somewhere not far beyond the wooded walls. "Get you out here, good fellow! For we've something to show you."

I pulled myself reluctantly from my seat beside the rocking preacher. His hand waved a willing release, and I left him there staring into the waning flames.

Outside, the noon sun painted the world bright green. The grass was yet tall and full of life. The trees held their shining, verdant leaves as tightly as ever in the autumn breeze. Summer still played, stubborn and carefree upon the earth, humming, *I am not tired and I will not go to bed,* turning deaf ears to the next season's righteous claims and weak complaints.

A thin, feathered shaft whispered in the golden air. I watched it fly, and as it ran its swift, straight course, the summers of my life flew with it, fast and true. It buried its head in a small scrap of paper tacked to an upright log that leaned against the rails that fenced the apple tree.

A young Praying Indian stood across the road, his face beaming brightly, rubbing a stinging wrist that had been slapped by a full-loosed bowstring. His brother stood at his side, leaping up and down like a dog that does tricks for its master. The eldest son of the preacher of Providence stood over them both, smiling, pointing to the target and the proud evidence of young John's aim and eye.

"Father!" cried the little bowman. "Daniel says it is a Bull's Eye!"

"And so it is, John," I said, walking to the log and pulling the shaft from the target.

"Let us go hunting!" pleaded the proud archer.

"We shall do so when we get home," I said, returning the arrow to my beaming boy. "But only if you promise not to shoot our neighbor's bull!"

A Glossary of Terms

assoko Literally "a fool" in Narragansett; one who is weak-minded, retarded, or simple. As applied to this principal character in *The Ransom*, there is no negative moral connotation attached to his name. The Indians, not understanding mental retardation or mental illness, had superstition concerning fools, and thought them to be especially close with the spirits. Our Assoko is a unique fellow who, though retarded, is "no fool."

backbaskets Small reeded, leather, or wooden baskets belted and worn on the back, for carrying food, pipe, and tobacco, and other items.

Cautantowwit (caw-TAN-tow-it) The Narragansett creator-god, who lived in the Southwest, and who oversaw the affairs of men and judged them at death.

Chepi (also *Hobomucko*) The devil of the Narragansett pantheon of gods. Not totally bad, Chepi nevertheless was associated with doom and gloom. He was also the patron spirit of the powwow, appearing in visions most often as a serpent (a very old trick!).

heel ball An author invention, so named in our novel as a distillation of any number of games the Indians played with balls of stone or wood—from a form of kickball or soccer, to lacrosse—upon the long shores of the sea.

Harvest Games (and Indian games in general) The Indians were very glad for any leisure activities that pulled them away from the grueling daily work of subsistence. But

375

their games were not all idle fun. Among young boys especially, many competitive games were played in preparation for manhood and war. Running and wrestling, throwing sticks and rolling stones, outwitting your opponent on the playfield: all helped develop the skills that a young boy would one day need in the battle. But everyone enjoyed the games, and much gambling accompanied them. There were special times of extended games (such as at the harvest) in which everyone was involved in the action—the men on the "playing field", the women and the children in the "grandstands," and many others laying bets on the side.

kaukant Literally "crow." In Narragansett mythology, the crow brought the Indians their first corn seed from the gardens of Cautantowwit. In gratitude, the Narragansett allowed the crow (but no other bird!) the freedom of the fields. If only kaukant could repay them for his centuries of mooching!

keesuckquand Literally "the sun."

manitoo General term for "a god." Besides the specific gods for whom the Indians had specific names, this term was often applied to any object, person, or happening the Indians found extraordinary. The English and the Dutch, when first encountered, were considered manitoos.

Massasoit (MASS-a-soyt) Grand Sachem of the Wampanoag Indians of Massachusetts, this great man was the first political ally and friend of the Pilgrims upon their arrival in the New World. It was he who, with ninety of his warriors, celebrated the first Thanksgiving with the people of Plymouth. Faithful to the English until his death in 1660 (his life was once saved by the compassionate doctoring of Edward Winslow), his son Metacomet (King Philip) led a united Indian uprising against the English in the mid 1670s.

medicine (of Latin and Middle English derivation) The supernatural powers and protection given to the Indians by the spirits.

Miantonomi (Mee-AN-ton-oh-mee) Historically, this great

sachem of the Narragansett is among the most famous of the New England Indians. Still quoted today, his words and recorded actions show us an intelligent man who did his very best to walk in peace with the English while leading his people in their ancient ways. He seems to have considered the truth of Christianity, and was a close and personal friend of Roger Williams. His murder at the height of his political power—at the hands of Uncas' Mohegan Indians and by the order of a few misguided English at Boston—is a black moment in the history of mid-seventeenth century New England.

Nanepaushat Literally "the moon."

Narragansett "People of the little points and bays," or "at the small narrow point of land." Inhabiting lands which encompass most of present-day Rhode Island, the Narragansett were the principal power among the New England Indians after the Great Dying—a plague which decimated the coastal tribes of New England a few years prior to the coming of the Pilgrims in 1620. Untouched by the sickness, the Narragansett were able to subject many previously independent tribes—including the Wampanoag, whose chief sachem Massasoit celebrated the famous first Thanksgiving with the colonists of Plymouth.

Nétop Literally "friend."

nokehick (or no-cake) Pounded, parched Indian corn. This simple food was the traveling sustenance of the hunter and the warrior. It was mixed with a little water, hot or cold, and made a tasty and fully adequate meal on the trail. Every brave carried a small basket of nokehick at his back or in a hollow leather belt about his waist—usually enough for three or four days. But forty days provision could be carried by any warrior with little inconvenience.

powwow The medicine man or shaman. The term has since come to mean any great tribal or intertribal gathering. In *The Ransom*, "powwow" is used only to refer to the medicine man.

sachem (SAY-chem) Chief, king, or prince; the head of a tribe or village. There were traditionally two main sachems among the Narragansett, one older and one younger. This co-rulership was unique among the New England tribes, but every tribe had at least one chief sachem, and all large tribes had many undersachems who ruled smaller groups of Indians.

sagamore Probably another name for sachem, but used sometimes in the same context as an undersachem or a lesser tribal leader (which is the context in which it is found in the novel).

snowsnake A winter game played with a long stick of maple that was very smooth and tapered near its "tail." The head of the stick was carved into some semblance of a snake. The game's object was to slide the snowsnake down a long, level track of packed snow. Men took turns flinging their snowsnakes, and the distances were marked. Whoever slid his snake the farthest won all the snakes. There were also many side bets.

sowwaniu Literally "the Southwest." Traditional dwelling of the great creator-god Cautantowwit. The New England Indian believed that his soul would fly to the Southwest upon death, and there be judged by Cautantowwit. A great dog guarded the gates of the courts of Cautantowwit, and only those souls who had lived righteously were allowed to enter those gates. In *The Ransom*, the word has been capitalized (Sowanniu) and used in a way to communicate the stronger sense of place and permanence (like Heaven or Paradise) that the Indian attached to it.

squaw Literally "woman."

wampum (from the Algonquian *wompompeague*) The small beads made from the shells of clam and whelk. The beads were white and—more rarely—purple ("black"). They were woven into belts or strung on leather thongs. *Wompompeague* literally means "white strings." Wampum was the major trade currency of the New England Indians, both among themselves and with the Europeans. It was also an integral part of all treaties, ransoms, and various ceremonies; wampum used in this way had "meaning" spoken into it, and people recalled the events by "reading" the wampum. The Narragansett and the Indians of Long Island were the principal producers of wampum.

Weetucks (called *Maushop* by the majority of the New England tribes) The humanlike giant of Algonquian tradition. He was believed to be responsible for the creation of Nantucket Island (he dumped the ashes of his great pipe into the sea, and Nantucket was the result). He was a good creature, and had been a great help to the Indians, chasing whales ashore for them to slay and eat. He lived on Martha's Vineyard at one time, and cooked whales whole over the smoking volcano that once stood on the isle. When too many Indians began to populate his lands, he packed up his backbasket and headed into the land of legend, never to be seen again.

wigwam The principal home structure of the New England Indian. It was built in two main forms: the domed wigwam (which was the most common), and the conical wigwam (which is more like the teepee of the western Indians). Constructed of poles and covered most often with bark of trees and mats of cattail rushes, wigwams could be moved from one location to another. Tribes and families moved several times yearly, according to the seasons and the need to be near the harvest, the hunt, the fishing grounds, or the shelter of a wooded valley in winter. Sometimes wigwams were moved simply because they became infested with vermin and needed to be set up anew on cleaner ground.

Crossing the Pocatuck

For the average reader of modern historical fiction, the river of objective history runs wide and muddy, often clouded by the opinions and imaginations of the author of the work. Sorting truth from tales is not an easy matter, even for the historian who blows the dust from ancient tomes to get the news and views of history's original correspondents. Nothing short of the Bible is inerrant recollection of days past. All history walks with feet of clay. We know in part. We see in part.

Yet the story of Kattenanit, though fictional, is based upon history as best I have seen it through the dark glass.

Characters

Most of the people you will meet in the pages of *The Ransom* are real people whose stories were first told in the journals, diaries, pamphlets, books, and town records of the seventeenth-century New England colonists. You will recognize a few of their names. Hopefully you will know them better when the tale is fully told.

With all of our historical cast—though I have invented eyes and noses and lips and mannerisms and figures of speech—I have attempted to portray the character of these folks as the record best reveals it. In many cases, the narrative is woven through with the recorded words, thoughts, and sentiments of the historical characters themselves. In some cases, the portraits differ greatly from the popular notions that many entertain today. My options were open. The waters were muddy. I picked my shoreline. I swam.

Many of the people in our tale—like Katanaquat the father of Kattenanit (the narrator and main character in *The Rain From God*)—are the product of the author's historically informed imagination. Yet, I have made every effort to be historically and culturally accurate in the depiction of all tribes and peoples.

Language

Since our narrator is portrayed as a Narragansett, I have sprinkled a good deal of the Narragansett language (with many other Algonquian words) throughout the text. Most of the places mentioned by name—the bays and rivers, the towns and villages—are real, and I have used Indian place-names (in a spelling of my own choosing—because spellings differ widely in original sources) wherever I could identify them. The Indian names for many animals, as well as objects in nature, also appear throughout the book.

Remarkably, many of the native phrases that have found their way into the popular Indian vocabulary of the twentieth century—and which many of us associate more with the Indians of America's west—are Narragansett (and generally Algonquian) in origin: i.e. *papoose, squaw, wigwam, moccasin, wampum, powwow, manitoo*. And of course a vast number of our rivers and lakes still maintain their original Indian appellations.

The longer the Indian and English cultures rubbed shoulders, the more Anglicized the Indian's personal names became. Many Indians had both an Indian and an English moniker. The Christian Indians especially took on English names, as well as names from the Bible, sometimes mixing them with their own Indian birthnames. Our main character, Job Kattenanit, is an example of this.

Culture

The culture of both the New England Indian and the New England colonist is widely documented in seventeenth-century sources. I have tried very hard to walk in the moccasins of the one and the shoes of the other, thinking their thoughts and speaking their hearts. I have tried very hard to reconstruct their physical and their spiritual worlds, their daily lives, and their family relationships from the details that are chronicled in the volumes of history.

I found that my own conception of both the Indian and the Puritan had been skewed by Hollywood and Hawthorne, and that the actual record tells us a tale far more complicated and fascinating. I found that the Puritan was a far better man than I had been led to believe, considering the day and age in which he lived, and that the Native American—though a distant son of Adam like us all—was not unlike the once-savage tribes of the Scottish Pict, the German Hun, or the Brazilian Head-hunter before the coming of the gospel among them. All nations and tribes were (and are) lost in darkness without the light of God's Son.

Though the New England Indian did not worship one Great Spirit as is often conceived—but had a virtual pantheon of gods they called *manitoos*—there is, amazingly, a distant memory of the One Great God in their mythology: a Creator and provider who made man and woman; a garden; a fall of sorts; a flood. The shadow of the truth often lies long upon the land even after the sun has fallen below the hills of time.

Events

The many events in *The Ransom*, both the fictional and the historical, follow an historically accurate chronology. I have not applied dates to anything before Kattenanit's personal submersion into English culture, however, because the European calendar was—in the childhood days of our narrator's life—a meaningless and unknown thing.

There is nothing in the fictional that could not have happened, and there is remarkably much that seems fictional—both natural and supernatural—that truly did happen:

The French captive and his curse, and the comet that preceded the Great Dying, are a matter of record.

The lives (excluding early childhood, which predates the Pilgrims and the Puritans) and deaths of our story's principal Indian sachems—Miantonomi, Uncas, Canonchet, Massasoit, Metacomet (King Philip) and others—are recorded history, as are the lives, conversions, and Christian confessions of our principal Praying Indian characters.

Wequash's conversion. Roger Williams' relationship to the Narragansett. The way the Indians fought and believed. The way the English fought and believed. John Eliot's tireless apostolic work among the Indians which began at Waban's wigwam and resulted ultimately in the phenomenon of the Praying Indians, their Indian-governed Praying Towns, and the Indian Bible. King Philip's War and the supernatural omens that preceded it. The murder of John Sassamon. Deer Island. The Great Swamp Fight. The incredible Christian haven of Capawack (Martha's Vineyard). Job Kattenanit's and James Quannapohit's courageous sojourn in the camp of Mautampe. Job's long run home. All this, and much more that is woven into our narrative, really happened. Folks who were there wrote it down. Through a dark glass we can see it still.

For a more in-depth discussion of the New England Indian's language and culture, see Part 1 of "The Muddy River and How I Swam It" in The Rain From God: *Book One of* The Cross and the Tomahawk.

A Summary of the Gospel among the New England Indians in the Seventeenth Century

When the Pilgrims first arrived on the windblown shores of the northeast coast of America, they had little time for evangelistic crusades among the Indians. They had their hands full just staying alive. God provided them a precious friend in the person of Tisquantum (Squanto), the sole survivor of the tribe of the Patuxet which perished in the Great Dying. Squanto lived only because he had been taken captive years earlier by an English ship captain named Hunt, and thus he wasn't home when the plague destroyed his people. When he finally found his way home (after having been to England, Spain, and possibly Newfoundland) he was a man without a country. He pitched a wigwam in the city of Massasoit of the Wampanoag. When a shipload of English Christians—men, women, and children—began to build rude huts on the coastal lands of the perished Patuxet, Squanto left the tents of Massasoit and offered himself as a friend and a temporal savior to the people of Plymouth.

Squanto may have trusted in Christ—he certainly heard the gospel many times—but the record shows a duplicitous man who played his own game. Though he was a Godsend to the Pilgrims—teaching them many things they needed to know in order to survive in this foreign wilderness—he seems to have also caused a good deal of trouble for both his Indian and his English neighbors by the schemes he contrived in order to win himself influence and power among the surrounding tribes. Upon his deathbed, he gave all of his worldly goods to his Plymouth friends and asked them to pray that he would go to Heaven.

The Pilgrims entered into a sincere pact of friendship with Massasoit that lasted more than forty years. It was Massasoit, with ninety of his warriors, who celebrated that famous first Thanksgiving with the English of Plymouth. But the impact of the gospel on the Wampanoag people was minimal, in part because of the strong opposition of their powwows, and in part because of the lack of any real effort on the part of the Pilgrims to evangelize their Indian neighbors. The language and cultural walls were high when it came to the things of religion, and there were few who attempted much to scale them.

Ten years after the *Mayflower* first hove into Plymouth Harbor, another wave of English Christians, larger and stronger than the first, rolled onto the shores of the New England frontier. The Great Puritan Migration was underway, and the towns of Salem and Boston in Massachusetts country began to rise as the trees fell at the eastern edge of the vast and ancient northeastern woods. Among some of the first to cross the Atlantic to this rugged Puritan Promised Land was a courageous and unorthodox young preacher named Roger Williams. A puritan among Puritans and a separatist among separatists, Williams saw things a bit differently than his peers, and very soon some of the principal colonial ministers and leaders were not so happy to have him among them. His faith and his character were beyond reproach, and he was much loved by the congregations that he served, but his ideas dangerously rocked the boat of the Puritan experiment. Williams was eventually banished from Massachusett Bay, and rather than be sent back to England (as the Bay authorities had decided) the radical preacher fled on foot in winter to the tents of the Wampanoag—and then to the Narragansett. He had always had a heart for the Indian, and already had learned a good deal more of their language and customs than most of his fellow English. Canonicus, grand sachem of the Narragansett, loved the English preacher, and gave him the land upon which he founded Providence and eventually the colony of Rhode Island.

Williams preached often to the Indians, but his gift was not that of the evangelist, and his own theology eventually led him to doubt the imminent possibility of native conversions. Though he was instrumental in the apparent faith of a Pequot sagamore named Wequash, Williams doubted whether the man was actually saved. And when the gospel began to enter the hearts of the Indians of Massachusetts nearly seven years after the death of Wequash, Roger William's colony saw hardly a conversion among its native population. The Narragansett, who loved the man and heard him speak of God and His Son often, never embraced the Savior. It would not be until the next century, during the Great Awakening, that God would apprehend the Narragansett people with His Word.

The Puritans, like the Pilgrims, had no evangelistic agenda. Their lives and their preaching were biblically saturated, but their vision did not embrace those outside their New Jerusalem. Though they had increasing trade and traffic with their Indian neighbors, they made little concerted effort to take the gospel into the forest. They, like Williams, came to believe that the Indian was not yet ripe for the Kingdom of God. They laid aside the Great Commission in order to build their earthly Zion, and God had to look mighty hard to find a man willing to carry the Good News to the soul-darkened native American.

But God found his man, and a few more. John Eliot arrived in Boston on the *Lyon,* the same ship that had carried Roger Williams across the Atlantic only one crossing earlier. He accepted the pulpit at Boston (which Williams had refused upon his recent arrival in the New World, saying that the Boston congregation was not yet fully separated from the Anglican Church). Eliot soon moved from there to a newborn town called Roxbury to lead a church of his former Nazick, England neighbors. As the years passed, God laid the burden of the souls of the Native American upon Eliot's heart. God also fired into that heart the first sharp arrow of cross-cultural mission wisdom: learning the language of those you are seeking to reach with the Good News.

By 1646, humbly stuttering in the tongue of the Massachusetts tribes, Eliot began his gospel work among the Indians at the wigwam of a minor Nipmuc sagamore named Waban. From that day on, until he died in 1690 at the age of eighty-five, John Eliot gave himself fully—in all things temporal and eternal—to two "congregations": that of his English neighbors and friends in Roxbury, and the Indians of the many scattered towns and tribes of New England. He eventually translated numerous Christian works into the Indian tongue, including the entire text of the Bible. His Indian Bible was the first Bible to be printed on the continent. There were many who helped him in this largely unlauded work (though the angels saw, and there are thousands of souls in Heaven today who laud it still, for it meant their very salvation), but none joined him so closely as a man named Daniel Gookin. A lawyer and a soldier, Gookin loved the Indians, and was made superintendent over their Praying Towns. Both Eliot and Gookin gave up comfort and reputation to slog the swampy trails in service of their Indian brothers and sisters.

And God found another man, a former merchant from Southampton, England, in whom there was love and vision for the Indian. Thomas Mayhew, Senior, obtained a grant from Lord Sterling for the island of Capawack, called Martha's Vineyard by the English. Though Mayhew considered his grant a right to the land by English law, he—like Williams—recognized the natural rights of the island's large native population. Mayhew lived as a good neighbor, and did not seek to impose his government upon any but the English who lived with him.

In very short order, the Indians took a liking to Thomas Mayhew, and as he assisted them in many practical ways, they
opened their hearts not only to the man but to the God he
served. The governor's son, Thomas Junior, began preaching
among the Indians of the island shortly before John Eliot began
the same upon the mainland. Eliot and the Mayhews very
quickly heard of the work that each was involved in, and they
often labored together in the overall task of bringing Christ to
the natives and pastoring the Indian believers ever after. They un-
dertook to elicit prayer and humanitarian aid from the churches
of both New England and Old England, oversaw the estab-
lishment of native churches and grammar schools, set up a printing press to publish Christian materials in the tongue of the
Indian, built an Indian college for native ministers at Cambridge,
and helped to establish Praying Indian towns that were governed
by the Christian Indians themselves. They traveled countless
miles by horse and boat and foot to preach and teach and pray
and encourage, and did all they could to bring their best understanding of civilization and a better life to their native neighbors.

By the dawn of King Philip's War in 1675, there were fourteen Praying Towns in Massachusetts and two covenanted In-
dian-led churches, totaling 1,100 native American Christians in
the Massachusetts Bay Colony. There were 497 Praying Indians in Plymouth Colony, with one Indian Church. In Connecticut, the Reverend James Fitch reported thirty converts among
the Mohegan. On Martha's Vineyard nearly all the Indian
population confessed Christ; there were three churches, ten Indian preachers, several smaller congregations, and six services
on the island each Sabbath. Chappiquidick and Nantucket
were Christianized also. The total number of Praying Indians
on the islands may have come close to 2,000. This incredible
growth of the gospel among the New England Indian gives us a
fair estimate of three to four thousand Christian Indians by the
year 1675. Satan was losing the war for men's souls.

But then men began to fight men. And the story of the gospel after the tragic war between the English and the son of
Massasoit is something that will have to wait for a future volume of *The Cross and the Tomahawk*.

A Bibliography

The resources utilized for the writing of *The Ransom* are too many and too varied to list fully in a popular novel of this kind. Yet the subject matter is so historically critical to the understanding of America's early heritage in the gospel that I cannot let Kattenanit simply tell his story and then say goodnight. Therefore, I have chosen to print an edited list of works that I found essential and most helpful in swimming the muddy river of the past. Some of these books are still in print, but most can only be found on the shelves at your local library or through interlibrary loan.

Beals, Carleton, *John Eliot, The Man Who Loved the Indians* (New York: Julian Messner, Inc., 1957).

Boissevain, Ethel, *The Narragansett People* (Phoenix, AZ: Indian Tribal Series, 1975).

Chapin, Howard M., *Sachems of the Narragansett* (Providence, RI: Rhode Island Historical Society, 1931).

DeForest, John W., *The History of the Indians of Connecticut from the Earliest Known Period to 1850* (Hartford, CT, 1852).

Earle, Alice Morse, *Home Life in Colonial Days* (Stockbridge, MA: Berkshire House, 1992). Originally published in 1898.

Eliot, John, *The Day-breaking, if not the Sun-rising, of the Gospell with the Indians in New England* (London,1649).

_____, *The Christian Commonwealth: or The Civil Policy of the Rising Kingdom of Jesus Christ* (New York: Arno Press, reprint, 1972). Originally published in London in 1659.

Gookin, Daniel, *Historical Collections of the Indians in New England. Of Their Several Nations, Numbers, Customs, Manners, Religion and Government, Before the English Planted There* (New York: Arno Press, reprint, 1972). Completed in 1674, it was first published in Boston by the Massachusetts Historical Society in 1792.

_____, *An Historical Account of the Doings and Sufferings of the Christian Indians in New England in the Years 1675, 1676, 1677* (New York: Arno Press, reprint, 1972). Completed shortly after King Philip's War (the dedicatory is dated 1677), it was not published until 1836, in Gookin's hometown of Cambridge.

Hare, Lloyd C.M., *Thomas Mayhew, Patriarch to the Indians (1593-1682)* (New York: AMS Press, 1969).

Mayhew, Experience, *Indian Converts* (London, 1727).

Mason, John, *A Brief History of the Pequot War* (Ann Arbor, MI: University Microfilms, Inc., reprint, 1966). Originally published in Boston in 1736.

Morgan, Edmund S., *The Puritan Family* (New York: Harper & Row, 1966).

Rider, Sidney S., *The Lands of Rhode Island As They Were Known to Caunounicus and Miantunnomu When Roger Williams Came in 1636* (Providence, RI: 1904).

Simmons, William S., *Cautantowwit's House: An Indian Burial Ground on the Island of Conanicut in Narragansett Bay* (Providence: Brown University Press, 1970).

_____, *The Narragansett* (New York/Philadelphia: Chelsea House Publishers, 1989).

_____, *Spirit of the New England Tribes: Indian History and Folklore, 1620-1984* (Hanover, NH: University Press of New England, 1986).

Tunis, Edwin, *Indians* (New York: Thomas Y. Crowell, 1979).

_____, *Colonial Living* (New York: Thomas Y. Crowell.

Various authors, *King Phillip's War Narratives,* a collection of five contemporary accounts of the war, first published separately between 1675 and 1677 in London (Ann Arbor, MI: University Microfilms, Inc., reprint, 1966).

Vaughn, Alden T., *New England Frontier, Puritans and Indians 1620-1675* (Boston: Little, Brown and Company, 1965).

Wilbur, Keith, *New England Indians* (Chester, CT: Globe-Pequot Press, 1978).

Williams, Roger, *A Key into the Language of America; Christenings Make Not Christians;* and *The Letters of Roger Williams*—all from *The Complete Writings of Roger Williams,* 7 vols. (New York: Russell & Russell, reprint, 1963). *Key* was first published in London in 1643. There was as yet no printing press on the continent of North America.

Willison, George F., *The Pilgrim Reader* (Garden City, NY: Doubleday, 1953).

Winslow, Edward, *The Glorious Progress of the Gospel Amongst the Indians of New England.* Originally printed in Popes-head Alley in London in 1649. Winslow compiled and published this book of two letters written by John Eliot and one by Thomas Mayhew, Jr.

Winslow, Elizabeth Ola, *John Eliot, "Apostle to the Indians"* (Boston: Houghton Mifflin, 1968).

Besides the above-mentioned materials, the following books and pamphlets (generally know as the "Eliot Tracts") were published in London between the years 1648 and 1671, chronicling the work of the gospel among the New England Indian: *New England's First Fruits* (1648), John Eliot; *The Clear Sunshine of the Gospel Breaking Forth Among the Indians in New England* (1648), Thomas Shepherd; *The Light Appearing More and More Towards the Perfect Day* (1651) and *Strength out of Weaknesse* (1652), both published by Rev. Henry Whitfield and containing accounts chiefly written by John Eliot; *Tears of Repentance* (1653), Eliot and Mayhew; *A Late and Further Manifestation of the Progress of the Gospel Amongst the Indians in New England* (1655), Eliot; *A Further Account of the Progresse of the*

Gospel (1659), Eliot—a collection of testimonies by several Indians; *A Further Account of the Progresse of the Gospel* (1660), Eliot—also a collection of testimonies by several Indians; *A Brief Narration of the Progesse of the Gospel Among the Indians in New England* (1671).